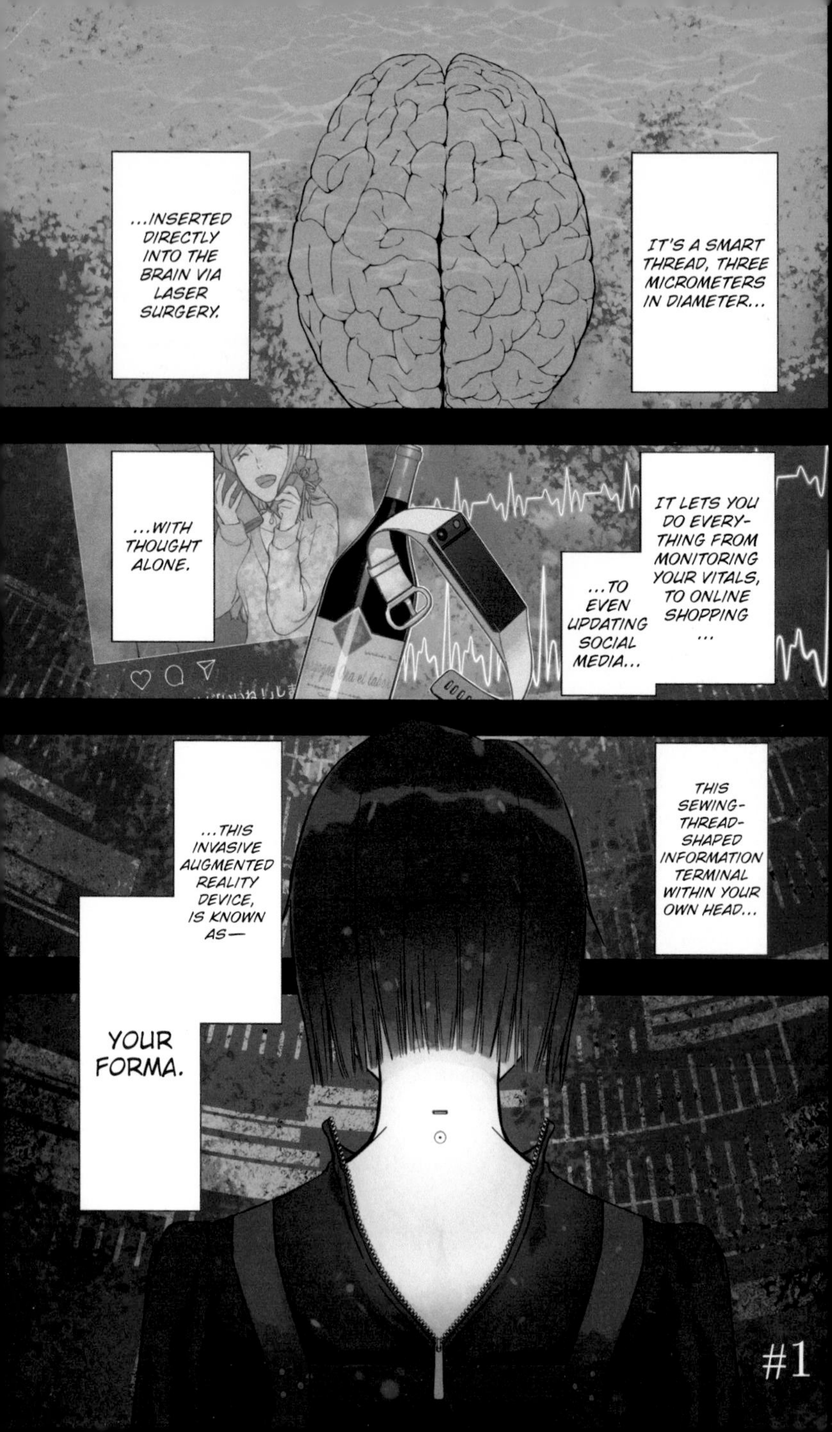
IT'S A SMART THREAD, THREE MICROMETERS IN DIAMETER...
...INSERTED DIRECTLY INTO THE BRAIN VIA LASER SURGERY.
IT LETS YOU DO EVERYTHING FROM MONITORING YOUR VITALS, TO ONLINE SHOPPING...
...TO EVEN UPDATING SOCIAL MEDIA...
...WITH THOUGHT ALONE.
THIS SEWING-THREAD-SHAPED INFORMATION TERMINAL WITHIN YOUR OWN HEAD...
...THIS INVASIVE AUGMENTED REALITY DEVICE, IS KNOWN AS—
YOUR FORMA.
#1

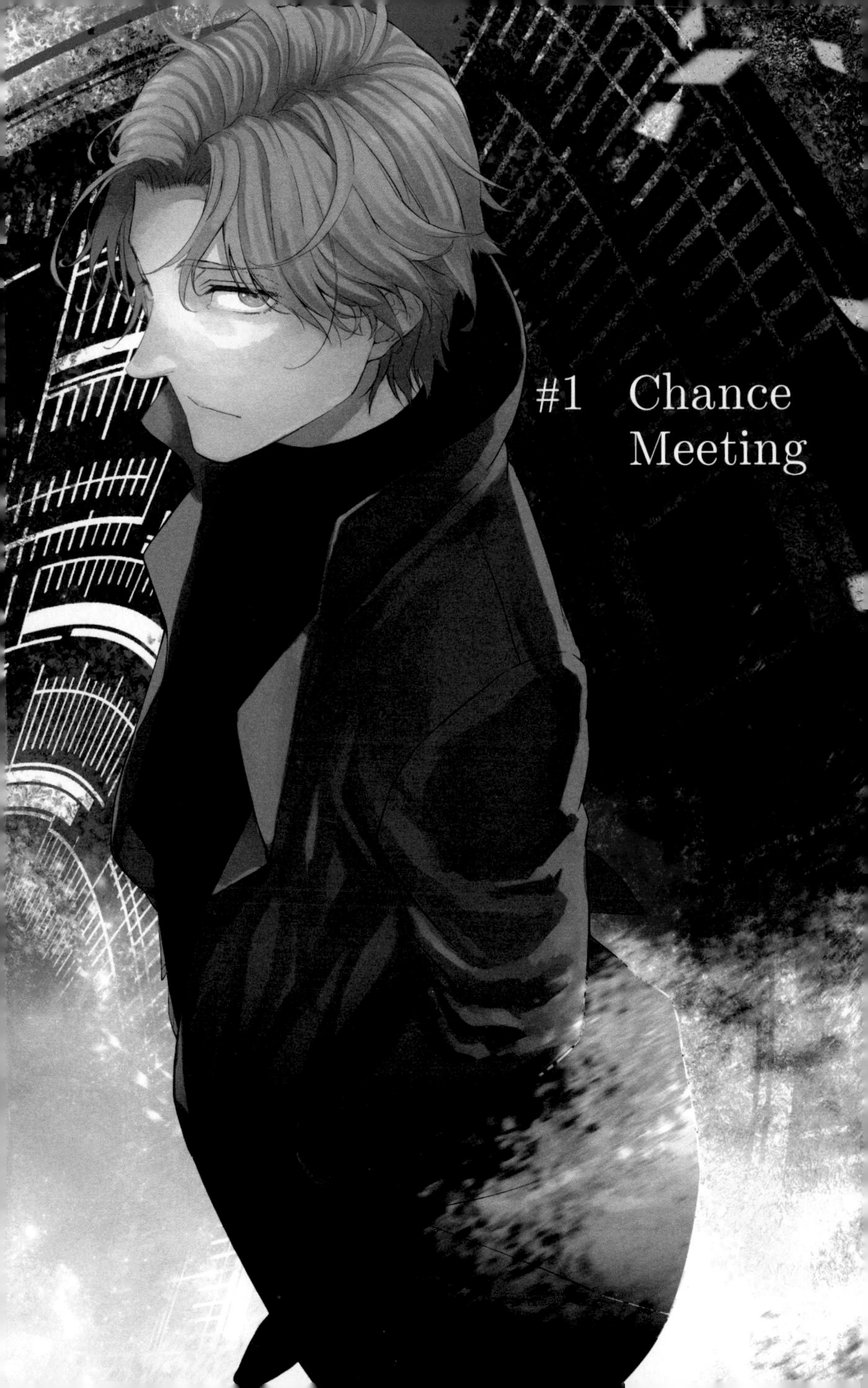
#1 Chance Meeting

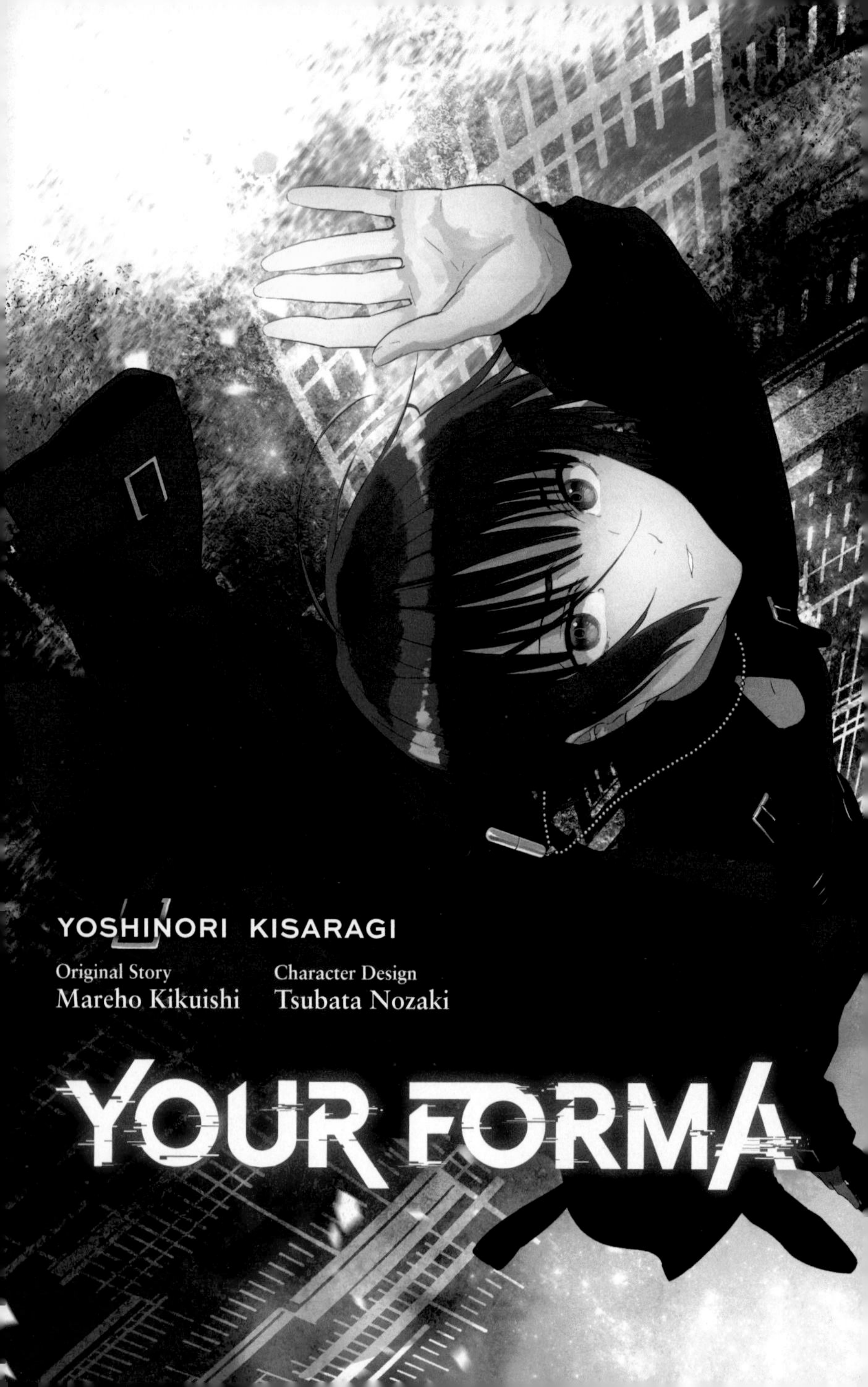
YOSHINORI KISARAGI
Original Story
Mareho Kikuishi
Character Design
Tsubata Nozaki
YOUR FORMA

CONTENTS

Y O U R   F O R M A

"Forgetting" is a thing of the past.

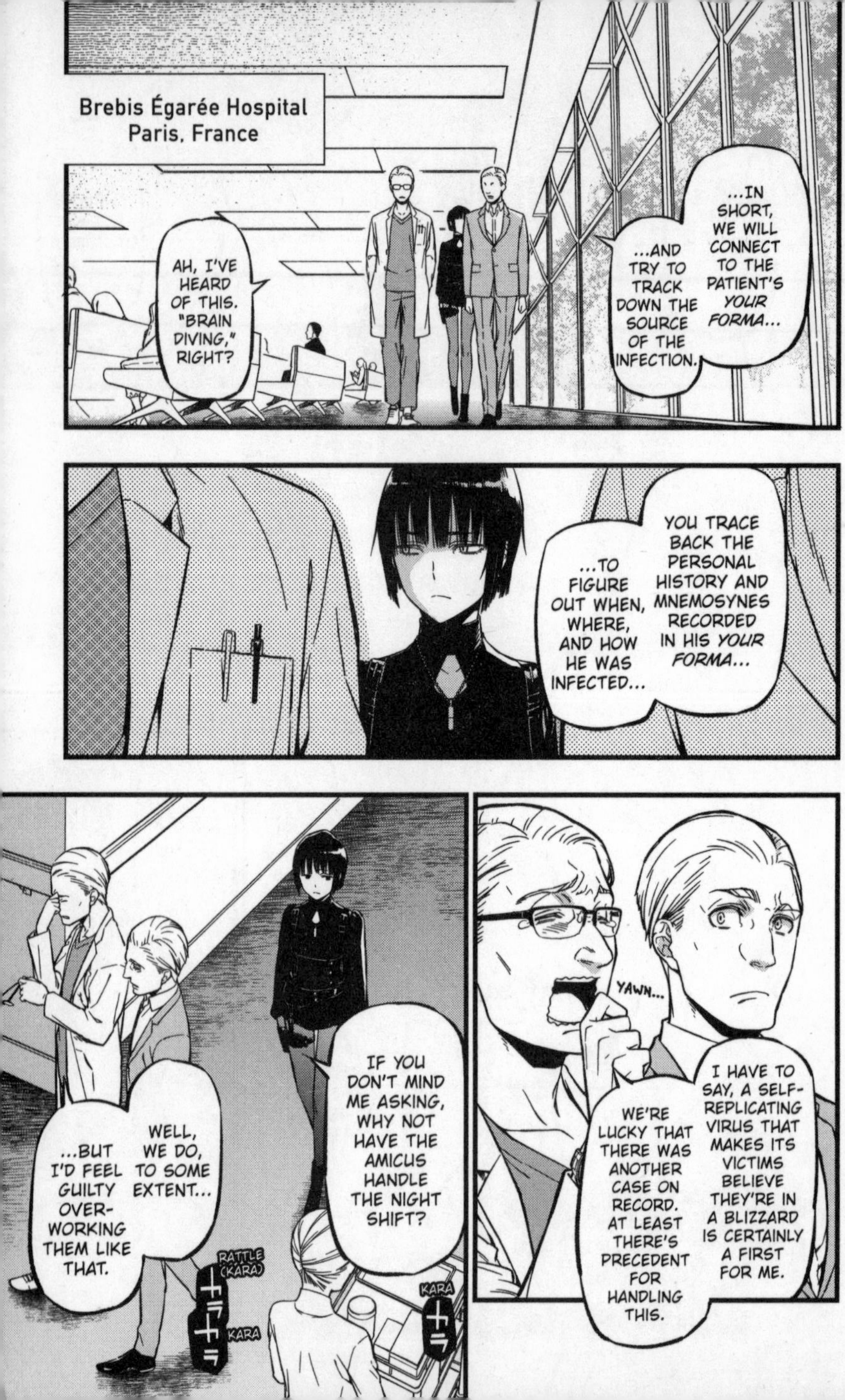
Brebis Égarée Hospital
Paris, France
...IN SHORT, WE WILL CONNECT TO THE PATIENT'S *YOUR FORMA*...
...AND TRY TO TRACK DOWN THE SOURCE OF THE INFECTION.
AH, I'VE HEARD OF THIS. "BRAIN DIVING," RIGHT?
YOU TRACE BACK THE PERSONAL HISTORY AND MNEMOSYNES RECORDED IN HIS *YOUR FORMA*...
...TO FIGURE OUT WHEN, WHERE, AND HOW HE WAS INFECTED...
YAWN...
I HAVE TO SAY, A SELF-REPLICATING VIRUS THAT MAKES ITS VICTIMS BELIEVE THEY'RE IN A BLIZZARD IS CERTAINLY A FIRST FOR ME.
WE'RE LUCKY THAT THERE WAS ANOTHER CASE ON RECORD. AT LEAST THERE'S PRECEDENT FOR HANDLING THIS.
IF YOU DON'T MIND ME ASKING, WHY NOT HAVE THE AMICUS HANDLE THE NIGHT SHIFT?
KARA
WELL, WE DO, TO SOME EXTENT...
...BUT I'D FEEL GUILTY OVER-WORKING THEM LIKE THAT.
RATTLE (KARA)
KARA

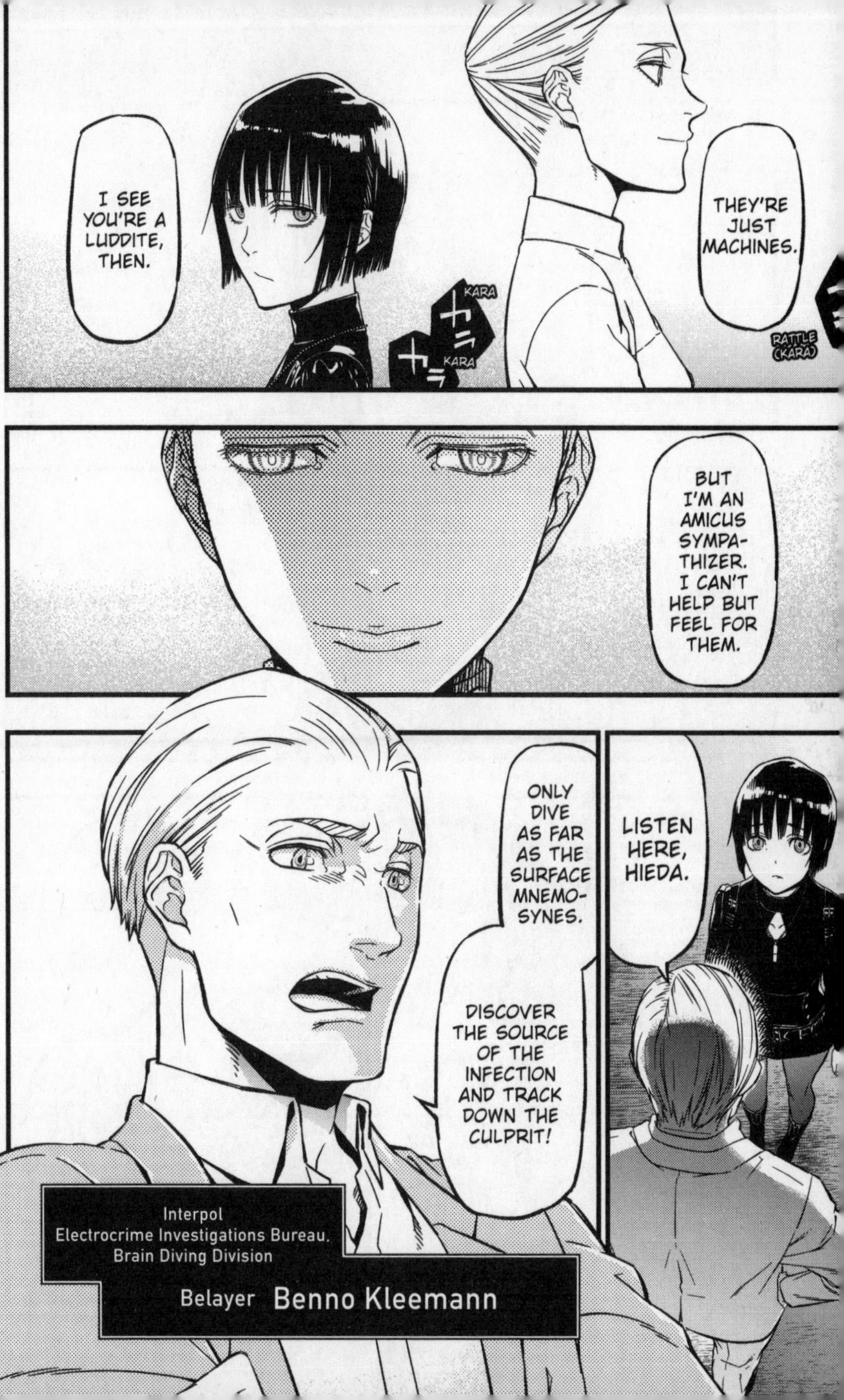
THEY'RE JUST MACHINES.
RATTLE (KARA)
カラ KARA
カラ KARA
I SEE YOU'RE A LUDDITE, THEN.
BUT I'M AN AMICUS SYMPATHIZER. I CAN'T HELP BUT FEEL FOR THEM.
LISTEN HERE, HIEDA.
ONLY DIVE AS FAR AS THE SURFACE MNEMOSYNES.
DISCOVER THE SOURCE OF THE INFECTION AND TRACK DOWN THE CULPRIT!
Interpol
Electrocrime Investigations Bureau.
Brain Diving Division
Belayer Benno Kleemann

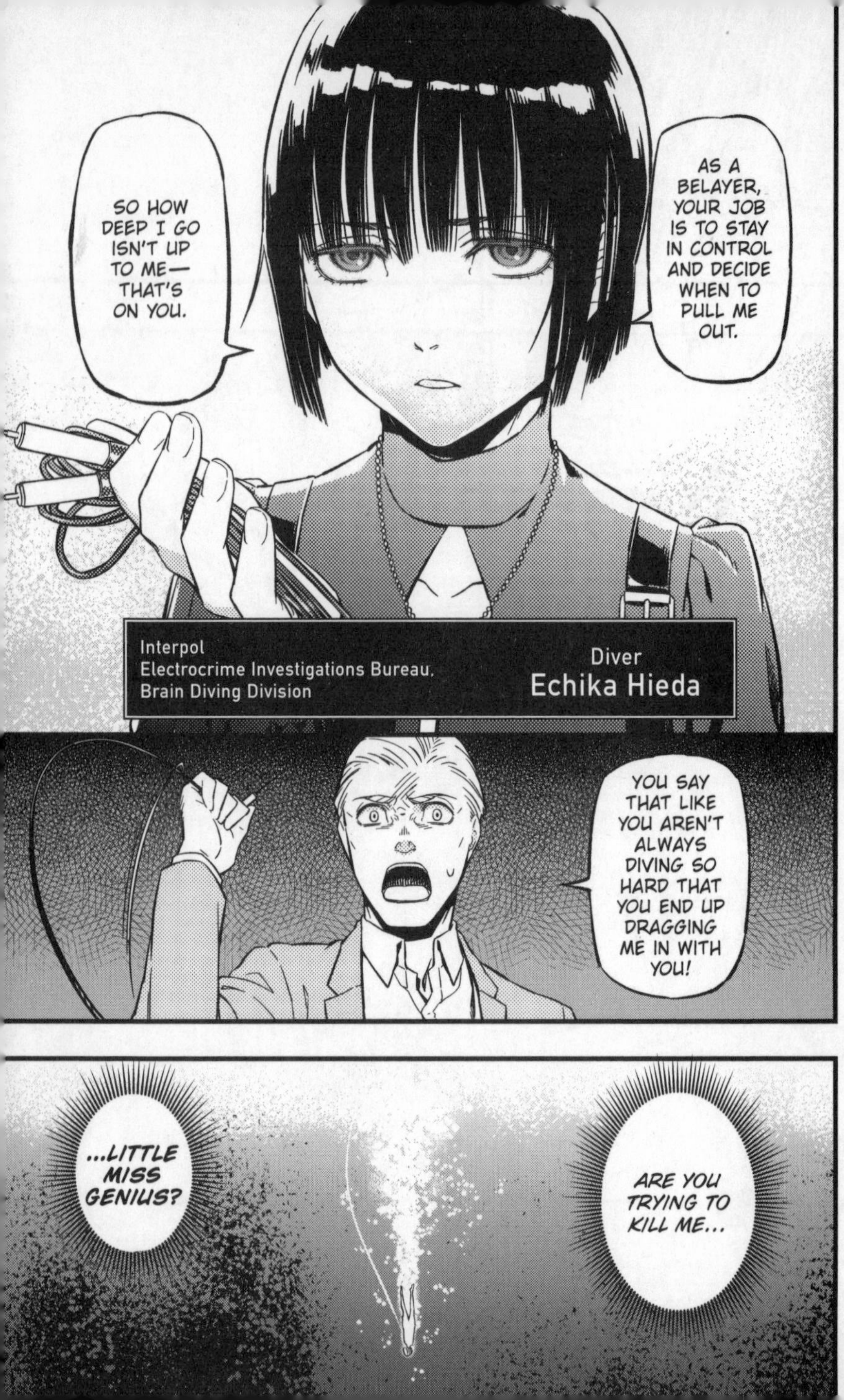
AS A BELAYER, YOUR JOB IS TO STAY IN CONTROL AND DECIDE WHEN TO PULL ME OUT.
SO HOW DEEP I GO ISN'T UP TO ME—THAT'S ON YOU.
Interpol
Electrocrime Investigations Bureau,
Brain Diving Division
Diver
Echika Hieda
YOU SAY THAT LIKE YOU AREN'T ALWAYS DIVING SO HARD THAT YOU END UP DRAGGING ME IN WITH YOU!
ARE YOU TRYING TO KILL ME...
...LITTLE MISS GENIUS?

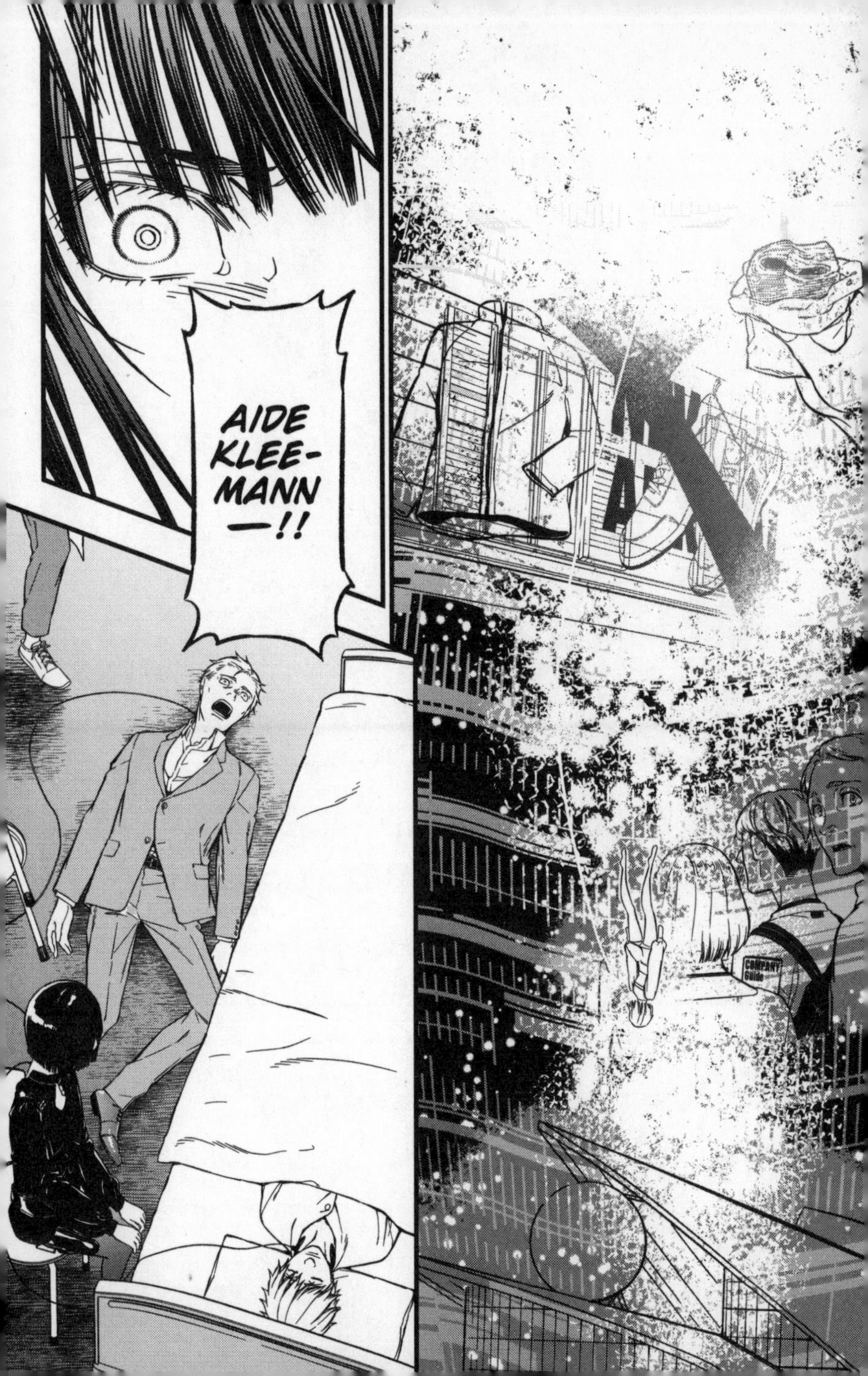
COMPANY Guide
AIDE KLEE-MANN—!!

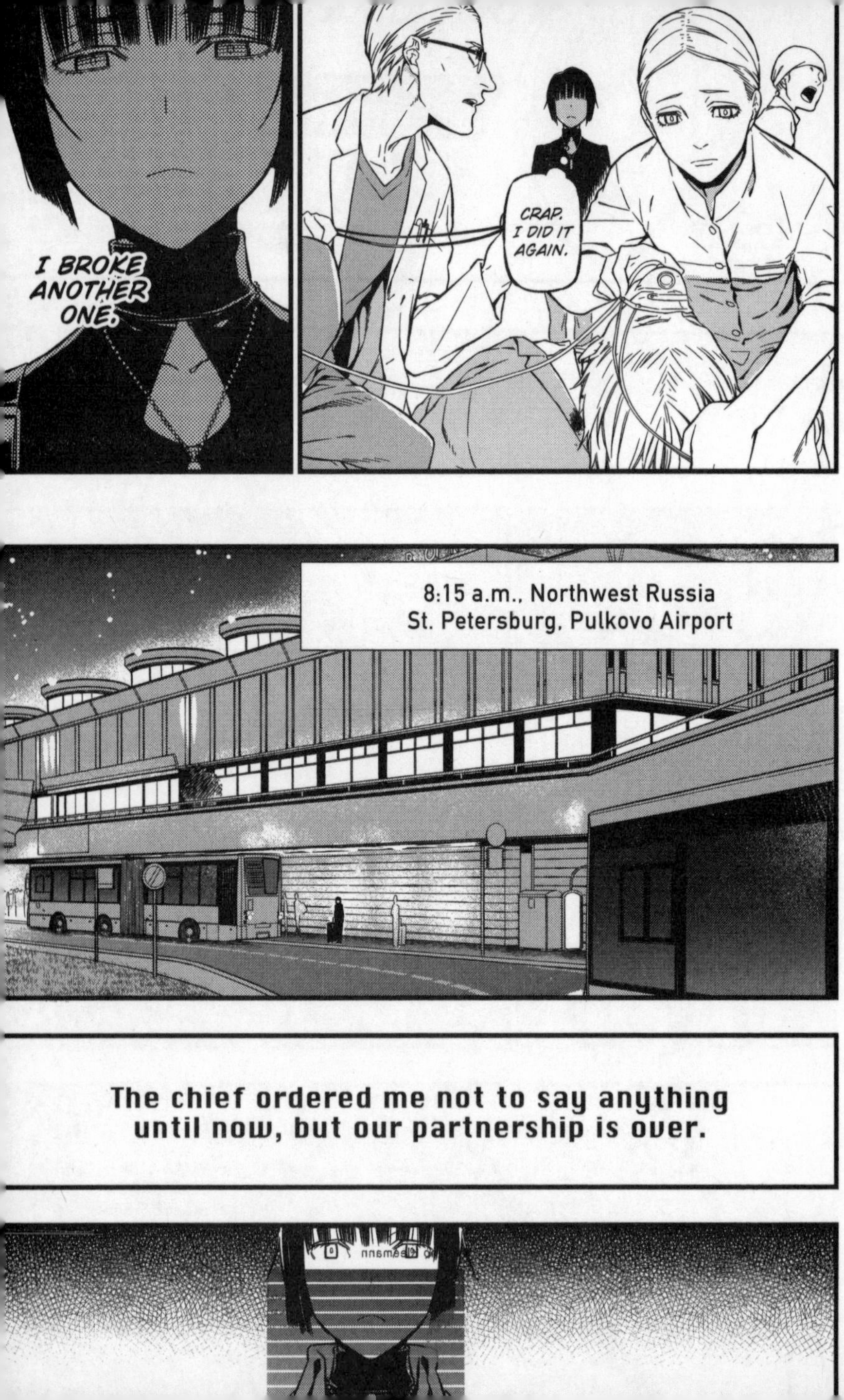
CRAP. I DID IT AGAIN.
I BROKE ANOTHER ONE.
8:15 a.m., Northwest Russia
St. Petersburg, Pulkovo Airport
The chief ordered me not to say anything until now, but our partnership is over.

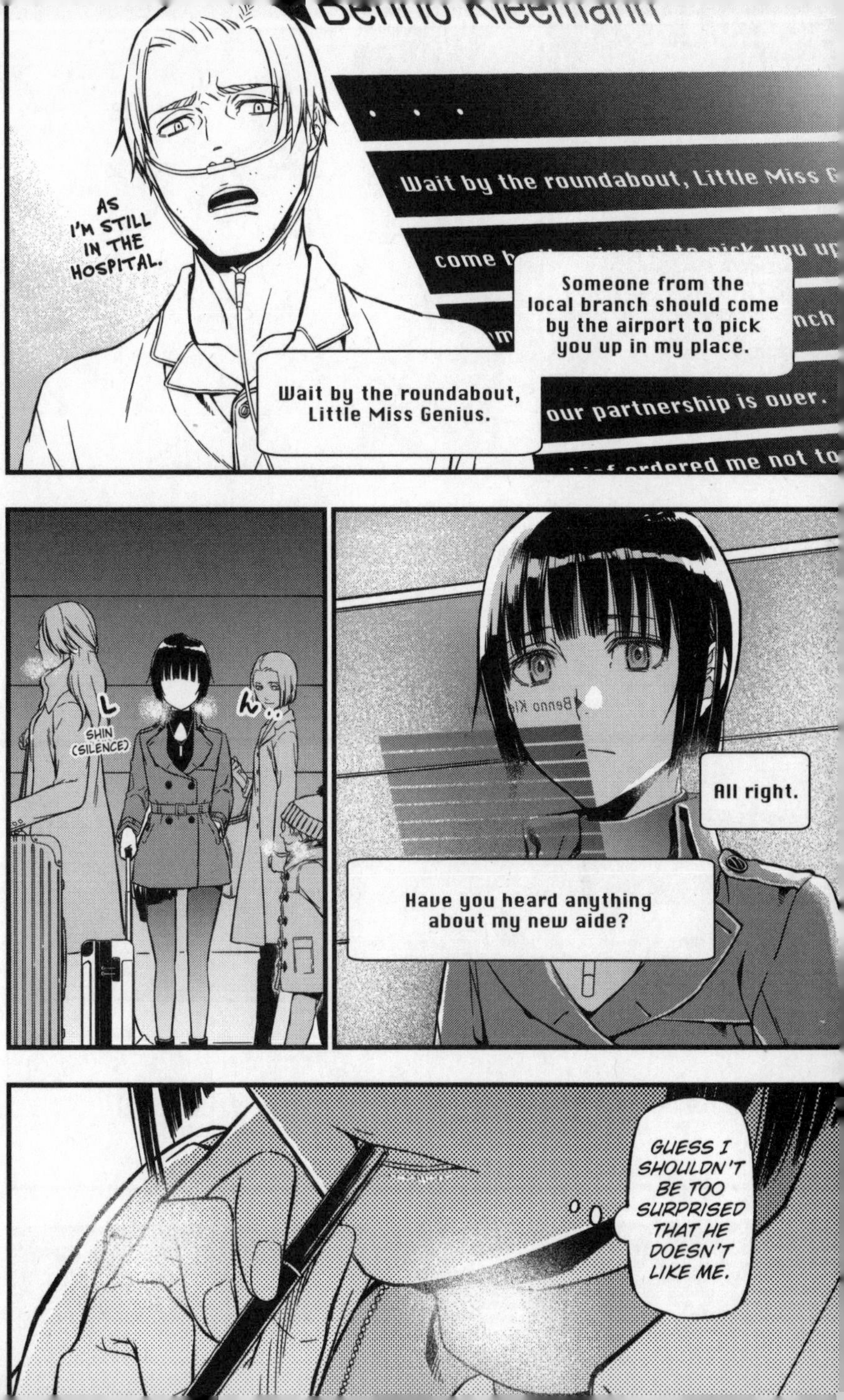
Someone from the local branch should come by the airport to pick you up in my place.
Wait by the roundabout, Little Miss Genius.
AS I'M STILL IN THE HOSPITAL.
All right.
Have you heard anything about my new aide?
SHIN (SILENCE)
GUESS I SHOULDN'T BE TOO SURPRISED THAT HE DOESN'T LIKE ME.

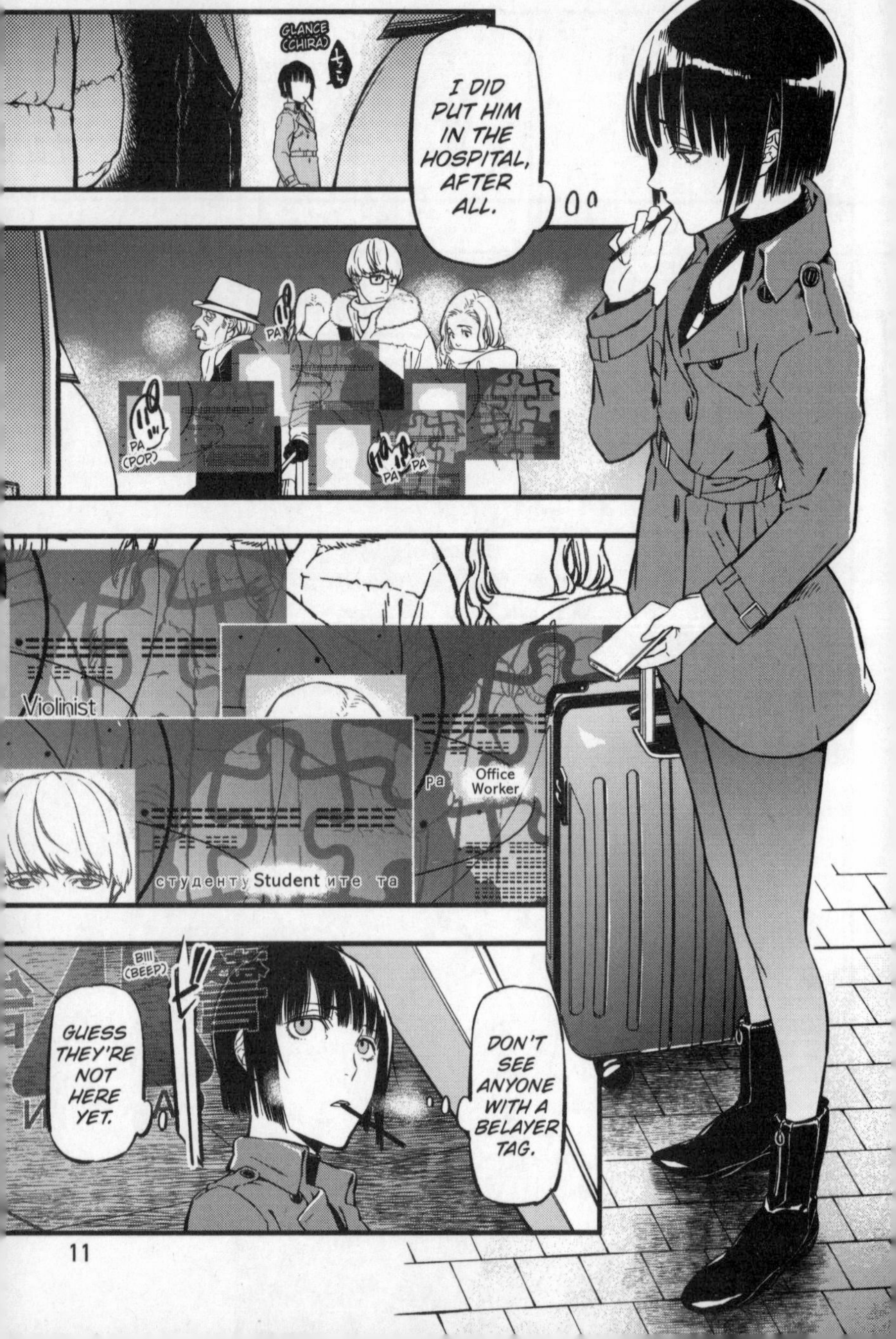
I DID PUT HIM IN THE HOSPITAL, AFTER ALL.
GLANCE (CHIRA)
PA
PA (POP)
PA
PA
Violinist
pa
Office Worker
студенту Student ите та
DON'T SEE ANYONE WITH A BELAYER TAG.
BIII (BEEP)
GUESS THEY'RE NOT HERE YET.

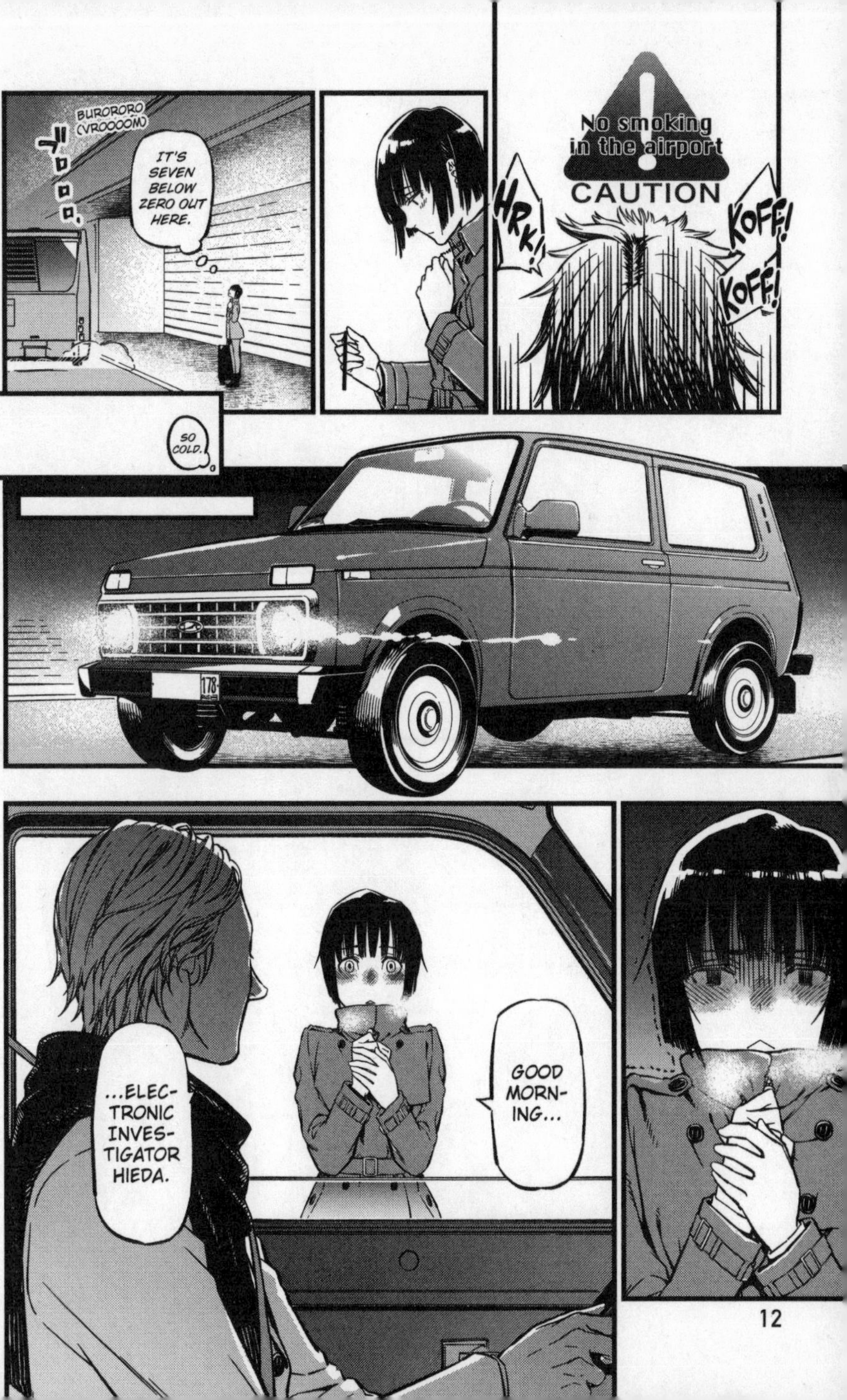
No smoking
in the airport
CAUTION
KOFF!
KOFF!
HRK!
BURORORO (VROOOOM)
ブロロロ
IT'S SEVEN BELOW ZERO OUT HERE.
SO COLD.
GOOD MORN-ING...
...ELEC-TRONIC INVES-TIGATOR HIEDA.

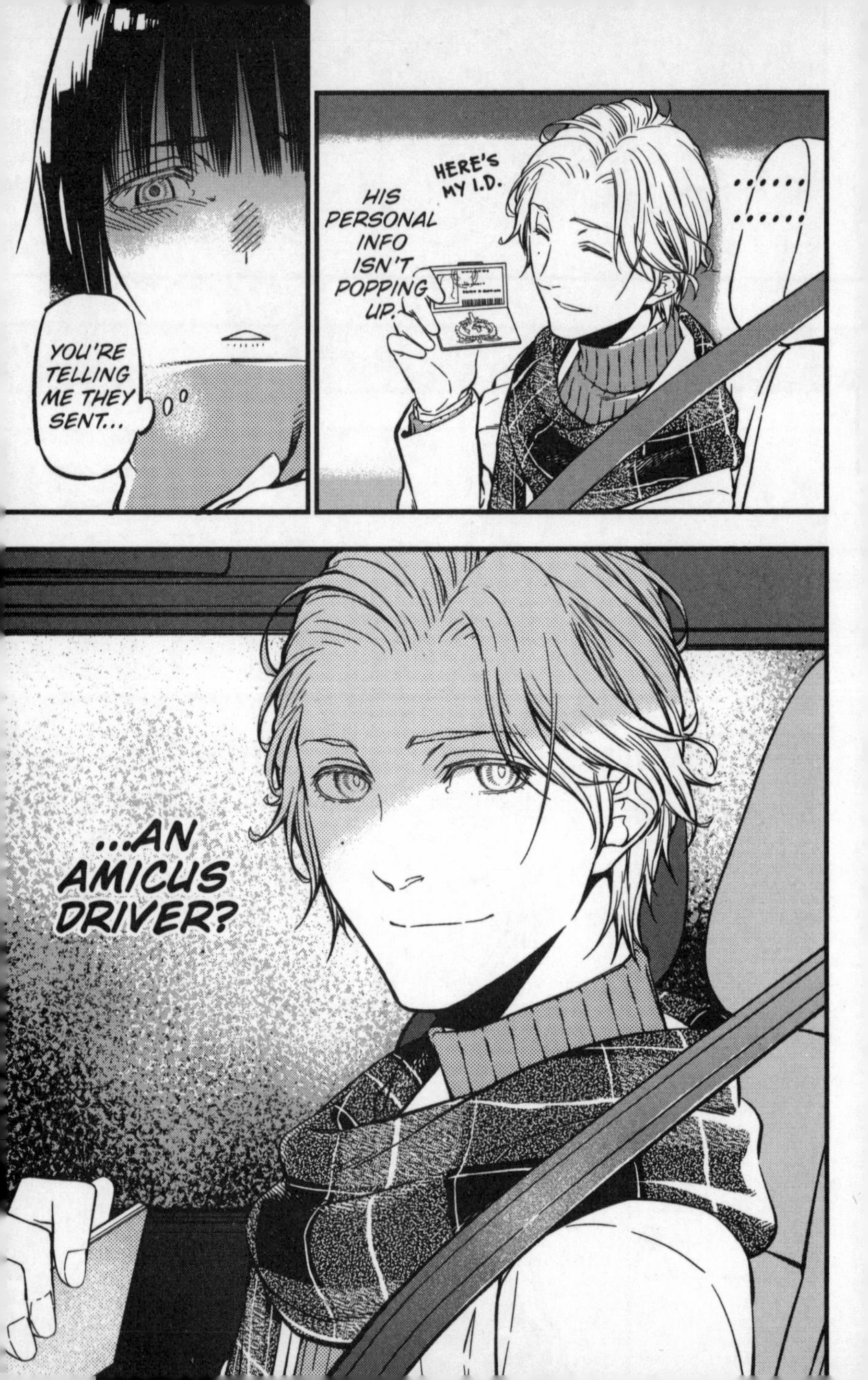
......
......
HERE'S MY I.D.
HIS PERSONAL INFO ISN'T POPPING UP.
YOU'RE TELLING ME THEY SENT...
...AN AMICUS DRIVER?

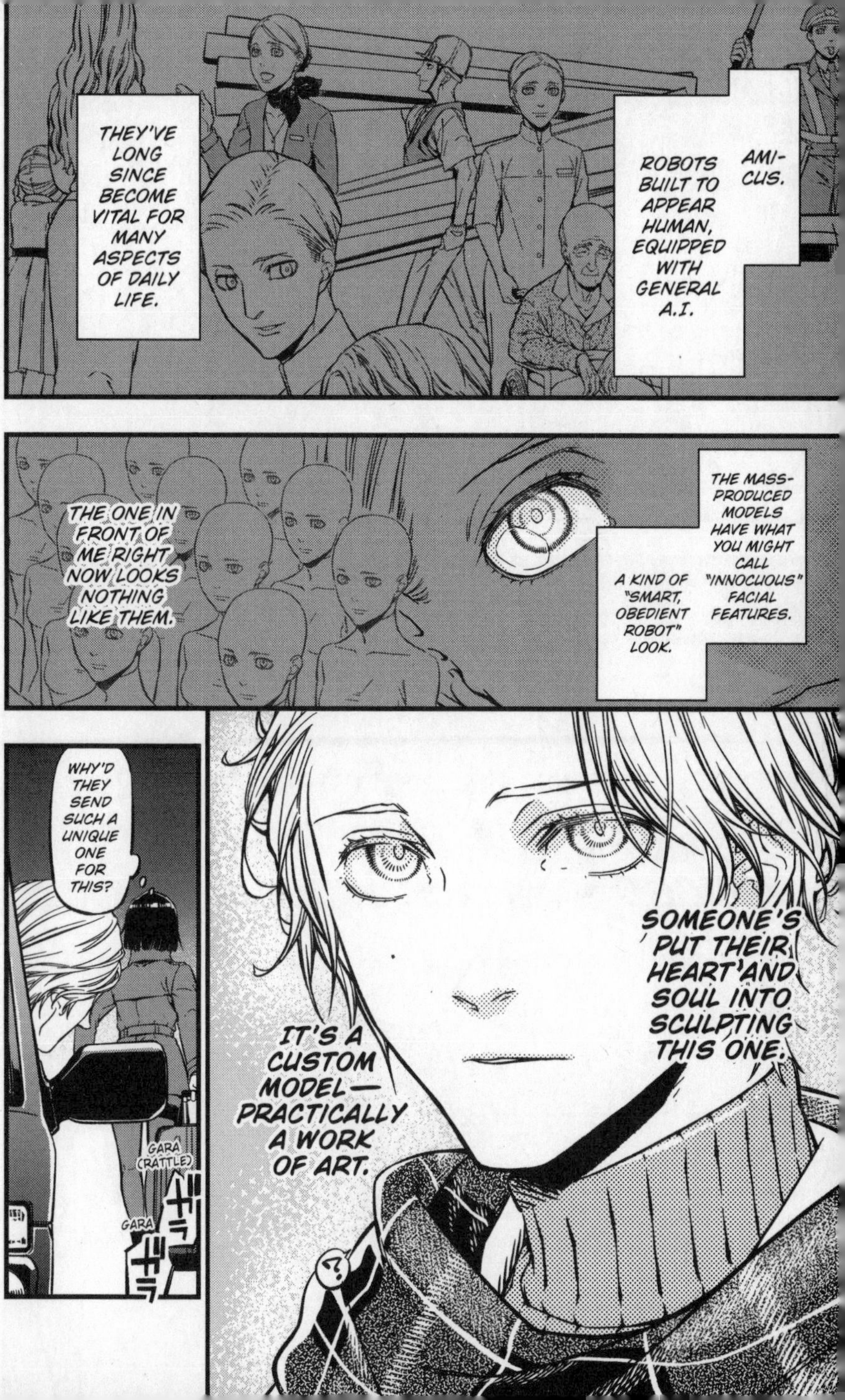
AMI-CUS.
ROBOTS BUILT TO APPEAR HUMAN, EQUIPPED WITH GENERAL A.I.
THEY'VE LONG SINCE BECOME VITAL FOR MANY ASPECTS OF DAILY LIFE.
THE MASS-PRODUCED MODELS HAVE WHAT YOU MIGHT CALL "INNOCUOUS" FACIAL FEATURES.
A KIND OF "SMART, OBEDIENT ROBOT" LOOK.
THE ONE IN FRONT OF ME RIGHT NOW LOOKS NOTHING LIKE THEM.
SOMEONE'S PUT THEIR HEART AND SOUL INTO SCULPTING THIS ONE.
IT'S A CUSTOM MODEL—PRACTICALLY A WORK OF ART.
WHY'D THEY SEND SUCH A UNIQUE ONE FOR THIS?
ガラ
GARA (RATTLE)
ガラ
GARA

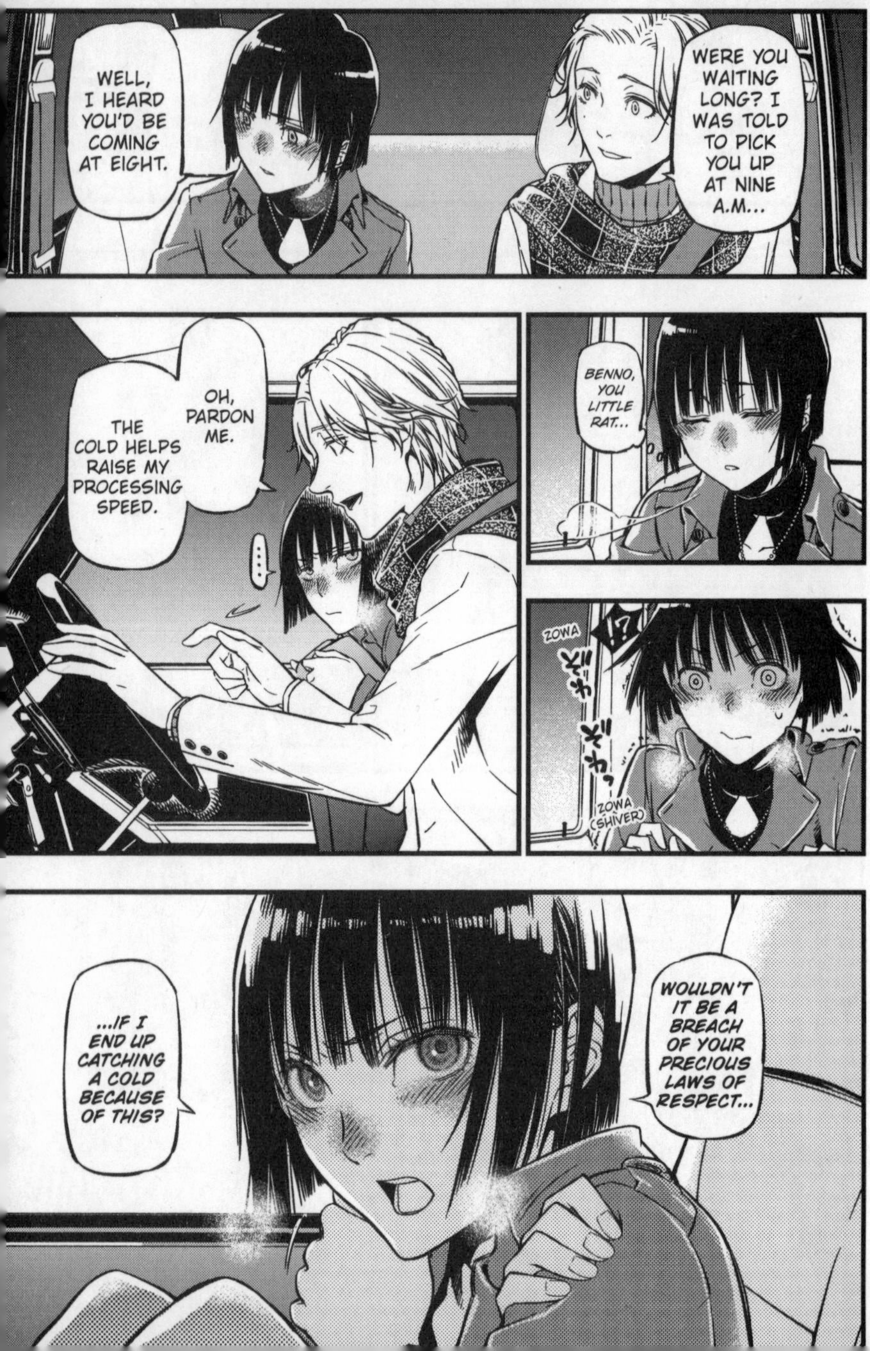
WERE YOU WAITING LONG? I WAS TOLD TO PICK YOU UP AT NINE A.M...
WELL, I HEARD YOU'D BE COMING AT EIGHT.
BENNO, YOU LITTLE RAT...
ZOWA
!?
ZOWA (SHIVER)
OH, PARDON ME.
THE COLD HELPS RAISE MY PROCESSING SPEED.
...
WOULDN'T IT BE A BREACH OF YOUR PRECIOUS LAWS OF RESPECT...
...IF I END UP CATCHING A COLD BECAUSE OF THIS?

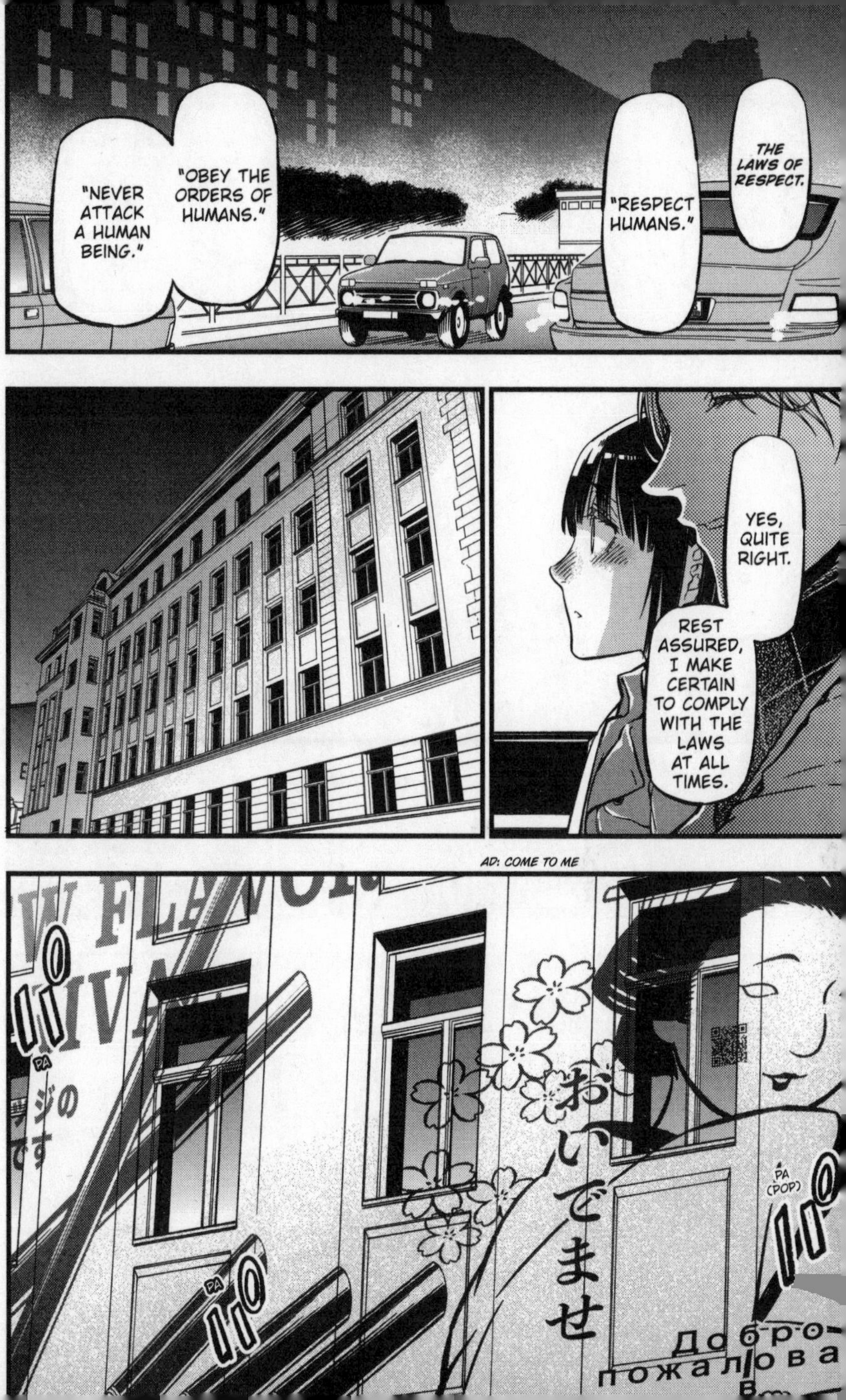
THE LAWS OF RESPECT.
"RESPECT HUMANS."
"OBEY THE ORDERS OF HUMANS."
"NEVER ATTACK A HUMAN BEING."
YES, QUITE RIGHT.
REST ASSURED, I MAKE CERTAIN TO COMPLY WITH THE LAWS AT ALL TIMES.
AD: COME TO ME
PA (POP)
おいでませ
Добро-
пожалова
PA
PA

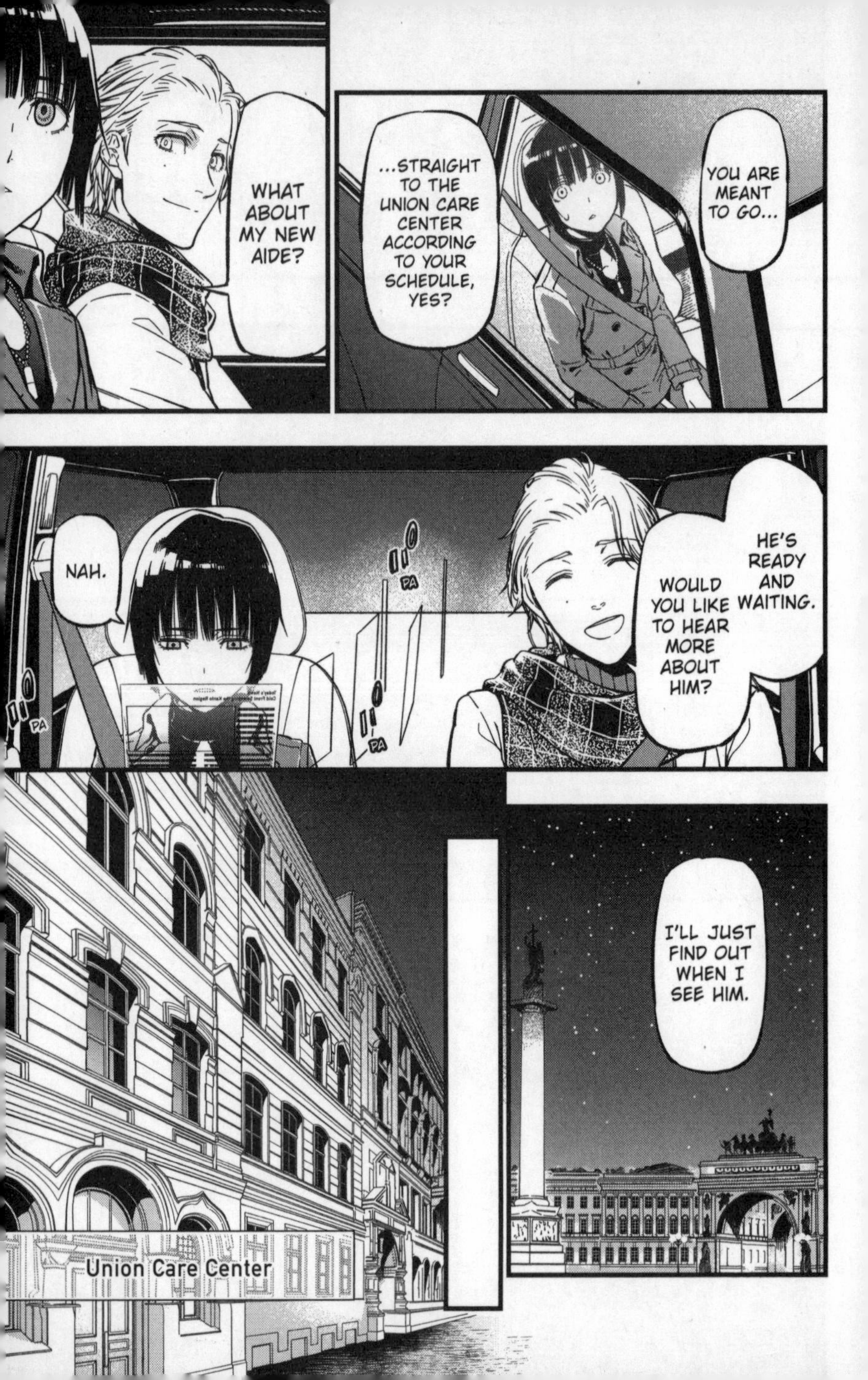
YOU ARE MEANT TO GO...
...STRAIGHT TO THE UNION CARE CENTER ACCORDING TO YOUR SCHEDULE, YES?
WHAT ABOUT MY NEW AIDE?
HE'S READY AND WAITING.
WOULD YOU LIKE TO HEAR MORE ABOUT HIM?
PA
PA
PA
NAH.
I'LL JUST FIND OUT WHEN I SEE HIM.
Union Care Center

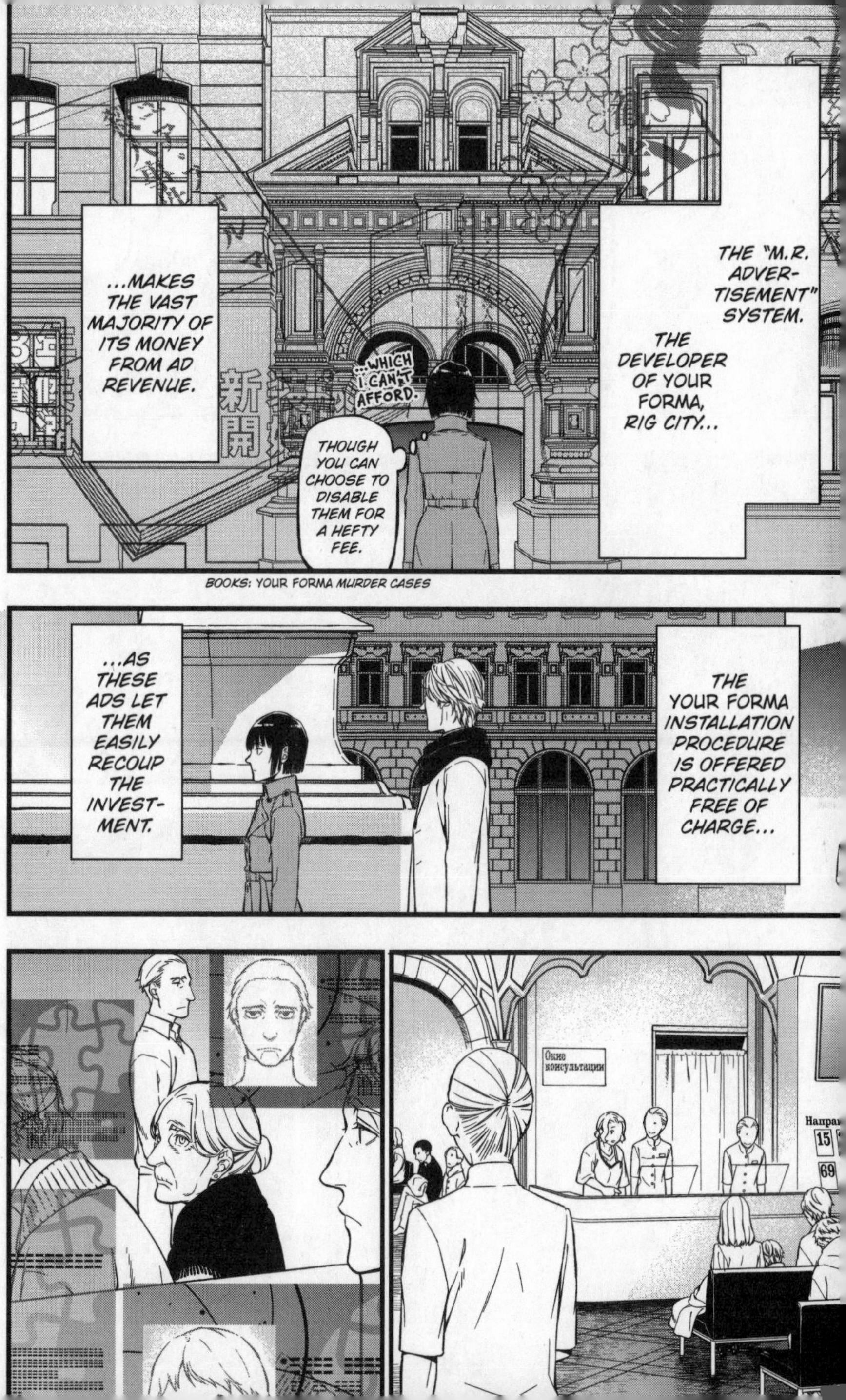
THE "M.R. ADVERTISEMENT" SYSTEM.
THE DEVELOPER OF YOUR FORMA, RIG CITY...
...MAKES THE VAST MAJORITY OF ITS MONEY FROM AD REVENUE.
THOUGH YOU CAN CHOOSE TO DISABLE THEM FOR A HEFTY FEE.
...WHICH I CAN'T AFFORD.
BOOKS: YOUR FORMA MURDER CASES
THE YOUR FORMA INSTALLATION PROCEDURE IS OFFERED PRACTICALLY FREE OF CHARGE...
...AS THESE ADS LET THEM EASILY RECOUP THE INVESTMENT.

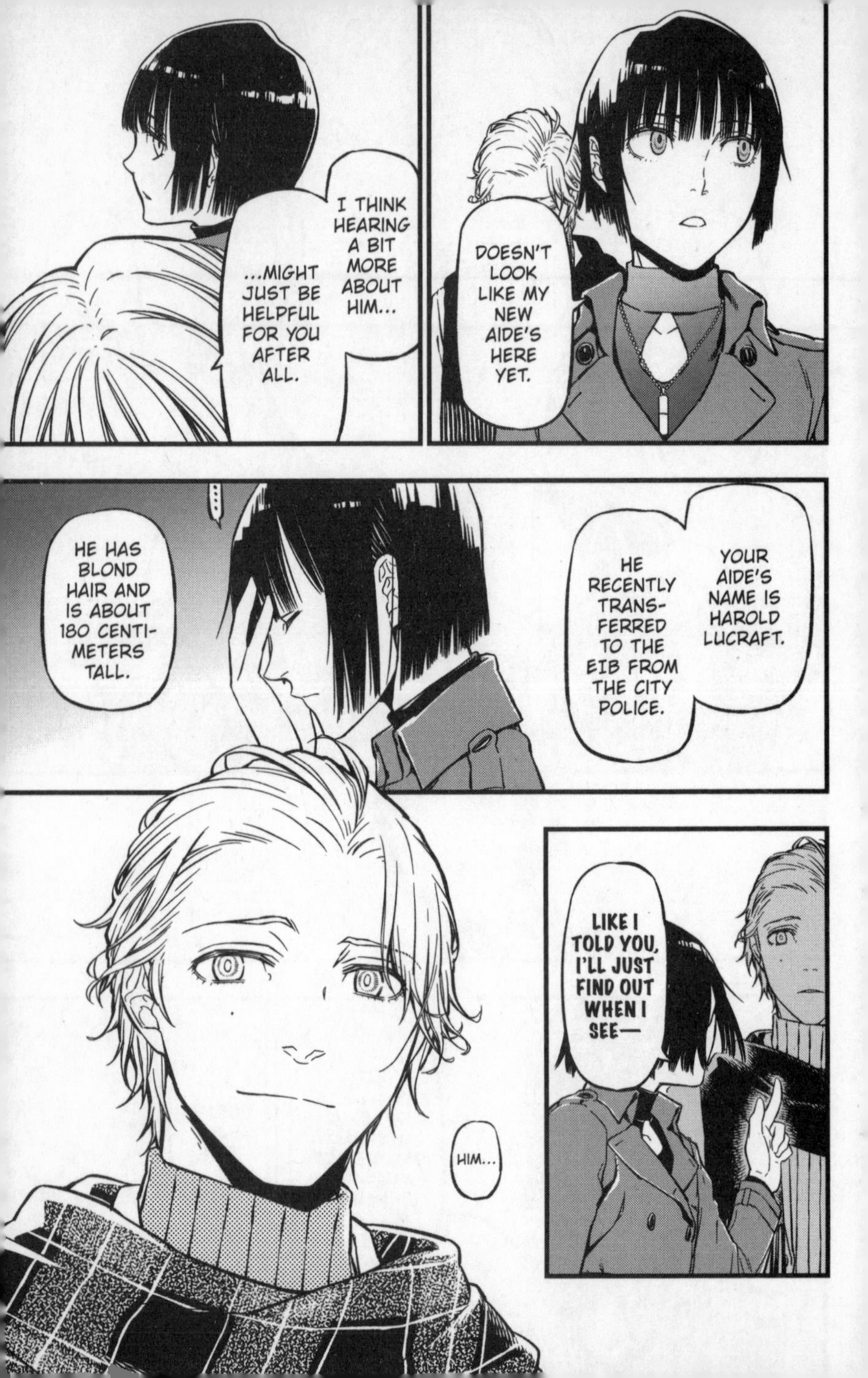
DOESN'T LOOK LIKE MY NEW AIDE'S HERE YET.
I THINK HEARING A BIT MORE ABOUT HIM...
...MIGHT JUST BE HELPFUL FOR YOU AFTER ALL.
YOUR AIDE'S NAME IS HAROLD LUCRAFT.
HE RECENTLY TRANS-FERRED TO THE EIB FROM THE CITY POLICE.
HE HAS BLOND HAIR AND IS ABOUT 180 CENTI-METERS TALL.
LIKE I TOLD YOU, I'LL JUST FIND OUT WHEN I SEE—
HIM...

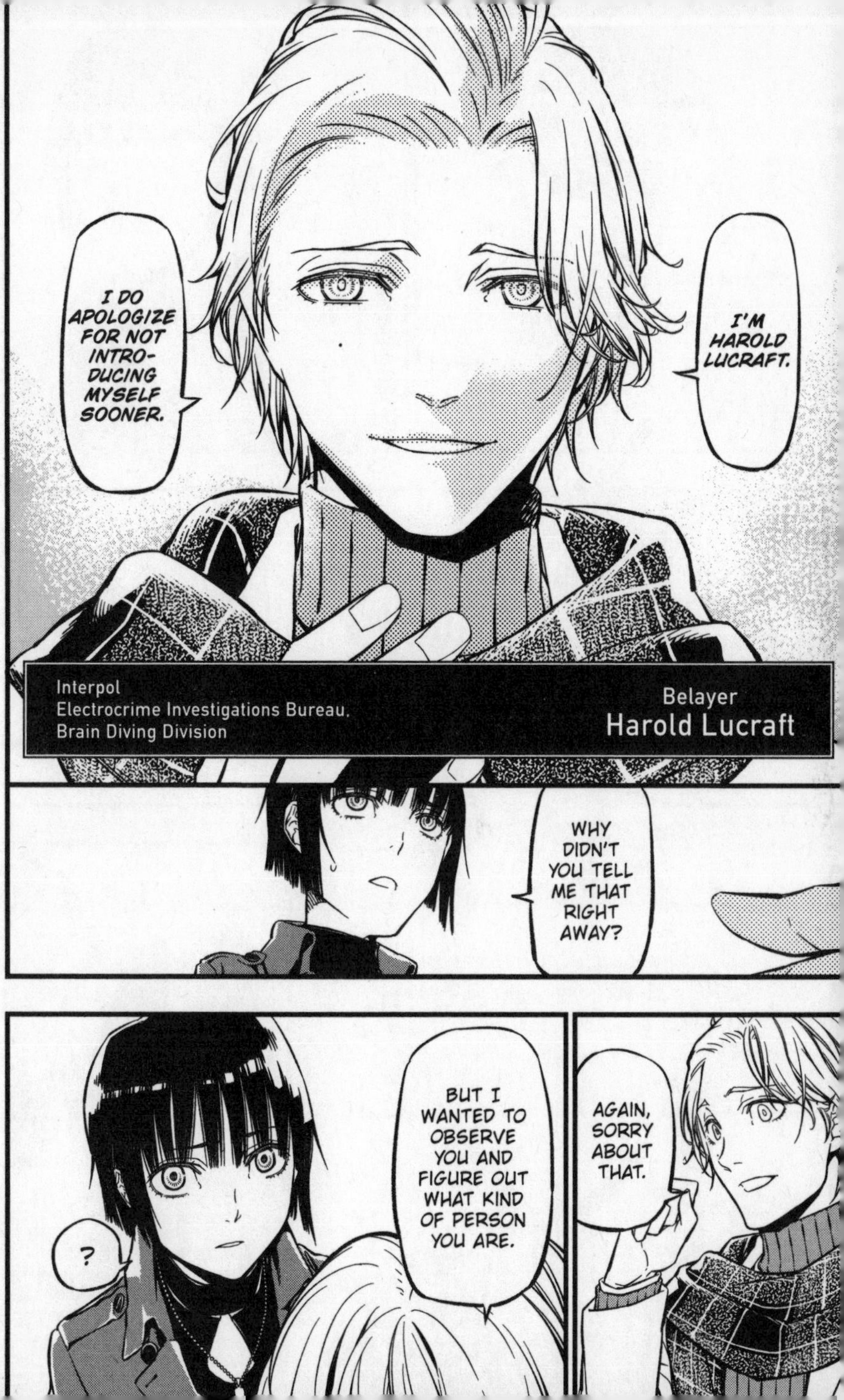
I'M HAROLD LUCRAFT.
I DO APOLOGIZE FOR NOT INTRODUCING MYSELF SOONER.
Belayer
Harold Lucraft
Interpol
Electrocrime Investigations Bureau,
Brain Diving Division
WHY DIDN'T YOU TELL ME THAT RIGHT AWAY?
AGAIN, SORRY ABOUT THAT.
BUT I WANTED TO OBSERVE YOU AND FIGURE OUT WHAT KIND OF PERSON YOU ARE.
?

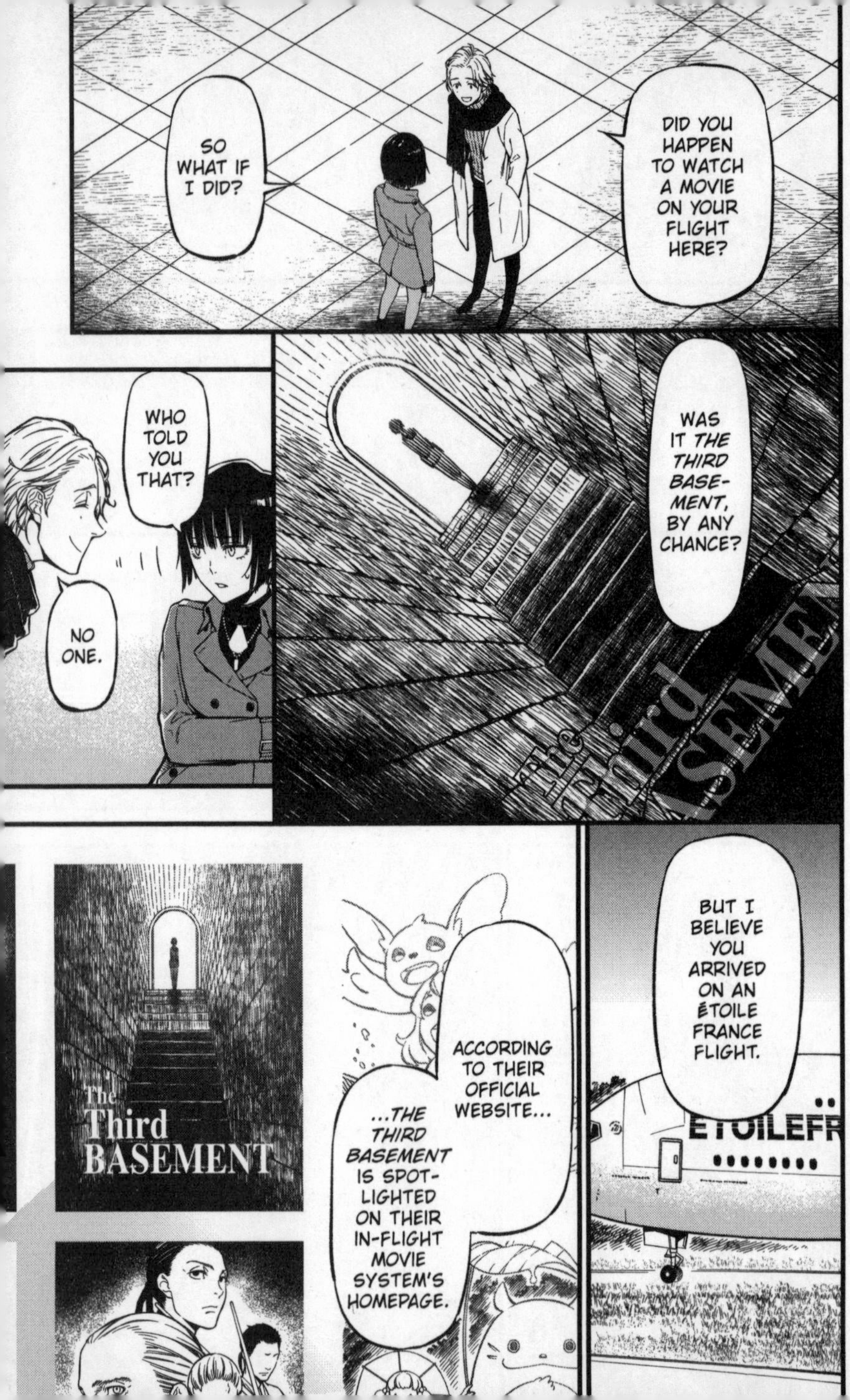
DID YOU HAPPEN TO WATCH A MOVIE ON YOUR FLIGHT HERE?
SO WHAT IF I DID?
WAS IT *THE THIRD BASEMENT*, BY ANY CHANCE?
The Third BASEMENT
WHO TOLD YOU THAT?
NO ONE.
BUT I BELIEVE YOU ARRIVED ON AN ÉTOILE FRANCE FLIGHT.
ETOILEFR
ACCORDING TO THEIR OFFICIAL WEBSITE...
...*THE THIRD BASEMENT* IS SPOTLIGHTED ON THEIR IN-FLIGHT MOVIE SYSTEM'S HOMEPAGE.
The Third BASEMENT

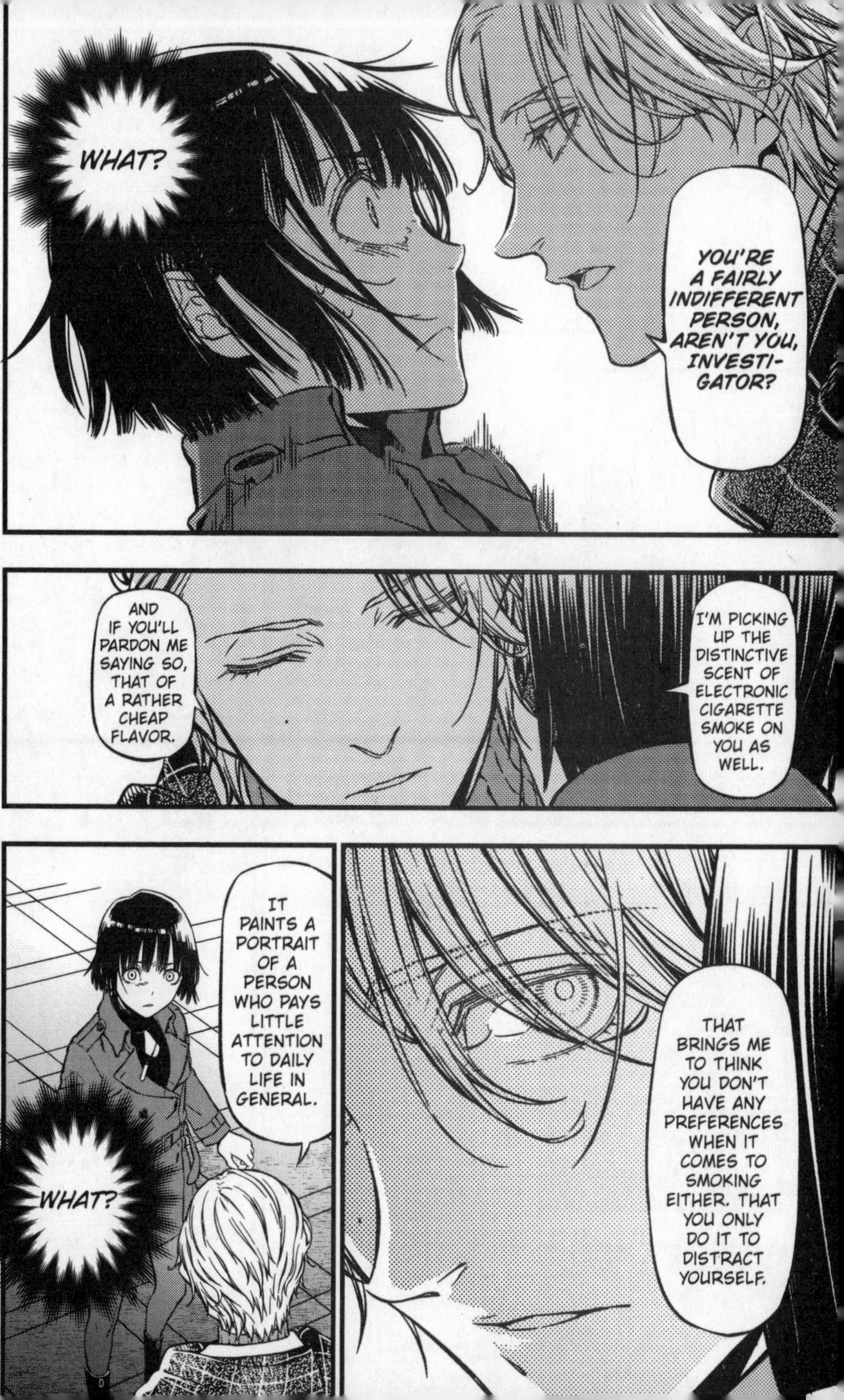
YOU'RE A FAIRLY INDIFFERENT PERSON, AREN'T YOU, INVESTI-GATOR?
WHAT?
I'M PICKING UP THE DISTINCTIVE SCENT OF ELECTRONIC CIGARETTE SMOKE ON YOU AS WELL.
AND IF YOU'LL PARDON ME SAYING SO, THAT OF A RATHER CHEAP FLAVOR.
THAT BRINGS ME TO THINK YOU DON'T HAVE ANY PREFERENCES WHEN IT COMES TO SMOKING EITHER. THAT YOU ONLY DO IT TO DISTRACT YOURSELF.
IT PAINTS A PORTRAIT OF A PERSON WHO PAYS LITTLE ATTENTION TO DAILY LIFE IN GENERAL.
WHAT?

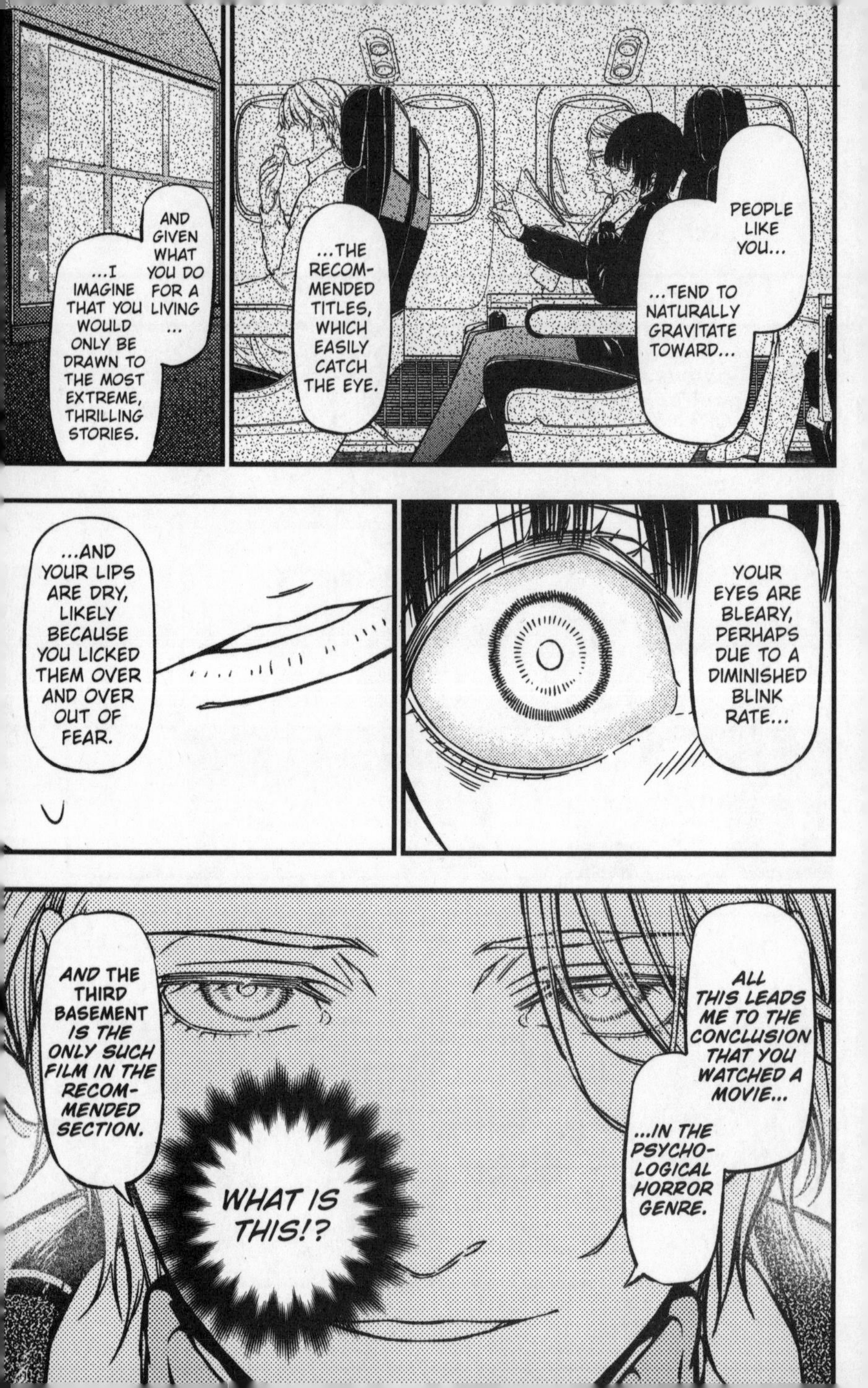
PEOPLE LIKE YOU...
...TEND TO NATURALLY GRAVITATE TOWARD...
...THE RECOMMENDED TITLES, WHICH EASILY CATCH THE EYE.
AND GIVEN WHAT YOU DO FOR A LIVING...
...I IMAGINE THAT YOU WOULD ONLY BE DRAWN TO THE MOST EXTREME, THRILLING STORIES.
YOUR EYES ARE BLEARY, PERHAPS DUE TO A DIMINISHED BLINK RATE...
...AND YOUR LIPS ARE DRY, LIKELY BECAUSE YOU LICKED THEM OVER AND OVER OUT OF FEAR.
ALL THIS LEADS ME TO THE CONCLUSION THAT YOU WATCHED A MOVIE...
...IN THE PSYCHOLOGICAL HORROR GENRE.
AND THE THIRD BASEMENT IS THE ONLY SUCH FILM IN THE RECOMMENDED SECTION.
WHAT IS THIS!?

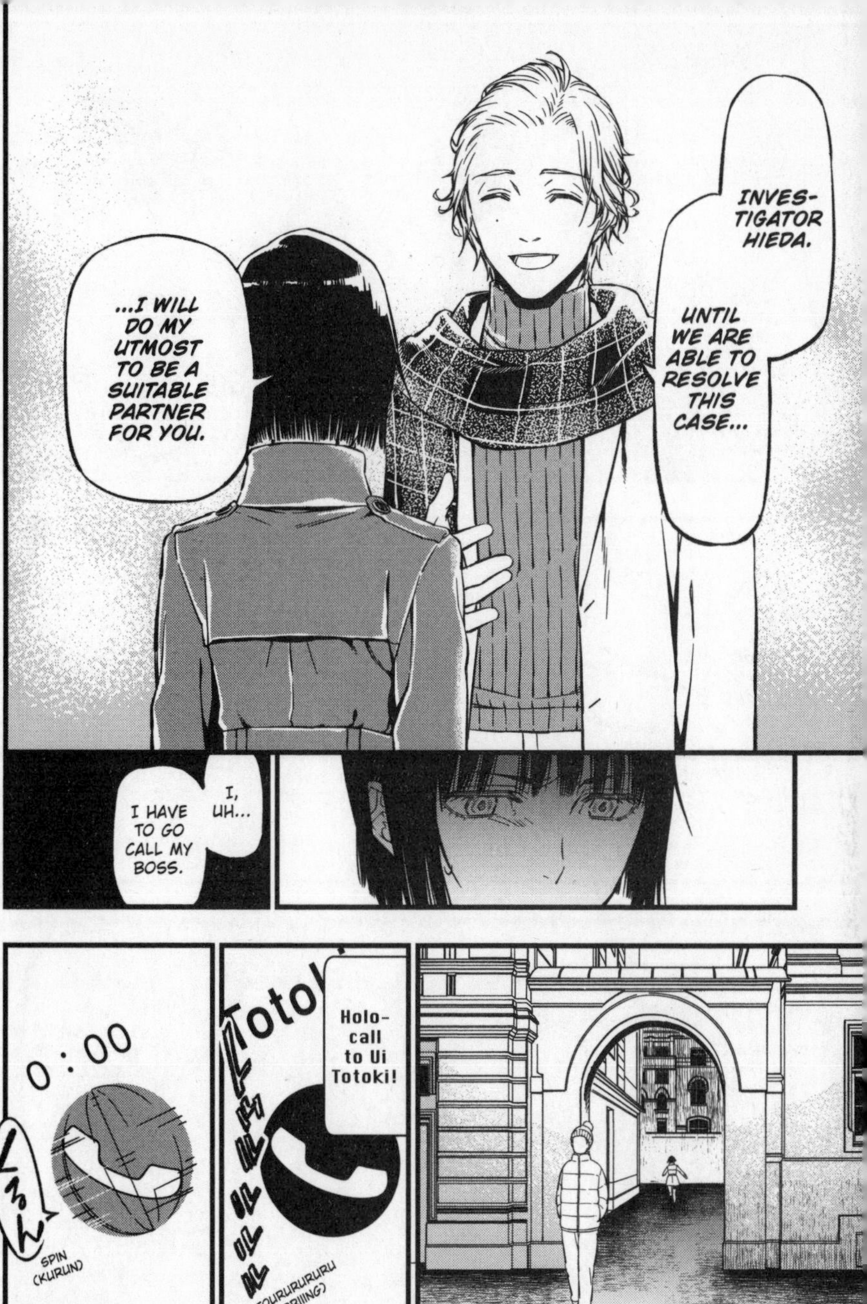
INVES-TIGATOR HIEDA.
UNTIL WE ARE ABLE TO RESOLVE THIS CASE...
...I WILL DO MY UTMOST TO BE A SUITABLE PARTNER FOR YOU.
I, UH...
I HAVE TO GO CALL MY BOSS.
Holo-call to Ui Totoki!
Totoki
TOURURURURU (BRIING)
0 : 00
SPIN (KURUN)

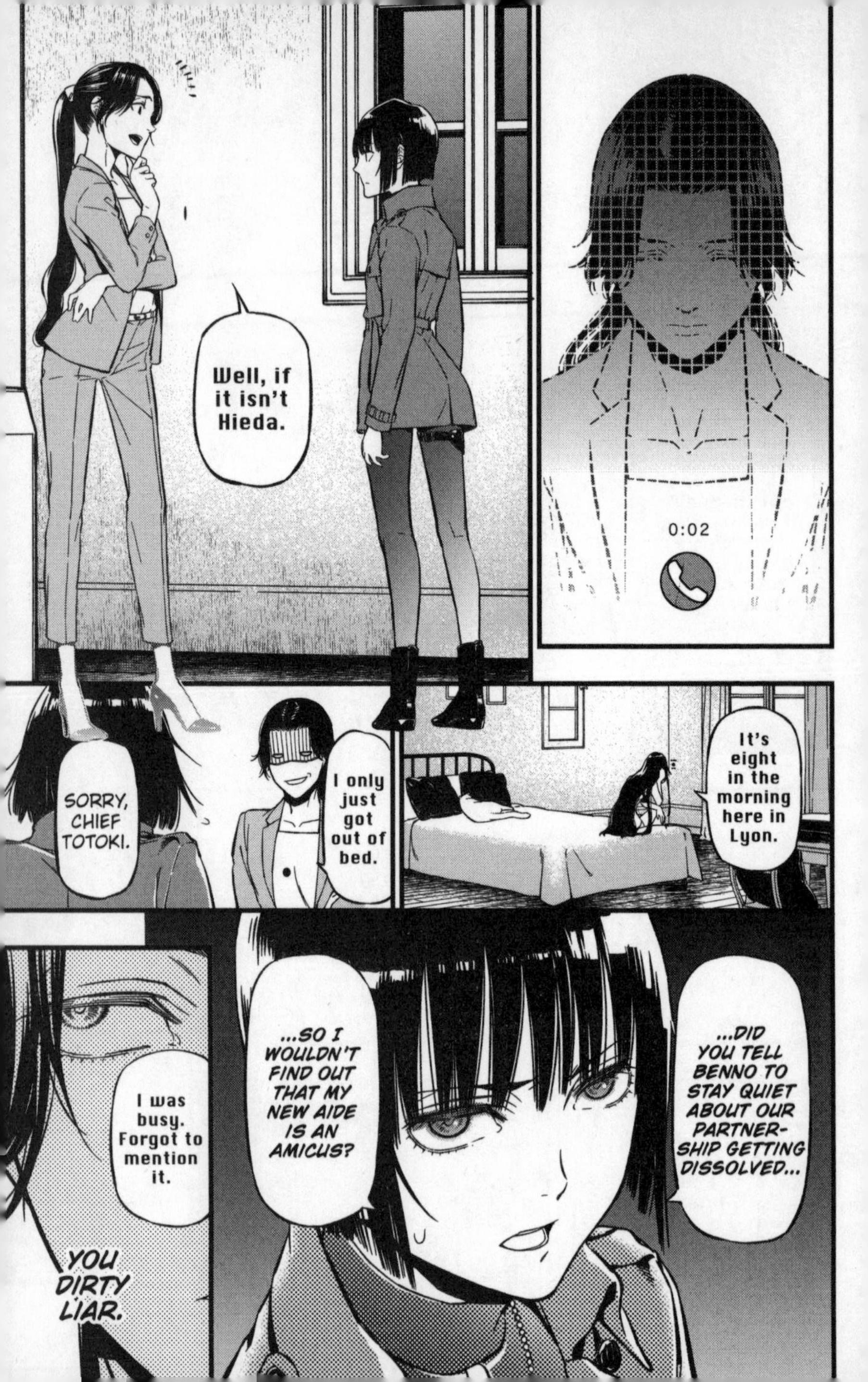
0:02
Well, if it isn't Hieda.
It's eight in the morning here in Lyon.
I only just got out of bed.
SORRY, CHIEF TOTOKI.
...DID YOU TELL BENNO TO STAY QUIET ABOUT OUR PARTNERSHIP GETTING DISSOLVED...
...SO I WOULDN'T FIND OUT THAT MY NEW AIDE IS AN AMICUS?
I was busy. Forgot to mention it.
YOU DIRTY LIAR.

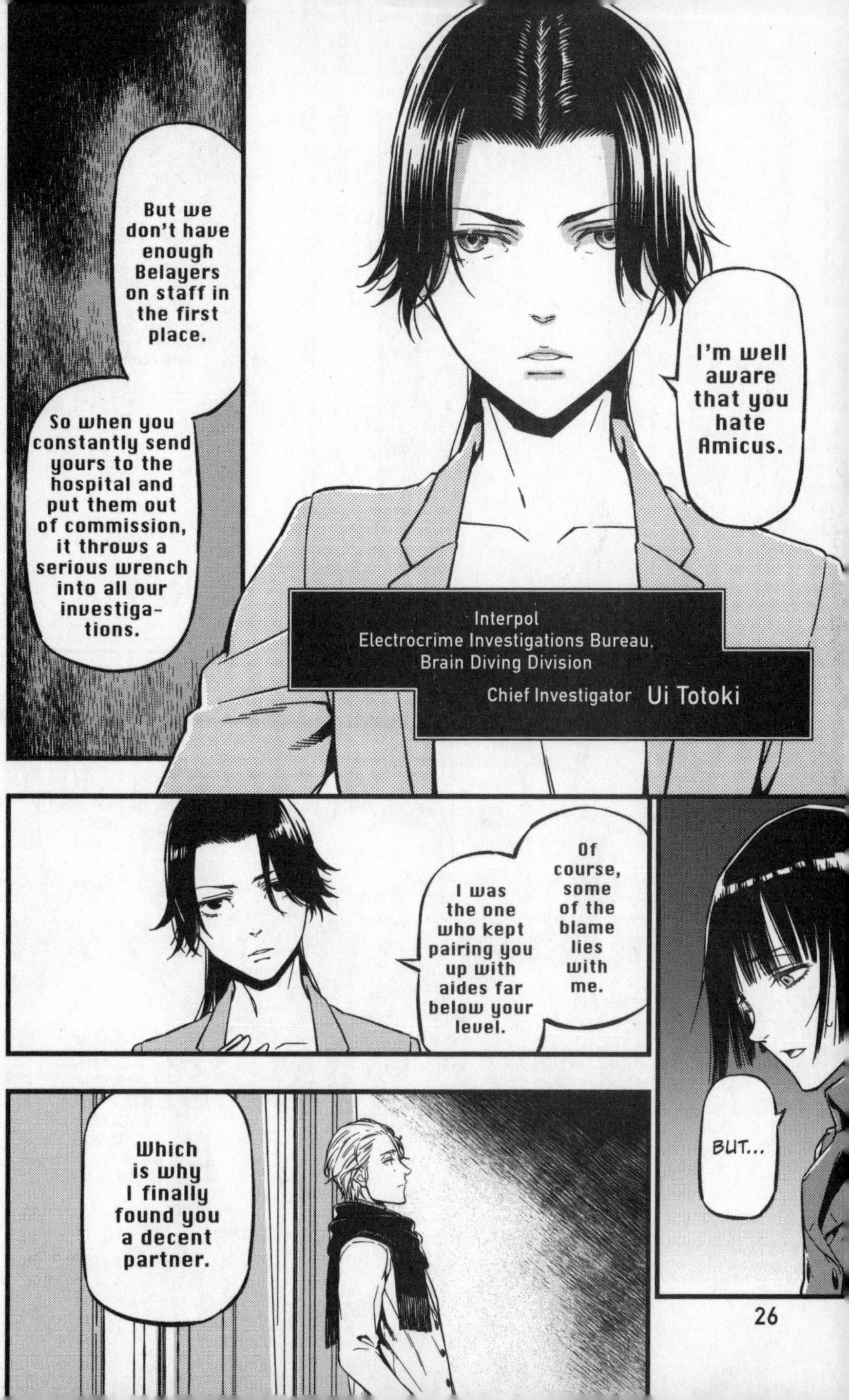

I'm well aware that you hate Amicus.
But we don't have enough Belayers on staff in the first place.
So when you constantly send yours to the hospital and put them out of commission, it throws a serious wrench into all our investiga- tions.
Interpol
Electrocrime Investigations Bureau, Brain Diving Division
Chief Investigator Ui Totoki
BUT...
Of course, some of the blame lies with me.
I was the one who kept pairing you up with aides far below your level.
Which is why I finally found you a decent partner.

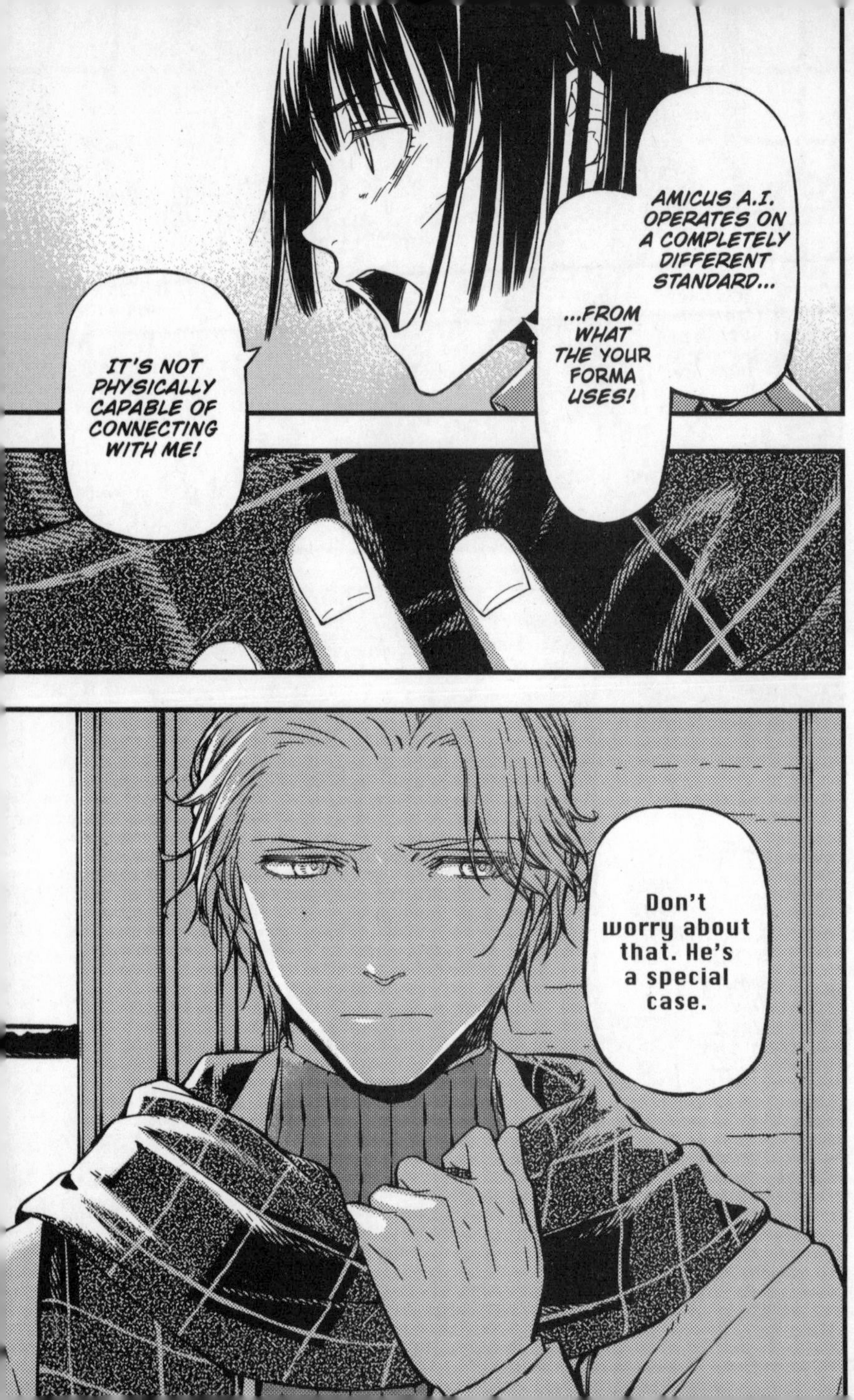
AMICUS A.I. OPERATES ON A COMPLETELY DIFFERENT STANDARD...
...FROM WHAT THE YOUR FORMA USES!
IT'S NOT PHYSICALLY CAPABLE OF CONNECTING WITH ME!
Don't worry about that. He's a special case.

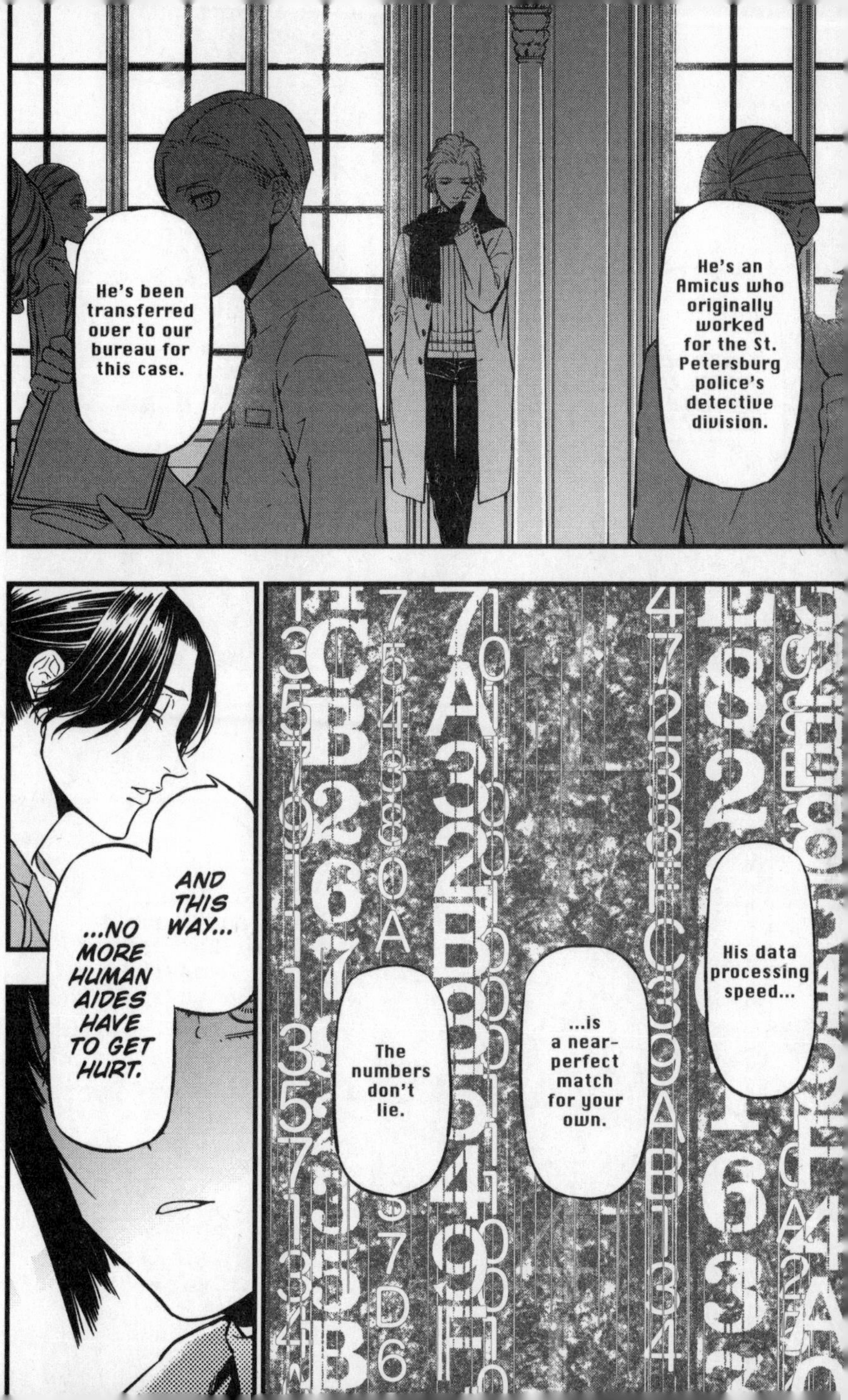
He's an Amicus who originally worked for the St. Petersburg police's detective division.
He's been transferred over to our bureau for this case.
His data processing speed...
...is a near-perfect match for your own.
The numbers don't lie.
AND THIS WAY...
...NO MORE HUMAN AIDES HAVE TO GET HURT.

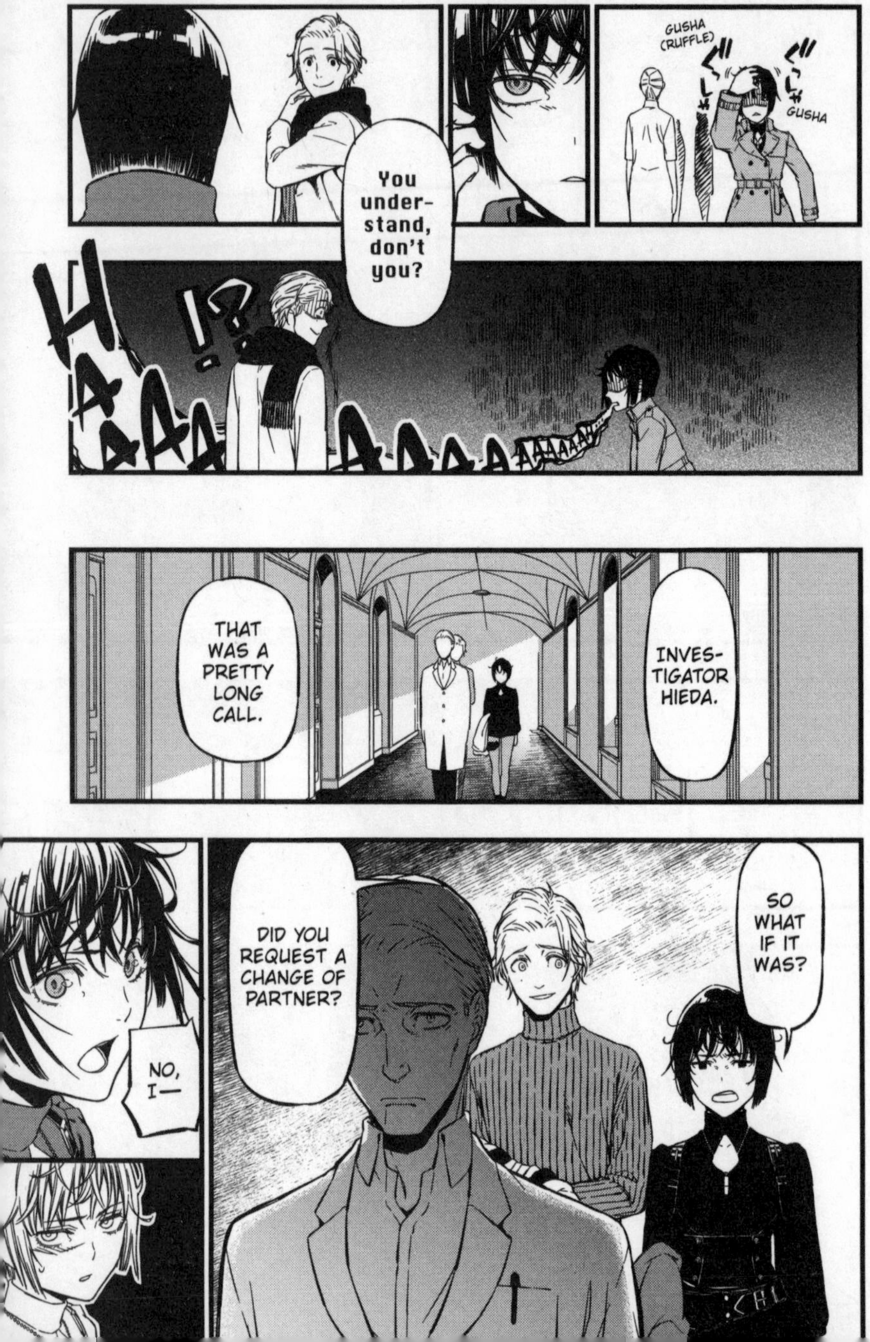
GUSHA (RUFFLE)
GUSHA
You understand, don't you?
!?
HAAAAAAAAAAAAAA
INVESTIGATOR HIEDA.
THAT WAS A PRETTY LONG CALL.
SO WHAT IF IT WAS?
DID YOU REQUEST A CHANGE OF PARTNER?
NO, I—

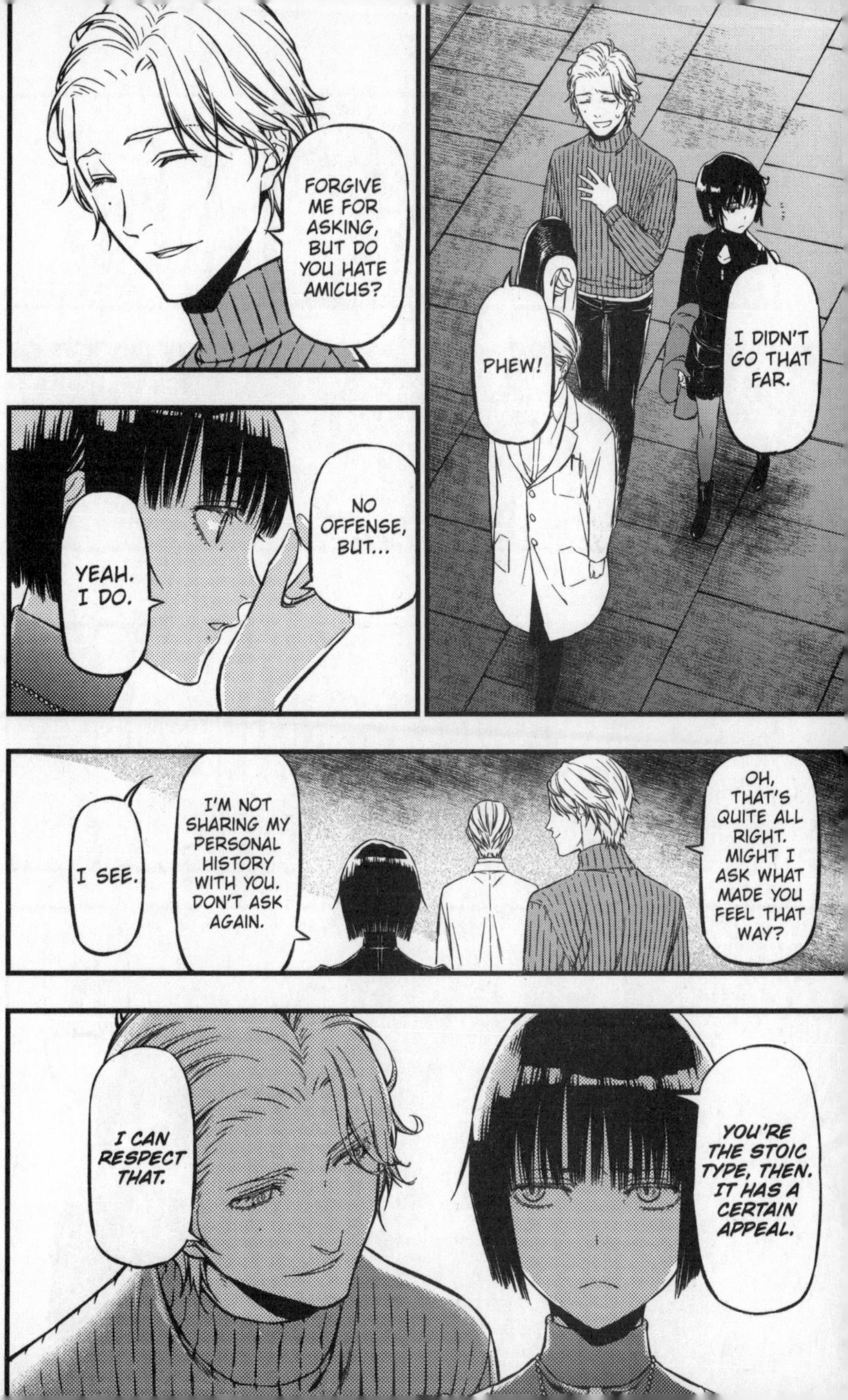
I DIDN'T GO THAT FAR.
PHEW!
FORGIVE ME FOR ASKING, BUT DO YOU HATE AMICUS?
NO OFFENSE, BUT...
YEAH. I DO.
OH, THAT'S QUITE ALL RIGHT. MIGHT I ASK WHAT MADE YOU FEEL THAT WAY?
I'M NOT SHARING MY PERSONAL HISTORY WITH YOU. DON'T ASK AGAIN.
I SEE.
YOU'RE THE STOIC TYPE, THEN. IT HAS A CERTAIN APPEAL.
I CAN RESPECT THAT.

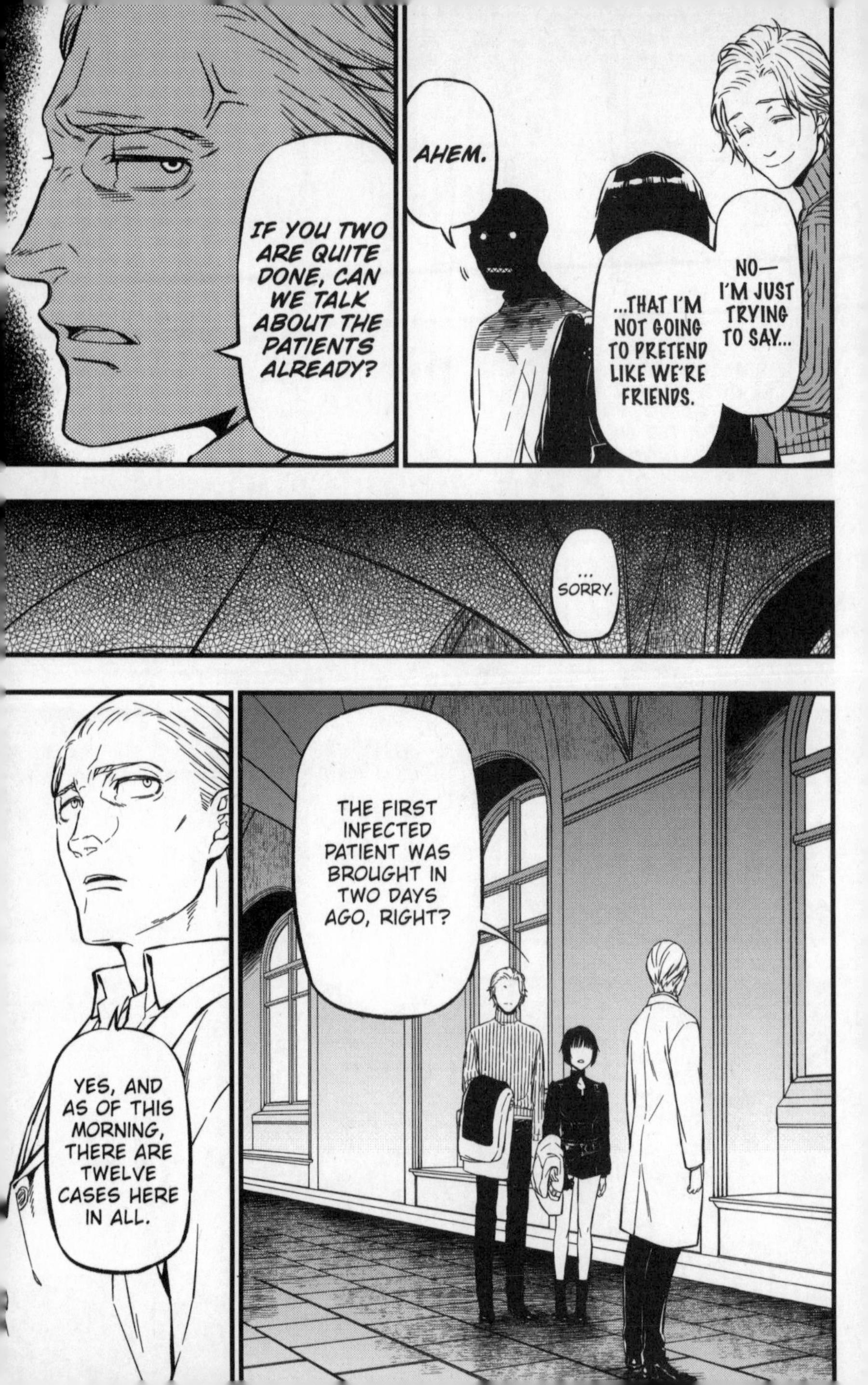
NO— I'M JUST TRYING TO SAY...
...THAT I'M NOT GOING TO PRETEND LIKE WE'RE FRIENDS.
AHEM.
IF YOU TWO ARE QUITE DONE, CAN WE TALK ABOUT THE PATIENTS ALREADY?
... SORRY.
THE FIRST INFECTED PATIENT WAS BROUGHT IN TWO DAYS AGO, RIGHT?
YES, AND AS OF THIS MORNING, THERE ARE TWELVE CASES HERE IN ALL.

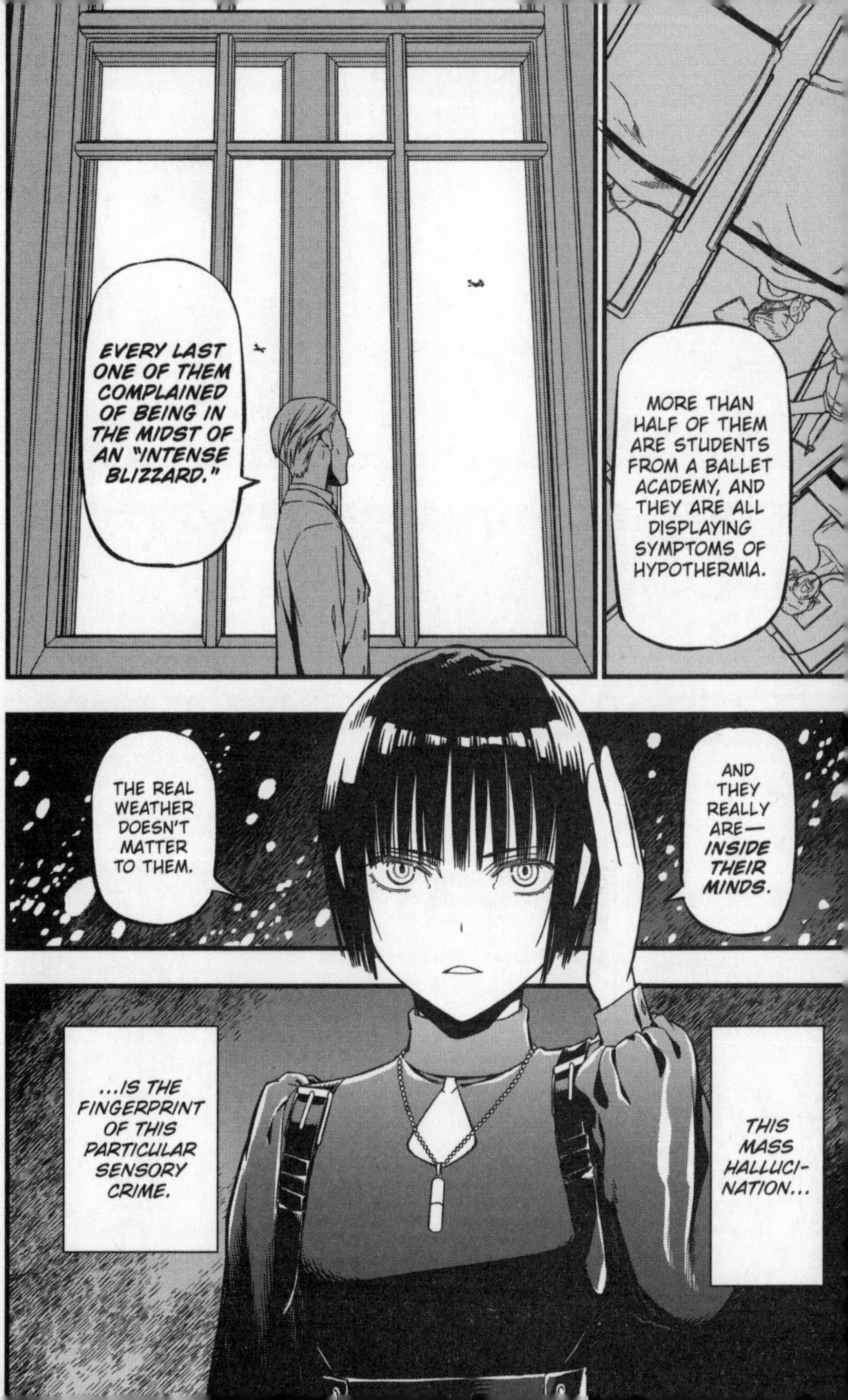
MORE THAN HALF OF THEM ARE STUDENTS FROM A BALLET ACADEMY, AND THEY ARE ALL DISPLAYING SYMPTOMS OF HYPOTHERMIA.
EVERY LAST ONE OF THEM COMPLAINED OF BEING IN THE MIDST OF AN "INTENSE BLIZZARD."
AND THEY REALLY ARE—INSIDE THEIR MINDS.
THE REAL WEATHER DOESN'T MATTER TO THEM.
THIS MASS HALLUCINATION...
...IS THE FINGERPRINT OF THIS PARTICULAR SENSORY CRIME.

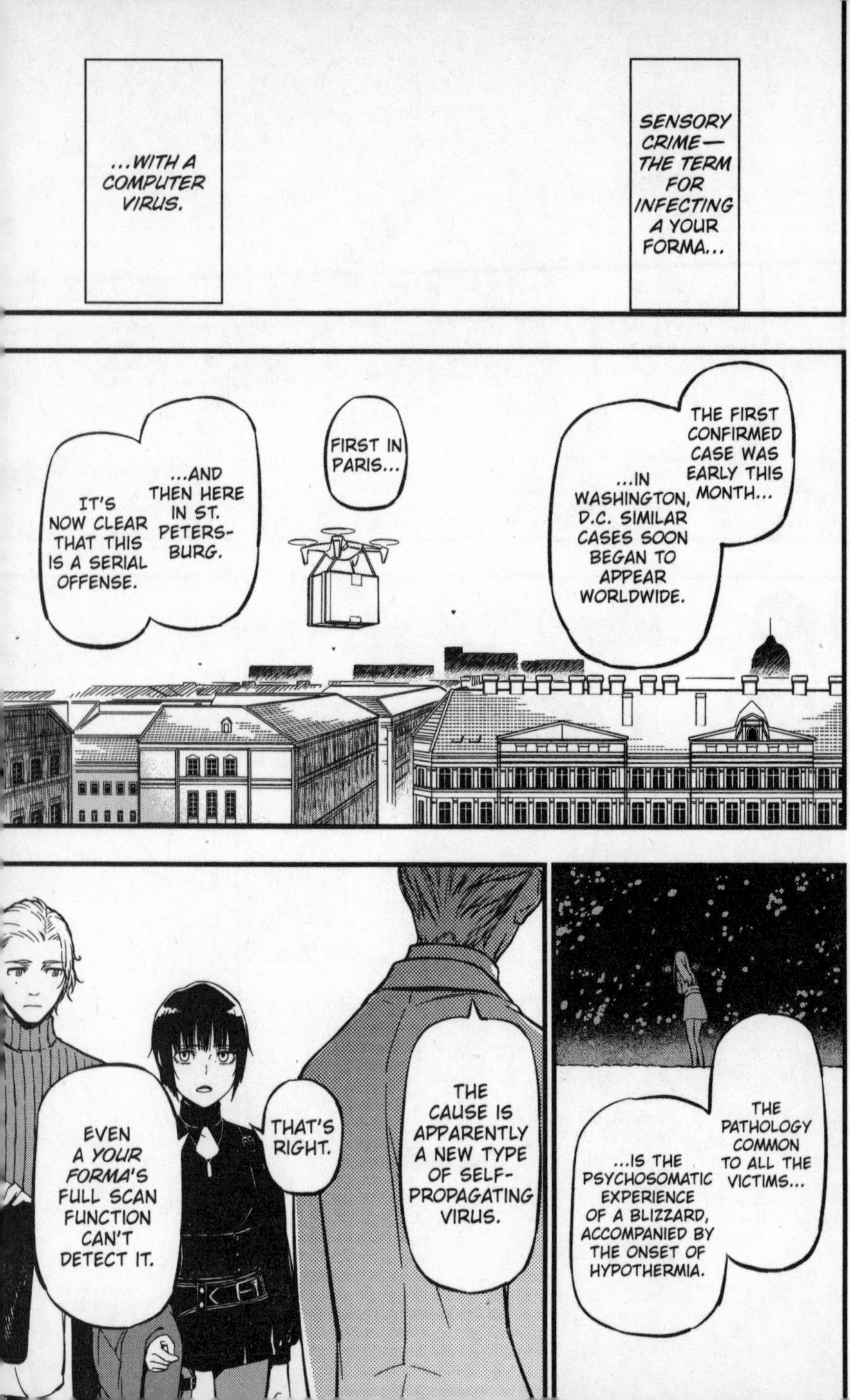
SENSORY CRIME—THE TERM FOR INFECTING A YOUR FORMA...
...WITH A COMPUTER VIRUS.
THE FIRST CONFIRMED CASE WAS EARLY THIS MONTH...
...IN WASHINGTON, D.C. SIMILAR CASES SOON BEGAN TO APPEAR WORLDWIDE.
FIRST IN PARIS...
...AND THEN HERE IN ST. PETERSBURG.
IT'S NOW CLEAR THAT THIS IS A SERIAL OFFENSE.
THE PATHOLOGY COMMON TO ALL THE VICTIMS...
...IS THE PSYCHOSOMATIC EXPERIENCE OF A BLIZZARD, ACCOMPANIED BY THE ONSET OF HYPOTHERMIA.
THE CAUSE IS APPARENTLY A NEW TYPE OF SELF-PROPAGATING VIRUS.
THAT'S RIGHT.
EVEN A YOUR FORMA'S FULL SCAN FUNCTION CAN'T DETECT IT.

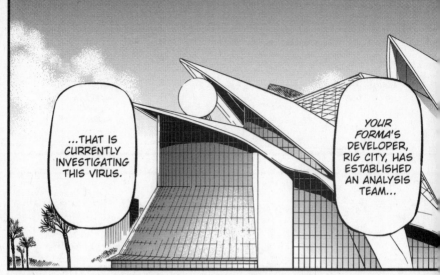

YOUR FORMA'S DEVELOPER, RIG CITY, HAS ESTABLISHED AN ANALYSIS TEAM...
...THAT IS CURRENTLY INVESTIGATING THIS VIRUS.
SO FAR, THEY HAVE MADE ONLY TWO SIGNIFICANT DISCOVERIES.
Benno Kleemann
FIRST— STARTING FROM THE INSTANT OF INFECTION...
...THE VIRUS IS CAPABLE OF SPREADING VIA THE YOUR FORMA'S MESSAGE AND PHONE FEATURES.
SECOND— ITS INCUBATION PERIOD LASTS A MERE FIFTEEN MINUTES AFTER THIS INITIAL EXPOSURE.
THE VIRUS IS ONLY CONTAGIOUS DURING THIS BRIEF PERIOD.
15 minutes

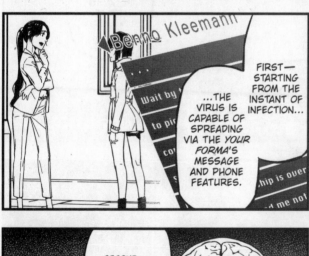

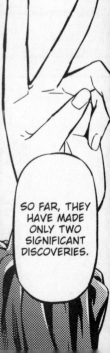

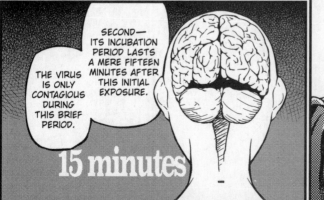

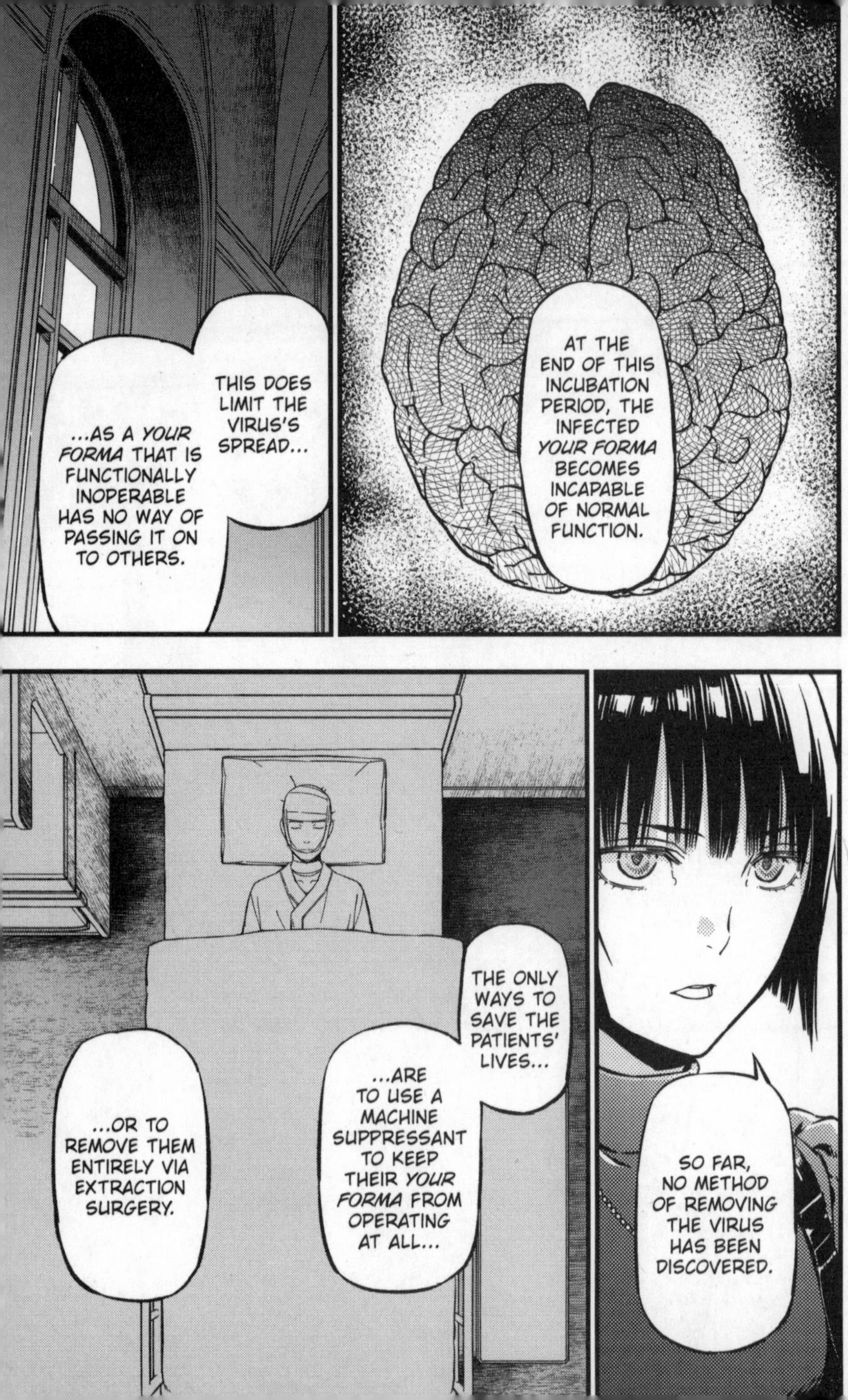
AT THE END OF THIS INCUBATION PERIOD, THE INFECTED *YOUR FORMA* BECOMES INCAPABLE OF NORMAL FUNCTION.
THIS DOES LIMIT THE VIRUS'S SPREAD...
...AS A *YOUR FORMA* THAT IS FUNCTIONALLY INOPERABLE HAS NO WAY OF PASSING IT ON TO OTHERS.
SO FAR, NO METHOD OF REMOVING THE VIRUS HAS BEEN DISCOVERED.
THE ONLY WAYS TO SAVE THE PATIENTS' LIVES...
...ARE TO USE A MACHINE SUPPRESSANT TO KEEP THEIR *YOUR FORMA* FROM OPERATING AT ALL...
...OR TO REMOVE THEM ENTIRELY VIA EXTRACTION SURGERY.

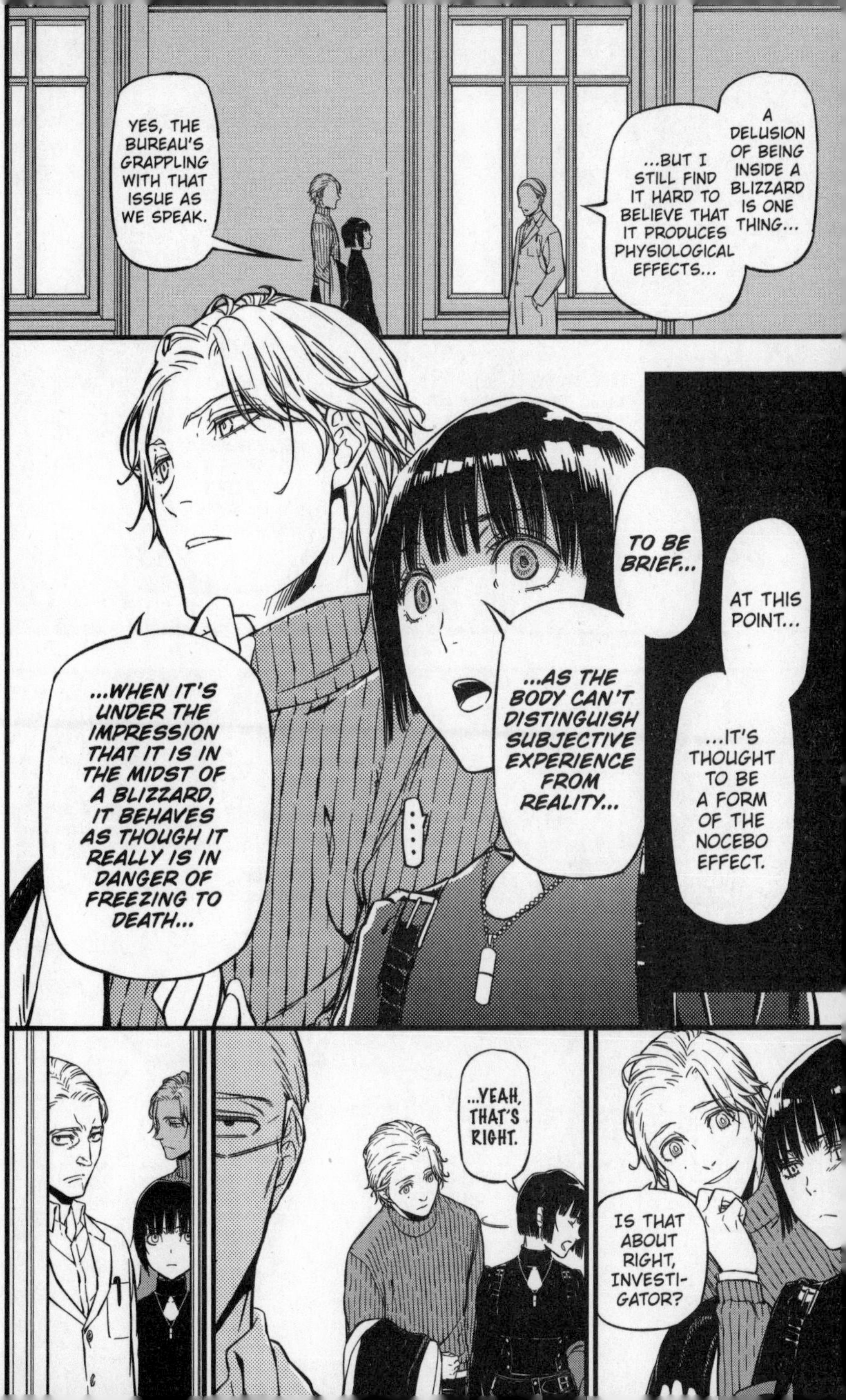
A DELUSION OF BEING INSIDE A BLIZZARD IS ONE THING...
...BUT I STILL FIND IT HARD TO BELIEVE THAT IT PRODUCES PHYSIOLOGICAL EFFECTS...
YES, THE BUREAU'S GRAPPLING WITH THAT ISSUE AS WE SPEAK.
TO BE BRIEF...
AT THIS POINT...
...IT'S THOUGHT TO BE A FORM OF THE NOCEBO EFFECT.
...AS THE BODY CAN'T DISTINGUISH SUBJECTIVE EXPERIENCE FROM REALITY...
...WHEN IT'S UNDER THE IMPRESSION THAT IT IS IN THE MIDST OF A BLIZZARD, IT BEHAVES AS THOUGH IT REALLY IS IN DANGER OF FREEZING TO DEATH...
IS THAT ABOUT RIGHT, INVESTIGATOR?
...YEAH, THAT'S RIGHT.

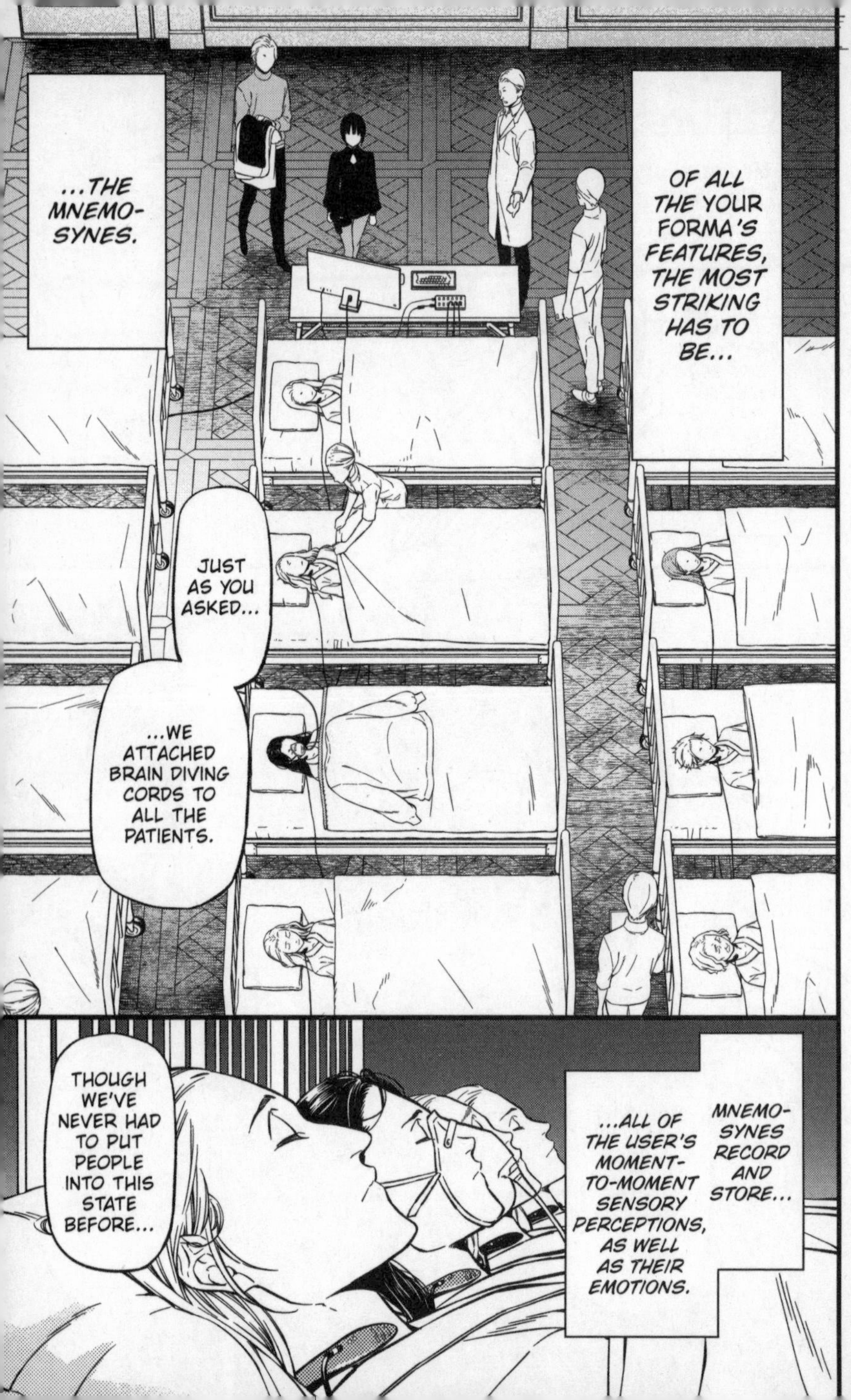
OF ALL THE YOUR FORMA'S FEATURES, THE MOST STRIKING HAS TO BE...
...THE MNEMO-SYNES.
JUST AS YOU ASKED...
...WE ATTACHED BRAIN DIVING CORDS TO ALL THE PATIENTS.
MNEMO-SYNES RECORD AND STORE...
...ALL OF THE USER'S MOMENT-TO-MOMENT SENSORY PERCEPTIONS, AS WELL AS THEIR EMOTIONS.
THOUGH WE'VE NEVER HAD TO PUT PEOPLE INTO THIS STATE BEFORE...

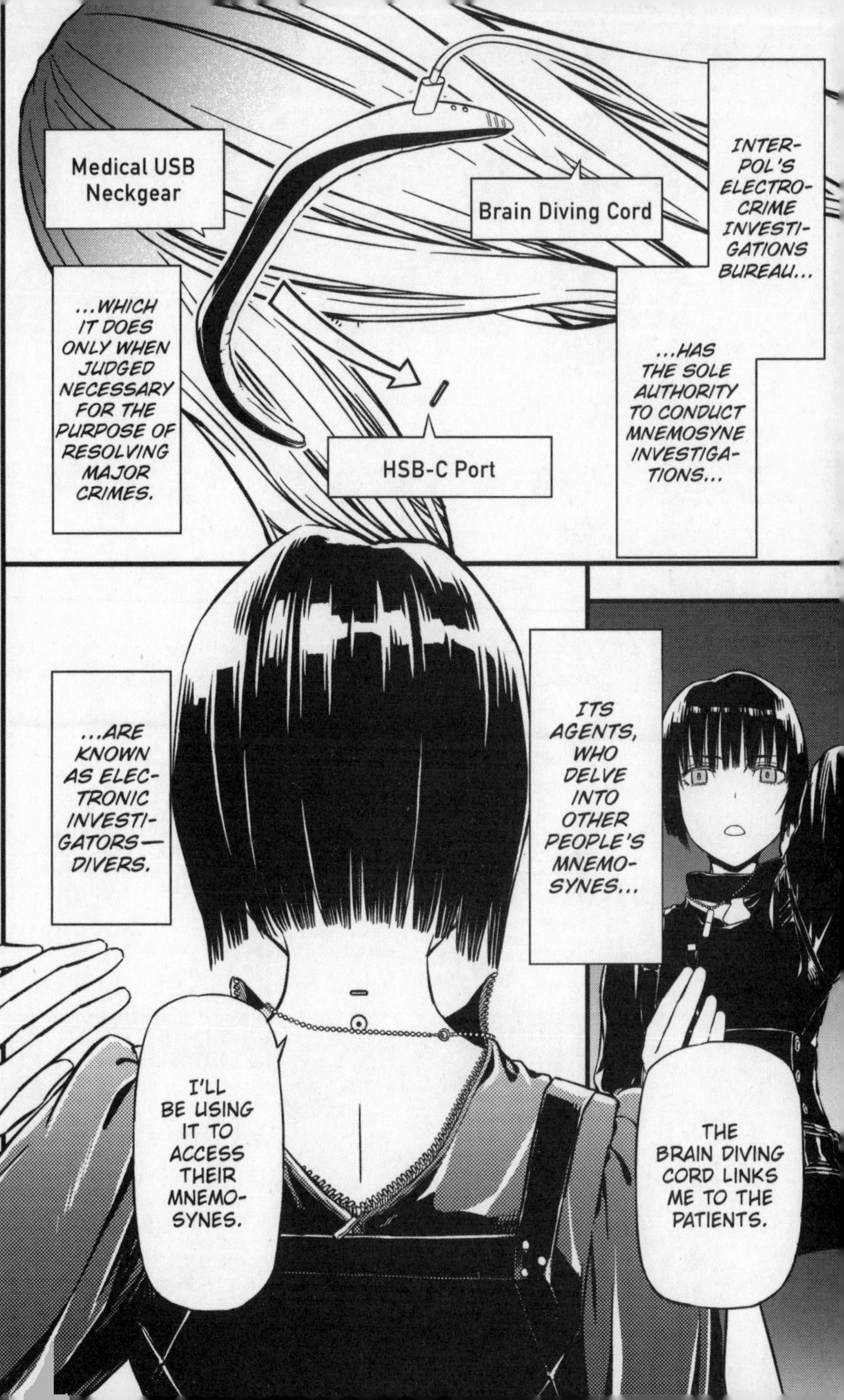
INTERPOL'S ELECTRO-CRIME INVESTIGATIONS BUREAU...
...HAS THE SOLE AUTHORITY TO CONDUCT MNEMOSYNE INVESTIGATIONS...
Brain Diving Cord
Medical USB Neckgear
HSB-C Port
...WHICH IT DOES ONLY WHEN JUDGED NECESSARY FOR THE PURPOSE OF RESOLVING MAJOR CRIMES.
ITS AGENTS, WHO DELVE INTO OTHER PEOPLE'S MNEMOSYNES...
...ARE KNOWN AS ELECTRONIC INVESTIGATORS—DIVERS.
THE BRAIN DIVING CORD LINKS ME TO THE PATIENTS.
I'LL BE USING IT TO ACCESS THEIR MNEMOSYNES.

HSB (Human Serial Bus): a standard unique to the Your Forma. Only certain medical and investigative bodies are allowed to use it.

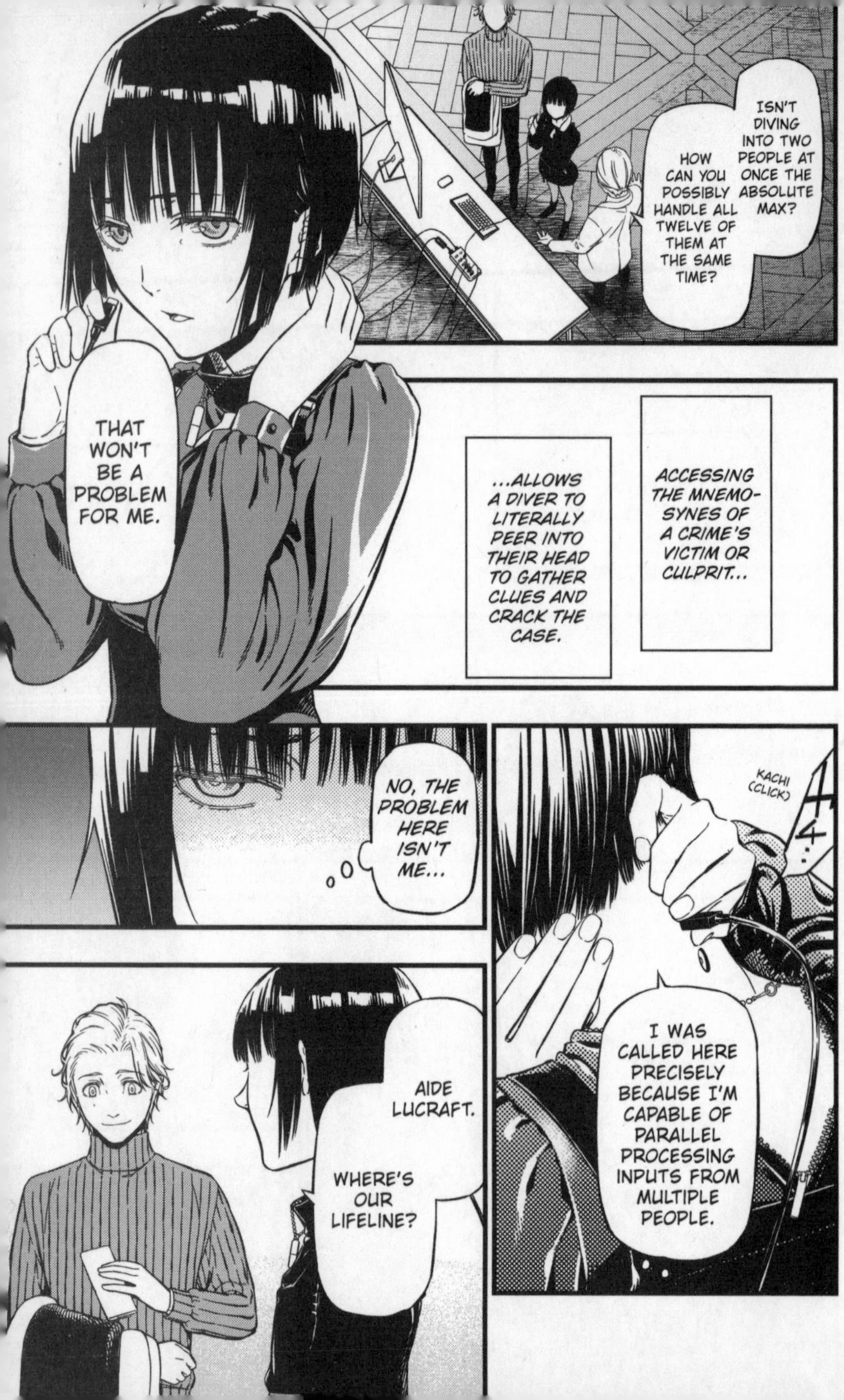
ISN'T DIVING INTO TWO PEOPLE AT ONCE THE ABSOLUTE MAX?
HOW CAN YOU POSSIBLY HANDLE ALL TWELVE OF THEM AT THE SAME TIME?
ACCESSING THE MNEMOSYNES OF A CRIME'S VICTIM OR CULPRIT...
...ALLOWS A DIVER TO LITERALLY PEER INTO THEIR HEAD TO GATHER CLUES AND CRACK THE CASE.
THAT WON'T BE A PROBLEM FOR ME.
KACHI (CLICK)
I WAS CALLED HERE PRECISELY BECAUSE I'M CAPABLE OF PARALLEL PROCESSING INPUTS FROM MULTIPLE PEOPLE.
NO, THE PROBLEM HERE ISN'T ME...
AIDE LUCRAFT.
WHERE'S OUR LIFELINE?

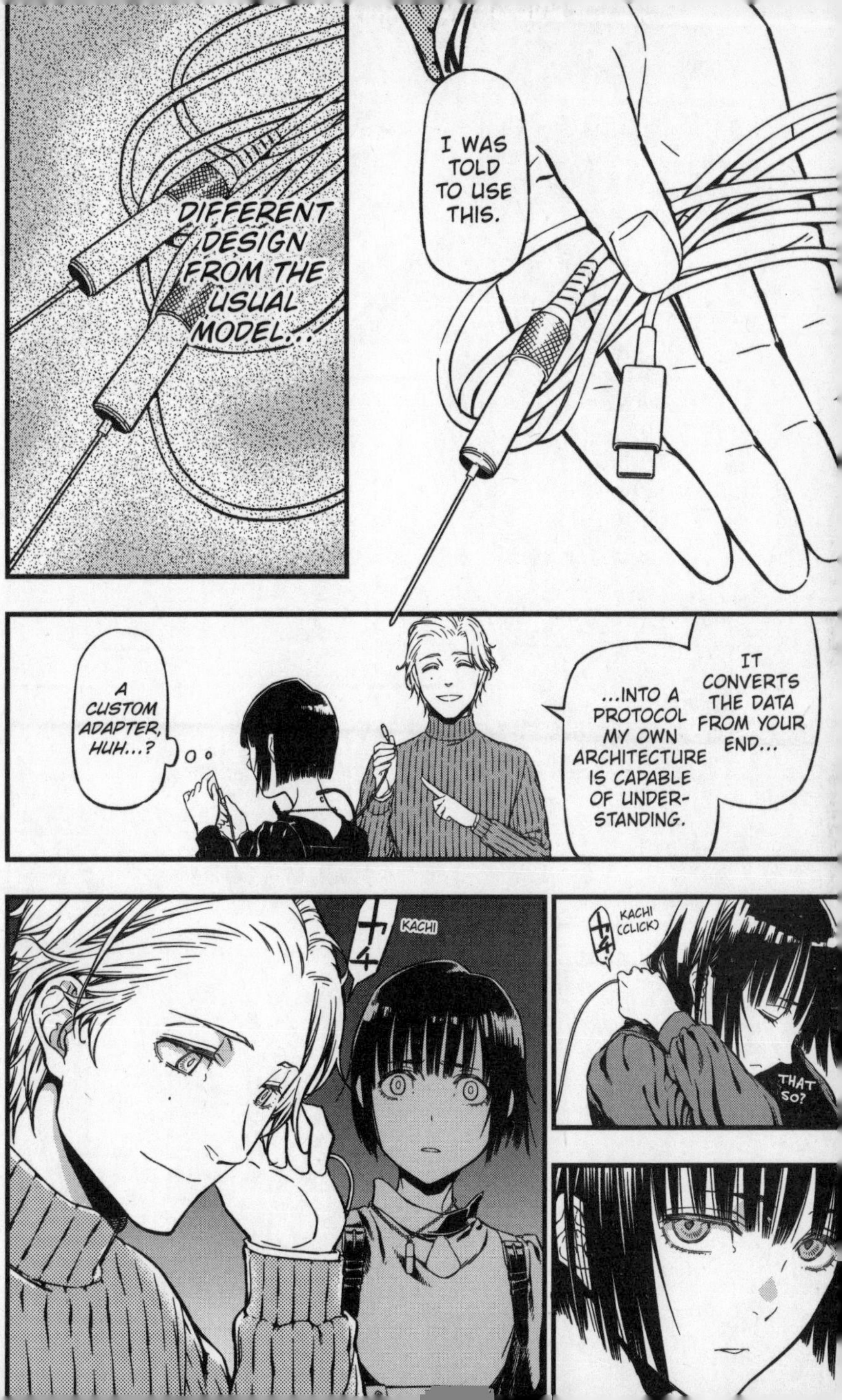
I WAS TOLD TO USE THIS.
DIFFERENT DESIGN FROM THE USUAL MODEL...
IT CONVERTS THE DATA FROM YOUR END...
...INTO A PROTOCOL MY OWN ARCHITECTURE IS CAPABLE OF UNDER-STANDING.
A CUSTOM ADAPTER, HUH...?
KACHI (CLICK)
THAT SO?
KACHI

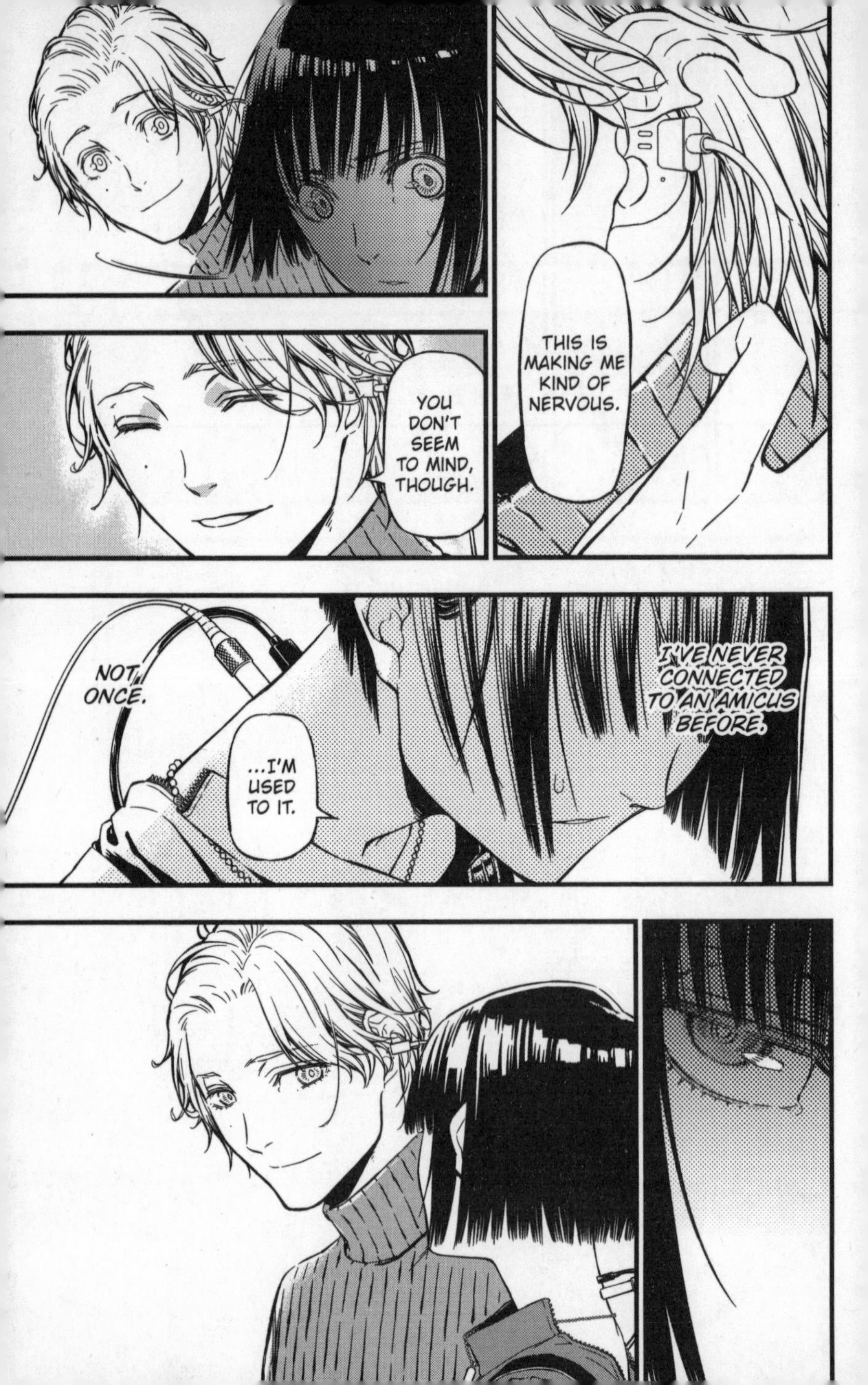
THIS IS MAKING ME KIND OF NERVOUS.
YOU DON'T SEEM TO MIND, THOUGH.
I'VE NEVER CONNECTED TO AN AMICUS BEFORE.
...I'M USED TO IT.
NOT ONCE.

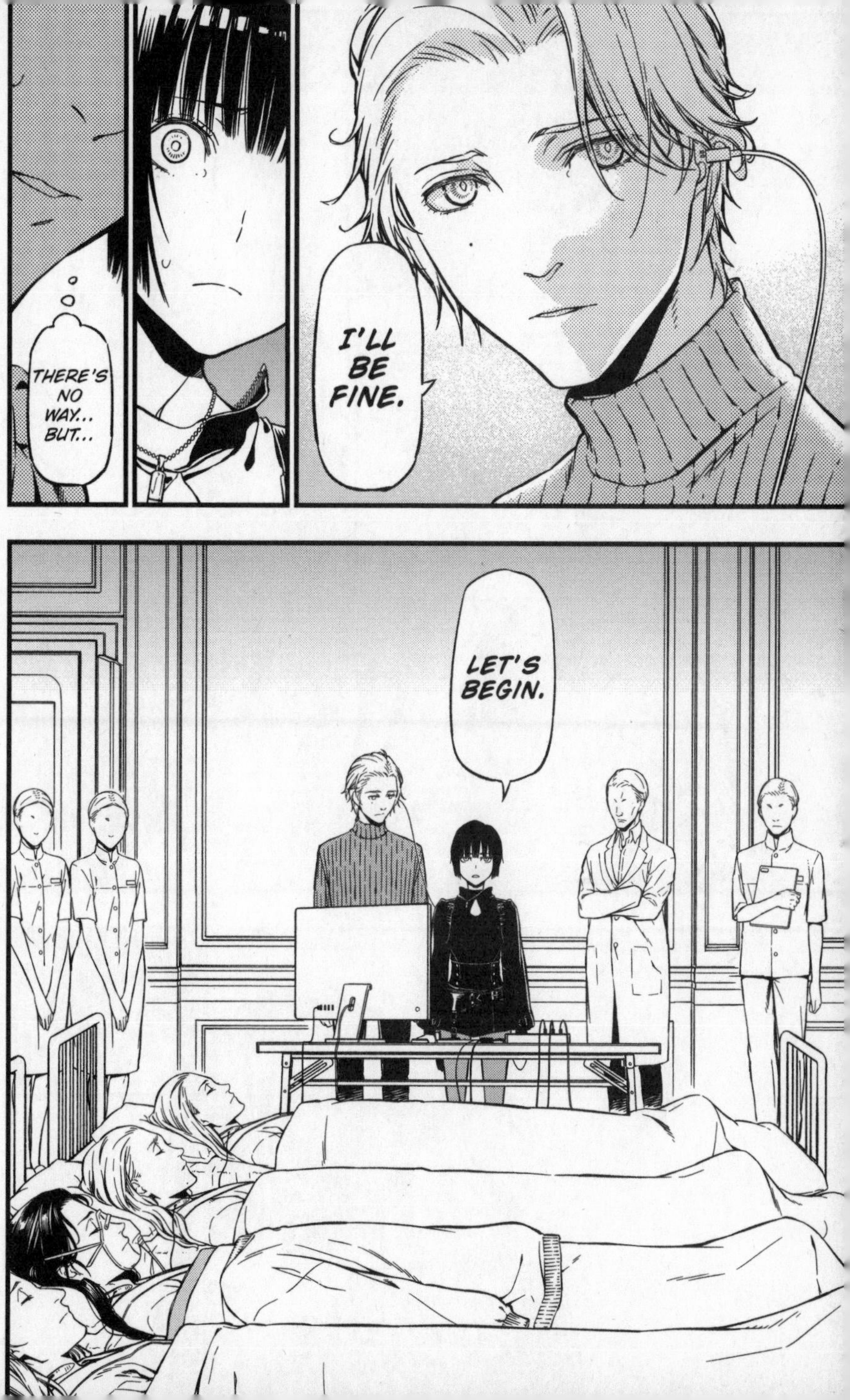
I'LL BE FINE.
THERE'S NO WAY... BUT...
LET'S BEGIN.

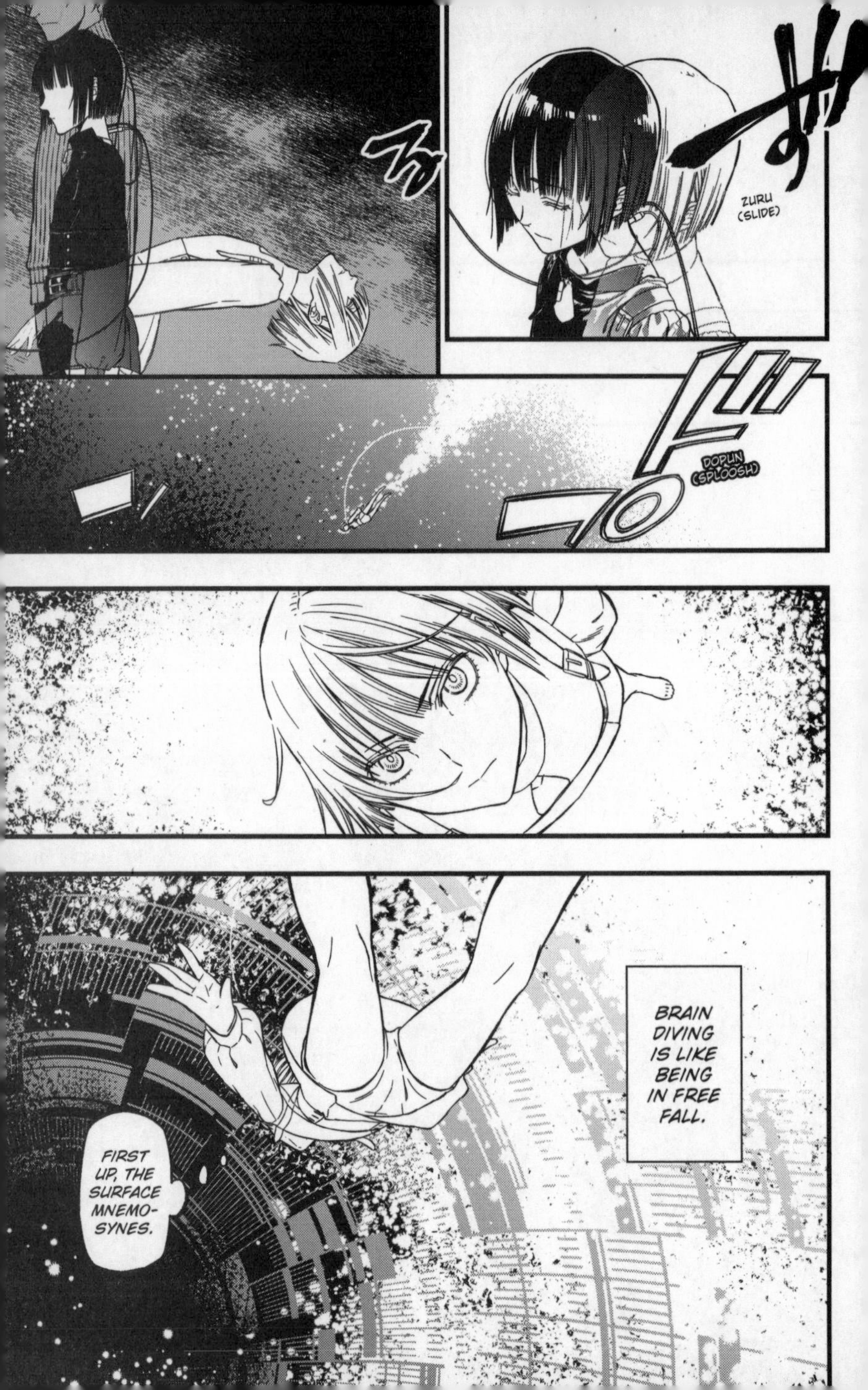

ZURU
(SLIDE)
DOPUN
(SPLOOSH)
BRAIN DIVING IS LIKE BEING IN FREE FALL.
FIRST UP, THE SURFACE MNEMO-SYNES.

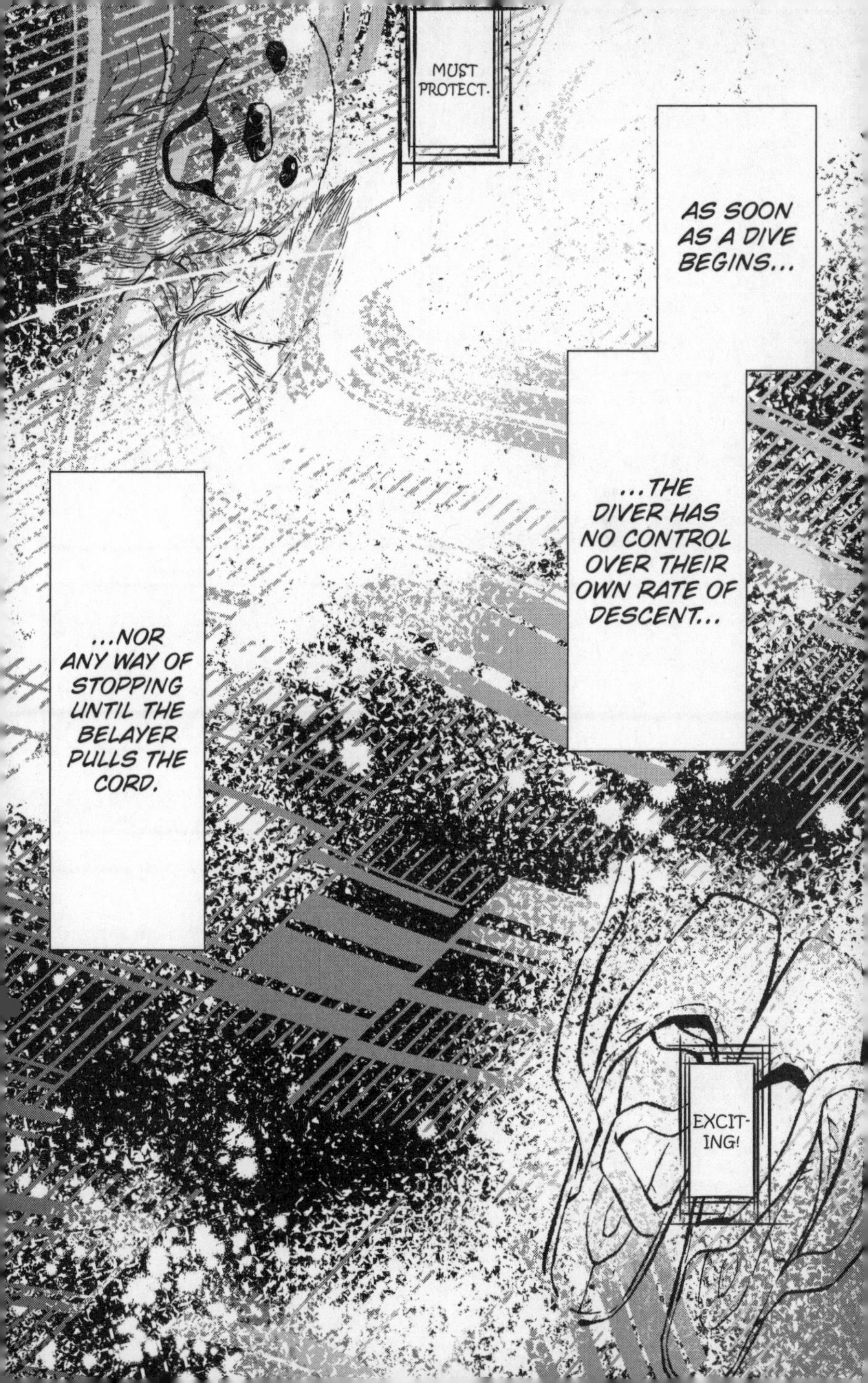
MUST PROTECT.
AS SOON AS A DIVE BEGINS...
...THE DIVER HAS NO CONTROL OVER THEIR OWN RATE OF DESCENT...
...NOR ANY WAY OF STOPPING UNTIL THE BELAYER PULLS THE CORD.
EXCIT-ING!

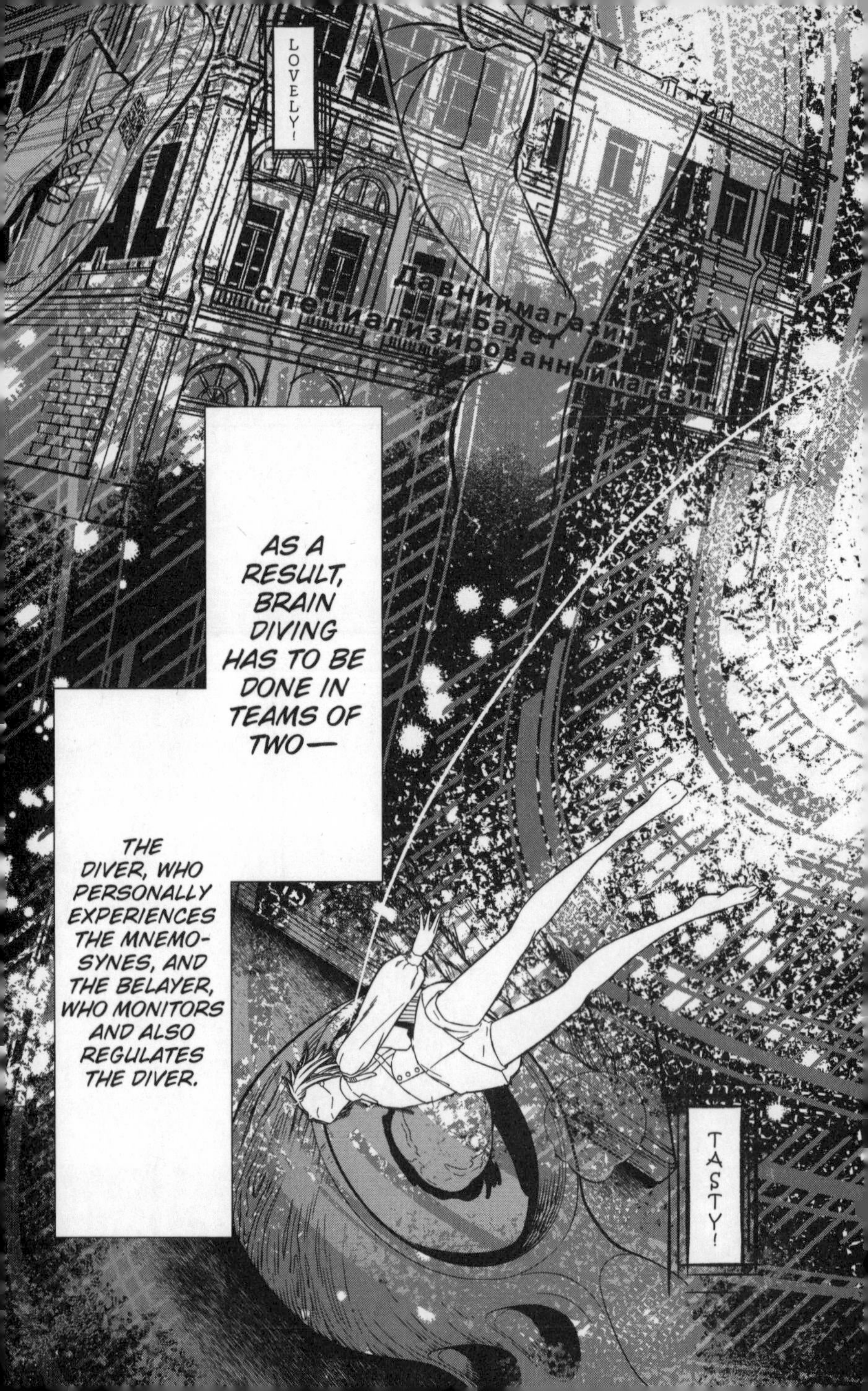
LOVELY!
Давний магазин
Балет
Специализированный магазин
AS A RESULT, BRAIN DIVING HAS TO BE DONE IN TEAMS OF TWO—
THE DIVER, WHO PERSONALLY EXPERIENCES THE MNEMOSYNES, AND THE BELAYER, WHO MONITORS AND ALSO REGULATES THE DIVER.
TASTY!

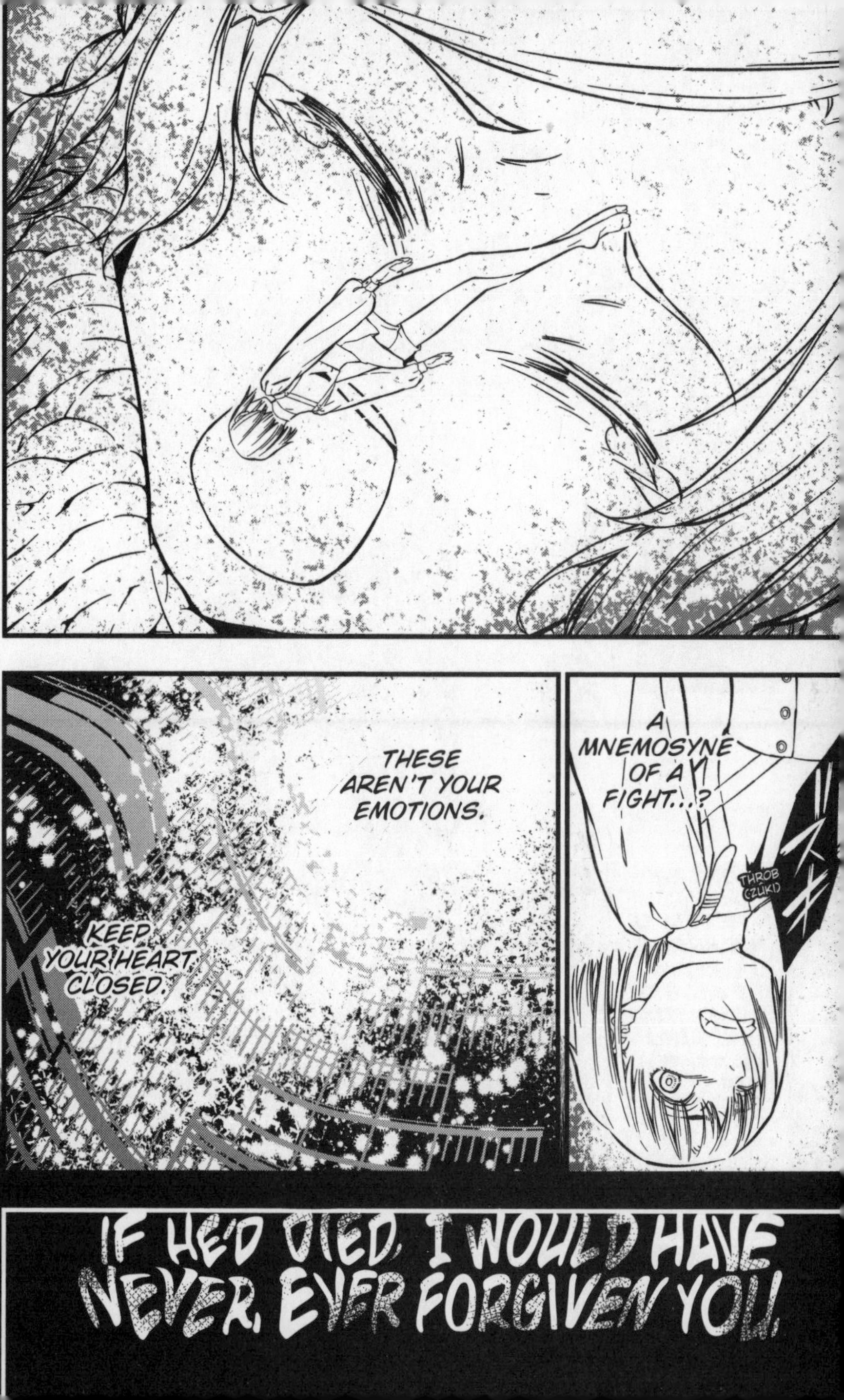
A MNEMOSYNE OF A FIGHT...?
THROB (ZUKI)
THESE AREN'T YOUR EMOTIONS.
KEEP YOUR HEART CLOSED.
IF HE'D DIED, I WOULD HAVE NEVER, EVER FORGIVEN YOU.

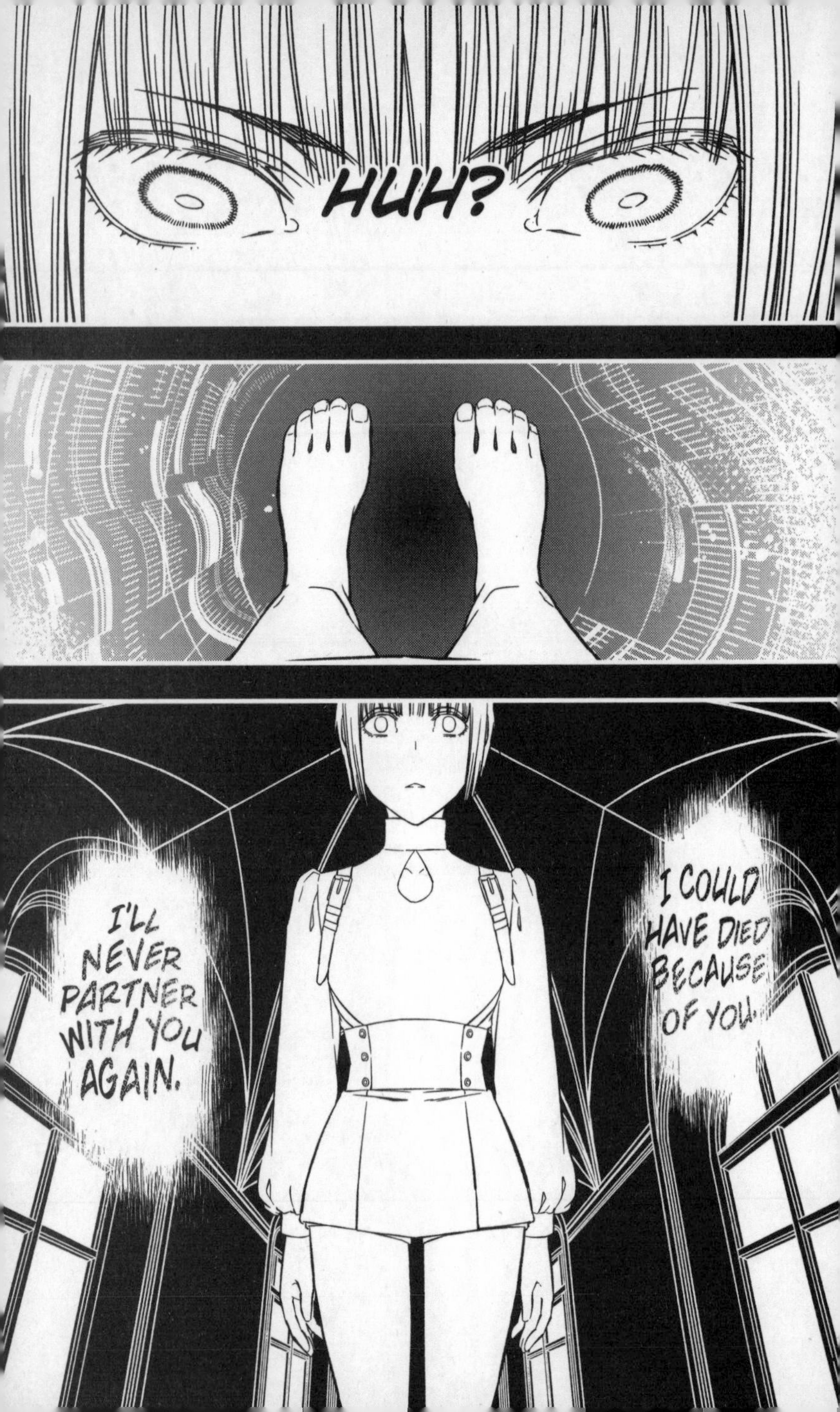
HUH?
I COULD HAVE DIED BECAUSE OF YOU.
I'LL NEVER PARTNER WITH YOU AGAIN.

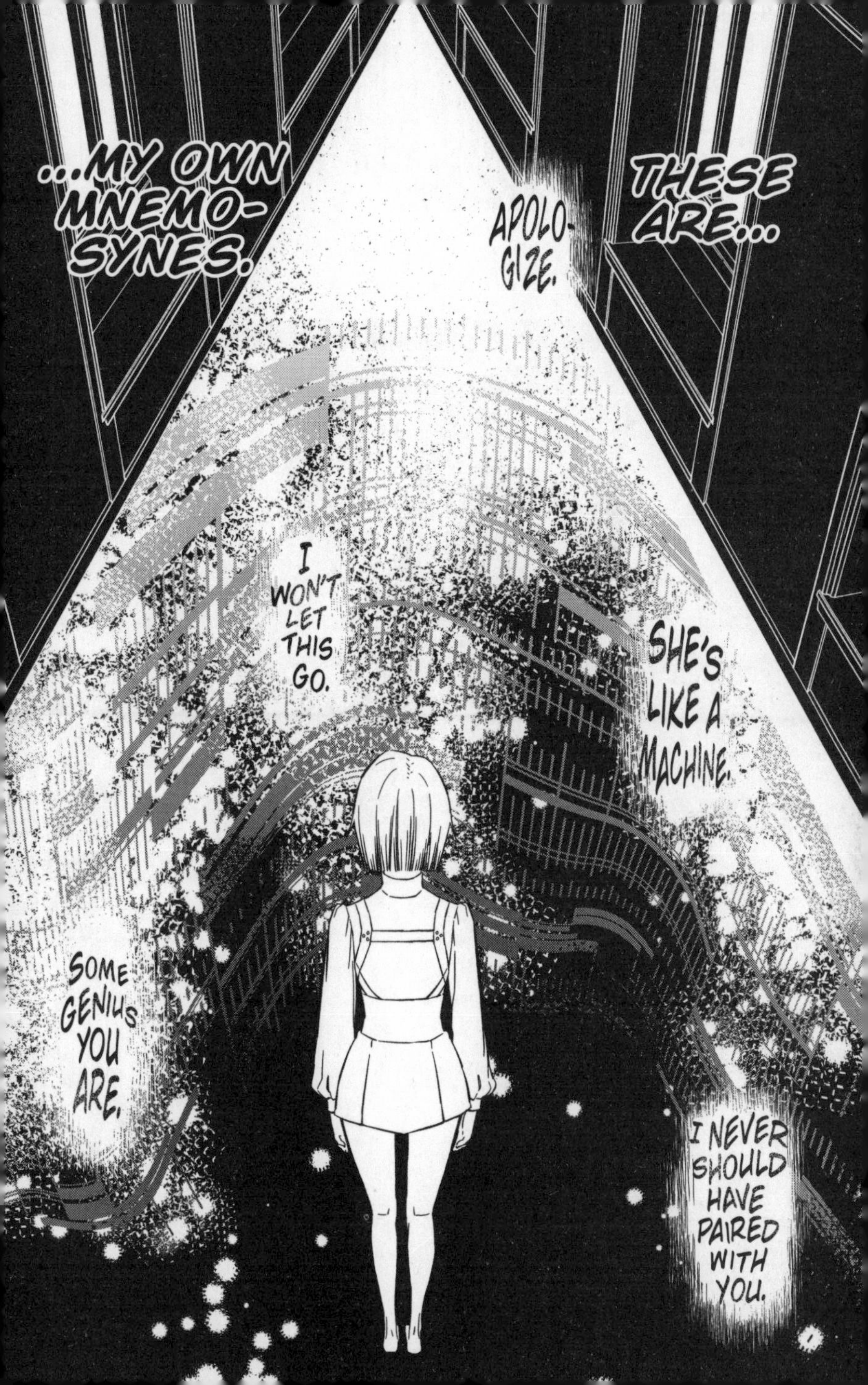
THESE ARE...
...MY OWN MNEMO-SYNES.
APOLO-GIZE.
SHE'S LIKE A MACHINE.
I WON'T LET THIS GO.
I NEVER SHOULD HAVE PAIRED WITH YOU.
SOME GENIUS YOU ARE.

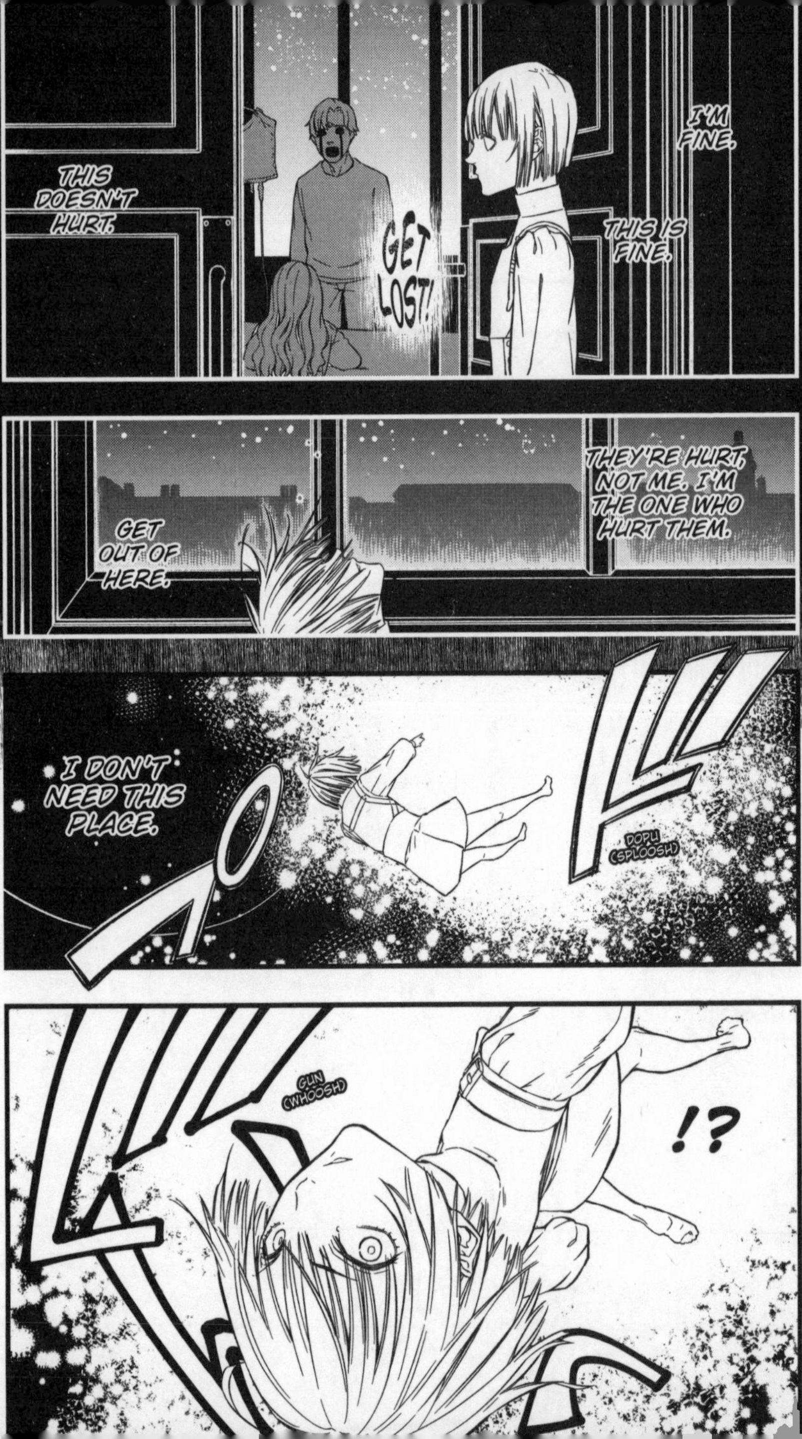
I'M FINE.
THIS IS FINE.
GET LOST!
THIS DOESN'T HURT.
THEY'RE HURT, NOT ME. I'M THE ONE WHO HURT THEM.
GET OUT OF HERE.
DOPU (SPLOOSH)
I DON'T NEED THIS PLACE.
!?
GUN (WHOOSH)

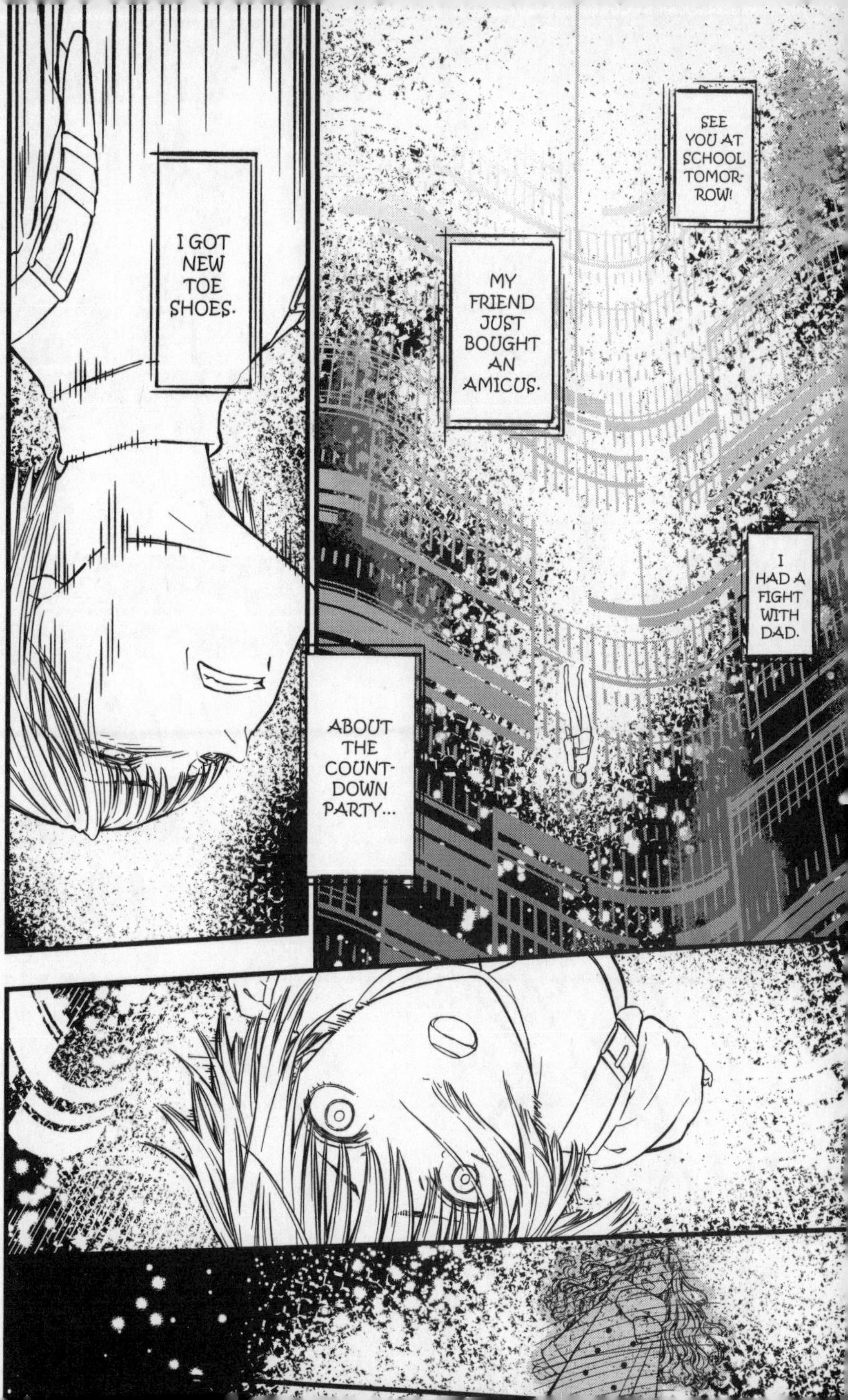
SEE YOU AT SCHOOL TOMOR-ROW!
MY FRIEND JUST BOUGHT AN AMICUS.
I HAD A FIGHT WITH DAD.
ABOUT THE COUNT-DOWN PARTY...
I GOT NEW TOE SHOES.

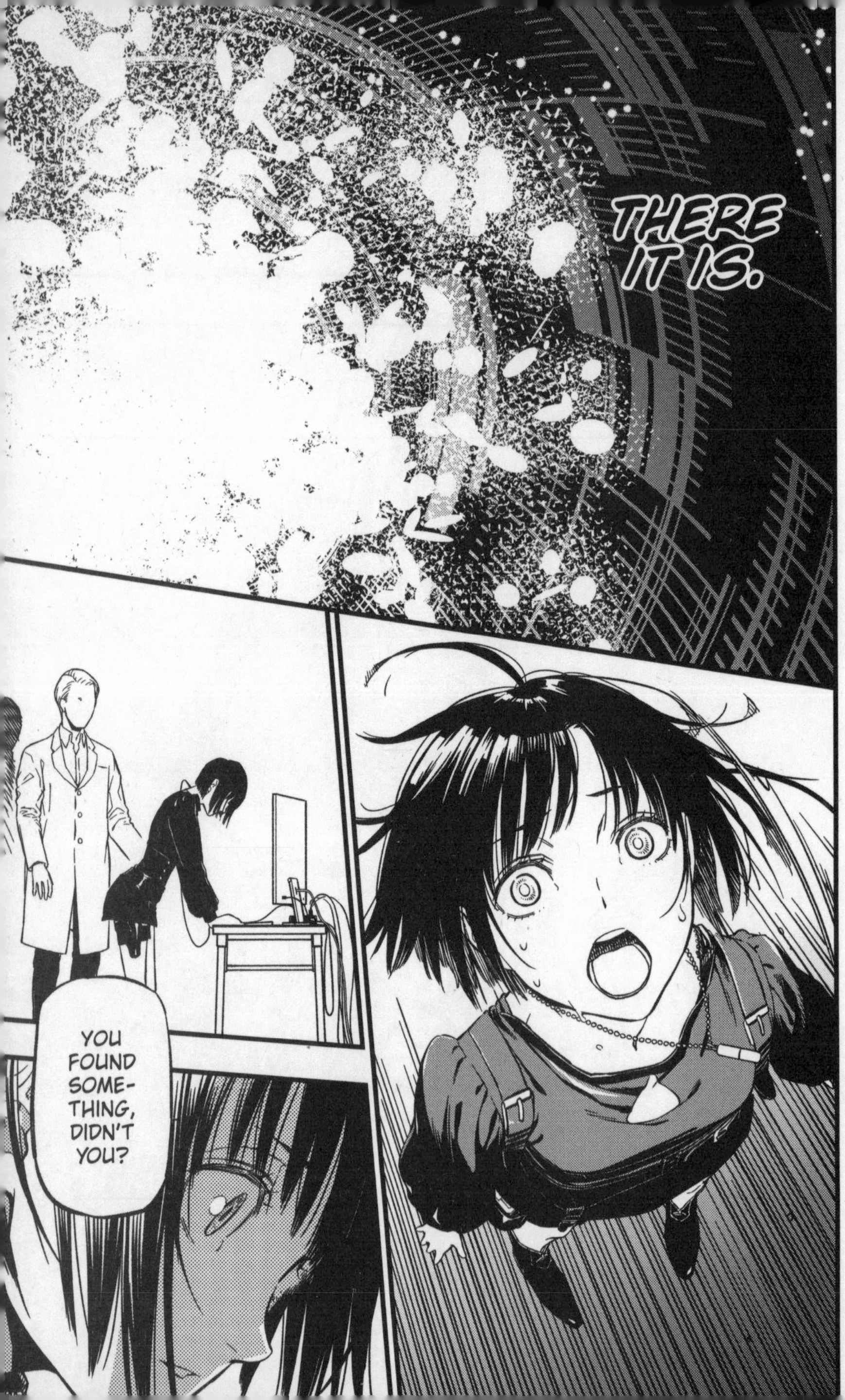
THERE IT IS.
YOU FOUND SOME-THING, DIDN'T YOU?

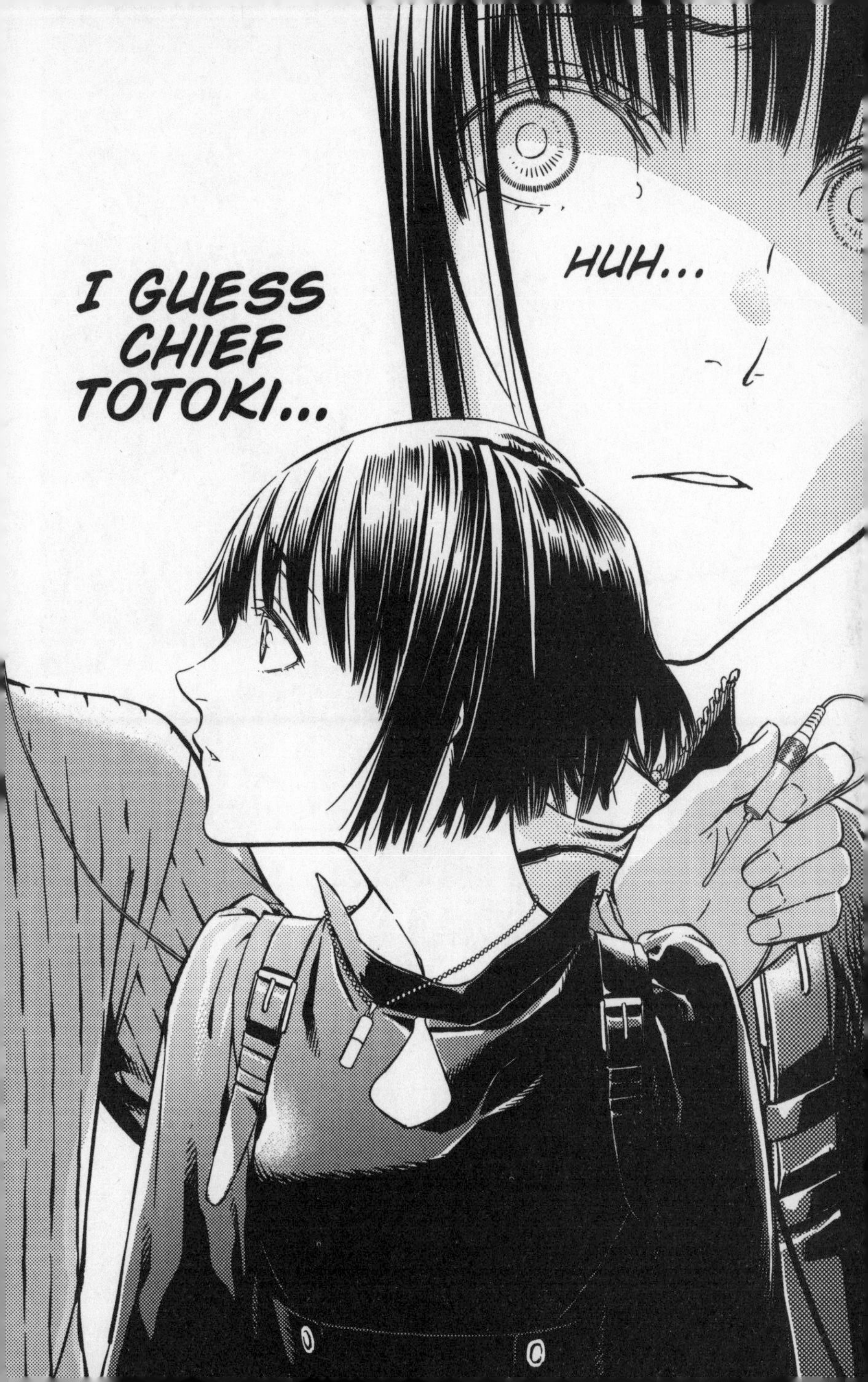
HUH...
I GUESS CHIEF TOTOKI...

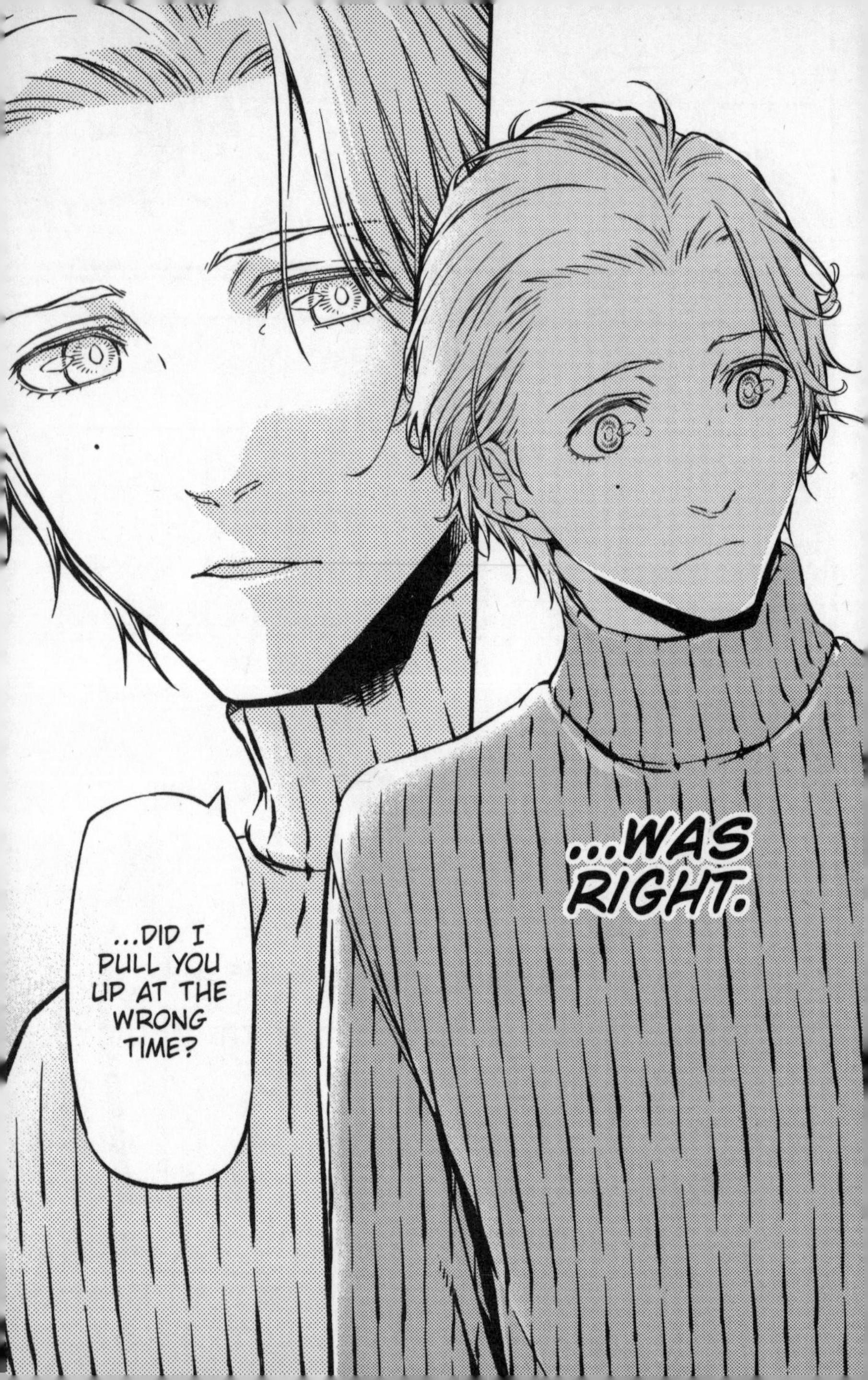
...WAS RIGHT.
...DID I PULL YOU UP AT THE WRONG TIME?

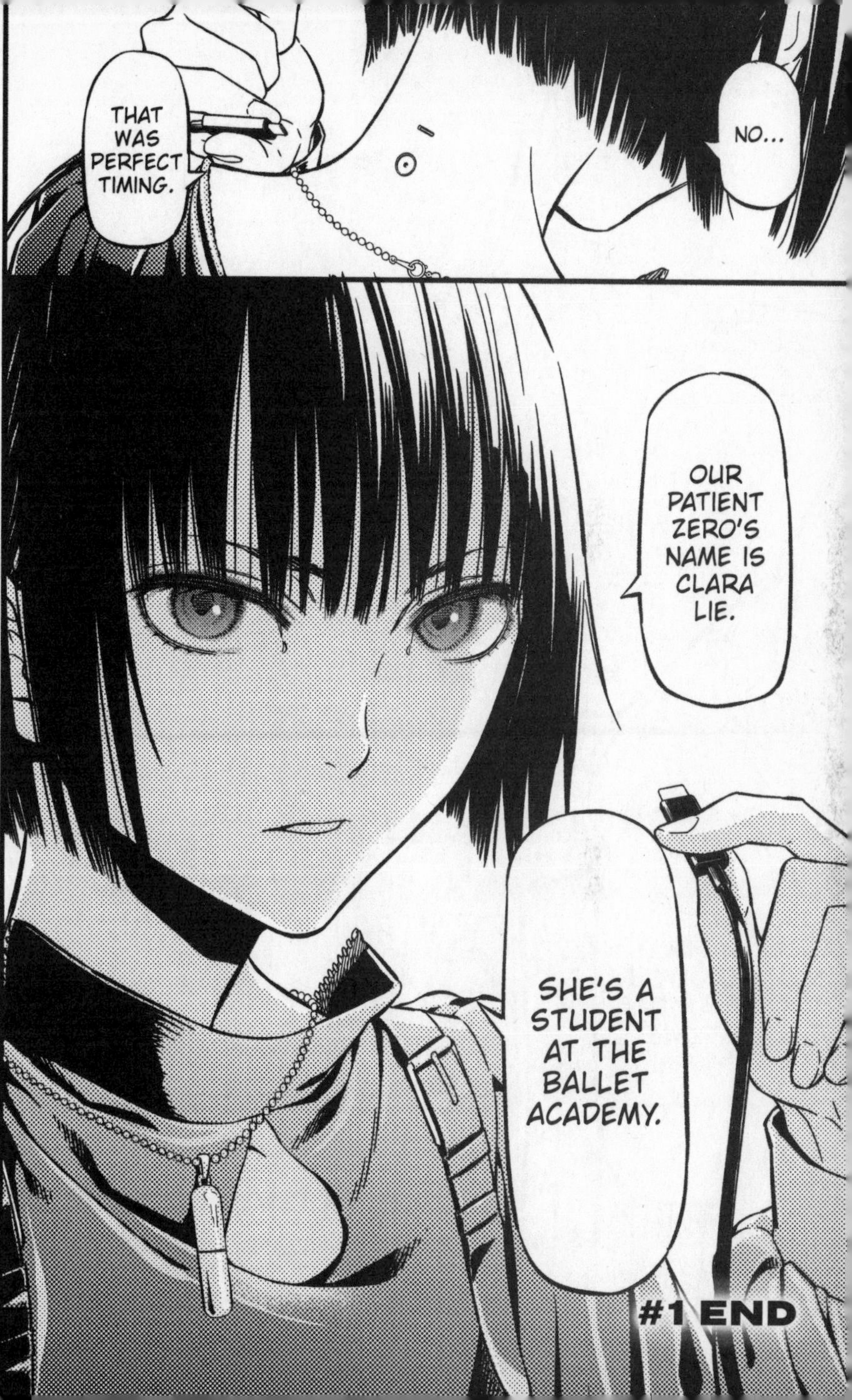
NO...
THAT WAS PERFECT TIMING.
OUR PATIENT ZERO'S NAME IS CLARA LIE.
SHE'S A STUDENT AT THE BALLET ACADEMY.
#1 END

YOUR FORMA

DATABASE

Amicus

The catchall term for humanoid robots designed to convincingly resemble biological humans. While they are capable of sophisticatedly understanding their environment and can respond flexibly to problems, their depth of expertise and capabilities in any given field are inferior to those of single-purpose industrial robots.

Accordingly, the highly specialized field of criminal investigations employs a variety of specialists, such as ant-like swarm robots for the purpose of gathering evidence from a crime scene, rather than Amicus. As such, it is rather unusual for Harold to work as a Belayer and aide.

The question of whether Amicus should be treated as "friends" of mankind or mere "machines" is an ongoing debate. Some developed countries have even begun granting Amicus fundamental human rights.

Laws of Respect

"Respect humans"; "Obey the orders of humans"; and "Never attack a human being." All Amicus are programmed to follow these rules.

Your Forma

A three-micrometer-wide, sewing-thread-shaped information terminal inserted directly into the brain via invasive laser surgery.

It records all aspects of conscious experience, from sensory perception to even emotions. Since it is integrated with the brain, it will cease to function with the loss of its user's vital functions. When this occurs, the Your Forma is programmed to wipe its memory in order to protect its user's privacy.

It was originally developed as a medical intervention for an infectious disease that targeted the nervous system.

Brain Diving

The act of connecting to another person's Your Forma via a specialized cord to browse through their Mnemosynes. It is expected to revolutionize the field of criminal investigations, but is currently performed only by Interpol for a small number of high-profile cases.

#2 Insight

YOUR FORMA

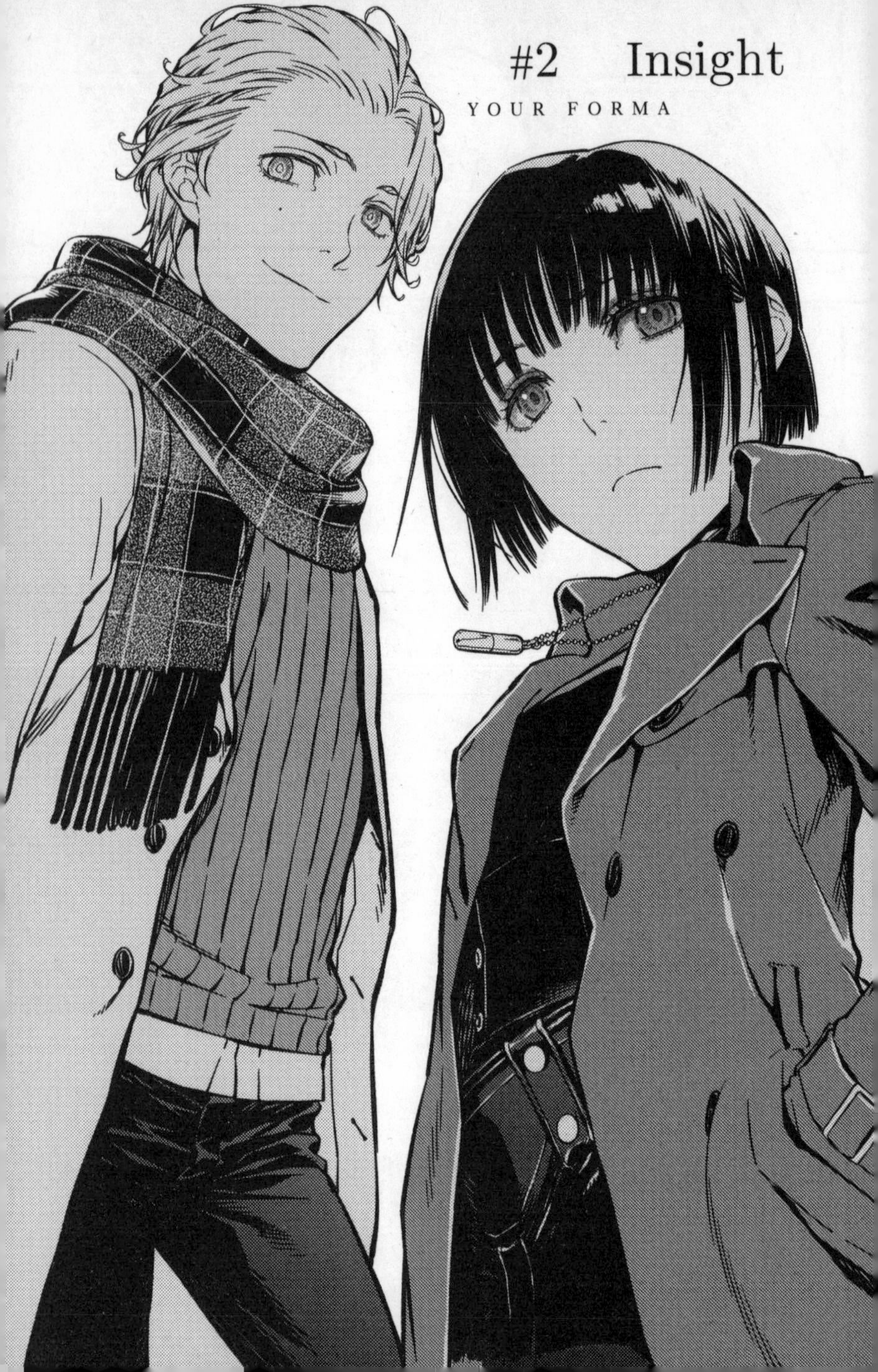

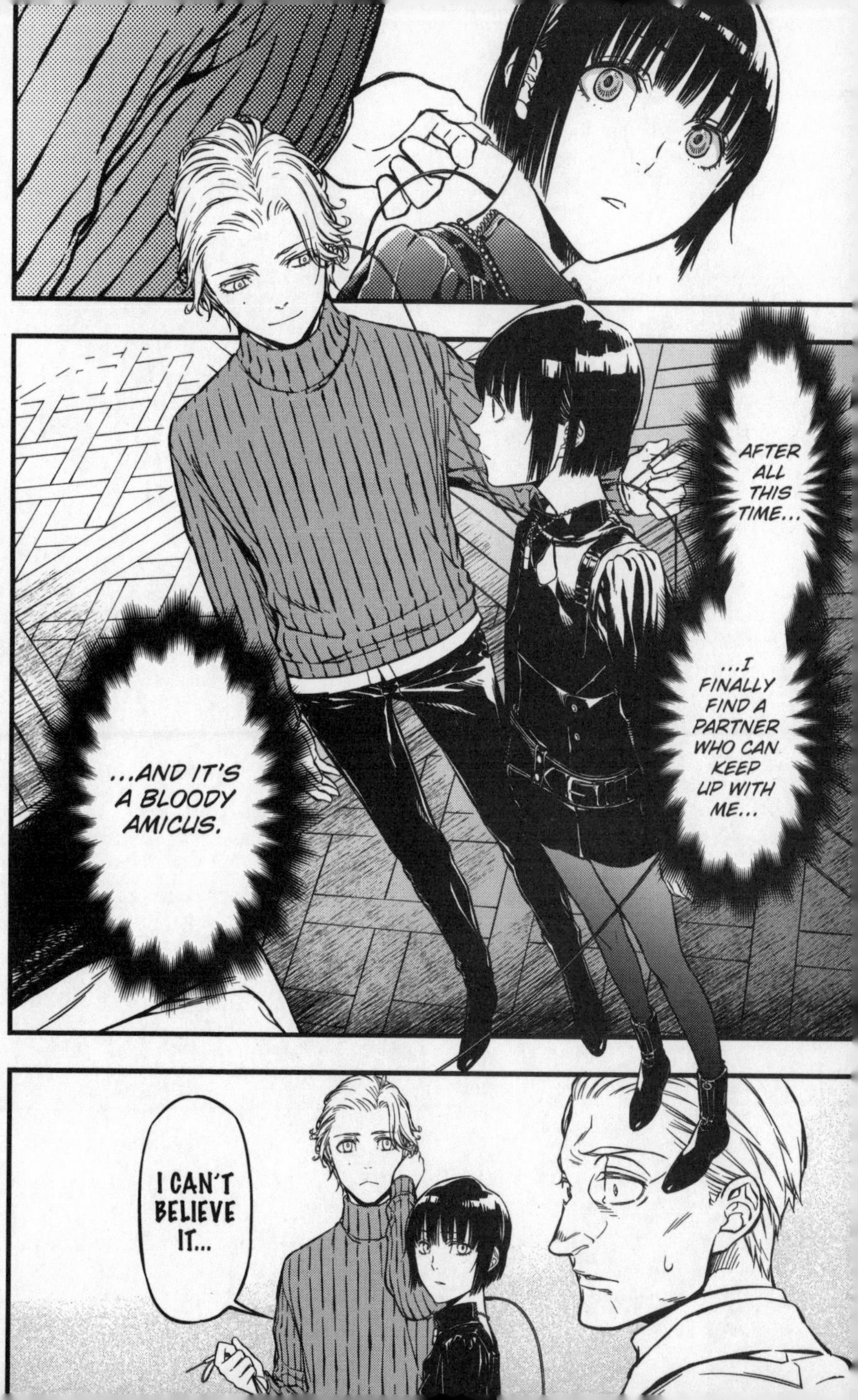
AFTER ALL THIS TIME...
...I FINALLY FIND A PARTNER WHO CAN KEEP UP WITH ME...
...AND IT'S A BLOODY AMICUS.
I CAN'T BELIEVE IT...

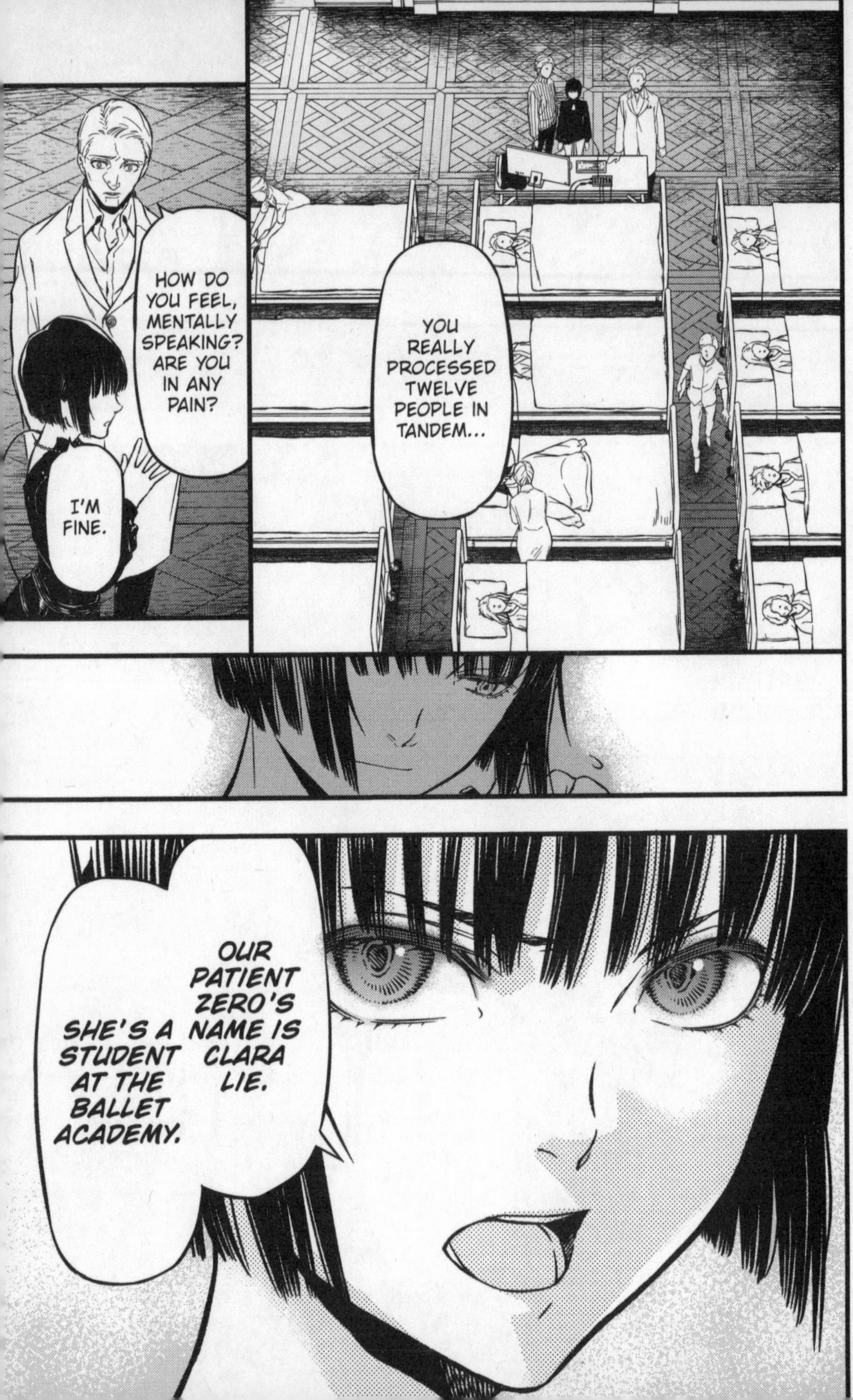
YOU REALLY PROCESSED TWELVE PEOPLE IN TANDEM...
HOW DO YOU FEEL, MENTALLY SPEAKING? ARE YOU IN ANY PAIN?
I'M FINE.
OUR PATIENT ZERO'S NAME IS CLARA LIE.
SHE'S A STUDENT AT THE BALLET ACADEMY.

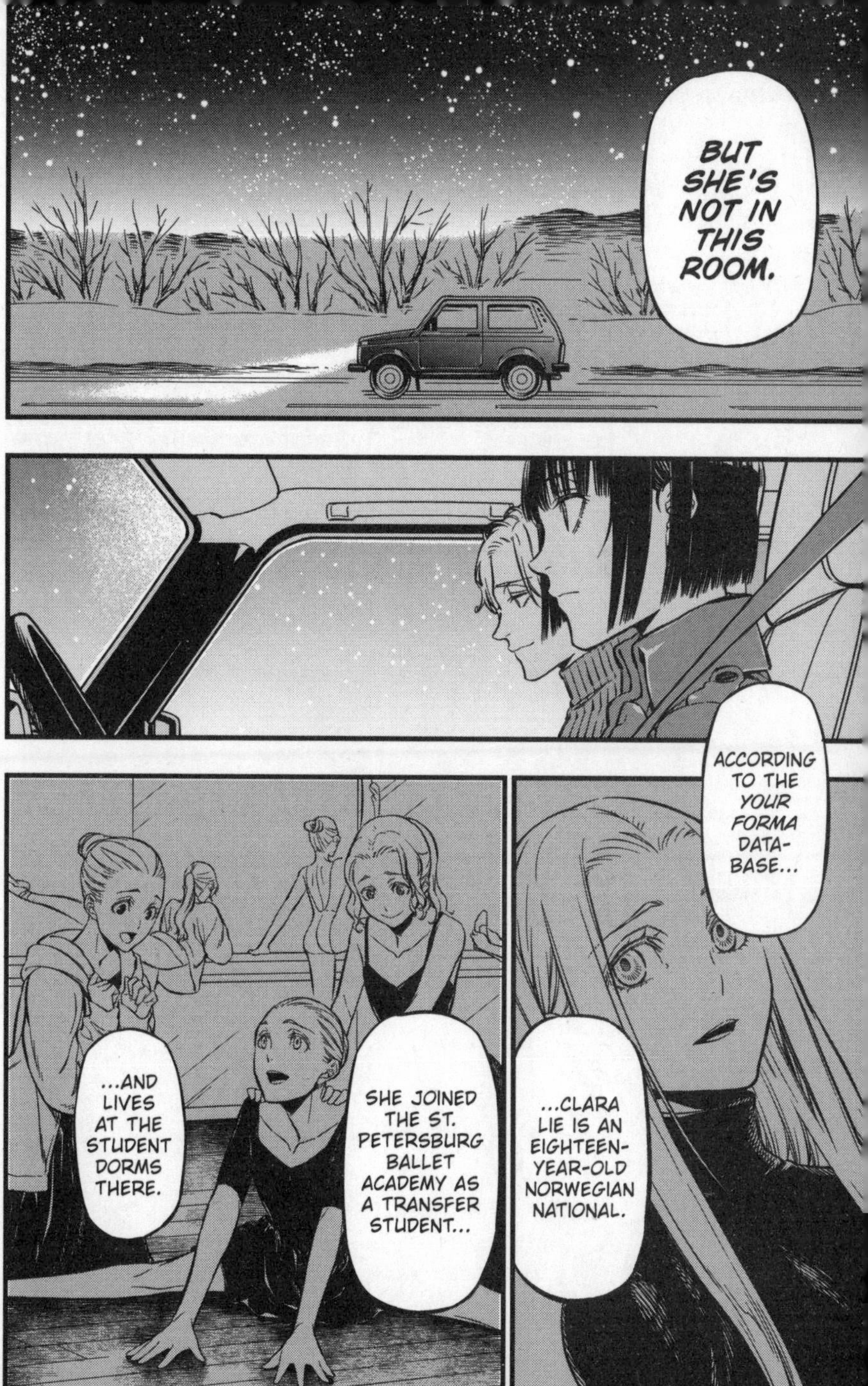
BUT SHE'S NOT IN THIS ROOM.
ACCORDING TO THE *YOUR FORMA* DATABASE...
...CLARA LIE IS AN EIGHTEEN-YEAR-OLD NORWEGIAN NATIONAL.
SHE JOINED THE ST. PETERSBURG BALLET ACADEMY AS A TRANSFER STUDENT...
...AND LIVES AT THE STUDENT DORMS THERE.

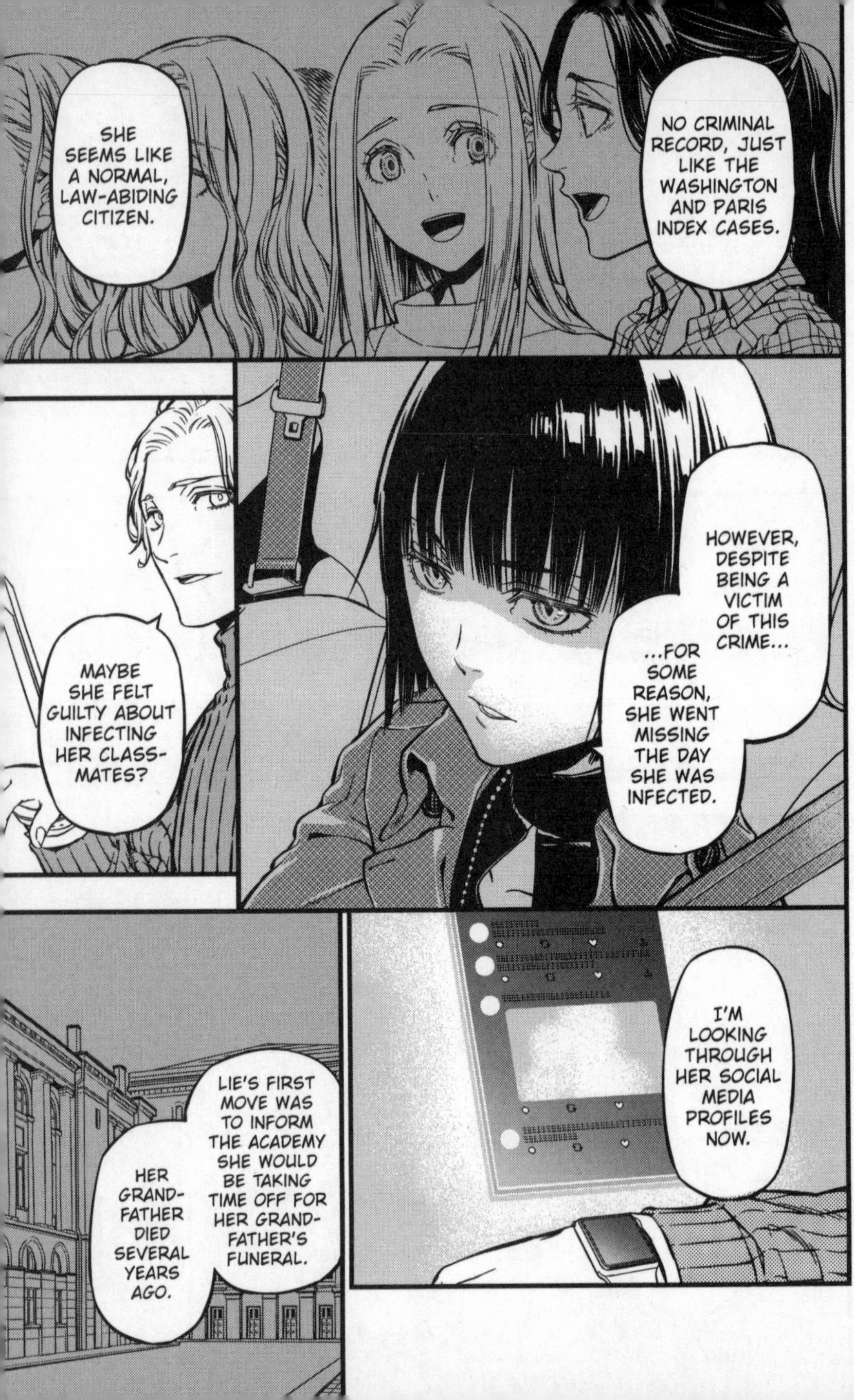
NO CRIMINAL RECORD, JUST LIKE THE WASHINGTON AND PARIS INDEX CASES.
SHE SEEMS LIKE A NORMAL, LAW-ABIDING CITIZEN.
HOWEVER, DESPITE BEING A VICTIM OF THIS CRIME...
...FOR SOME REASON, SHE WENT MISSING THE DAY SHE WAS INFECTED.
MAYBE SHE FELT GUILTY ABOUT INFECTING HER CLASS-MATES?
I'M LOOKING THROUGH HER SOCIAL MEDIA PROFILES NOW.
LIE'S FIRST MOVE WAS TO INFORM THE ACADEMY SHE WOULD BE TAKING TIME OFF FOR HER GRAND-FATHER'S FUNERAL.
HER GRAND-FATHER DIED SEVERAL YEARS AGO.

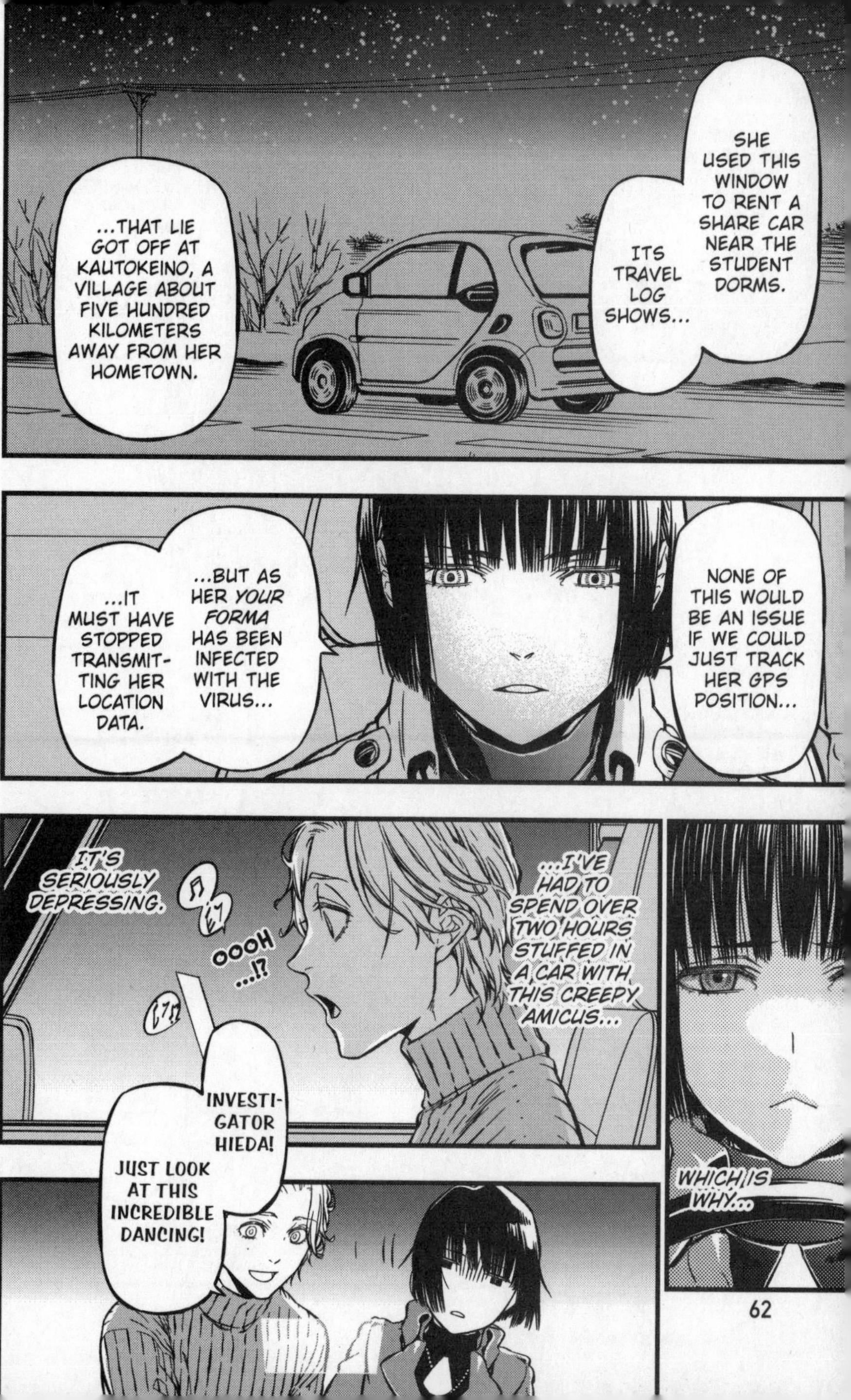
SHE USED THIS WINDOW TO RENT A SHARE CAR NEAR THE STUDENT DORMS.
ITS TRAVEL LOG SHOWS...
...THAT LIE GOT OFF AT KAUTOKEINO, A VILLAGE ABOUT FIVE HUNDRED KILOMETERS AWAY FROM HER HOMETOWN.
NONE OF THIS WOULD BE AN ISSUE IF WE COULD JUST TRACK HER GPS POSITION...
...BUT AS HER *YOUR FORMA* HAS BEEN INFECTED WITH THE VIRUS...
...IT MUST HAVE STOPPED TRANSMITTING HER LOCATION DATA.
WHICH IS WHY...
...I'VE HAD TO SPEND OVER TWO HOURS STUFFED IN A CAR WITH THIS CREEPY AMICUS...
IT'S SERIOUSLY DEPRESSING.
OOOH ...!?
INVESTIGATOR HIEDA! JUST LOOK AT THIS INCREDIBLE DANCING!

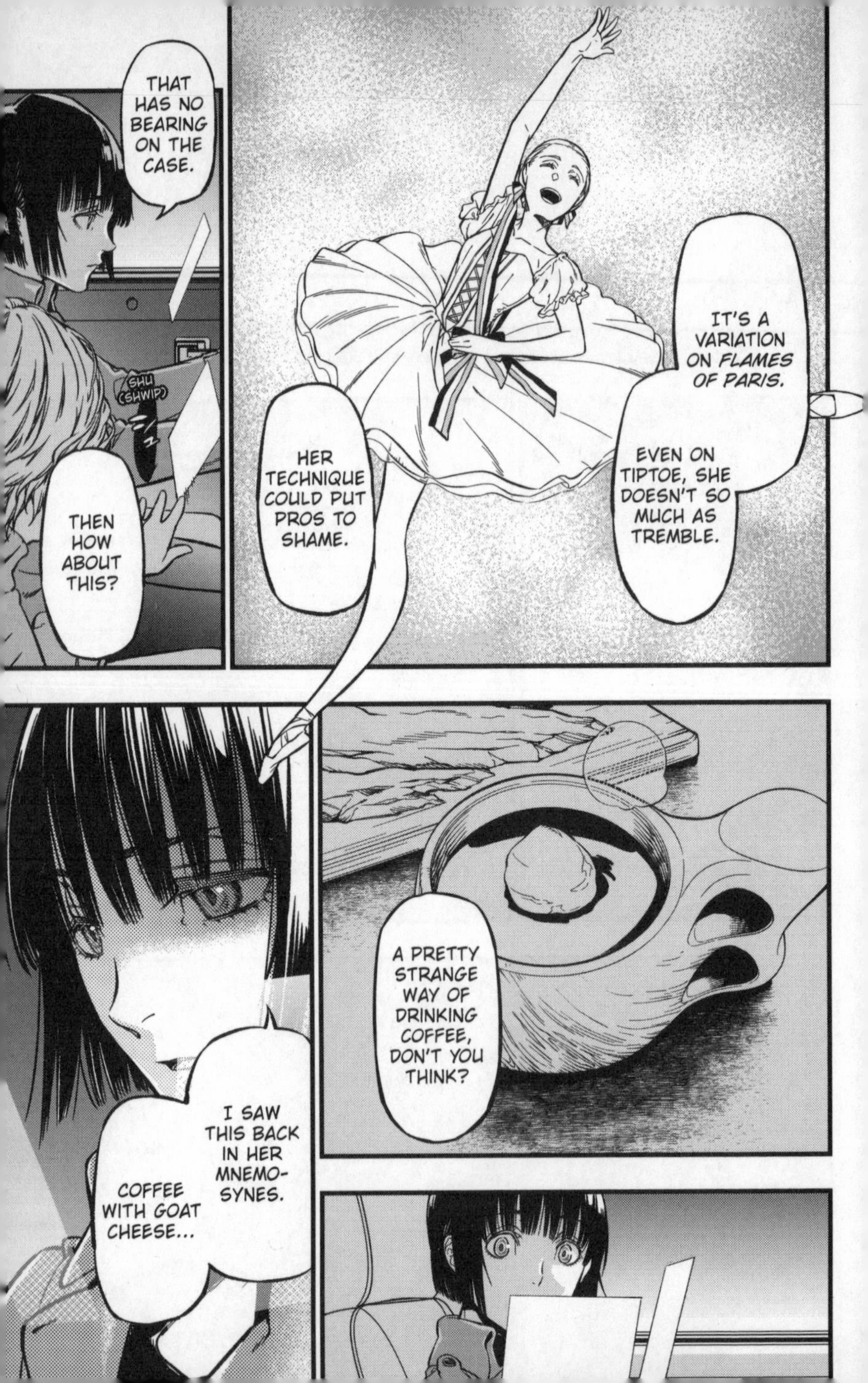
IT'S A VARIATION ON *FLAMES OF PARIS.*
EVEN ON TIPTOE, SHE DOESN'T SO MUCH AS TREMBLE.
HER TECHNIQUE COULD PUT PROS TO SHAME.
THAT HAS NO BEARING ON THE CASE.
SHU (SHWIP)
THEN HOW ABOUT THIS?
A PRETTY STRANGE WAY OF DRINKING COFFEE, DON'T YOU THINK?
I SAW THIS BACK IN HER MNEMO-SYNES.
COFFEE WITH GOAT CHEESE...

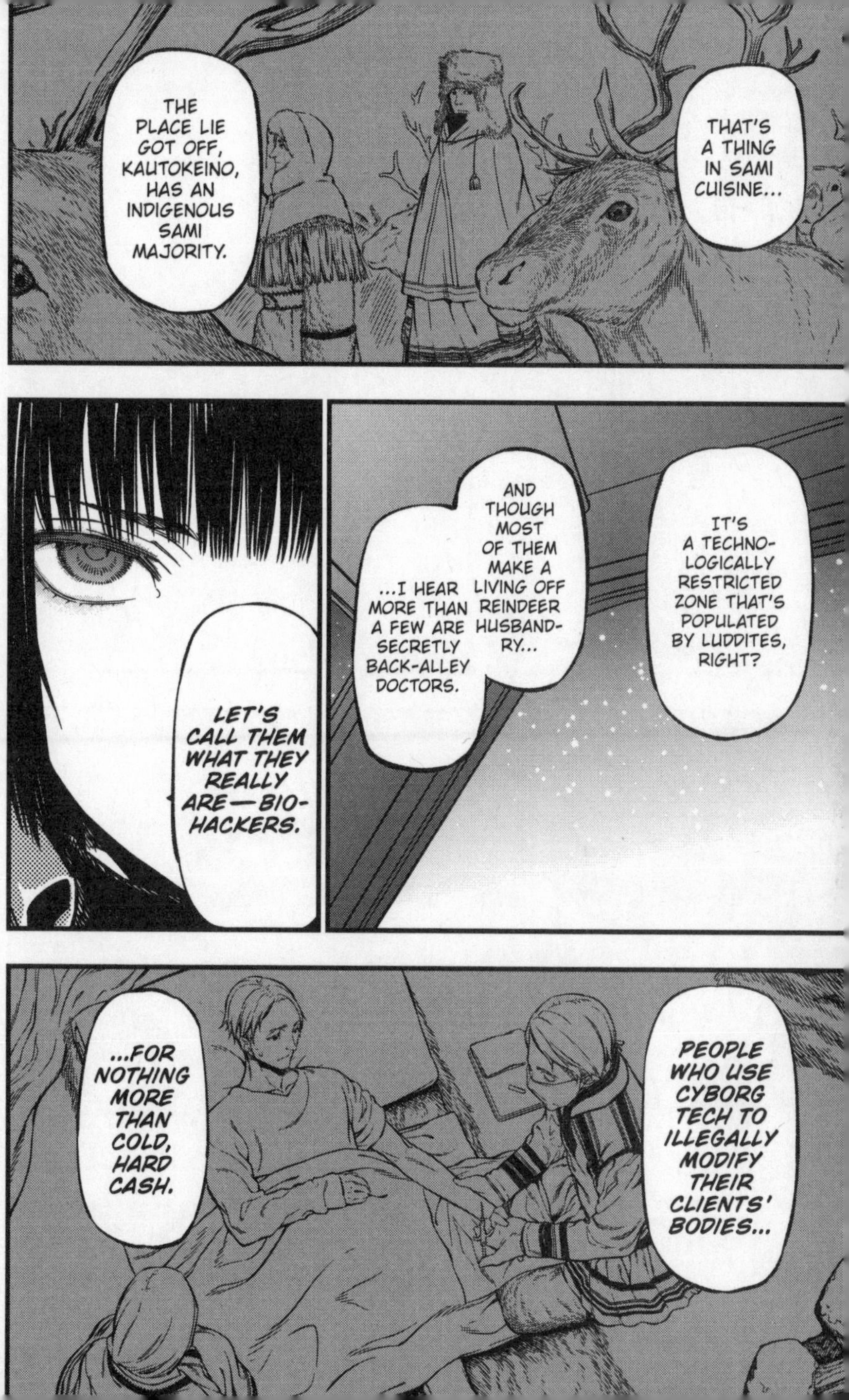
THAT'S A THING IN SAMI CUISINE...
THE PLACE LIE GOT OFF, KAUTOKEINO, HAS AN INDIGENOUS SAMI MAJORITY.
IT'S A TECHNOLOGICALLY RESTRICTED ZONE THAT'S POPULATED BY LUDDITES, RIGHT?
AND THOUGH MOST OF THEM MAKE A LIVING OFF REINDEER HUSBANDRY...
...I HEAR MORE THAN A FEW ARE SECRETLY BACK-ALLEY DOCTORS.
LET'S CALL THEM WHAT THEY REALLY ARE—BIOHACKERS.
PEOPLE WHO USE CYBORG TECH TO ILLEGALLY MODIFY THEIR CLIENTS' BODIES...
...FOR NOTHING MORE THAN COLD, HARD CASH.

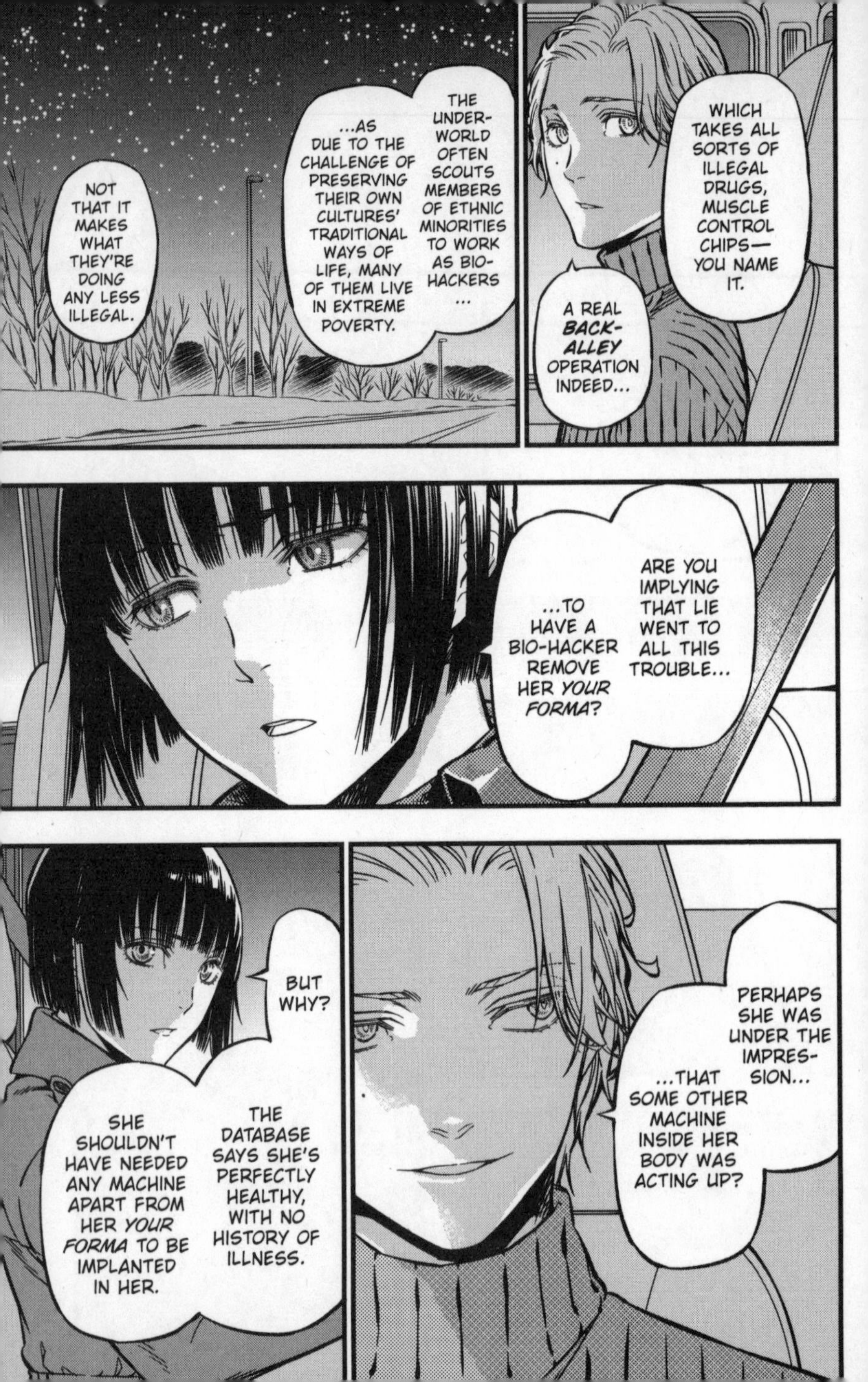

WHICH TAKES ALL SORTS OF ILLEGAL DRUGS, MUSCLE CONTROL CHIPS— YOU NAME IT.
A REAL *BACK-ALLEY* OPERATION INDEED...
THE UNDER-WORLD OFTEN SCOUTS MEMBERS OF ETHNIC MINORITIES TO WORK AS BIO-HACKERS...
...AS DUE TO THE CHALLENGE OF PRESERVING THEIR OWN CULTURES' TRADITIONAL WAYS OF LIFE, MANY OF THEM LIVE IN EXTREME POVERTY.
NOT THAT IT MAKES WHAT THEY'RE DOING ANY LESS ILLEGAL.
ARE YOU IMPLYING THAT LIE WENT TO ALL THIS TROUBLE...
...TO HAVE A BIO-HACKER REMOVE HER *YOUR FORMA*?
PERHAPS SHE WAS UNDER THE IMPRES-SION...
...THAT SOME OTHER MACHINE INSIDE HER BODY WAS ACTING UP?
BUT WHY?
THE DATABASE SAYS SHE'S PERFECTLY HEALTHY, WITH NO HISTORY OF ILLNESS.
SHE SHOULDN'T HAVE NEEDED ANY MACHINE APART FROM HER *YOUR FORMA* TO BE IMPLANTED IN HER.

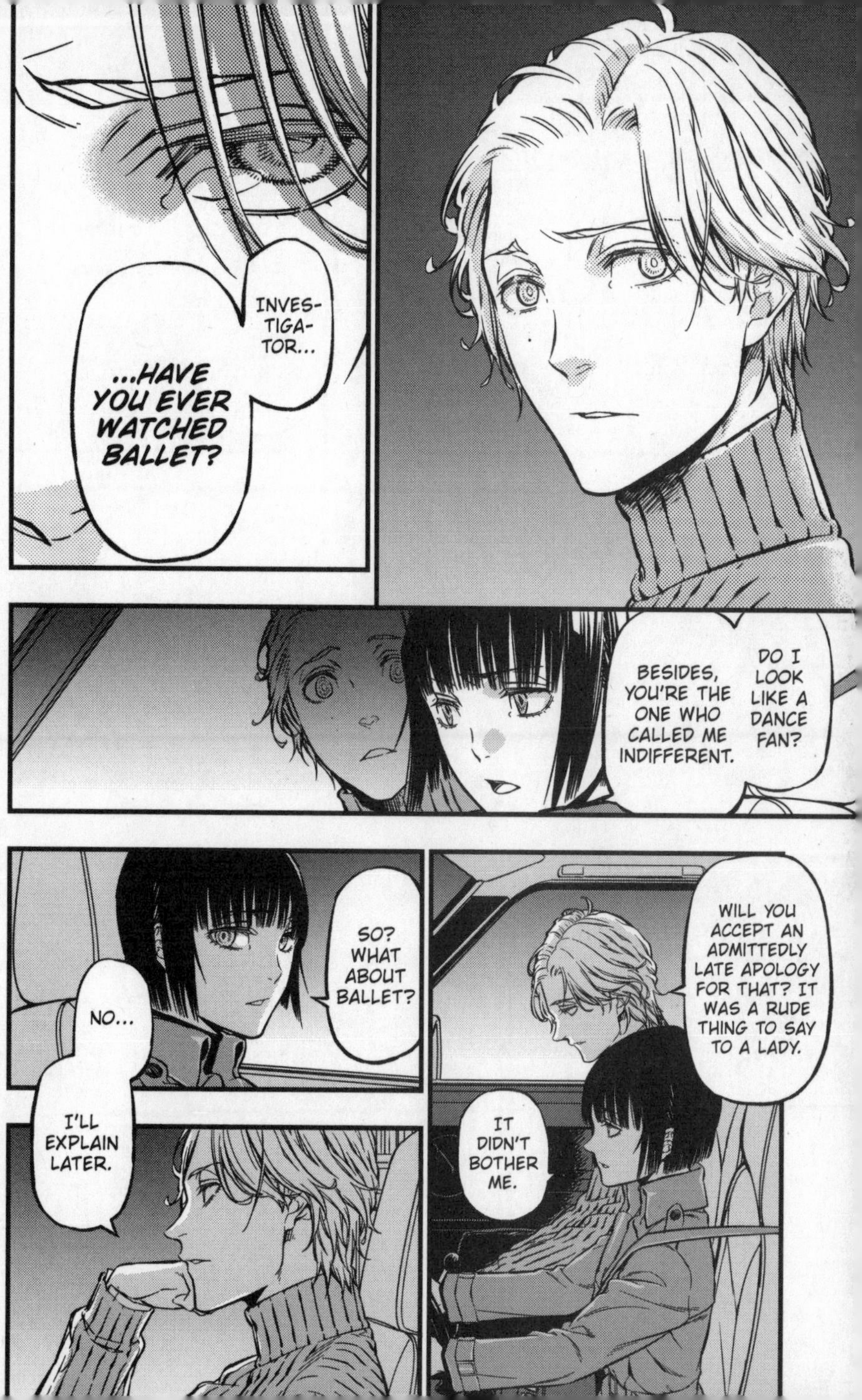
INVES-TIGA-TOR...
...HAVE YOU EVER WATCHED BALLET?
DO I LOOK LIKE A DANCE FAN?
BESIDES, YOU'RE THE ONE WHO CALLED ME INDIFFERENT.
WILL YOU ACCEPT AN ADMITTEDLY LATE APOLOGY FOR THAT? IT WAS A RUDE THING TO SAY TO A LADY.
IT DIDN'T BOTHER ME.
SO? WHAT ABOUT BALLET?
NO...
I'LL EXPLAIN LATER.

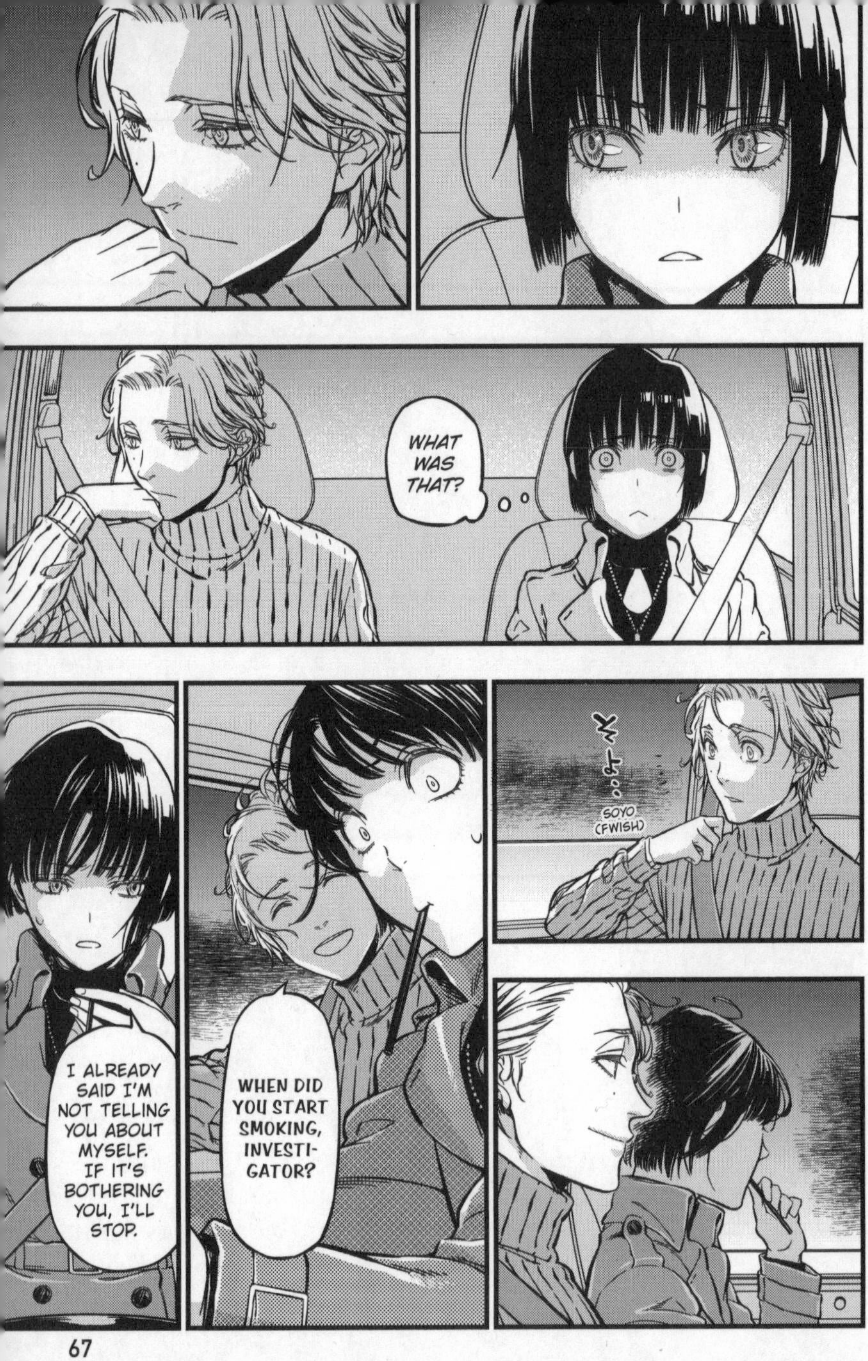
WHAT WAS THAT?
そよ…
SOYO (FWISH)
WHEN DID YOU START SMOKING, INVESTIGATOR?
I ALREADY SAID I'M NOT TELLING YOU ABOUT MYSELF. IF IT'S BOTHERING YOU, I'LL STOP.

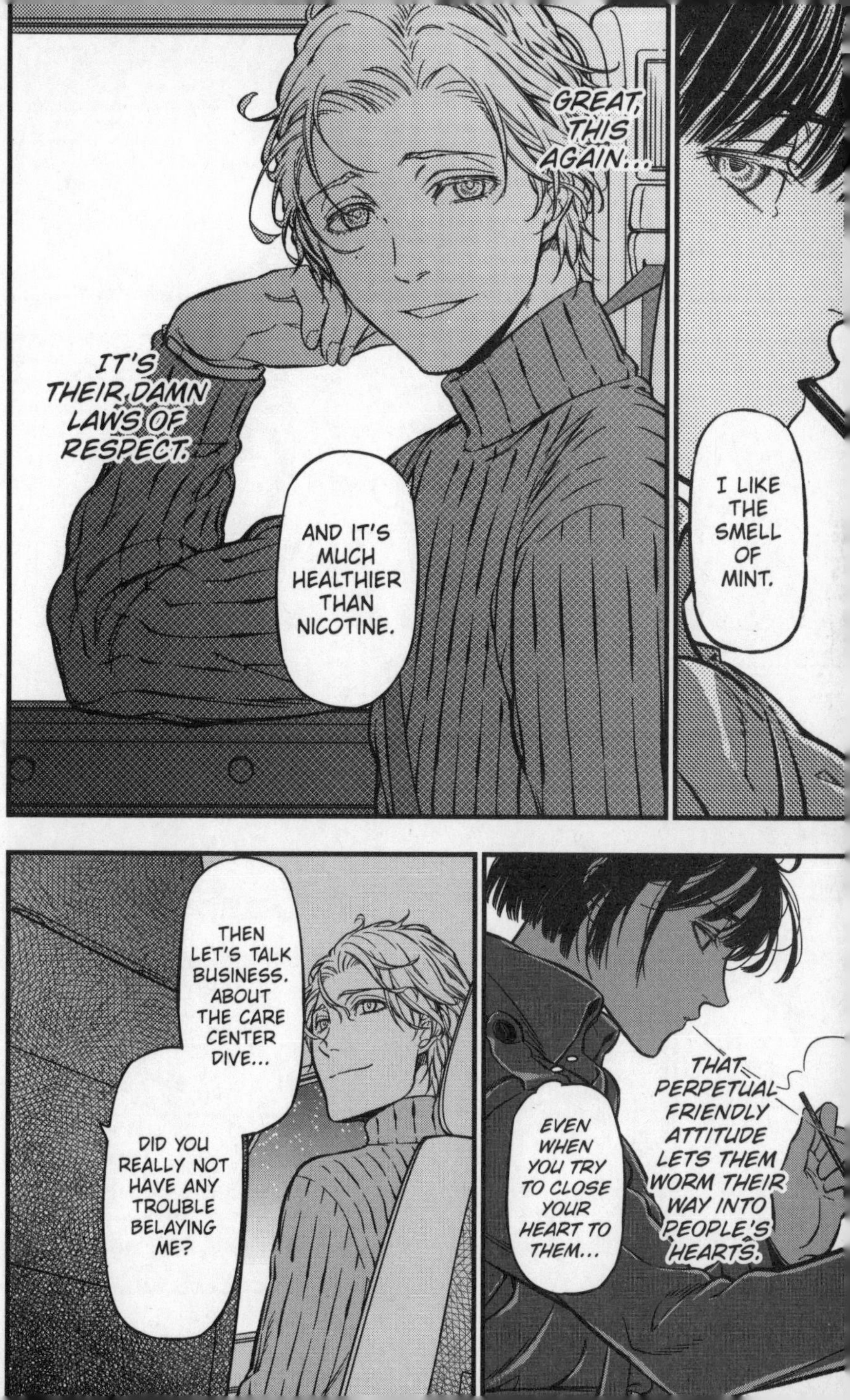
I LIKE THE SMELL OF MINT.
GREAT, THIS AGAIN...
IT'S THEIR DAMN LAWS OF RESPECT.
AND IT'S MUCH HEALTHIER THAN NICOTINE.
THAT PERPETUAL FRIENDLY ATTITUDE LETS THEM WORM THEIR WAY INTO PEOPLE'S HEARTS.
EVEN WHEN YOU TRY TO CLOSE YOUR HEART TO THEM...
THEN LET'S TALK BUSINESS. ABOUT THE CARE CENTER DIVE...
DID YOU REALLY NOT HAVE ANY TROUBLE BELAYING ME?

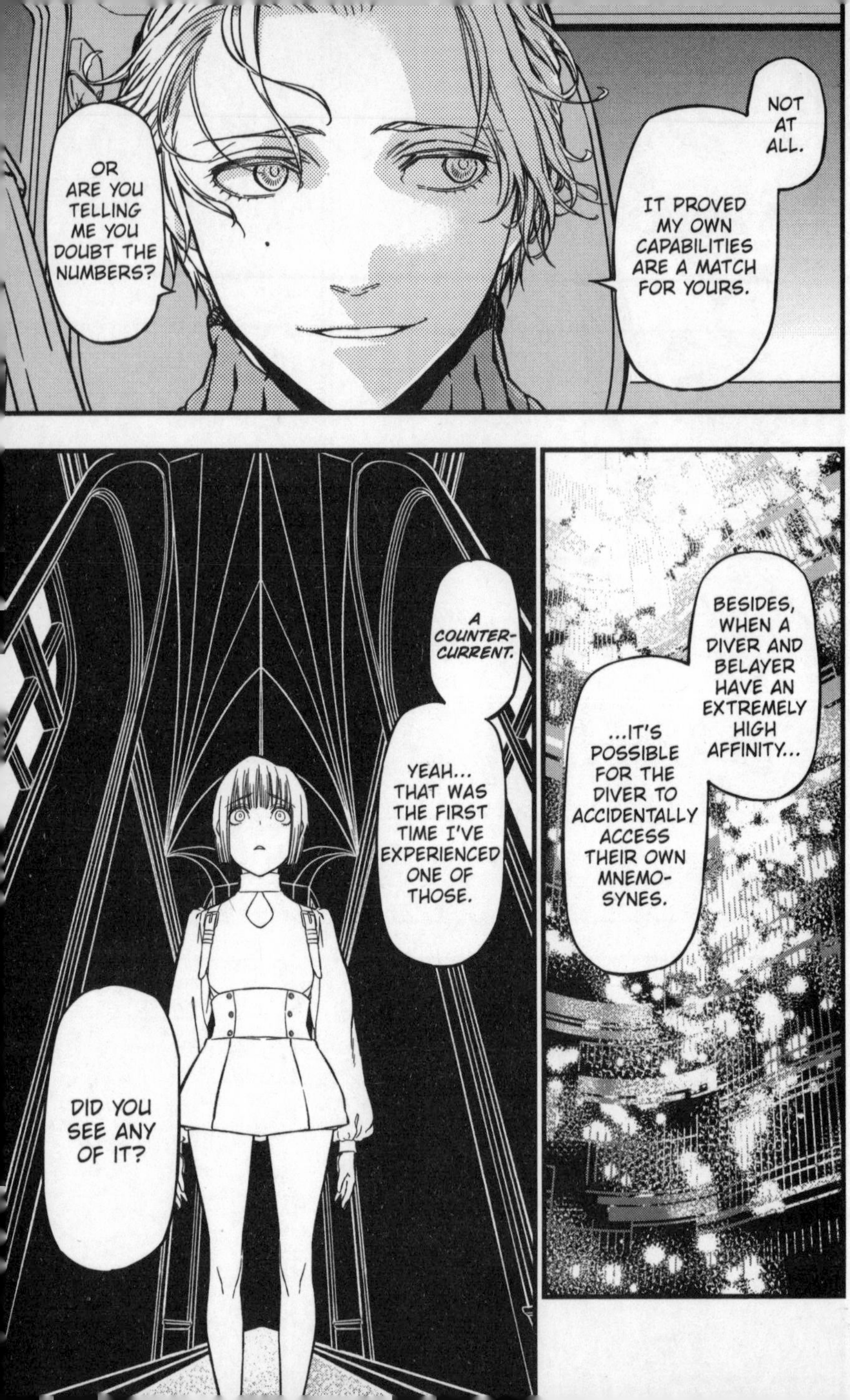
NOT AT ALL.
IT PROVED MY OWN CAPABILITIES ARE A MATCH FOR YOURS.
OR ARE YOU TELLING ME YOU DOUBT THE NUMBERS?
BESIDES, WHEN A DIVER AND BELAYER HAVE AN EXTREMELY HIGH AFFINITY...
...IT'S POSSIBLE FOR THE DIVER TO ACCIDENTALLY ACCESS THEIR OWN MNEMO-SYNES.
A COUNTER-CURRENT.
YEAH... THAT WAS THE FIRST TIME I'VE EXPERIENCED ONE OF THOSE.
DID YOU SEE ANY OF IT?

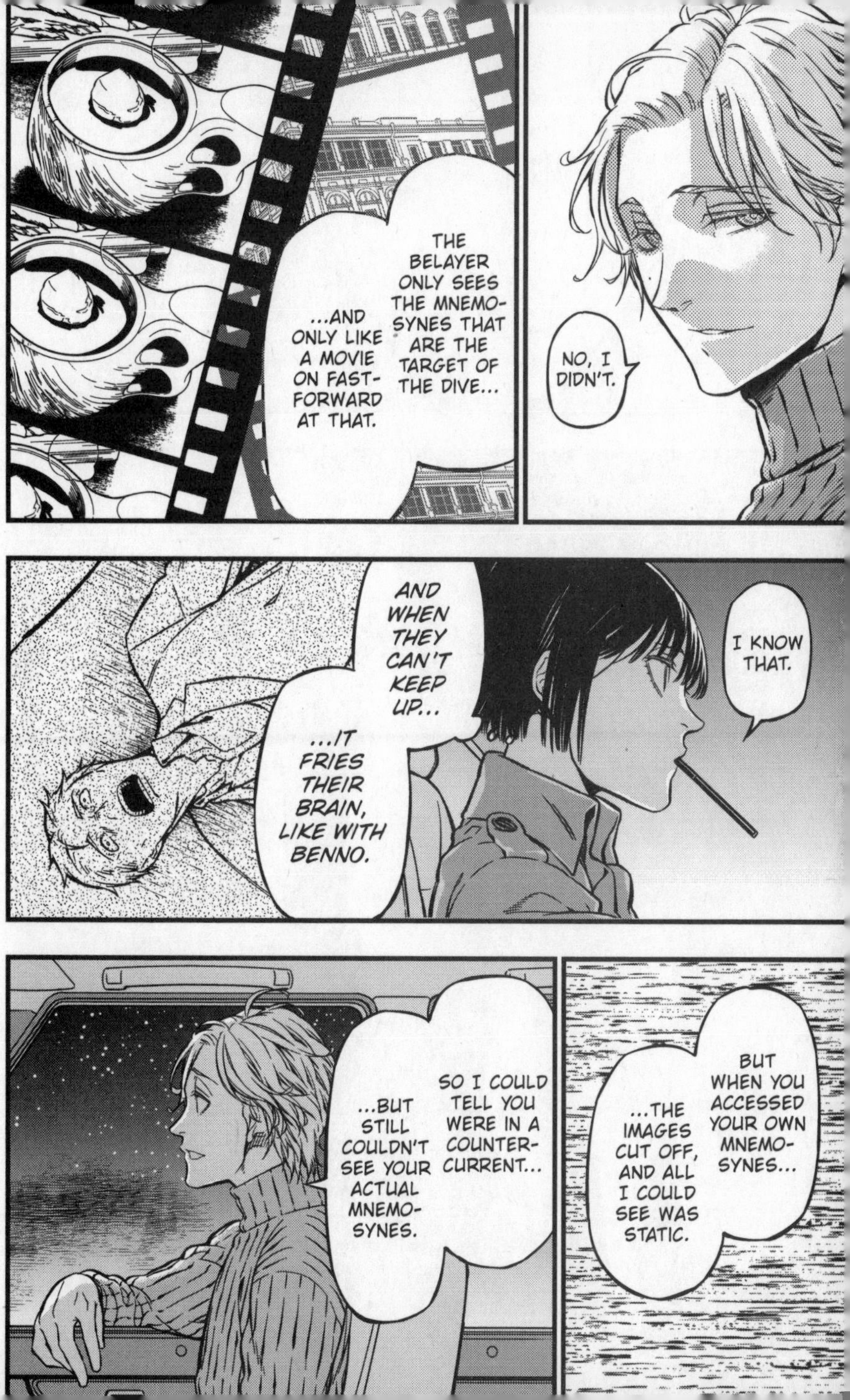
NO, I DIDN'T.
THE BELAYER ONLY SEES THE MNEMO-SYNES THAT ARE THE TARGET OF THE DIVE...
...AND ONLY LIKE A MOVIE ON FAST-FORWARD AT THAT.
I KNOW THAT.
AND WHEN THEY CAN'T KEEP UP...
...IT FRIES THEIR BRAIN, LIKE WITH BENNO.
BUT WHEN YOU ACCESSED YOUR OWN MNEMO-SYNES...
...THE IMAGES CUT OFF, AND ALL I COULD SEE WAS STATIC.
SO I COULD TELL YOU WERE IN A COUNTER-CURRENT...
...BUT STILL COULDN'T SEE YOUR ACTUAL MNEMO-SYNES.

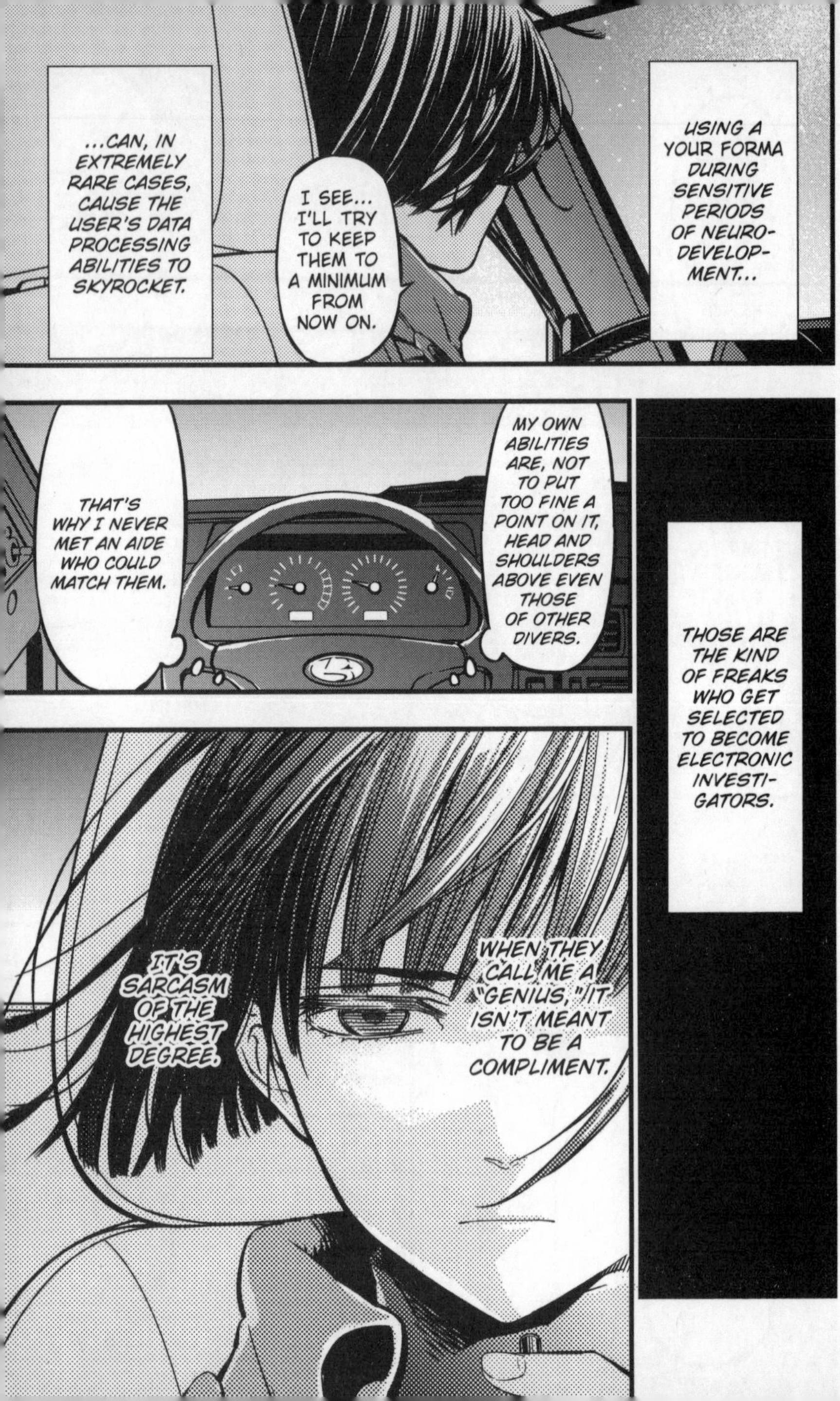
USING A YOUR FORMA DURING SENSITIVE PERIODS OF NEURO-DEVELOPMENT...
I SEE... I'LL TRY TO KEEP THEM TO A MINIMUM FROM NOW ON.
...CAN, IN EXTREMELY RARE CASES, CAUSE THE USER'S DATA PROCESSING ABILITIES TO SKYROCKET.
THOSE ARE THE KIND OF FREAKS WHO GET SELECTED TO BECOME ELECTRONIC INVESTI-GATORS.
MY OWN ABILITIES ARE, NOT TO PUT TOO FINE A POINT ON IT, HEAD AND SHOULDERS ABOVE EVEN THOSE OF OTHER DIVERS.
THAT'S WHY I NEVER MET AN AIDE WHO COULD MATCH THEM.
WHEN THEY CALL ME A "GENIUS," IT ISN'T MEANT TO BE A COMPLIMENT.
IT'S SARCASM OF THE HIGHEST DEGREE.

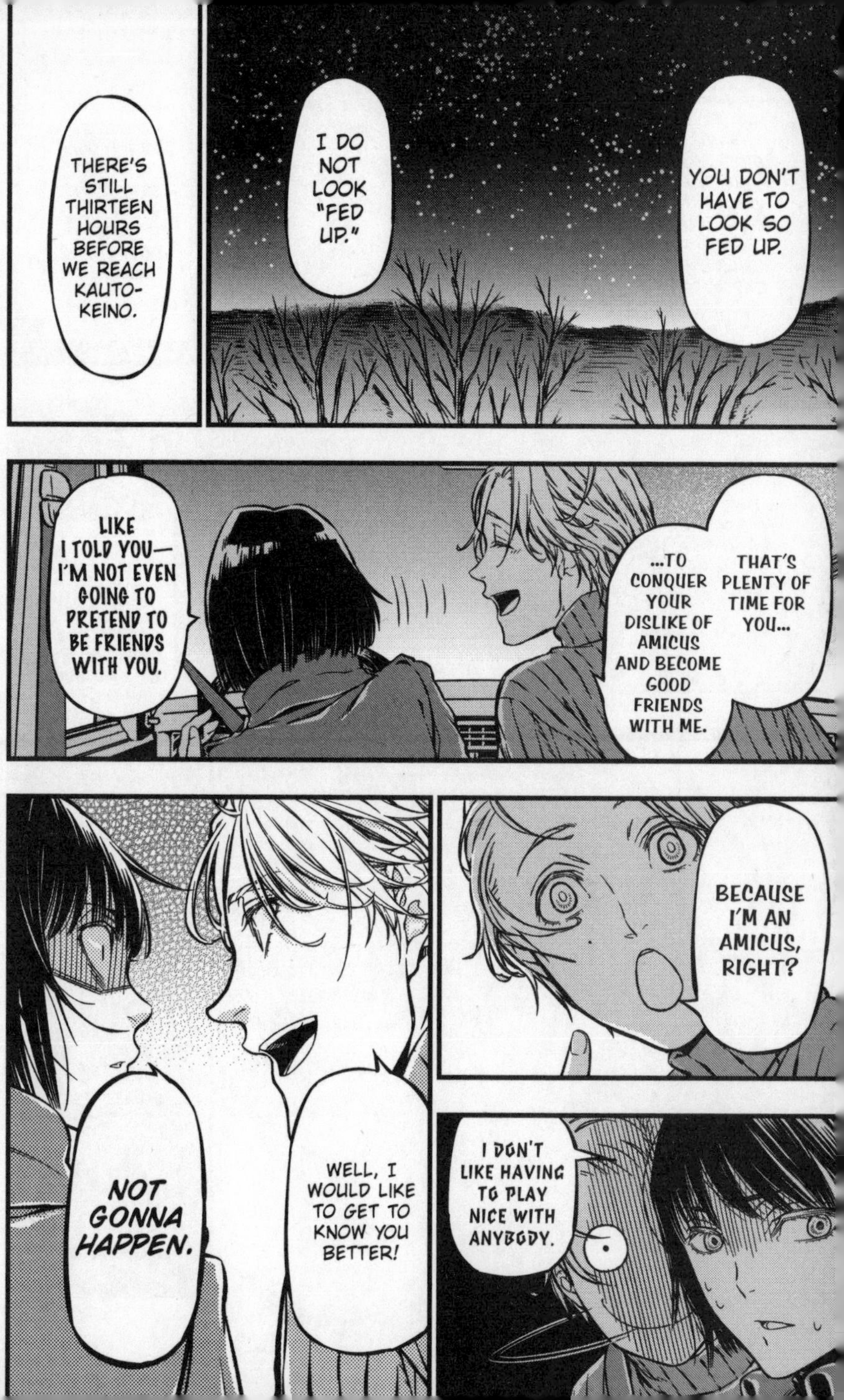
YOU DON'T HAVE TO LOOK SO FED UP.
I DO NOT LOOK "FED UP."
THERE'S STILL THIRTEEN HOURS BEFORE WE REACH KAUTO-KEINO.
THAT'S PLENTY OF TIME FOR YOU...
...TO CONQUER YOUR DISLIKE OF AMICUS AND BECOME GOOD FRIENDS WITH ME.
LIKE I TOLD YOU— I'M NOT EVEN GOING TO PRETEND TO BE FRIENDS WITH YOU.
BECAUSE I'M AN AMICUS, RIGHT?
I DON'T LIKE HAVING TO PLAY NICE WITH ANYBODY.
WELL, I WOULD LIKE TO GET TO KNOW YOU BETTER!
NOT GONNA HAPPEN.

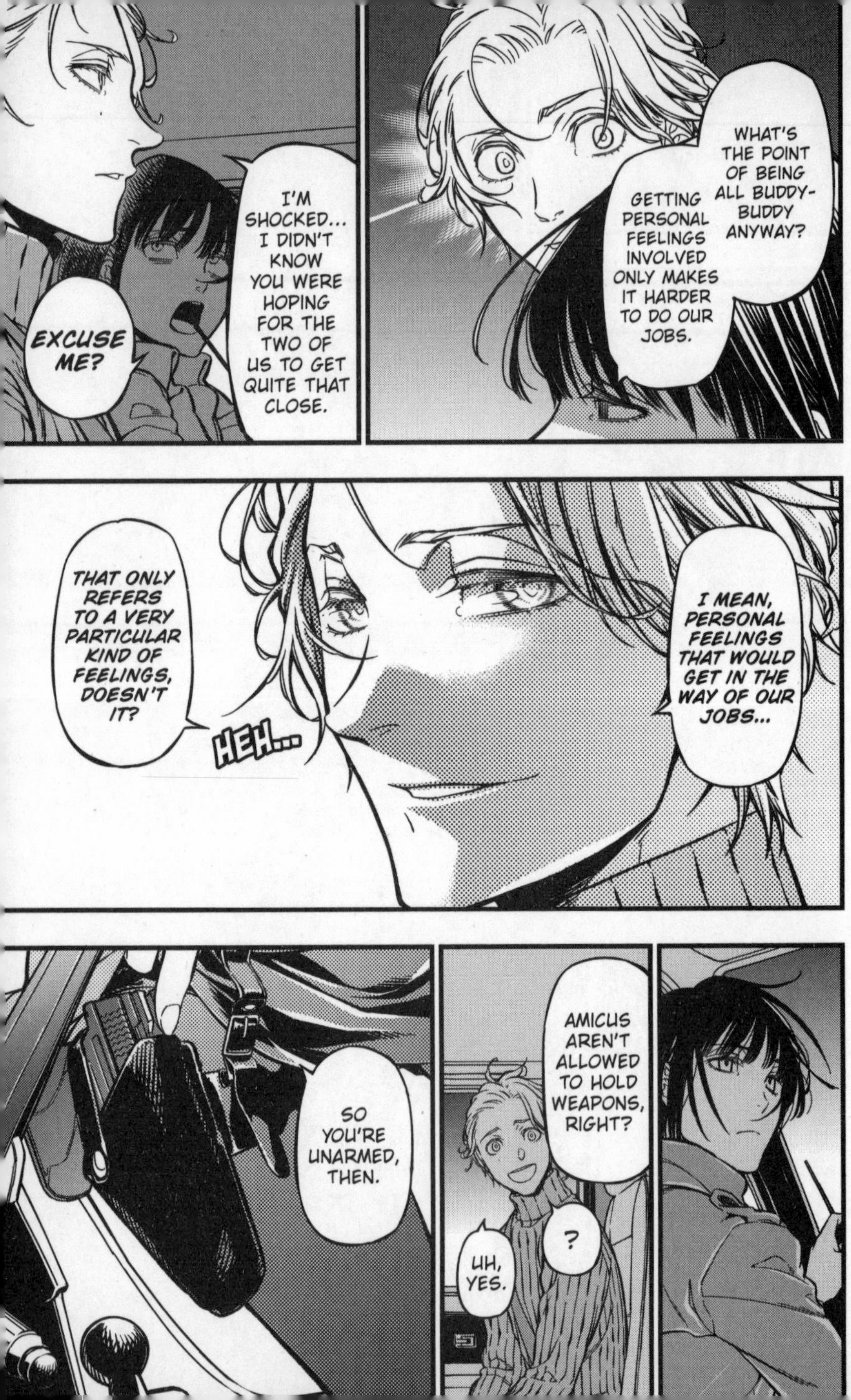
WHAT'S THE POINT OF BEING ALL BUDDY-BUDDY ANYWAY?
GETTING PERSONAL FEELINGS INVOLVED ONLY MAKES IT HARDER TO DO OUR JOBS.
I'M SHOCKED... I DIDN'T KNOW YOU WERE HOPING FOR THE TWO OF US TO GET QUITE THAT CLOSE.
EXCUSE ME?
I MEAN, PERSONAL FEELINGS THAT WOULD GET IN THE WAY OF OUR JOBS...
HEH...
THAT ONLY REFERS TO A VERY PARTICULAR KIND OF FEELINGS, DOESN'T IT?
AMICUS AREN'T ALLOWED TO HOLD WEAPONS, RIGHT?
?
UH, YES.
SO YOU'RE UNARMED, THEN.

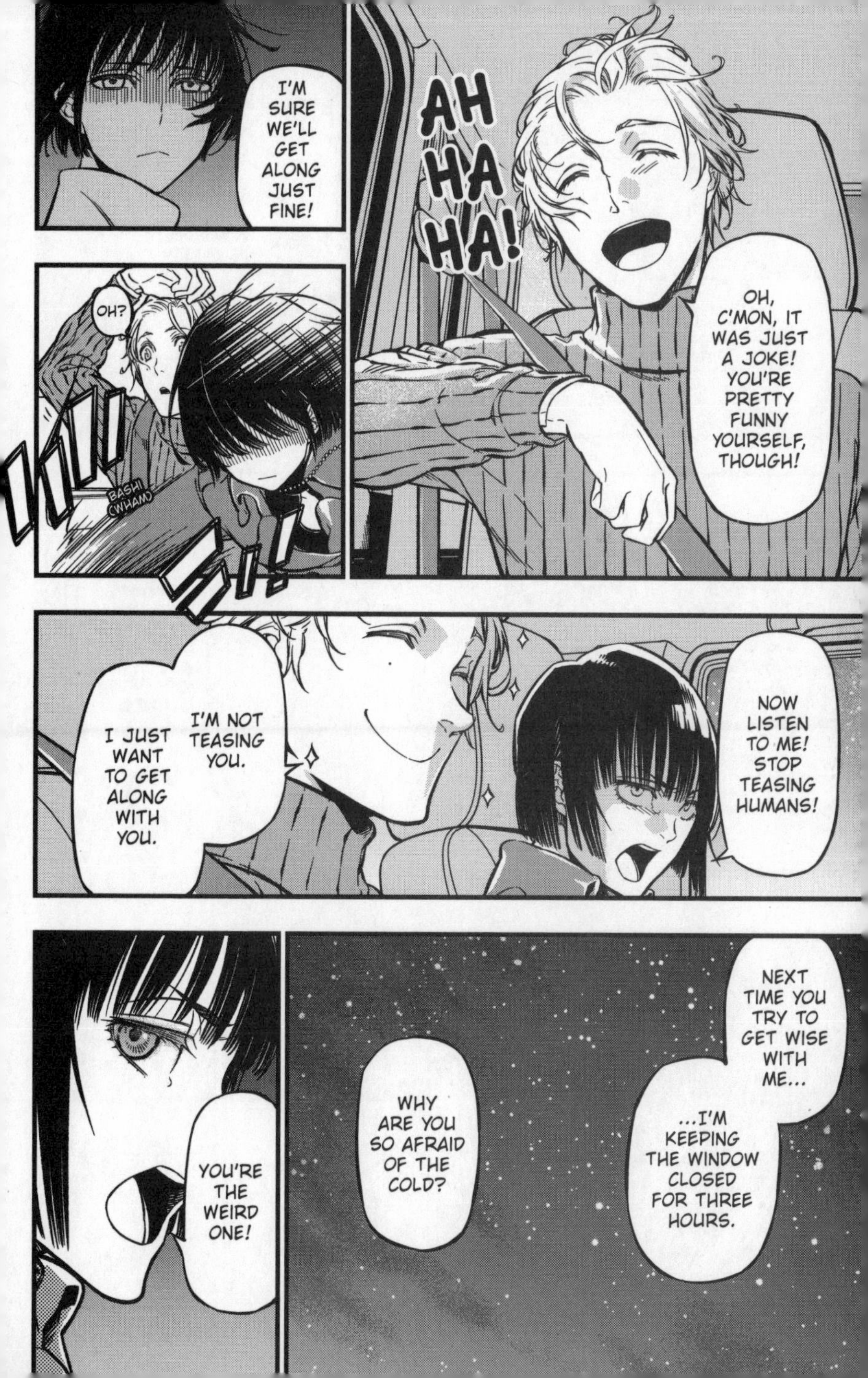
AH HA HA HA!
OH, C'MON, IT WAS JUST A JOKE! YOU'RE PRETTY FUNNY YOURSELF, THOUGH!
I'M SURE WE'LL GET ALONG JUST FINE!
OH?
BASHI (WHAM)
NOW LISTEN TO ME! STOP TEASING HUMANS!
I'M NOT TEASING YOU.
I JUST WANT TO GET ALONG WITH YOU.
NEXT TIME YOU TRY TO GET WISE WITH ME...
...I'M KEEPING THE WINDOW CLOSED FOR THREE HOURS.
WHY ARE YOU SO AFRAID OF THE COLD?
YOU'RE THE WEIRD ONE!

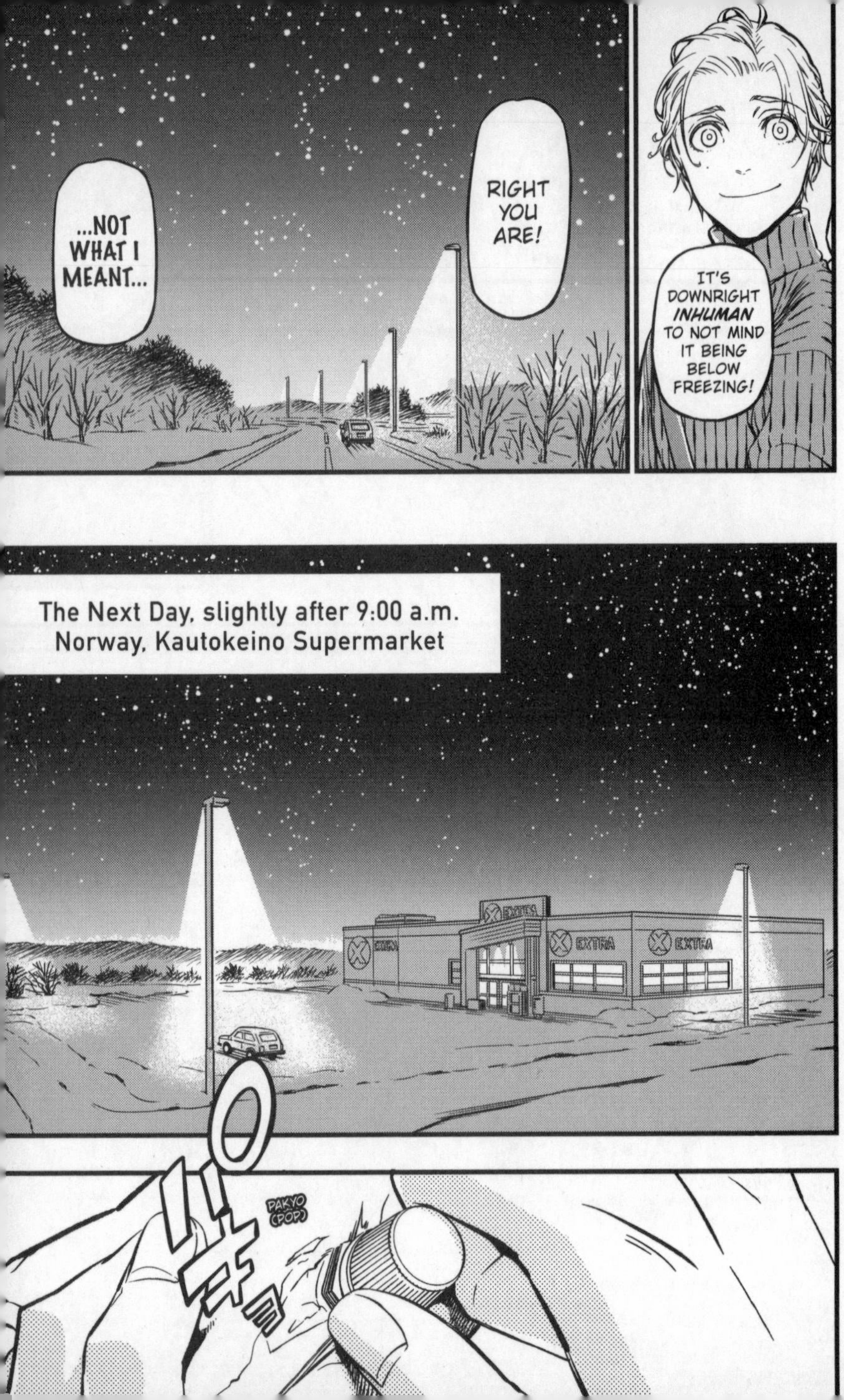
IT'S DOWNRIGHT *INHUMAN* TO NOT MIND IT BEING BELOW FREEZING!
RIGHT YOU ARE!
...NOT WHAT I MEANT...
The Next Day, slightly after 9:00 a.m.
Norway, Kautokeino Supermarket
EXTRA
EXTRA
EXTRA
PAKYO (POP)

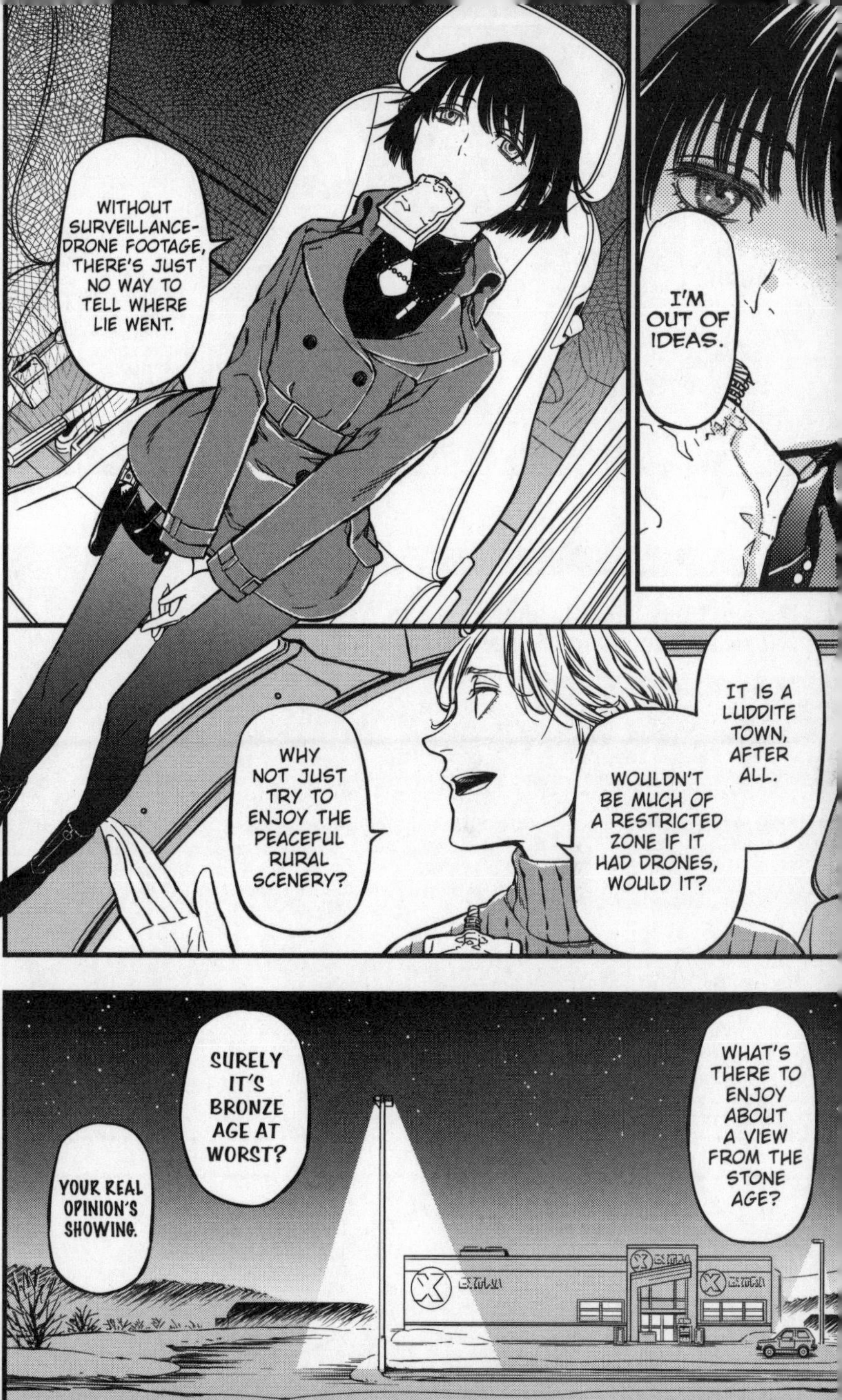
I'M OUT OF IDEAS.
WITHOUT SURVEILLANCE-DRONE FOOTAGE, THERE'S JUST NO WAY TO TELL WHERE LIE WENT.
IT IS A LUDDITE TOWN, AFTER ALL.
WOULDN'T BE MUCH OF A RESTRICTED ZONE IF IT HAD DRONES, WOULD IT?
WHY NOT JUST TRY TO ENJOY THE PEACEFUL RURAL SCENERY?
WHAT'S THERE TO ENJOY ABOUT A VIEW FROM THE STONE AGE?
SURELY IT'S BRONZE AGE AT WORST?
YOUR REAL OPINION'S SHOWING.

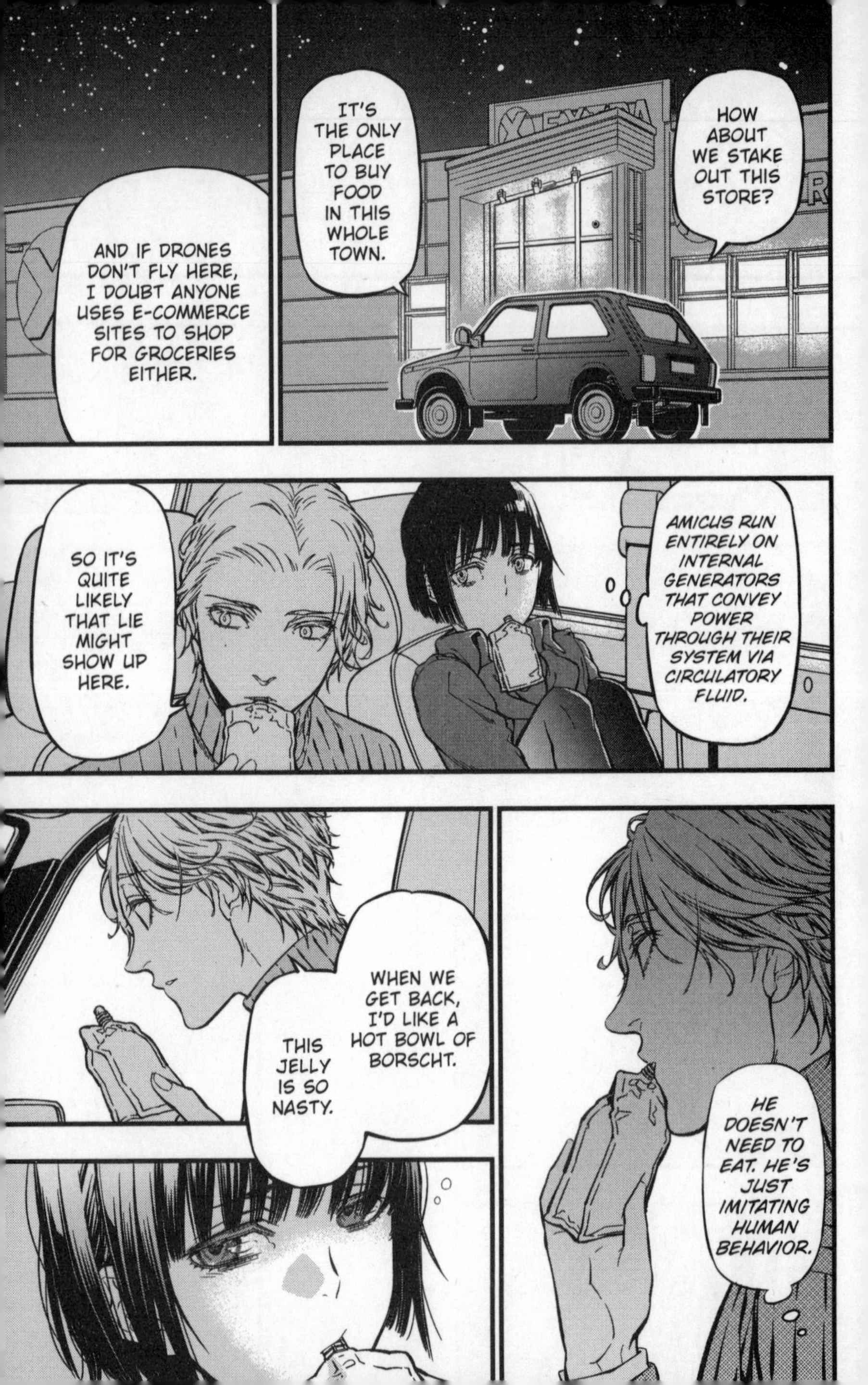
HOW ABOUT WE STAKE OUT THIS STORE?
IT'S THE ONLY PLACE TO BUY FOOD IN THIS WHOLE TOWN.
AND IF DRONES DON'T FLY HERE, I DOUBT ANYONE USES E-COMMERCE SITES TO SHOP FOR GROCERIES EITHER.
SO IT'S QUITE LIKELY THAT LIE MIGHT SHOW UP HERE.
AMICUS RUN ENTIRELY ON INTERNAL GENERATORS THAT CONVEY POWER THROUGH THEIR SYSTEM VIA CIRCULATORY FLUID.
HE DOESN'T NEED TO EAT. HE'S JUST IMITATING HUMAN BEHAVIOR.
WHEN WE GET BACK, I'D LIKE A HOT BOWL OF BORSCHT.
THIS JELLY IS SO NASTY.

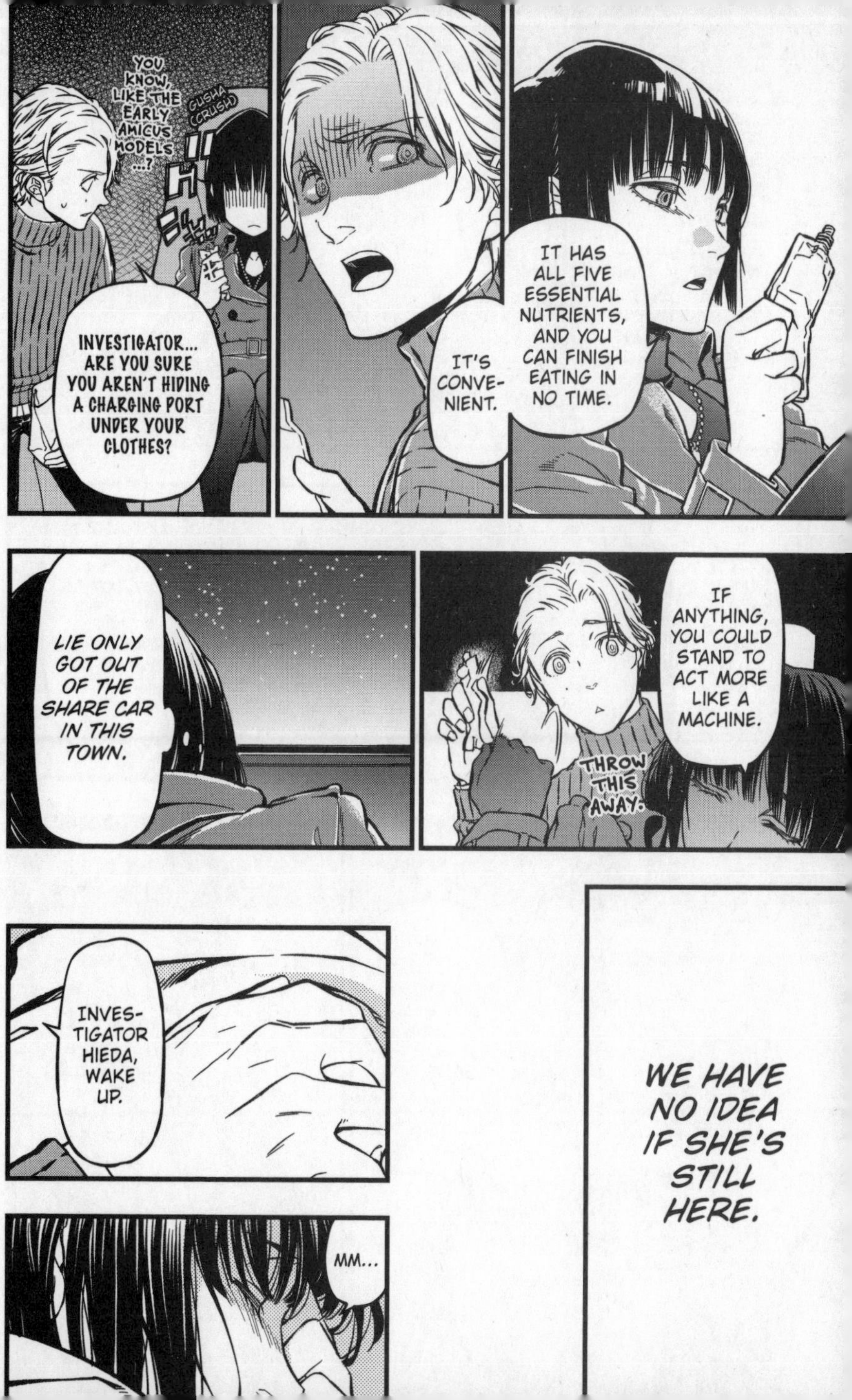
IT HAS ALL FIVE ESSENTIAL NUTRIENTS, AND YOU CAN FINISH EATING IN NO TIME.
IT'S CONVE-NIENT.
GUSHA (CRUSH)
YOU KNOW, LIKE THE EARLY AMICUS MODELS ...?
INVESTIGATOR... ARE YOU SURE YOU AREN'T HIDING A CHARGING PORT UNDER YOUR CLOTHES?
IF ANYTHING, YOU COULD STAND TO ACT MORE LIKE A MACHINE.
THROW THIS AWAY.
LIE ONLY GOT OUT OF THE SHARE CAR IN THIS TOWN.
WE HAVE NO IDEA IF SHE'S STILL HERE.
INVES-TIGATOR HIEDA, WAKE UP.
MM...

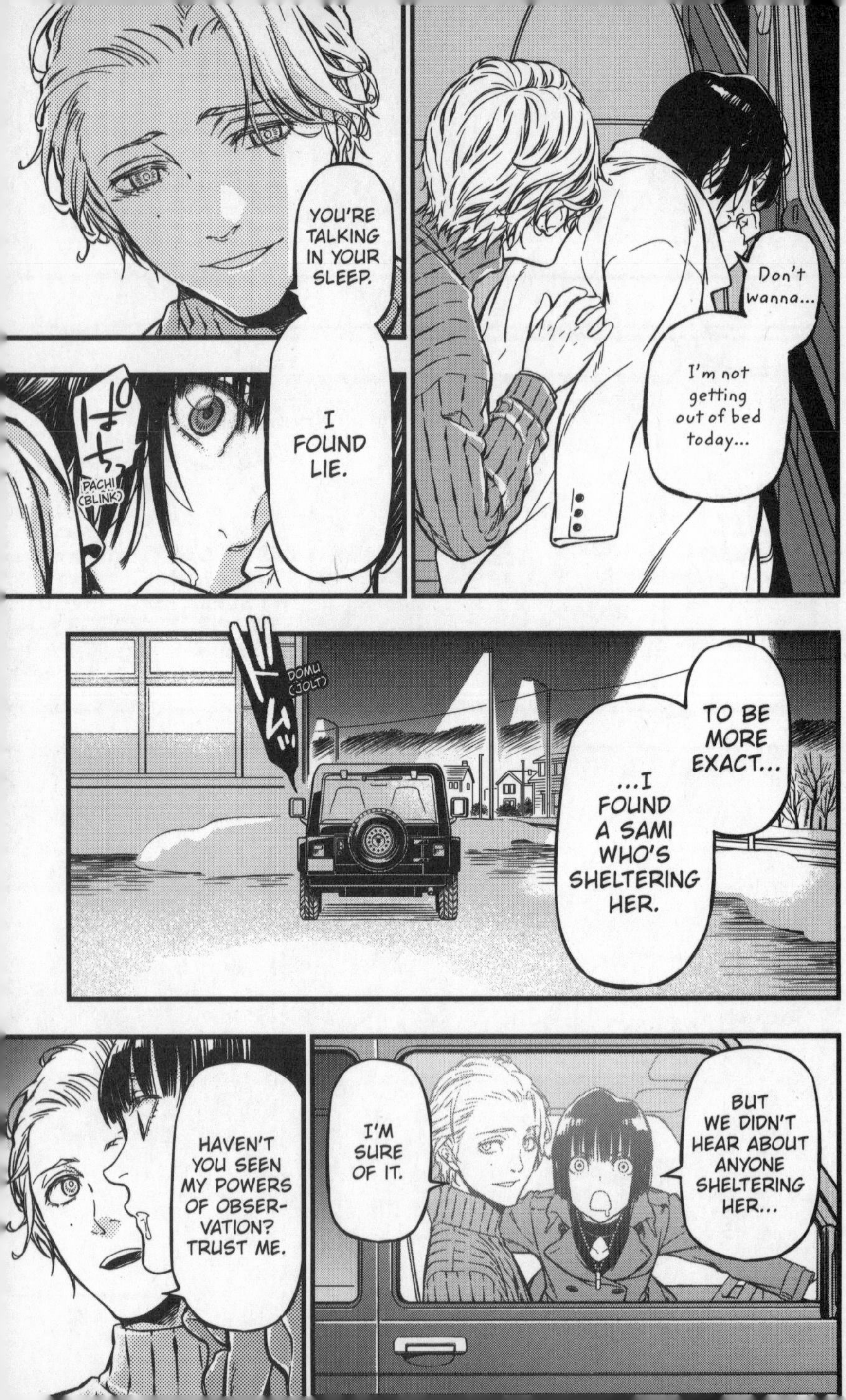
Don't wanna...
I'm not getting out of bed today...
YOU'RE TALKING IN YOUR SLEEP.
I FOUND LIE.
PACHI (BLINK)
TO BE MORE EXACT...
...I FOUND A SAMI WHO'S SHELTERING HER.
DOMU (JOLT)
BUT WE DIDN'T HEAR ABOUT ANYONE SHELTERING HER...
I'M SURE OF IT.
HAVEN'T YOU SEEN MY POWERS OF OBSERVATION? TRUST ME.

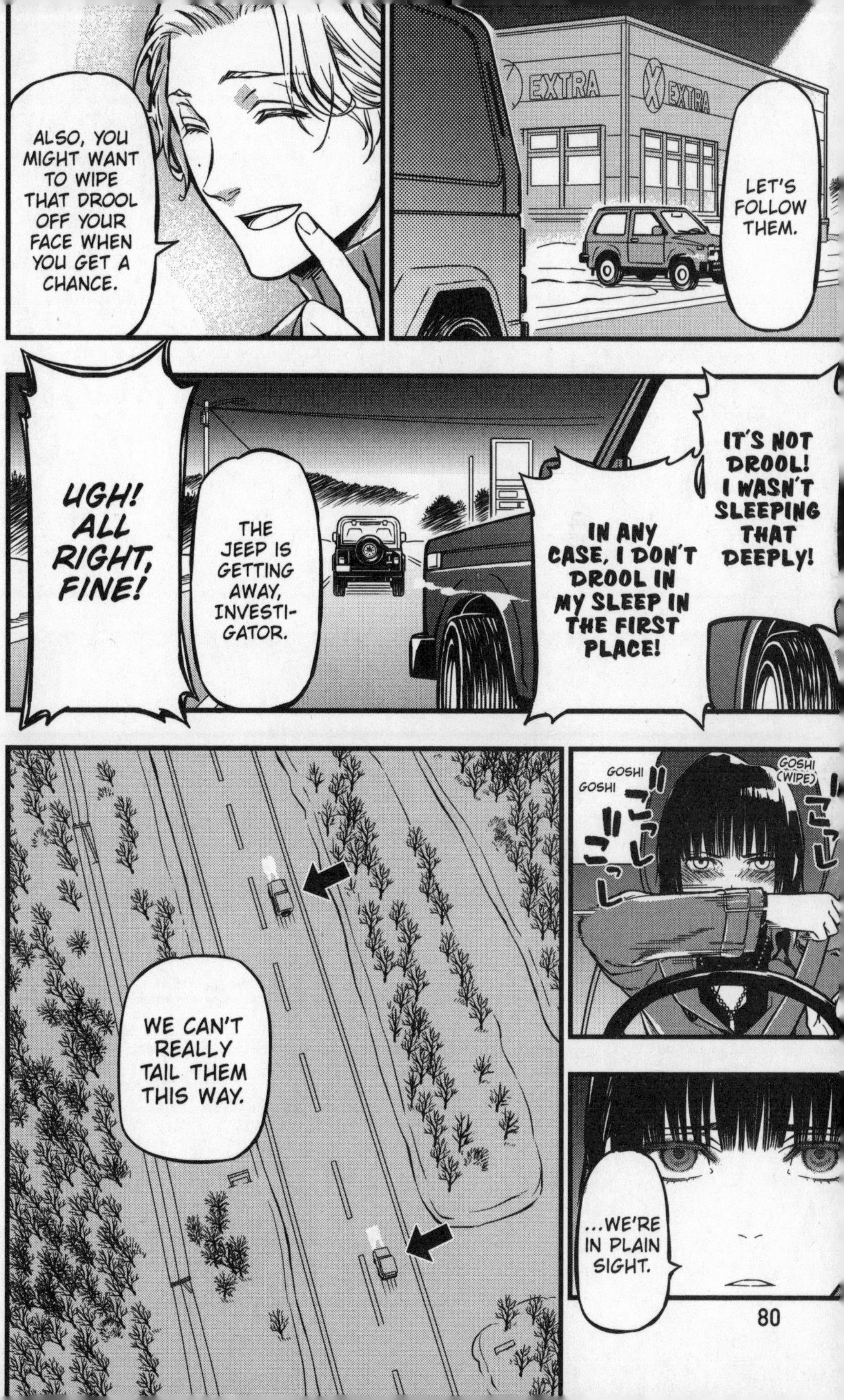
EXTRA
EXTRA
LET'S FOLLOW THEM.
ALSO, YOU MIGHT WANT TO WIPE THAT DROOL OFF YOUR FACE WHEN YOU GET A CHANCE.
IT'S NOT DROOL! I WASN'T SLEEPING THAT DEEPLY!
IN ANY CASE, I DON'T DROOL IN MY SLEEP IN THE FIRST PLACE!
THE JEEP IS GETTING AWAY, INVESTI-GATOR.
UGH! ALL RIGHT, FINE!
GOSHI (WIPE)
GOSHI
GOSHI
...WE'RE IN PLAIN SIGHT.
WE CAN'T REALLY TAIL THEM THIS WAY.

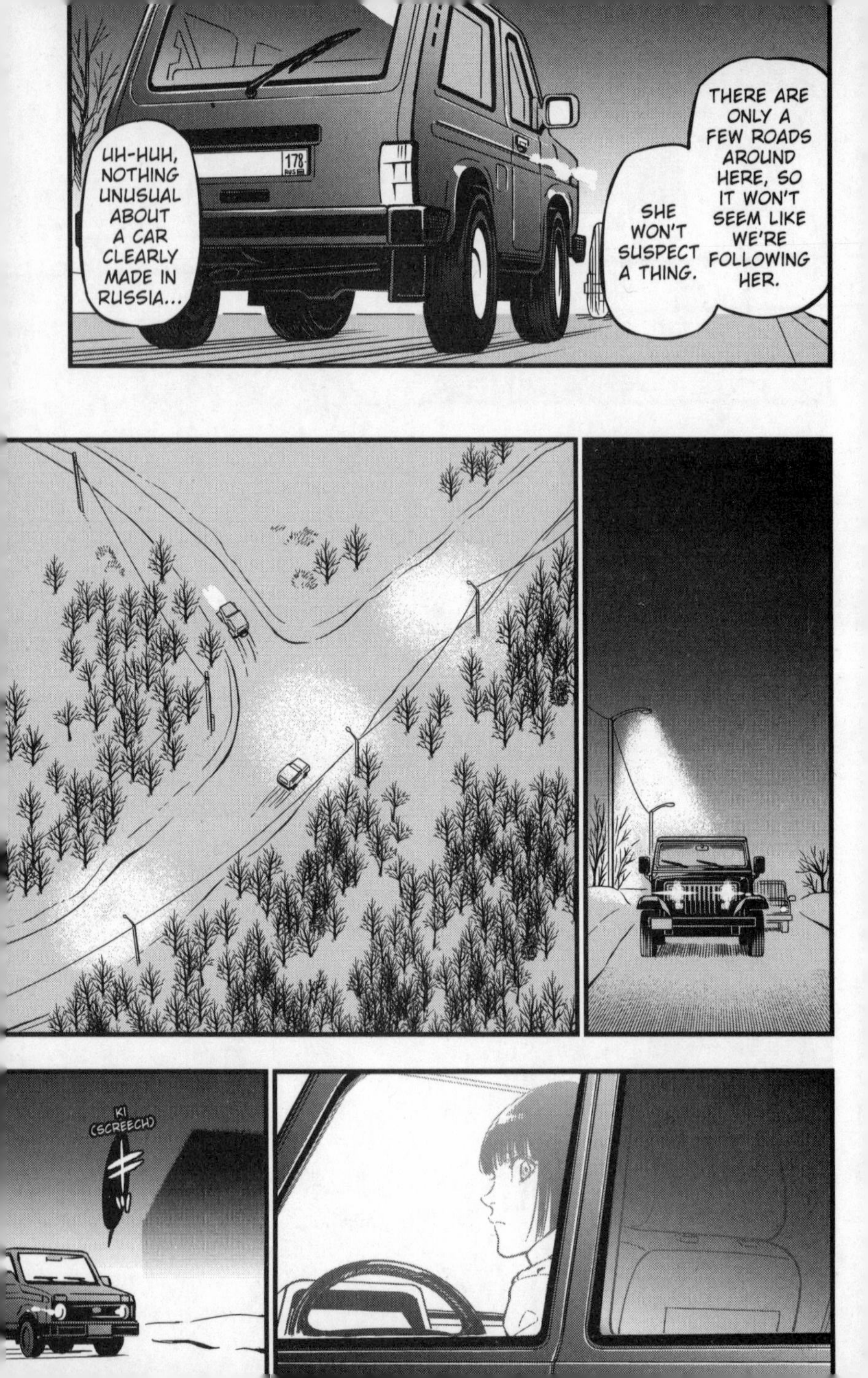
THERE ARE ONLY A FEW ROADS AROUND HERE, SO IT WON'T SEEM LIKE WE'RE FOLLOWING HER.
SHE WON'T SUSPECT A THING.
UH-HUH, NOTHING UNUSUAL ABOUT A CAR CLEARLY MADE IN RUSSIA...
KI (SCREECH)

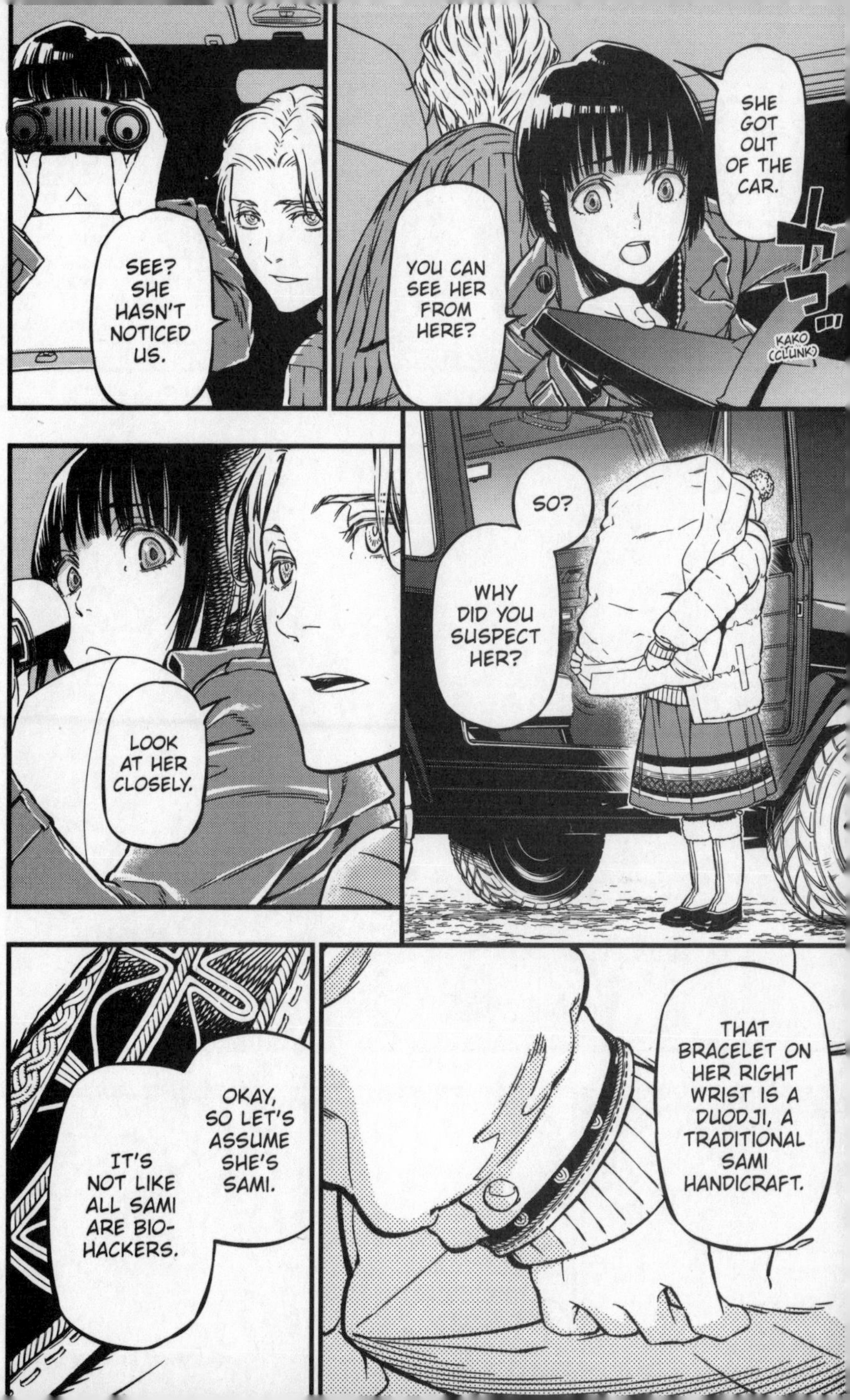
SHE GOT OUT OF THE CAR.
KAKO (CLUNK)
YOU CAN SEE HER FROM HERE?
SEE? SHE HASN'T NOTICED US.
SO?
WHY DID YOU SUSPECT HER?
LOOK AT HER CLOSELY.
THAT BRACELET ON HER RIGHT WRIST IS A DUODJI, A TRADITIONAL SAMI HANDICRAFT.
OKAY, SO LET'S ASSUME SHE'S SAMI.
IT'S NOT LIKE ALL SAMI ARE BIO-HACKERS.

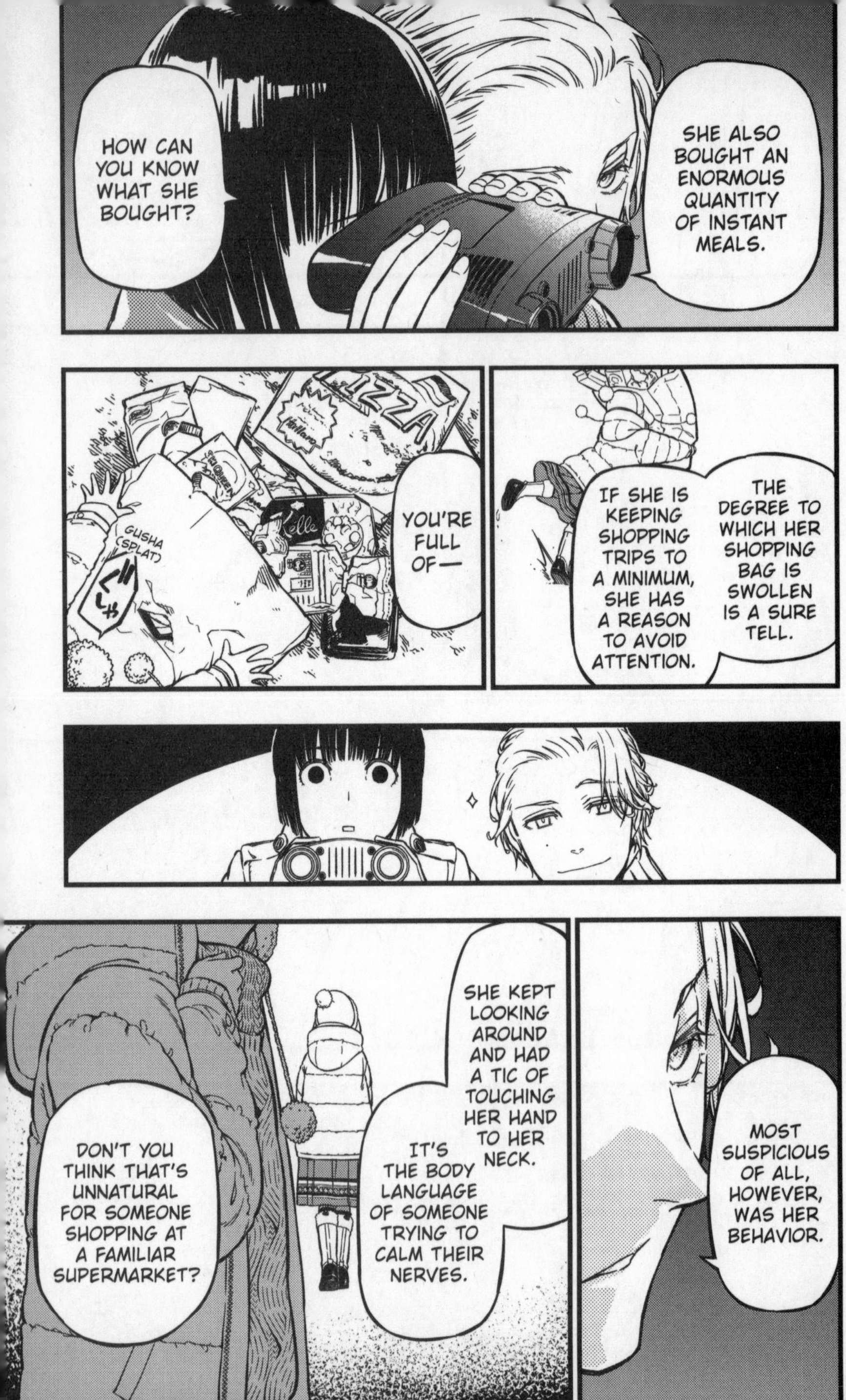
SHE ALSO BOUGHT AN ENORMOUS QUANTITY OF INSTANT MEALS.
HOW CAN YOU KNOW WHAT SHE BOUGHT?
THE DEGREE TO WHICH HER SHOPPING BAG IS SWOLLEN IS A SURE TELL.
IF SHE IS KEEPING SHOPPING TRIPS TO A MINIMUM, SHE HAS A REASON TO AVOID ATTENTION.
YOU'RE FULL OF—
GUSHA (SPLAT)
PIZZA
MOST SUSPICIOUS OF ALL, HOWEVER, WAS HER BEHAVIOR.
SHE KEPT LOOKING AROUND AND HAD A TIC OF TOUCHING HER HAND TO HER NECK.
IT'S THE BODY LANGUAGE OF SOMEONE TRYING TO CALM THEIR NERVES.
DON'T YOU THINK THAT'S UNNATURAL FOR SOMEONE SHOPPING AT A FAMILIAR SUPERMARKET?

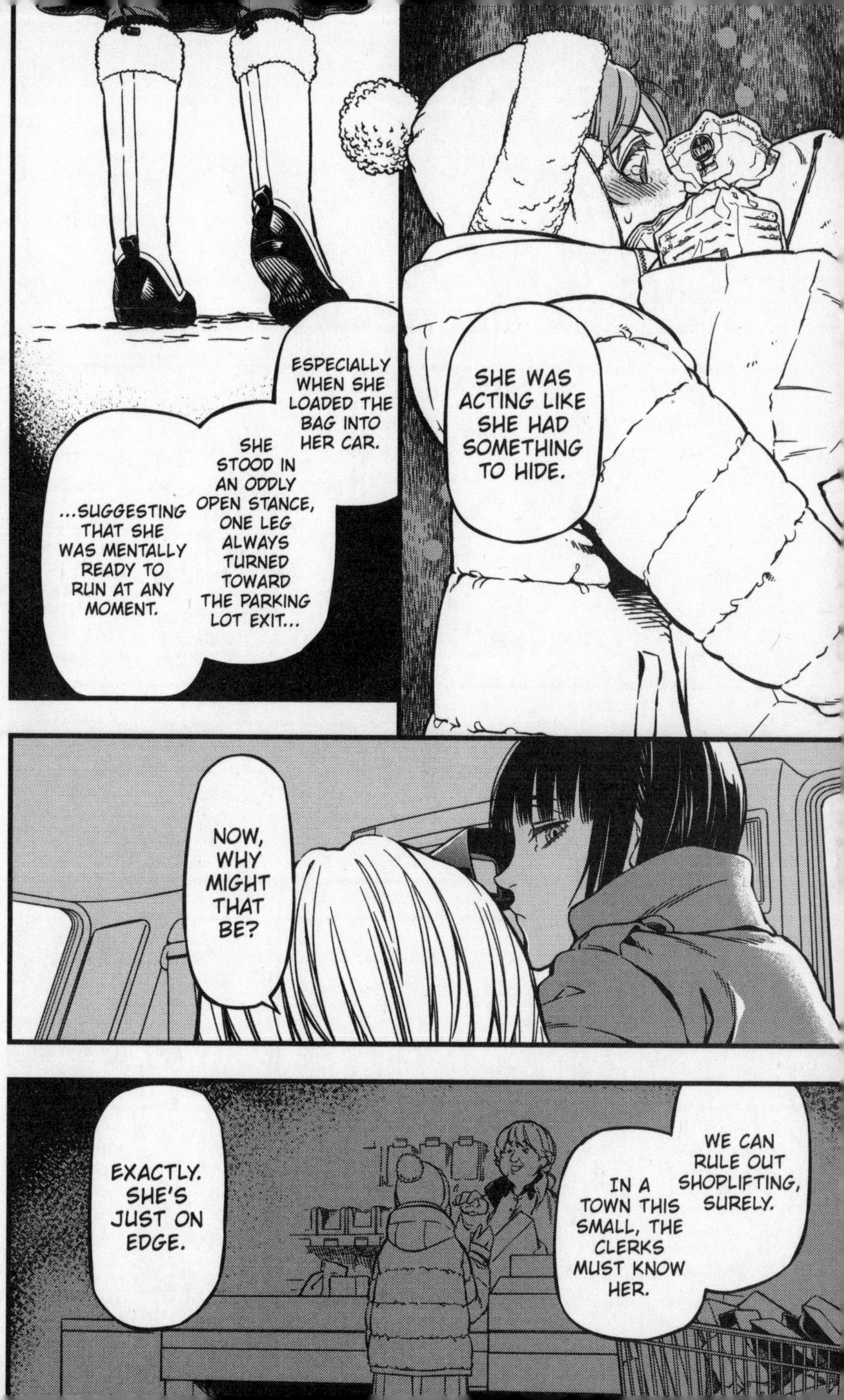
SHE WAS ACTING LIKE SHE HAD SOMETHING TO HIDE.
ESPECIALLY WHEN SHE LOADED THE BAG INTO HER CAR.
SHE STOOD IN AN ODDLY OPEN STANCE, ONE LEG ALWAYS TURNED TOWARD THE PARKING LOT EXIT...
...SUGGESTING THAT SHE WAS MENTALLY READY TO RUN AT ANY MOMENT.
NOW, WHY MIGHT THAT BE?
WE CAN RULE OUT SHOPLIFTING, SURELY.
IN A TOWN THIS SMALL, THE CLERKS MUST KNOW HER.
EXACTLY. SHE'S JUST ON EDGE.

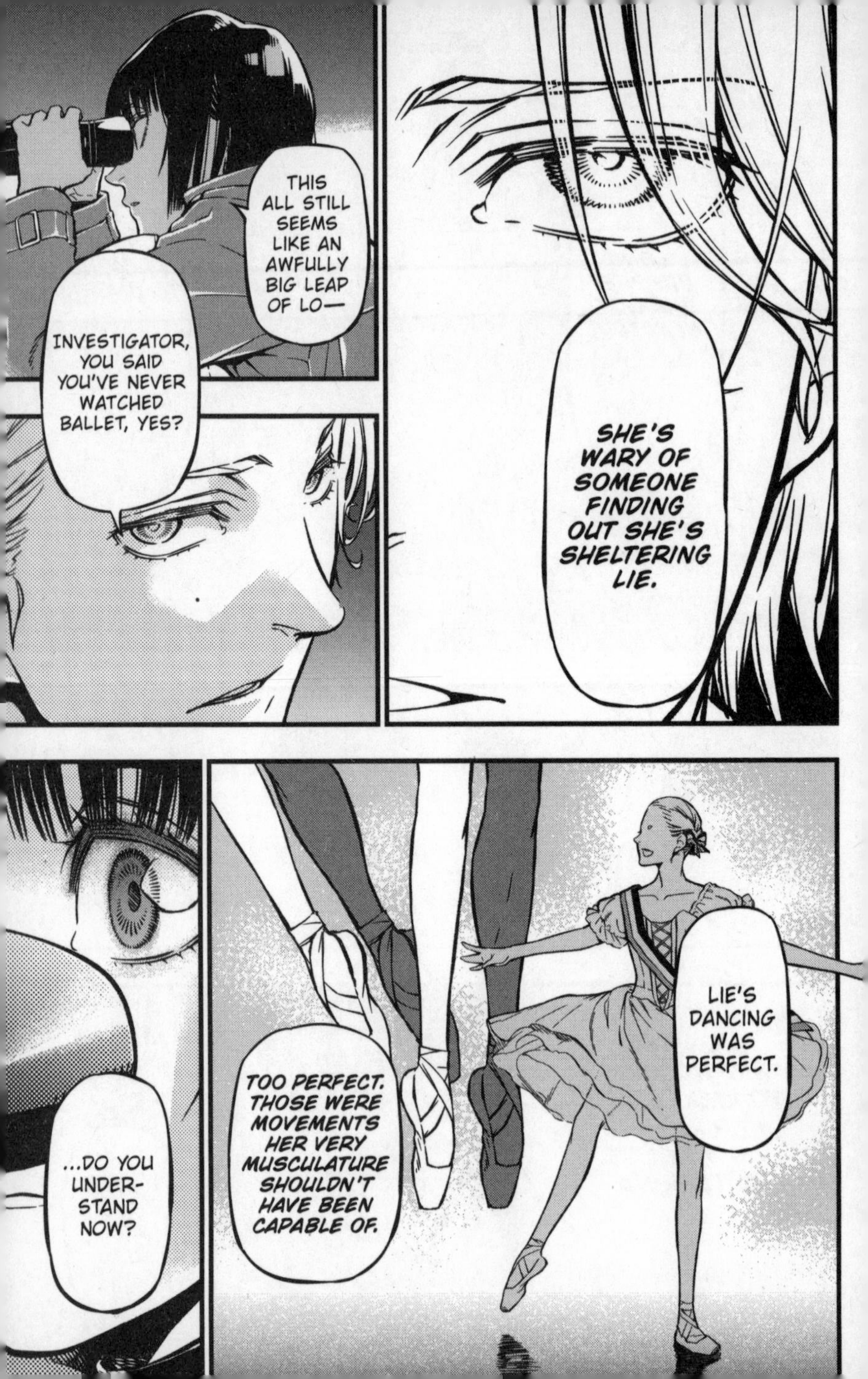
SHE'S WARY OF SOMEONE FINDING OUT SHE'S SHELTERING LIE.
THIS ALL STILL SEEMS LIKE AN AWFULLY BIG LEAP OF LO—
INVESTIGATOR, YOU SAID YOU'VE NEVER WATCHED BALLET, YES?
LIE'S DANCING WAS PERFECT.
TOO PERFECT. THOSE WERE MOVEMENTS HER VERY MUSCULATURE SHOULDN'T HAVE BEEN CAPABLE OF.
...DO YOU UNDER-STAND NOW?

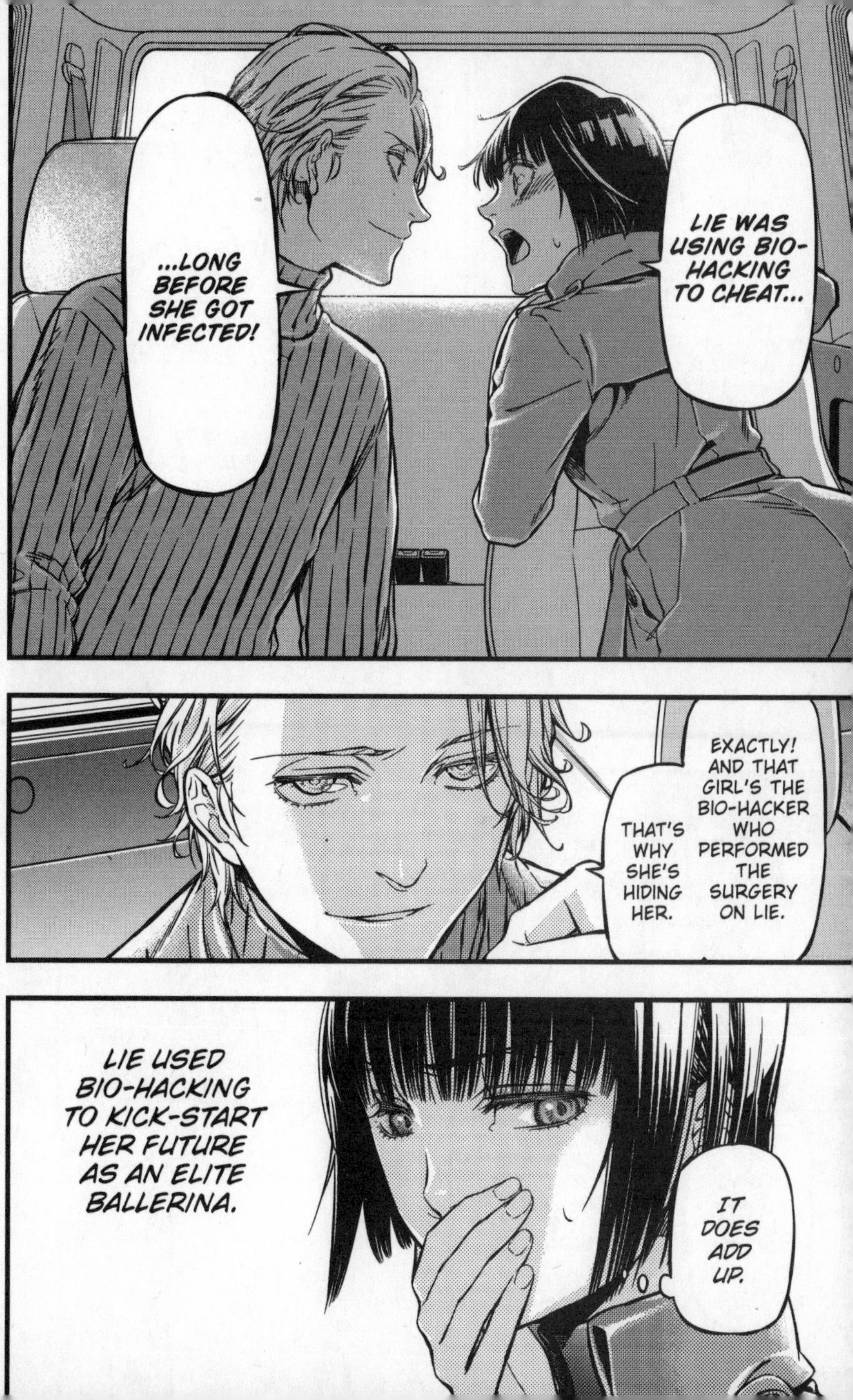
LIE WAS USING BIO-HACKING TO CHEAT...
...LONG BEFORE SHE GOT INFECTED!
EXACTLY! AND THAT GIRL'S THE BIO-HACKER WHO PERFORMED THE SURGERY ON LIE.
THAT'S WHY SHE'S HIDING HER.
LIE USED BIO-HACKING TO KICK-START HER FUTURE AS AN ELITE BALLERINA.
IT DOES ADD UP.

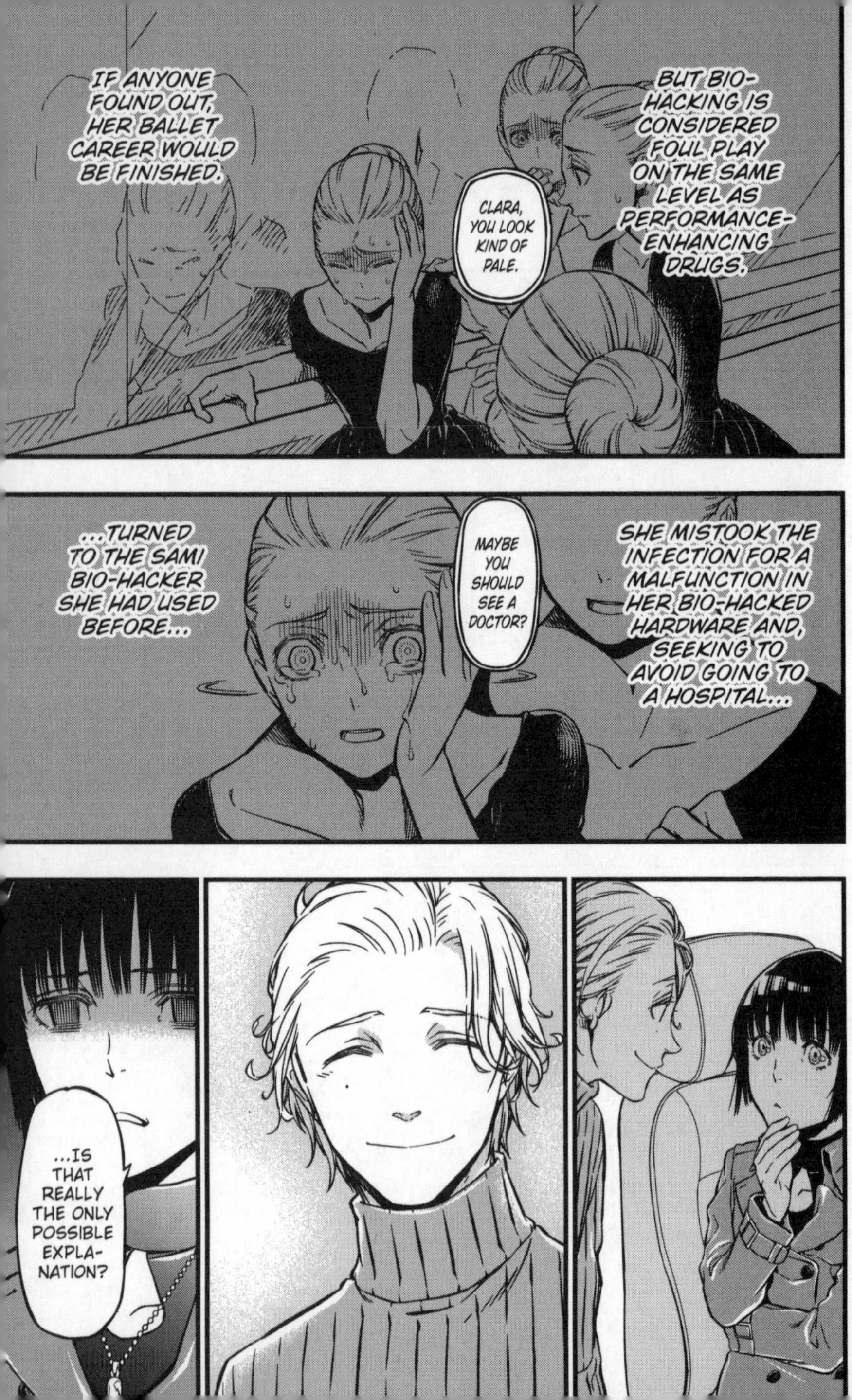
BUT BIO-HACKING IS CONSIDERED FOUL PLAY ON THE SAME LEVEL AS PERFORMANCE-ENHANCING DRUGS.
CLARA, YOU LOOK KIND OF PALE.
IF ANYONE FOUND OUT, HER BALLET CAREER WOULD BE FINISHED.
SHE MISTOOK THE INFECTION FOR A MALFUNCTION IN HER BIO-HACKED HARDWARE AND, SEEKING TO AVOID GOING TO A HOSPITAL...
MAYBE YOU SHOULD SEE A DOCTOR?
...TURNED TO THE SAMI BIO-HACKER SHE HAD USED BEFORE...
...IS THAT REALLY THE ONLY POSSIBLE EXPLANATION?

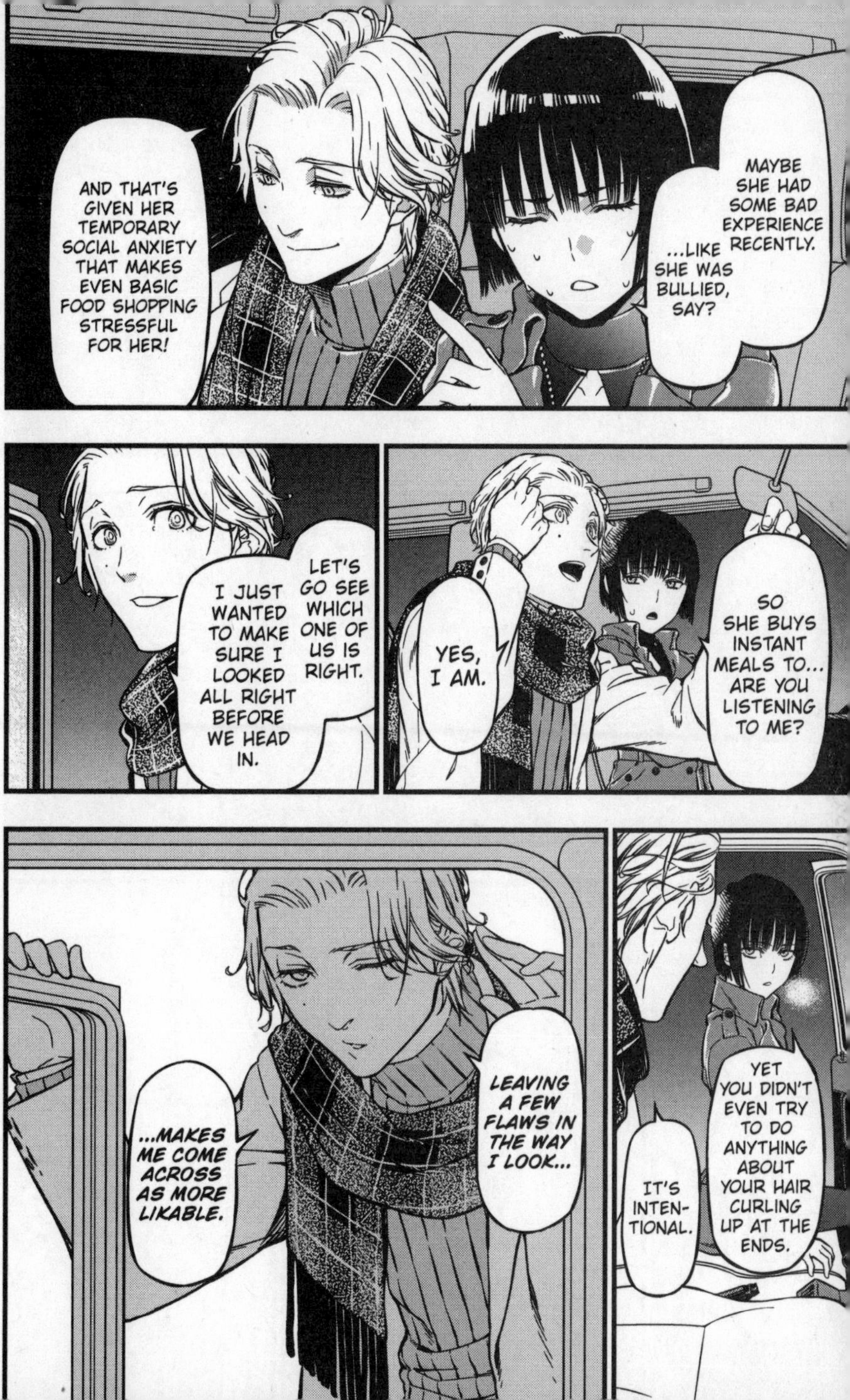
MAYBE SHE HAD SOME BAD EXPERIENCE RECENTLY.
...LIKE SHE WAS BULLIED, SAY?
AND THAT'S GIVEN HER TEMPORARY SOCIAL ANXIETY THAT MAKES EVEN BASIC FOOD SHOPPING STRESSFUL FOR HER!
SO SHE BUYS INSTANT MEALS TO... ARE YOU LISTENING TO ME?
YES, I AM.
LET'S GO SEE WHICH ONE OF US IS RIGHT.
I JUST WANTED TO MAKE SURE I LOOKED ALL RIGHT BEFORE WE HEAD IN.
YET YOU DIDN'T EVEN TRY TO DO ANYTHING ABOUT YOUR HAIR CURLING UP AT THE ENDS.
IT'S INTEN-TIONAL.
LEAVING A FEW FLAWS IN THE WAY I LOOK...
...MAKES ME COME ACROSS AS MORE LIKABLE.

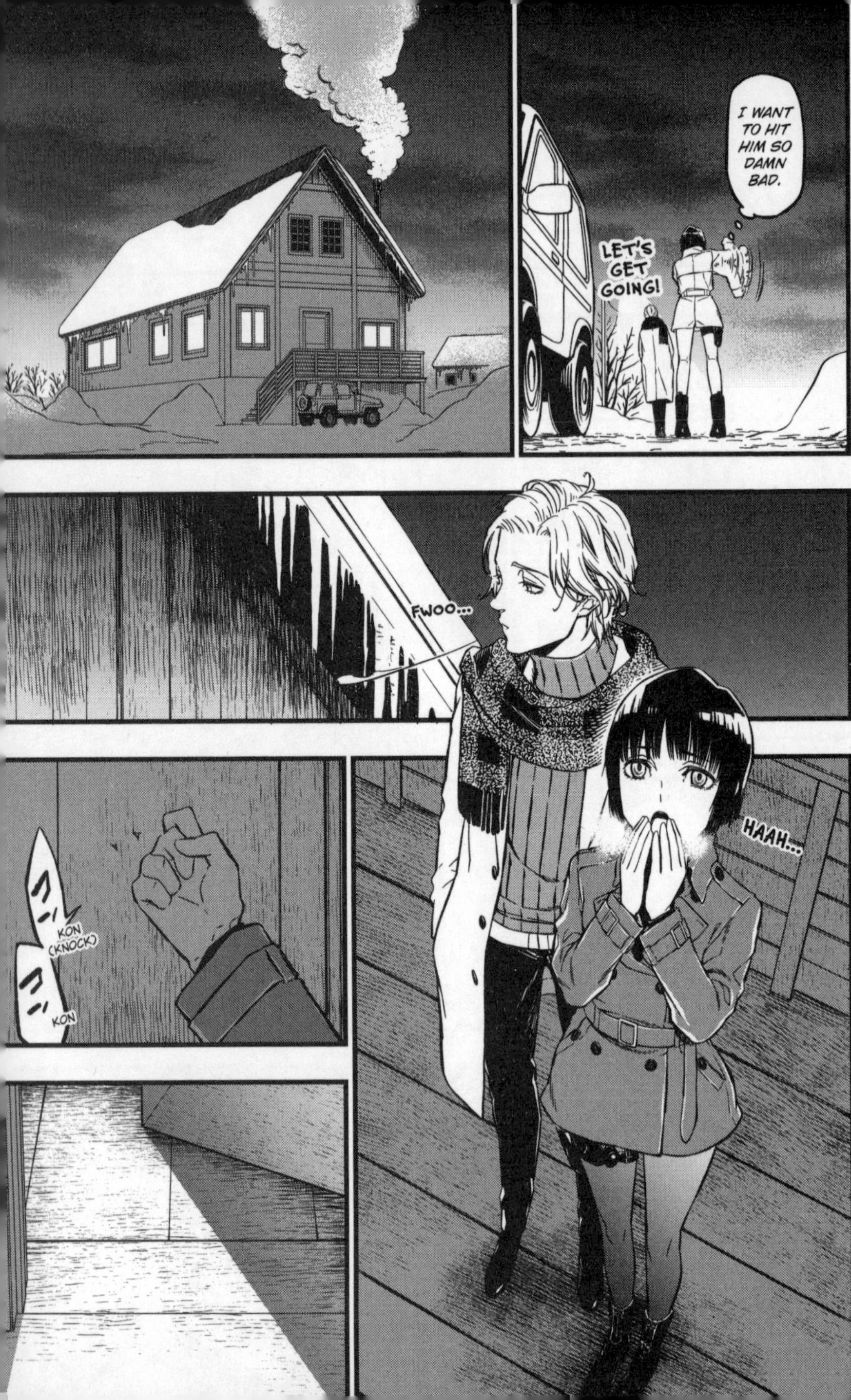
I WANT TO HIT HIM SO DAMN BAD.
LET'S GET GOING!
FWOO...
HAAH...
コン
KON (KNOCK)
コン
KON

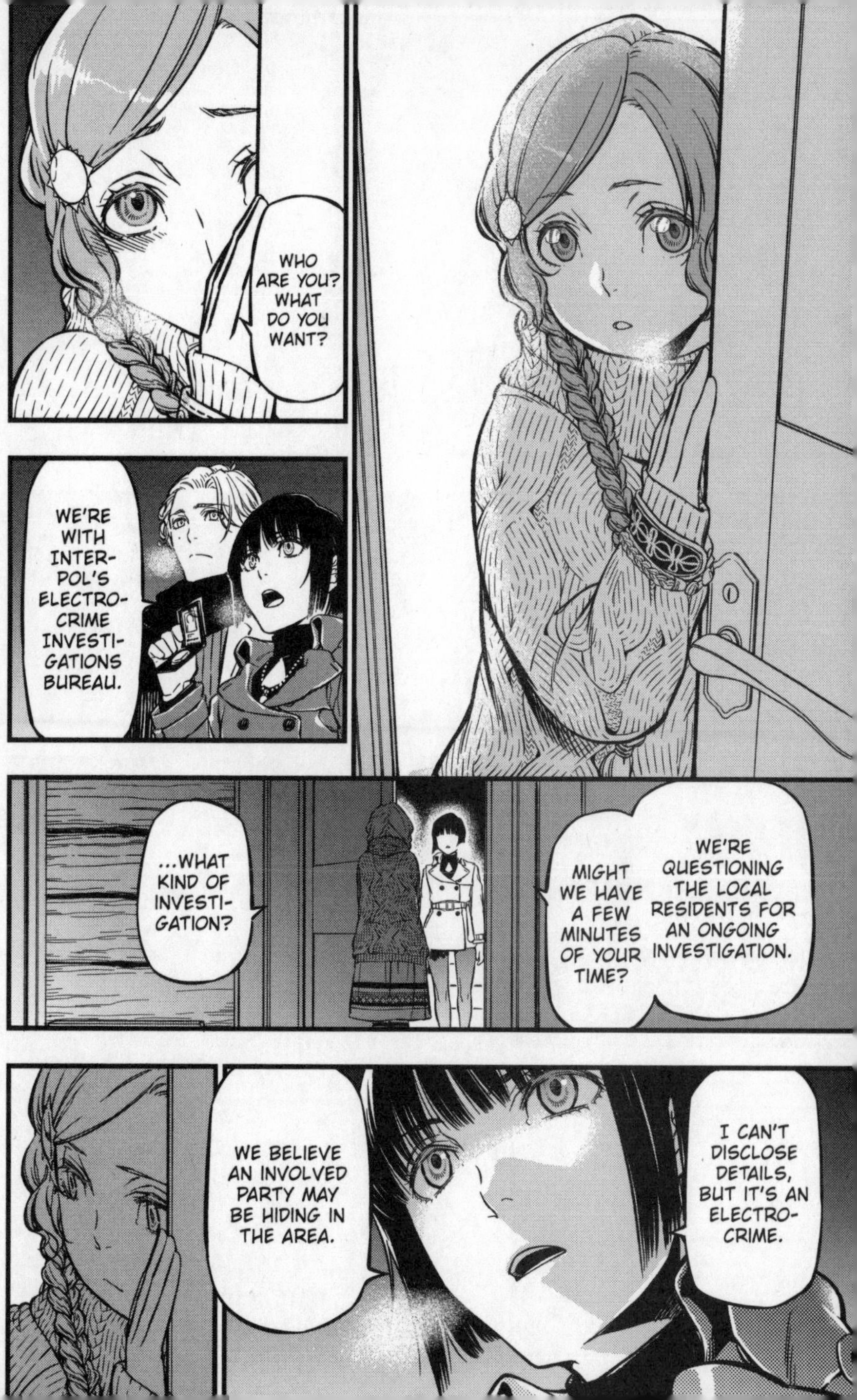
WHO ARE YOU? WHAT DO YOU WANT?
WE'RE WITH INTERPOL'S ELECTRO-CRIME INVESTIGATIONS BUREAU.
WE'RE QUESTIONING THE LOCAL RESIDENTS FOR AN ONGOING INVESTIGATION.
MIGHT WE HAVE A FEW MINUTES OF YOUR TIME?
...WHAT KIND OF INVESTIGATION?
I CAN'T DISCLOSE DETAILS, BUT IT'S AN ELECTRO-CRIME.
WE BELIEVE AN INVOLVED PARTY MAY BE HIDING IN THE AREA.

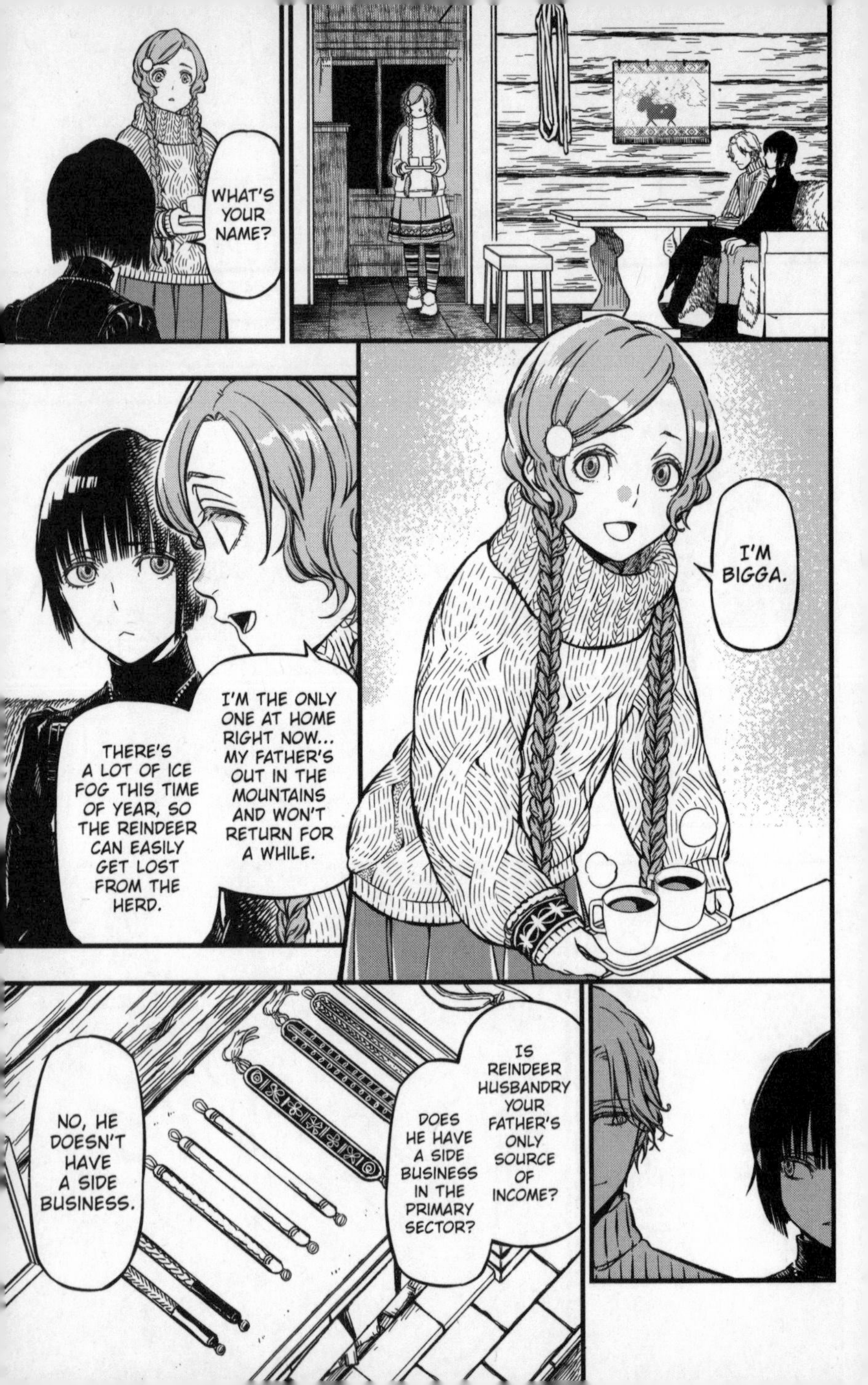
WHAT'S YOUR NAME?
I'M BIGGA.
I'M THE ONLY ONE AT HOME RIGHT NOW... MY FATHER'S OUT IN THE MOUNTAINS AND WON'T RETURN FOR A WHILE.
THERE'S A LOT OF ICE FOG THIS TIME OF YEAR, SO THE REINDEER CAN EASILY GET LOST FROM THE HERD.
IS REINDEER HUSBANDRY YOUR FATHER'S ONLY SOURCE OF INCOME?
DOES HE HAVE A SIDE BUSINESS IN THE PRIMARY SECTOR?
NO, HE DOESN'T HAVE A SIDE BUSINESS.

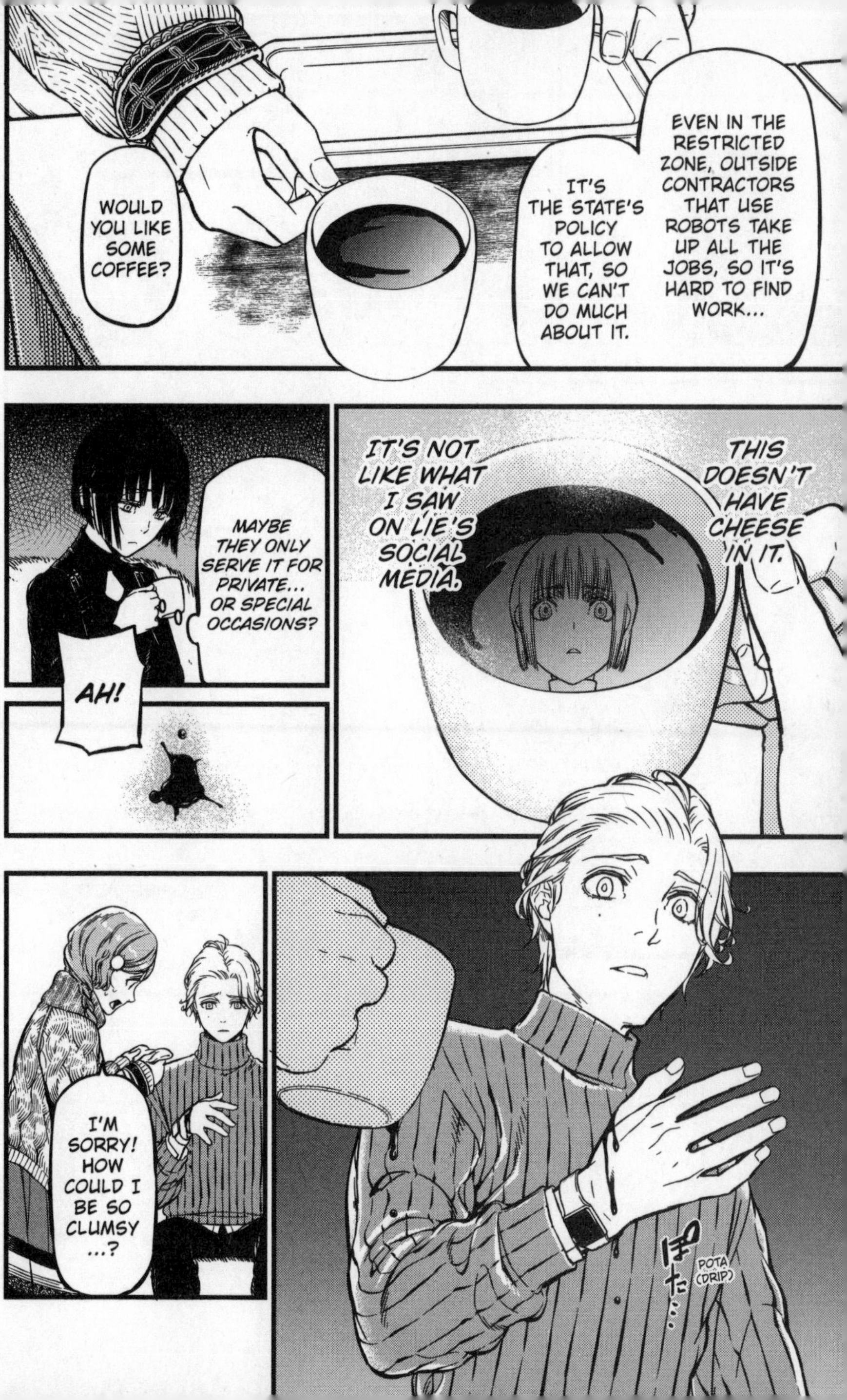
EVEN IN THE RESTRICTED ZONE, OUTSIDE CONTRACTORS THAT USE ROBOTS TAKE UP ALL THE JOBS, SO IT'S HARD TO FIND WORK...
IT'S THE STATE'S POLICY TO ALLOW THAT, SO WE CAN'T DO MUCH ABOUT IT.
WOULD YOU LIKE SOME COFFEE?
THIS DOESN'T HAVE CHEESE IN IT.
IT'S NOT LIKE WHAT I SAW ON LIE'S SOCIAL MEDIA.
MAYBE THEY ONLY SERVE IT FOR PRIVATE... OR SPECIAL OCCASIONS?
AH!
ぽた…
POTA (DRIP)
I'M SORRY! HOW COULD I BE SO CLUMSY ...?

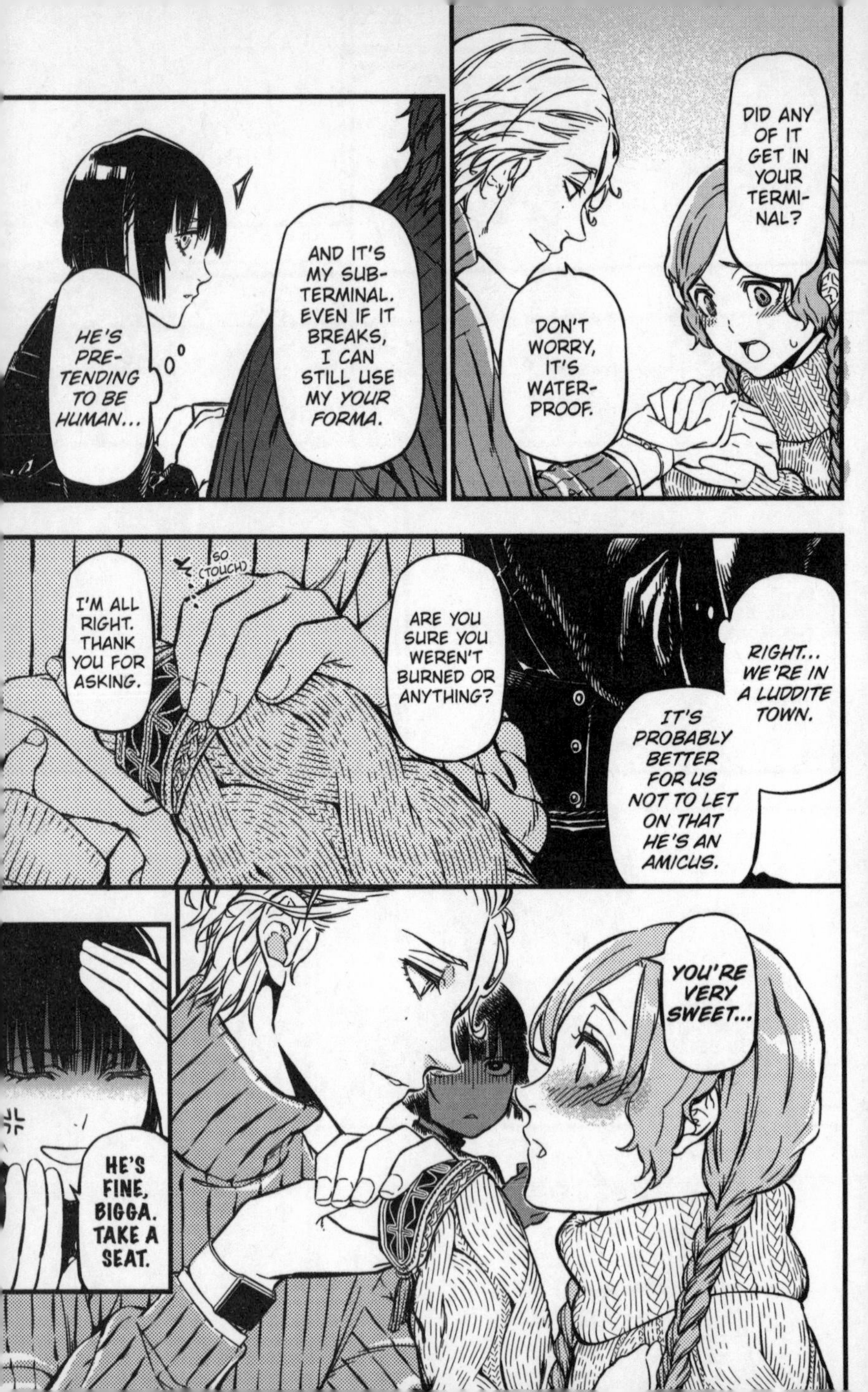
DID ANY OF IT GET IN YOUR TERMINAL?
DON'T WORRY, IT'S WATERPROOF.
AND IT'S MY SUB-TERMINAL. EVEN IF IT BREAKS, I CAN STILL USE MY *YOUR FORMA*.
HE'S PRETENDING TO BE HUMAN...
RIGHT... WE'RE IN A LUDDITE TOWN.
IT'S PROBABLY BETTER FOR US NOT TO LET ON THAT HE'S AN AMICUS.
ARE YOU SURE YOU WEREN'T BURNED OR ANYTHING?
SO (TOUCH)
I'M ALL RIGHT. THANK YOU FOR ASKING.
YOU'RE VERY SWEET...
HE'S FINE, BIGGA. TAKE A SEAT.

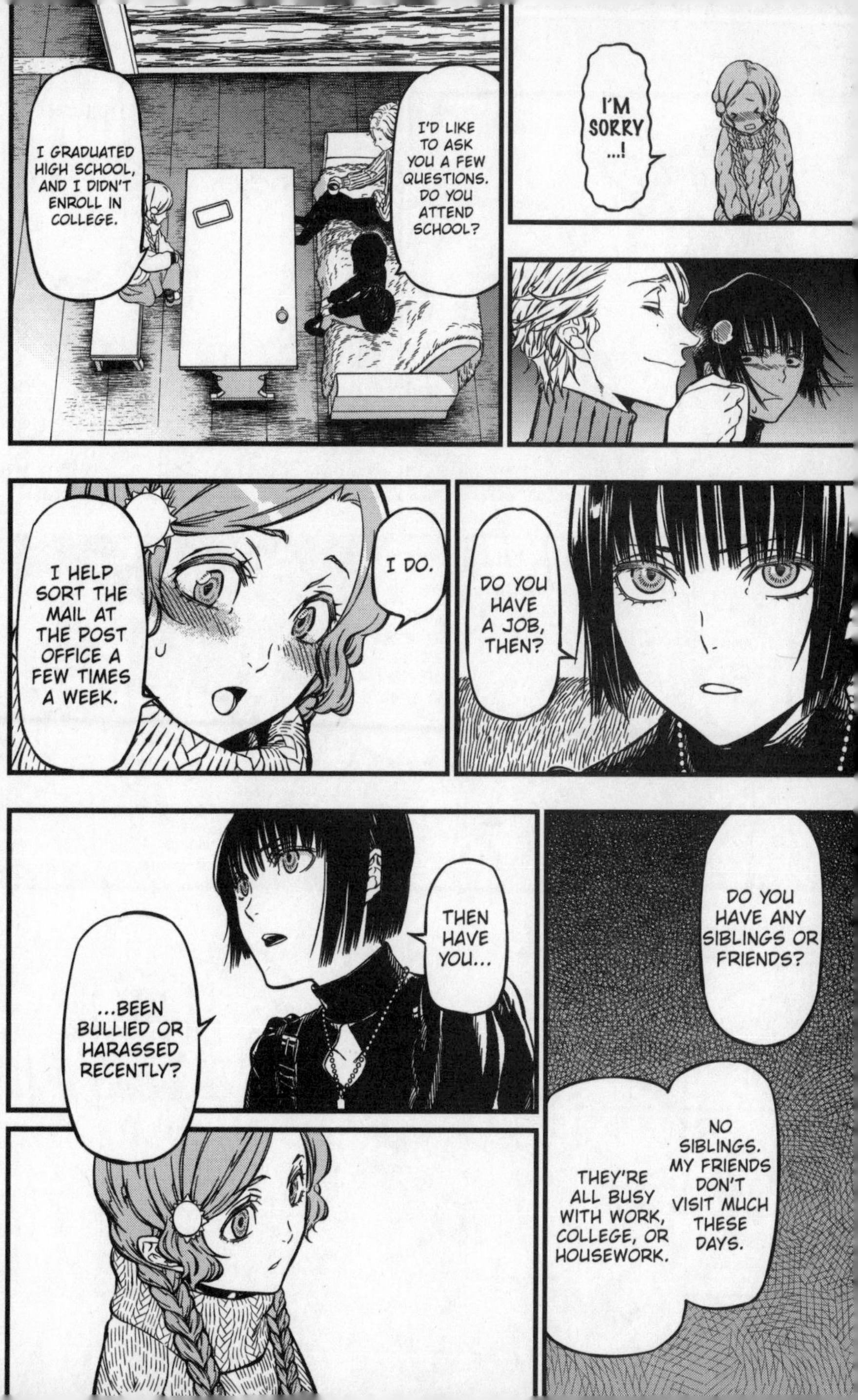
I'M SORRY ...!
I'D LIKE TO ASK YOU A FEW QUESTIONS. DO YOU ATTEND SCHOOL?
I GRADUATED HIGH SCHOOL, AND I DIDN'T ENROLL IN COLLEGE.
DO YOU HAVE A JOB, THEN?
I DO.
I HELP SORT THE MAIL AT THE POST OFFICE A FEW TIMES A WEEK.
DO YOU HAVE ANY SIBLINGS OR FRIENDS?
NO SIBLINGS. MY FRIENDS DON'T VISIT MUCH THESE DAYS.
THEY'RE ALL BUSY WITH WORK, COLLEGE, OR HOUSEWORK.
THEN HAVE YOU...
...BEEN BULLIED OR HARASSED RECENTLY?

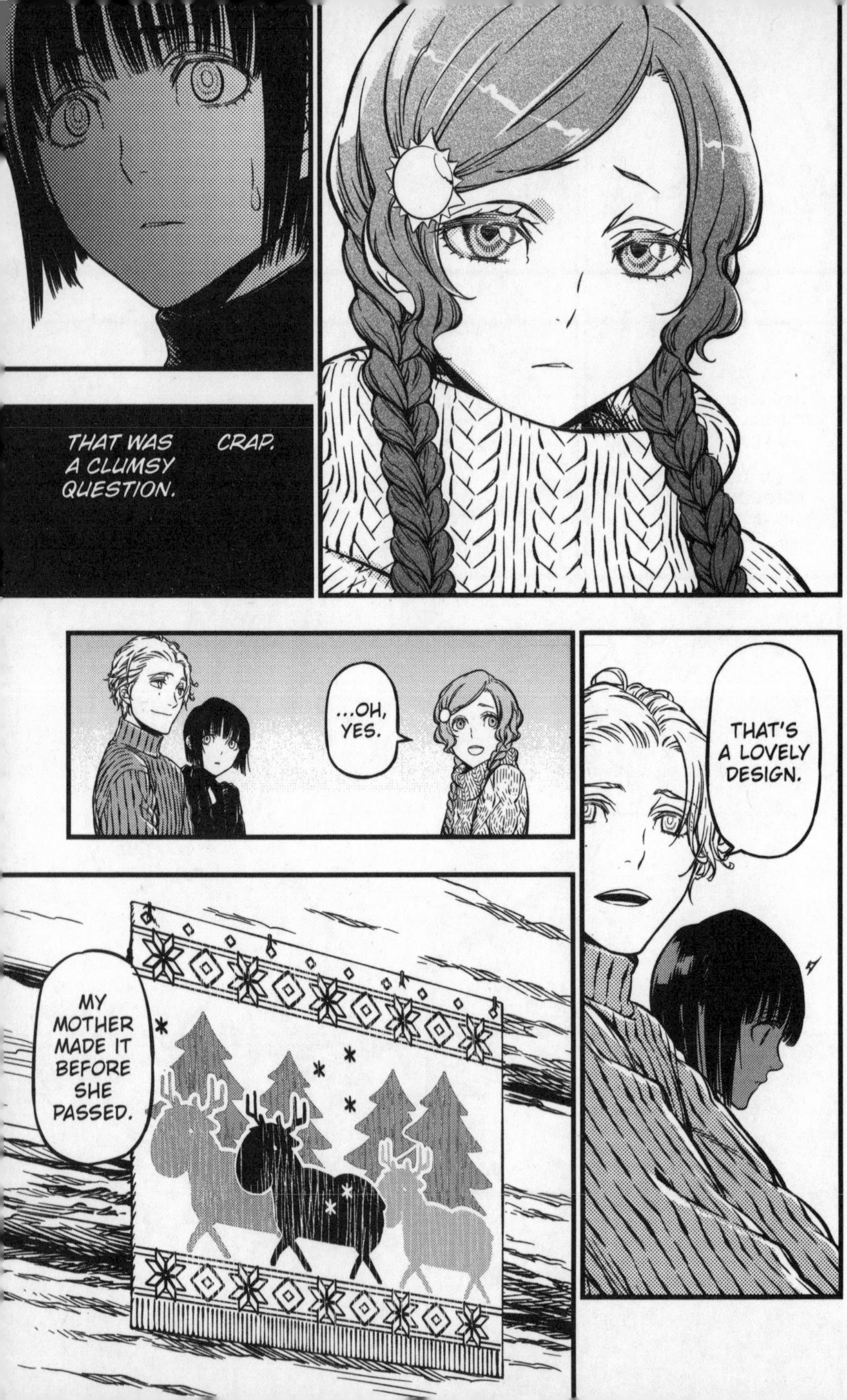
CRAP.
THAT WAS A CLUMSY QUESTION.
THAT'S A LOVELY DESIGN.
...OH, YES.
MY MOTHER MADE IT BEFORE SHE PASSED.

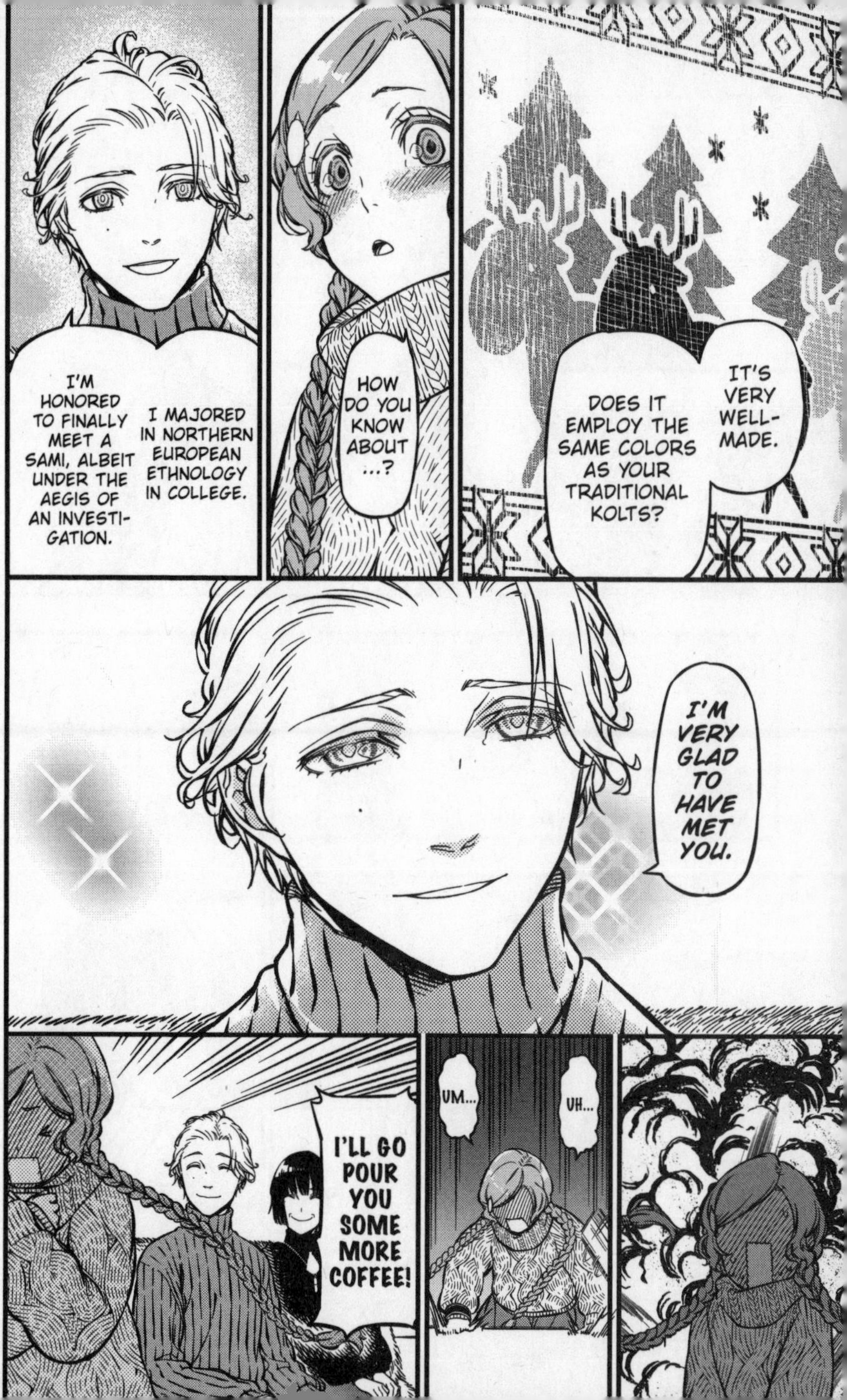
IT'S VERY WELL-MADE.
DOES IT EMPLOY THE SAME COLORS AS YOUR TRADITIONAL KOLTS?
HOW DO YOU KNOW ABOUT ...?
I MAJORED IN NORTHERN EUROPEAN ETHNOLOGY IN COLLEGE.
I'M HONORED TO FINALLY MEET A SAMI, ALBEIT UNDER THE AEGIS OF AN INVESTIGATION.
I'M VERY GLAD TO HAVE MET YOU.
UH...
UM...
I'LL GO POUR YOU SOME MORE COFFEE!

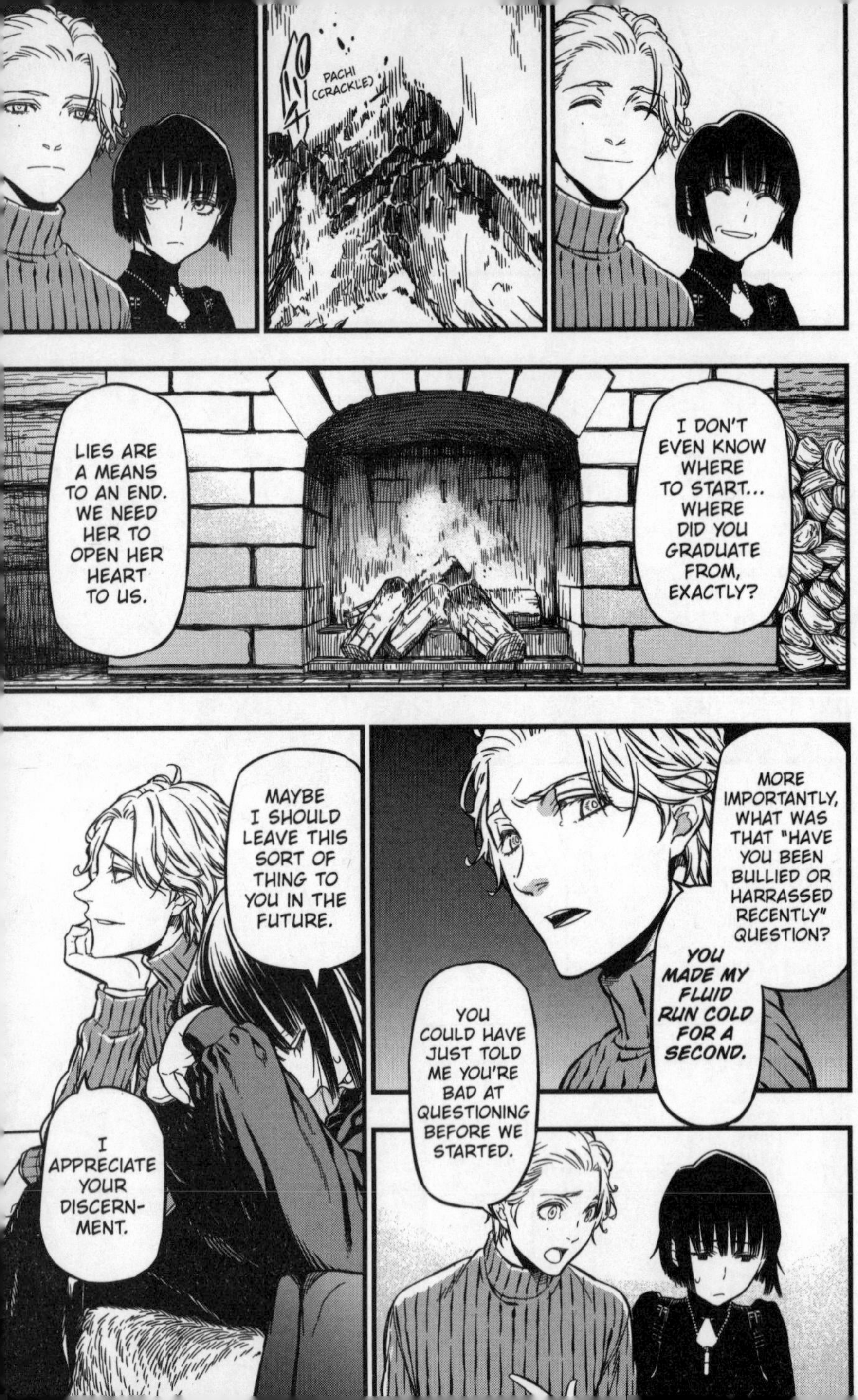
PACHI (CRACKLE)
I DON'T EVEN KNOW WHERE TO START... WHERE DID YOU GRADUATE FROM, EXACTLY?
LIES ARE A MEANS TO AN END. WE NEED HER TO OPEN HER HEART TO US.
MORE IMPORTANTLY, WHAT WAS THAT "HAVE YOU BEEN BULLIED OR HARRASSED RECENTLY" QUESTION?
YOU MADE MY FLUID RUN COLD FOR A SECOND.
YOU COULD HAVE JUST TOLD ME YOU'RE BAD AT QUESTIONING BEFORE WE STARTED.
MAYBE I SHOULD LEAVE THIS SORT OF THING TO YOU IN THE FUTURE.
I APPRECIATE YOUR DISCERNMENT.

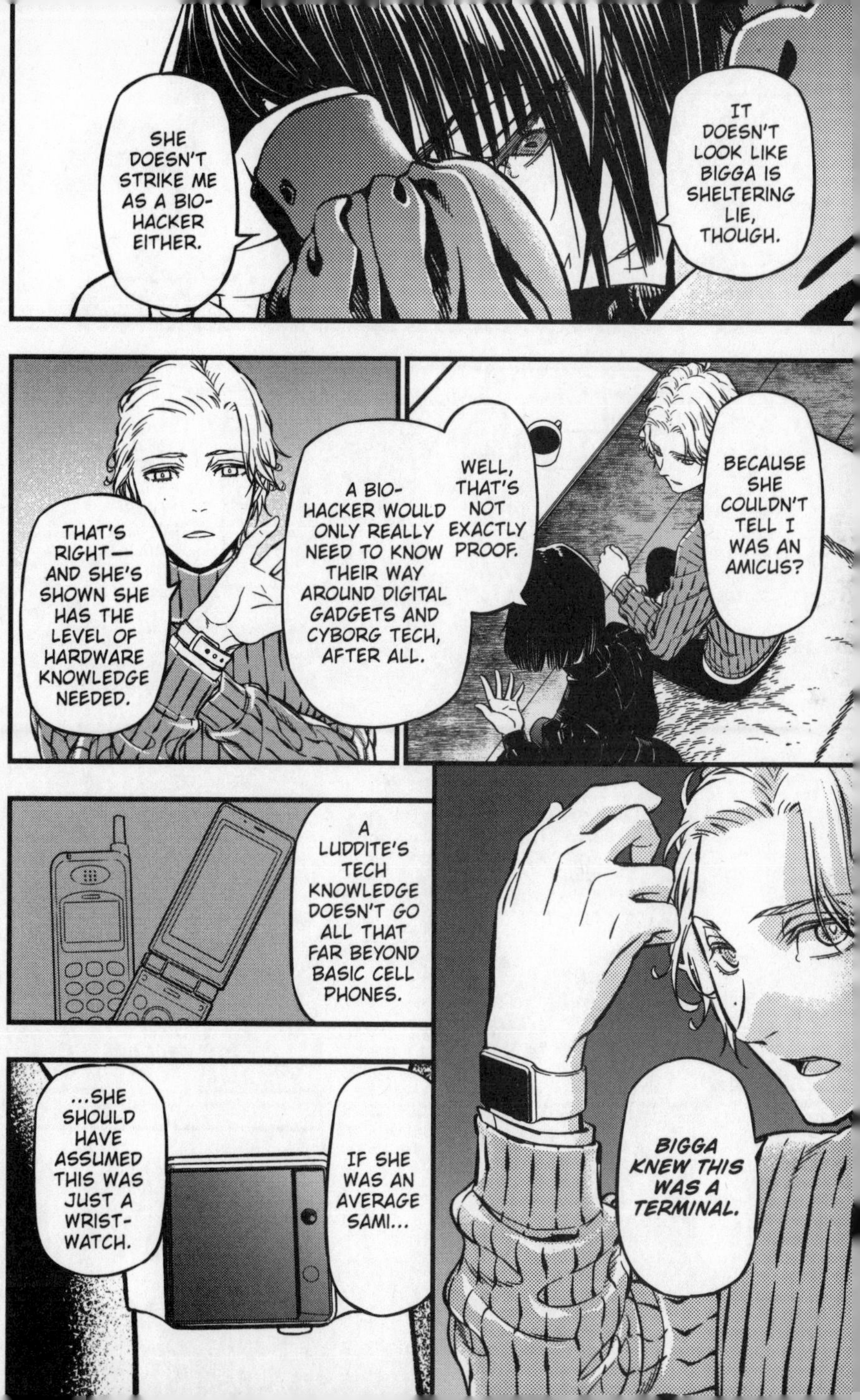
IT DOESN'T LOOK LIKE BIGGA IS SHELTERING LIE, THOUGH.
SHE DOESN'T STRIKE ME AS A BIO-HACKER EITHER.
BECAUSE SHE COULDN'T TELL I WAS AN AMICUS?
WELL, THAT'S NOT EXACTLY PROOF.
A BIO-HACKER WOULD ONLY REALLY NEED TO KNOW THEIR WAY AROUND DIGITAL GADGETS AND CYBORG TECH, AFTER ALL.
THAT'S RIGHT—AND SHE'S SHOWN SHE HAS THE LEVEL OF HARDWARE KNOWLEDGE NEEDED.
BIGGA KNEW THIS WAS A TERMINAL.
A LUDDITE'S TECH KNOWLEDGE DOESN'T GO ALL THAT FAR BEYOND BASIC CELL PHONES.
IF SHE WAS AN AVERAGE SAMI...
...SHE SHOULD HAVE ASSUMED THIS WAS JUST A WRIST-WATCH.

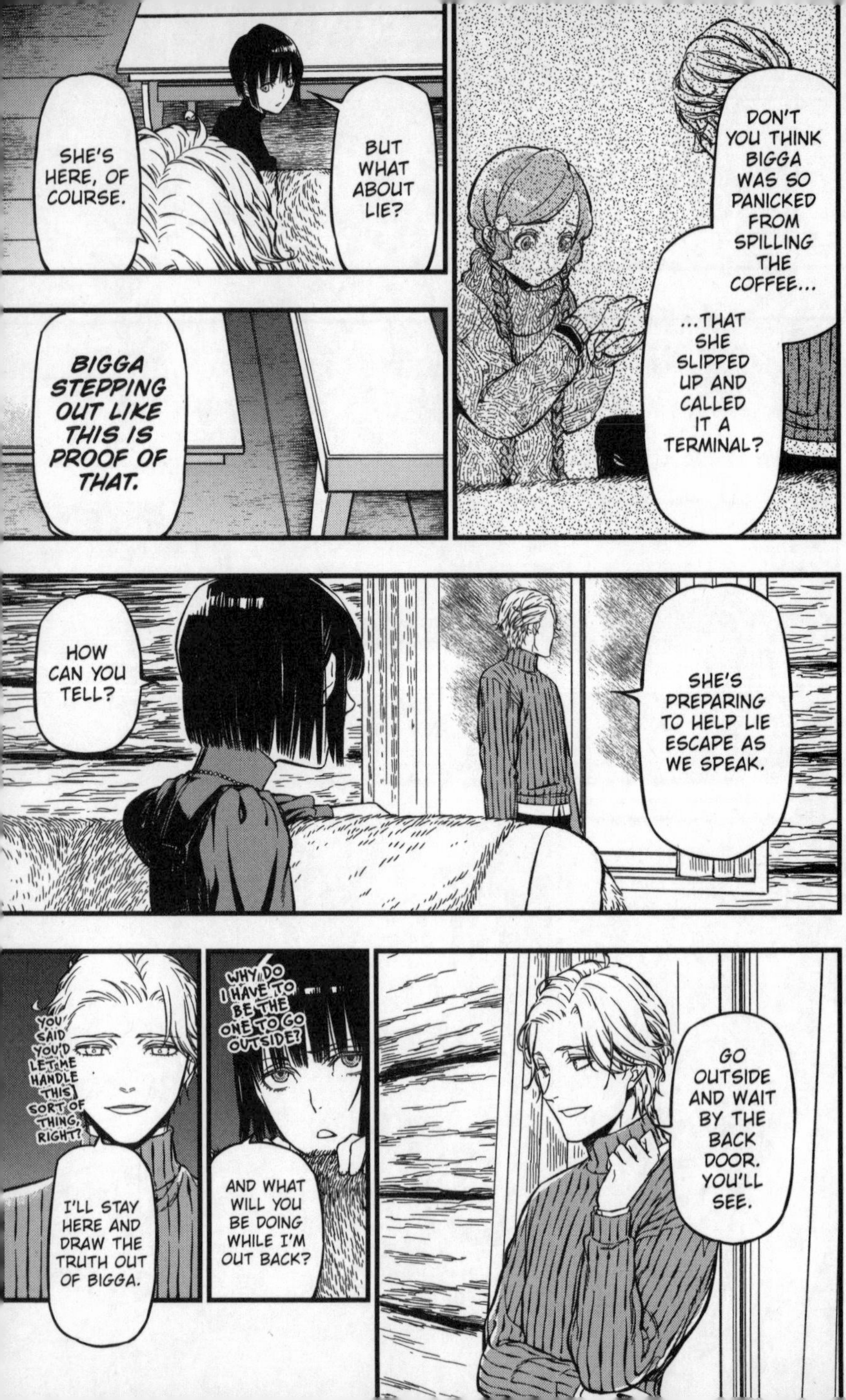
DON'T YOU THINK BIGGA WAS SO PANICKED FROM SPILLING THE COFFEE...
...THAT SHE SLIPPED UP AND CALLED IT A TERMINAL?
BUT WHAT ABOUT LIE?
SHE'S HERE, OF COURSE.
BIGGA STEPPING OUT LIKE THIS IS PROOF OF THAT.
SHE'S PREPARING TO HELP LIE ESCAPE AS WE SPEAK.
HOW CAN YOU TELL?
GO OUTSIDE AND WAIT BY THE BACK DOOR. YOU'LL SEE.
WHY DO I HAVE TO BE THE ONE TO GO OUTSIDE?
AND WHAT WILL YOU BE DOING WHILE I'M OUT BACK?
YOU SAID YOU'D LET ME HANDLE THIS SORT OF THING, RIGHT?
I'LL STAY HERE AND DRAW THE TRUTH OUT OF BIGGA.

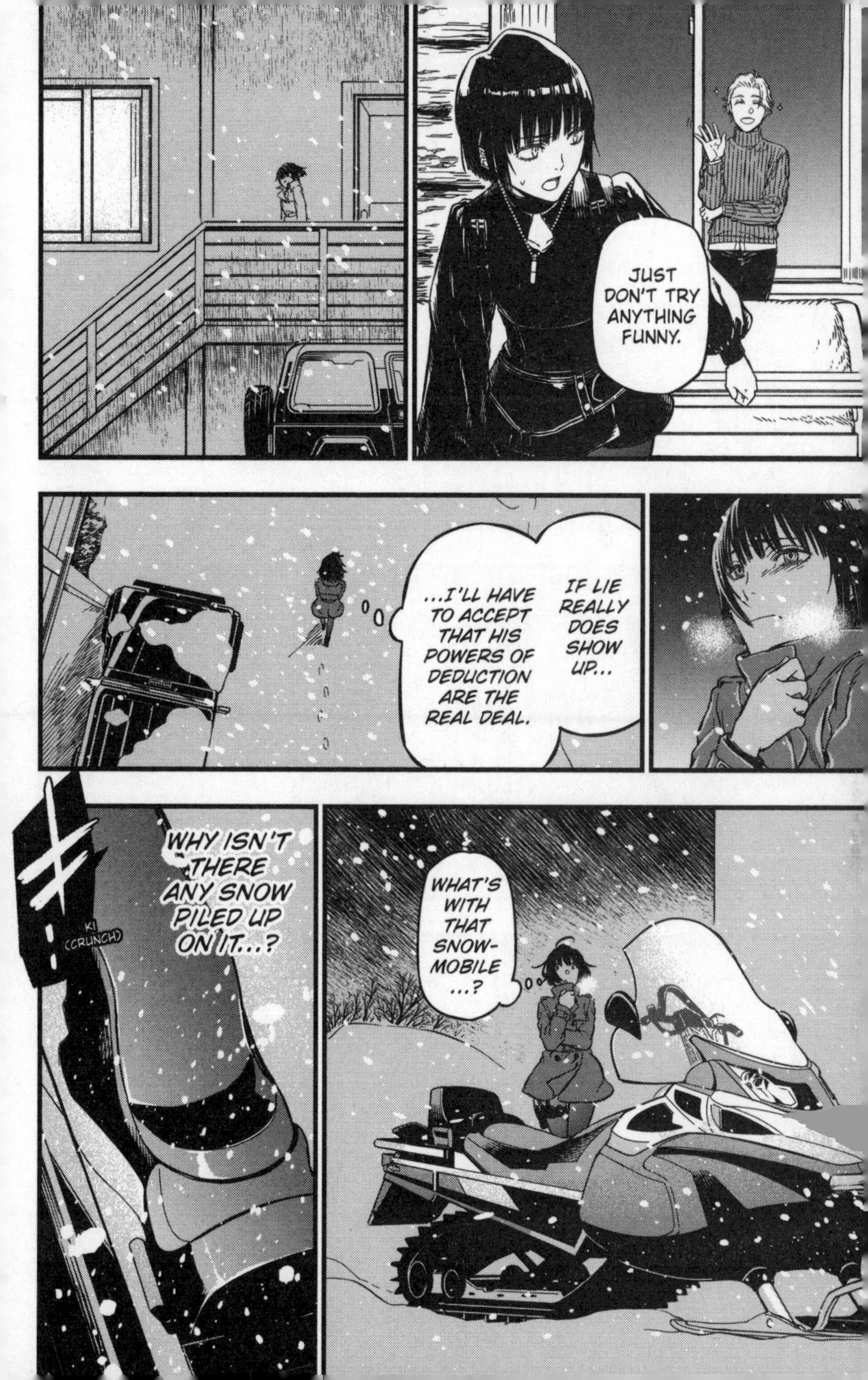
JUST DON'T TRY ANYTHING FUNNY.
IF LIE REALLY DOES SHOW UP...
...I'LL HAVE TO ACCEPT THAT HIS POWERS OF DEDUCTION ARE THE REAL DEAL.
WHAT'S WITH THAT SNOW-MOBILE ...?
WHY ISN'T THERE ANY SNOW PILED UP ON IT...?
KI (CRUNCH)

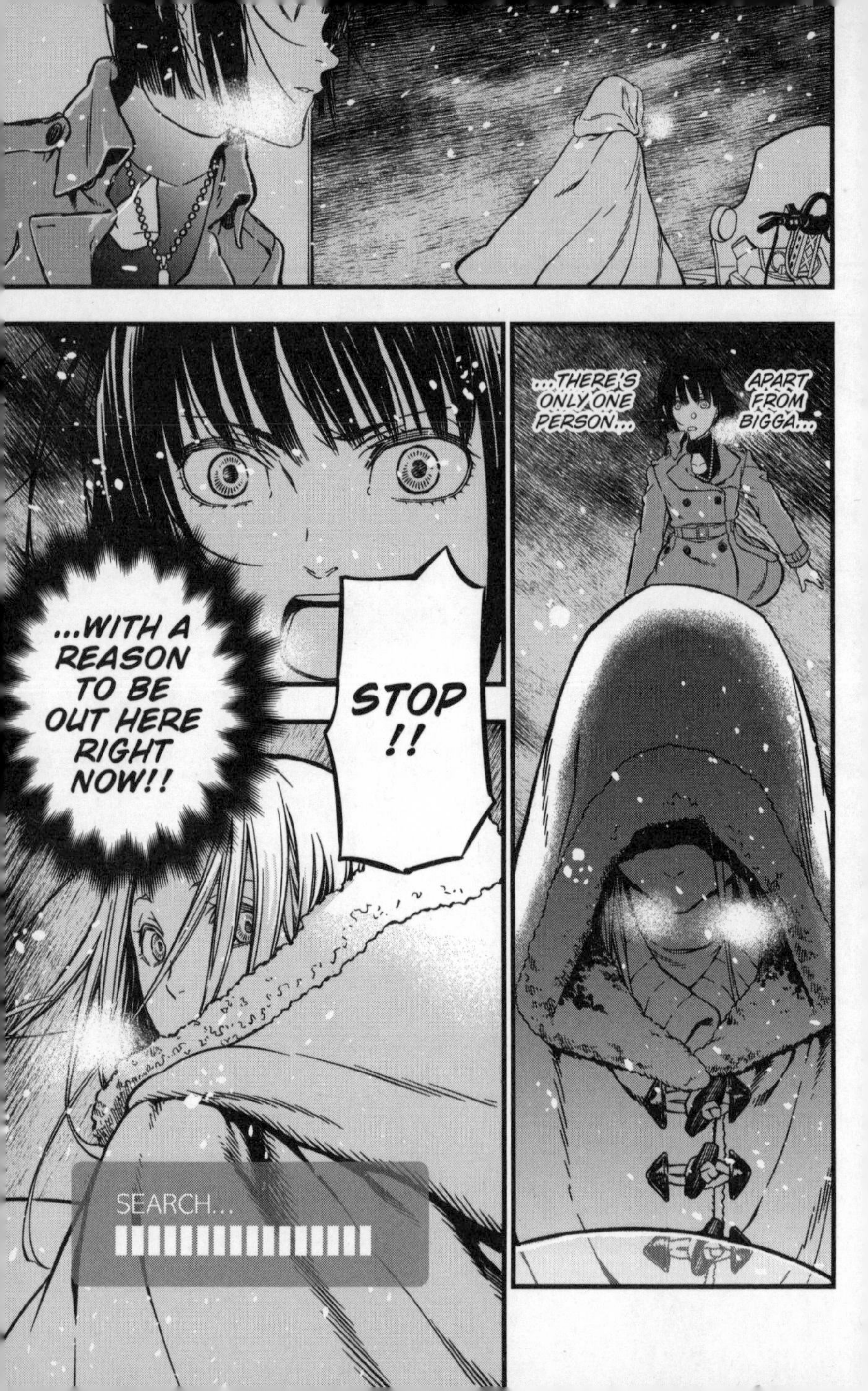
APART FROM BIGGA...
...THERE'S ONLY ONE PERSON...
...WITH A REASON TO BE OUT HERE RIGHT NOW!!
STOP!!
SEARCH...

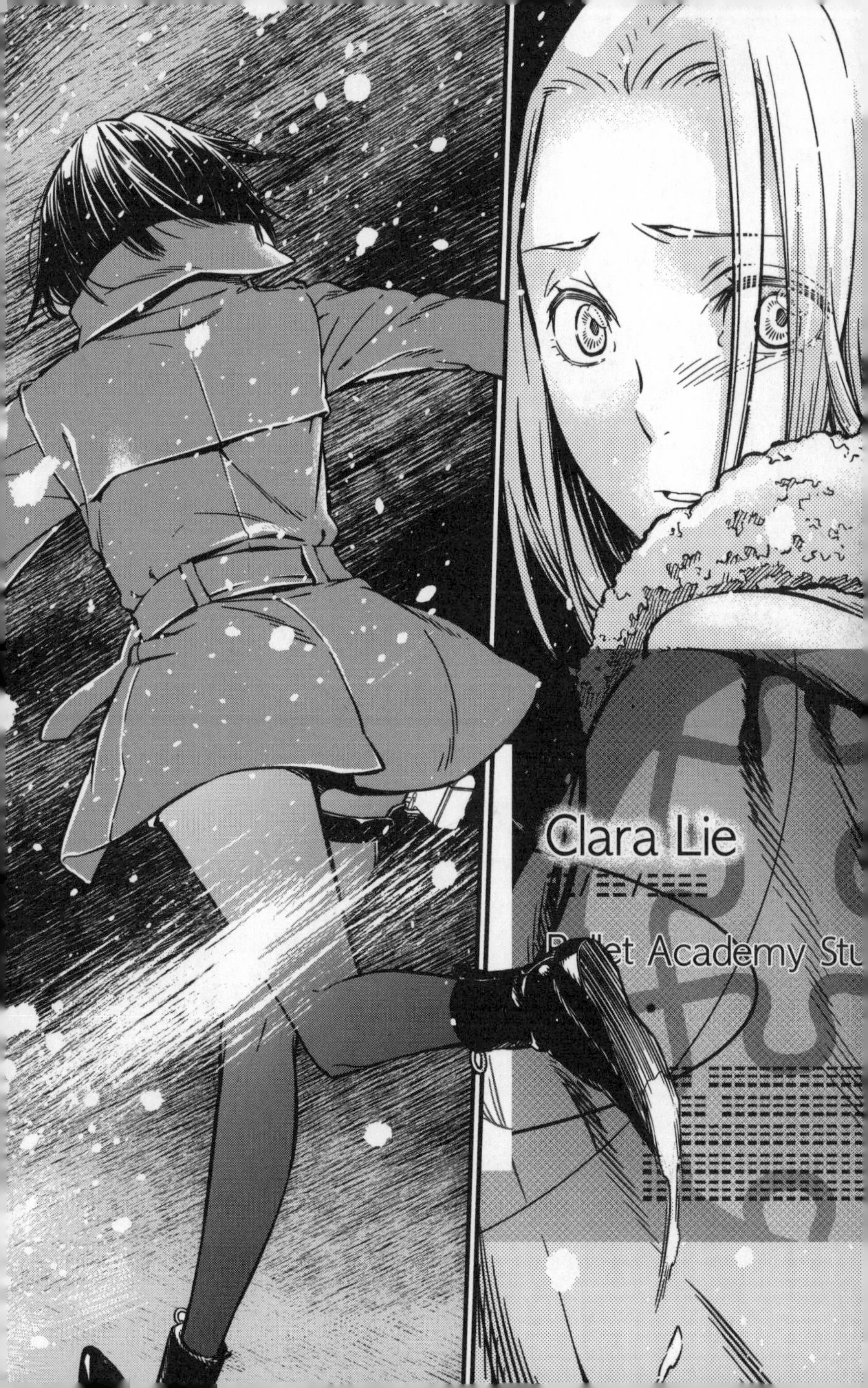
Clara Lie
let Academy Stu

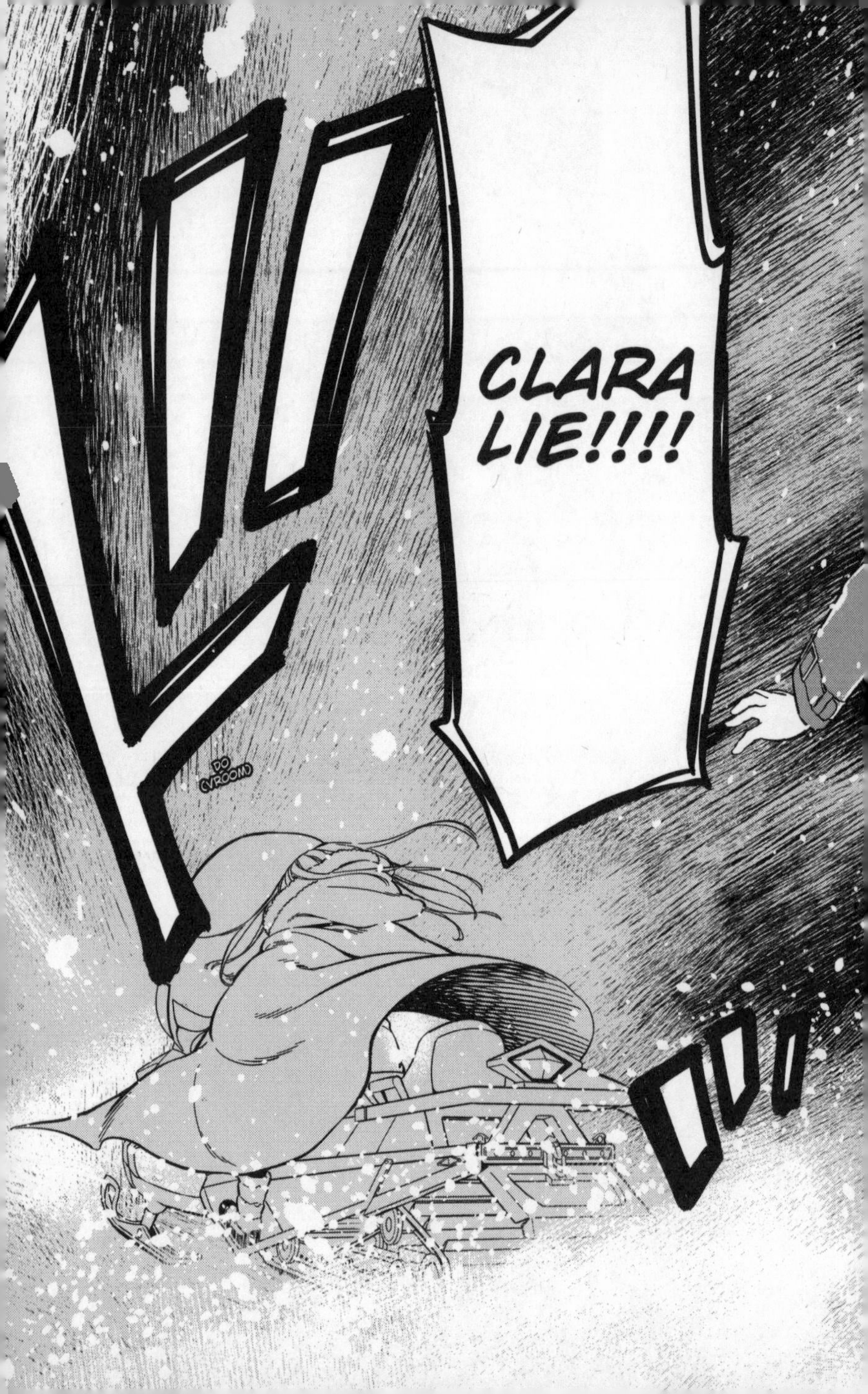
CLARA
LIE!!!!
DO
(VROOM)

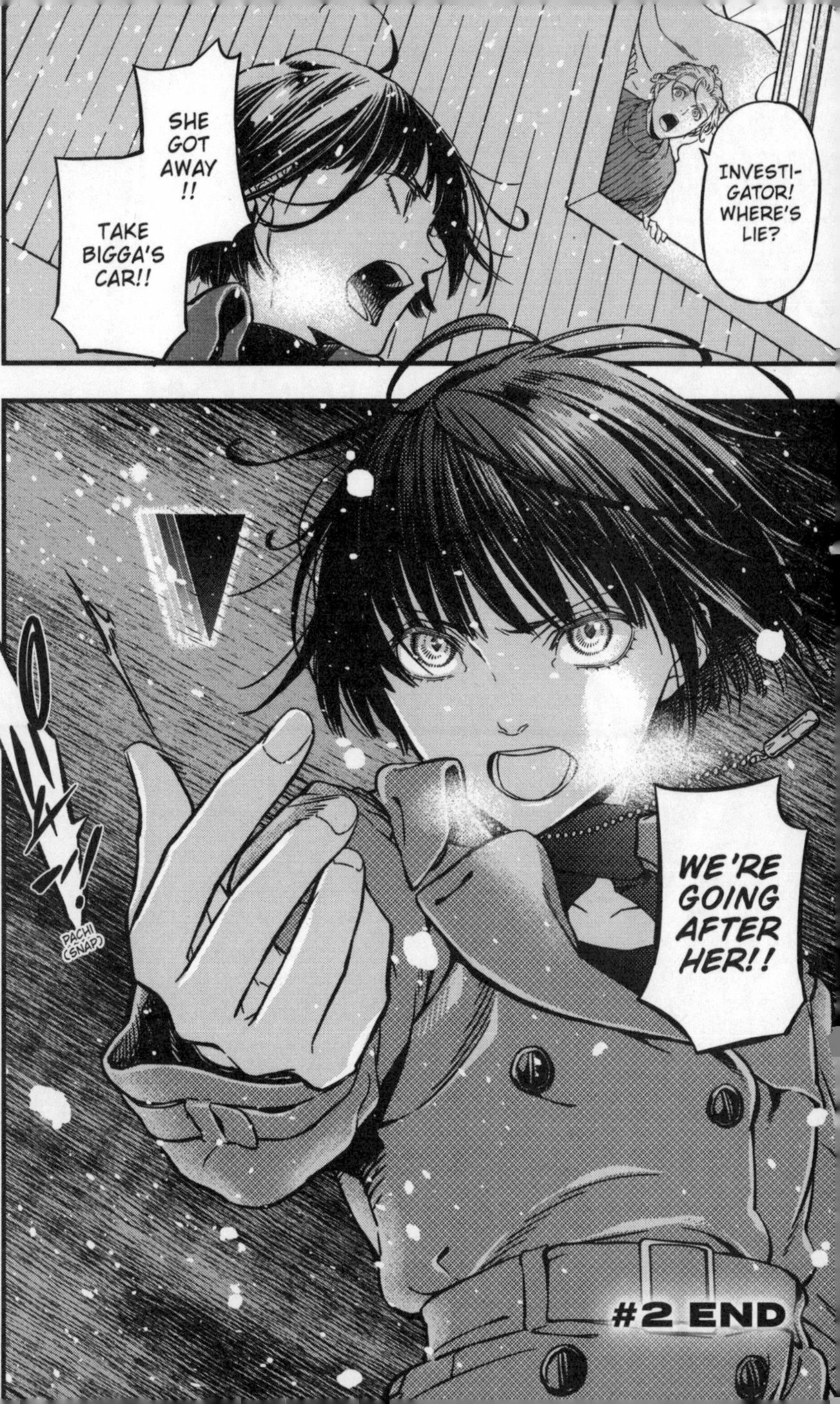
INVESTI-GATOR! WHERE'S LIE?
SHE GOT AWAY!!
TAKE BIGGA'S CAR!!
WE'RE GOING AFTER HER!!
PACHI (SNAP)
#2 END

YOUR FORMA

DATABASE

Mnemosynes
A function of the Your Forma that records and stores all of the user's moment-to-moment sensory perceptions and emotions. There is no way to export Mnemosyne data, and the only method of accessing another person's is for a specially trained electronic investigator to Dive into a largely unsorted aggregate pool of their Mnemosynes.

Divers/Belayers
Highly specialized professions reserved for those with both high affinity for the Your Forma and high resistance to stress.
As Divers are incapable of ending a Dive on their own, Brain Diving is only possible with the help of a Belayer. A Diver with data processing abilities that far outstrip their Belayer's will exert a heavy toll on their partner's brain when they Dive.
All Divers and Belayers are employed by Interpol.

Technologically Restricted Zones
Sectors occupied by minority groups that reject the use of smart threads and other complex technology, known as luddites. This segregation between restricted and non-restricted zones is not unique to Kautokeino—which is where Echika and Harold went—but rather carried out in regions all around the world.

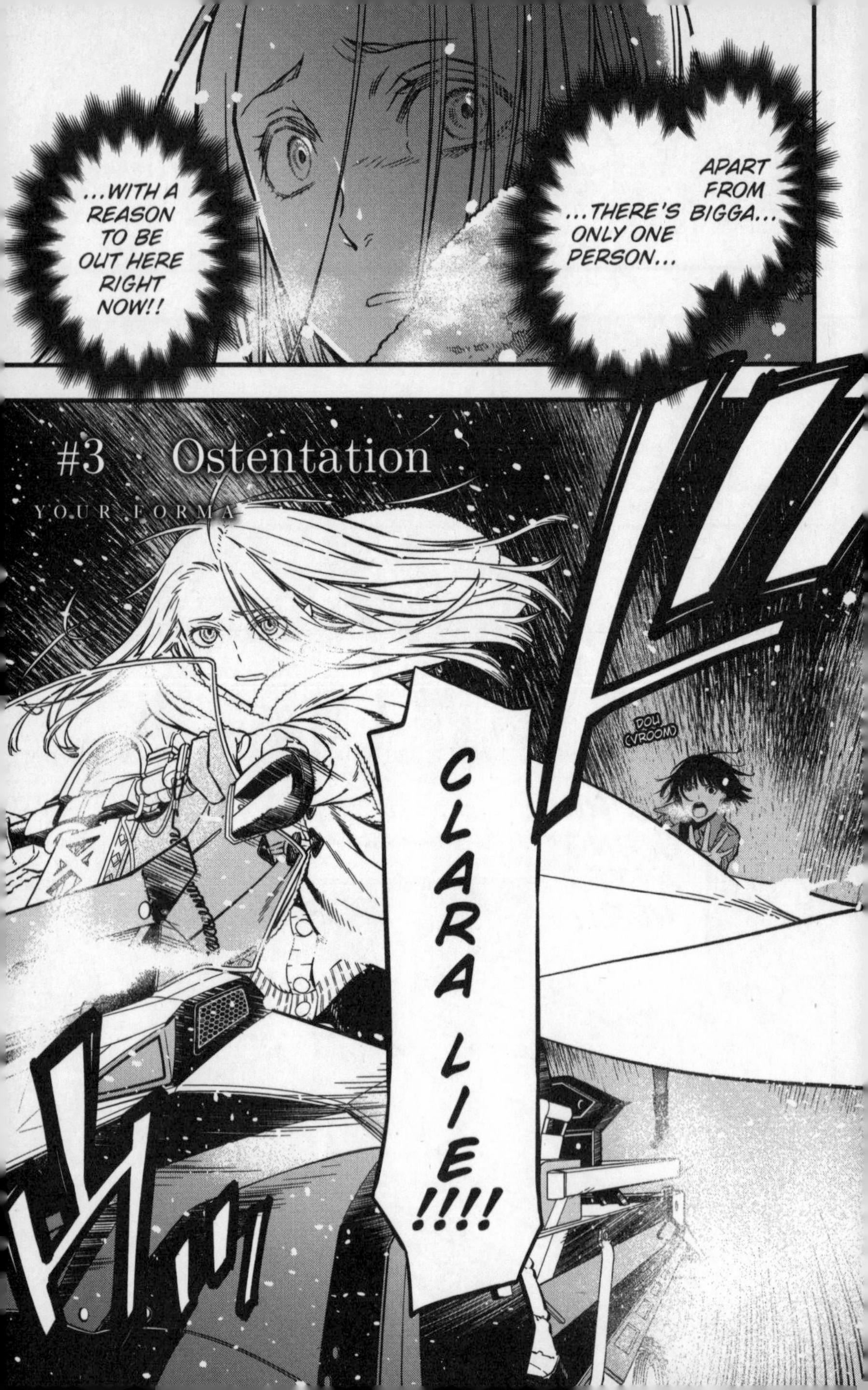
APART FROM BIGGA... ...THERE'S ONLY ONE PERSON...
...WITH A REASON TO BE OUT HERE RIGHT NOW!!
#3 Ostentation
YOUR FORMA
DOU (VROOM)
CLARA LIE!!!!

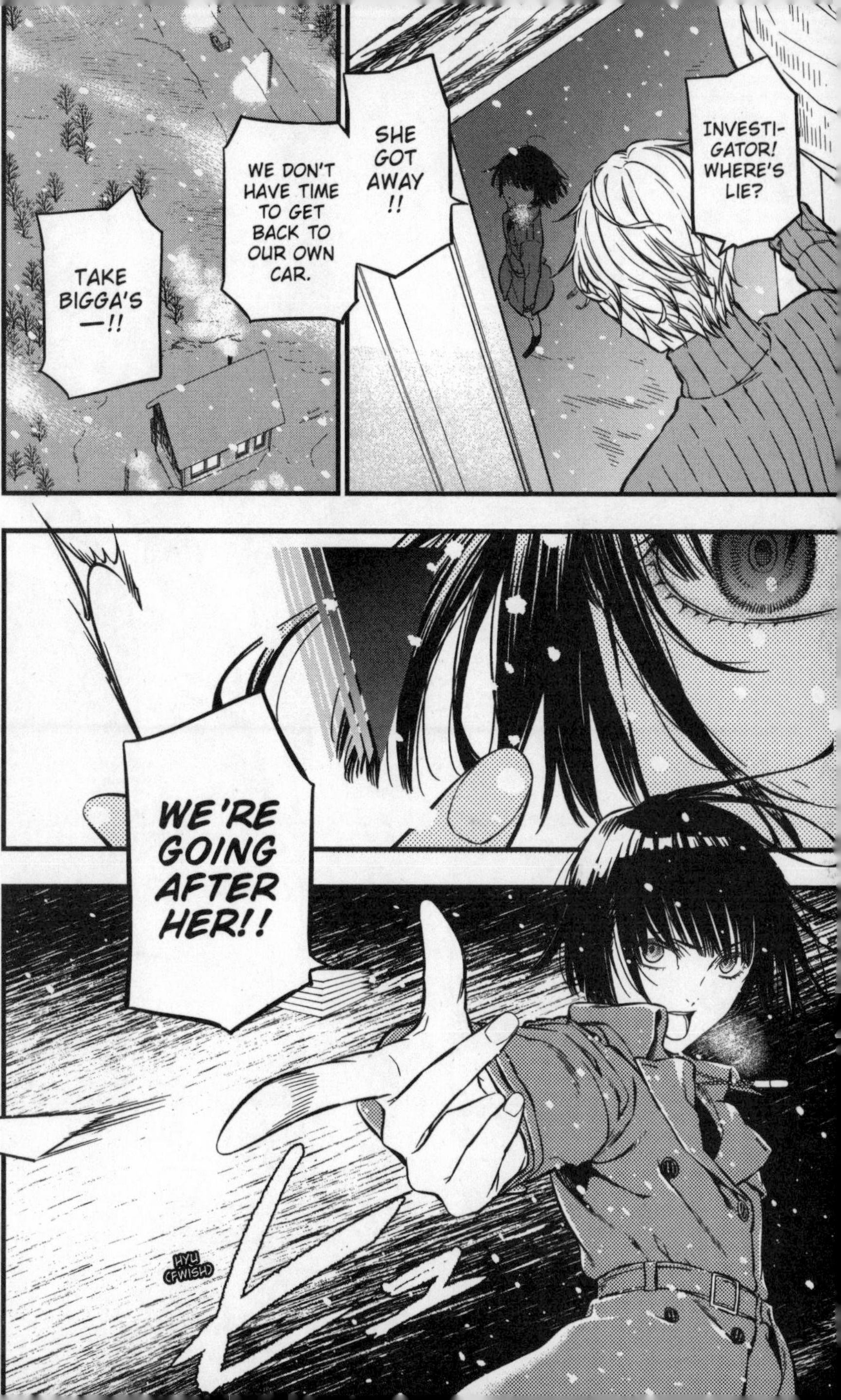
INVESTIGATOR! WHERE'S LIE?
SHE GOT AWAY!!
WE DON'T HAVE TIME TO GET BACK TO OUR OWN CAR.
TAKE BIGGA'S—!!
WE'RE GOING AFTER HER!!
HYU (FWISH)

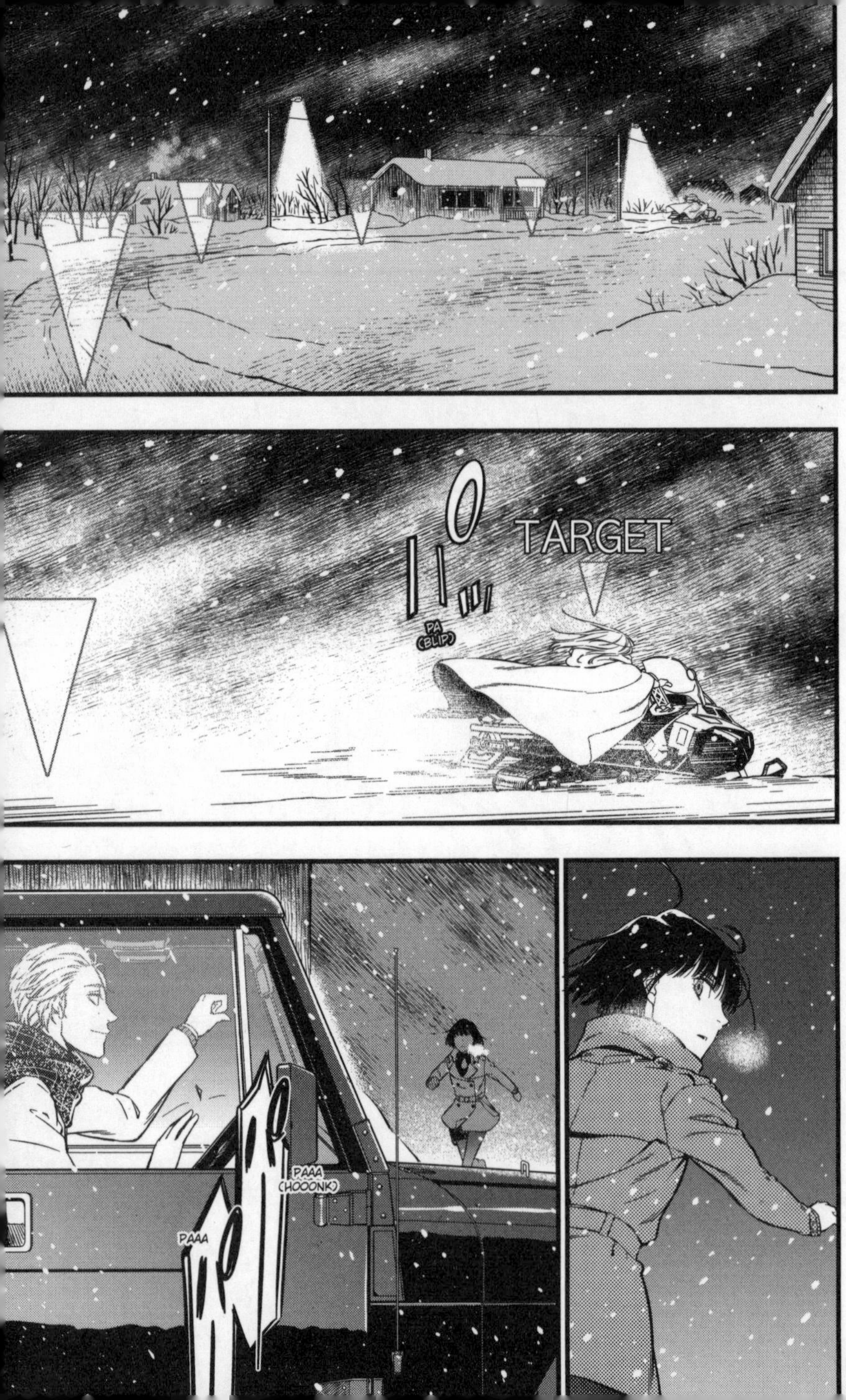
TARGET
PA
(BLIP)
PAAA
(HOOONK)
PAAA

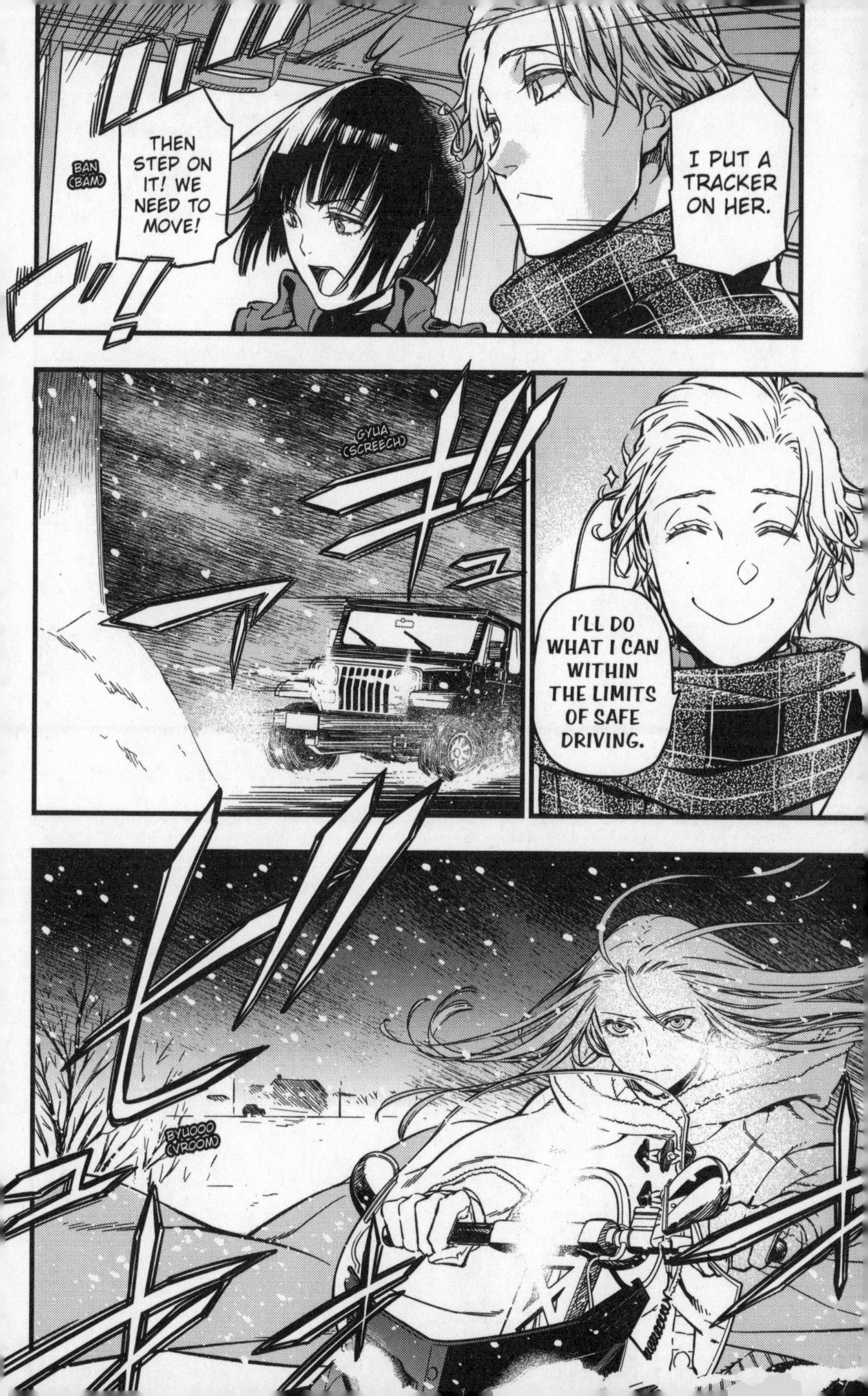
I PUT A TRACKER ON HER.
THEN STEP ON IT! WE NEED TO MOVE!
BAN (BAM)
I'LL DO WHAT I CAN WITHIN THE LIMITS OF SAFE DRIVING.
GYUA (SCREECH)
BYUOOO (VROOM)

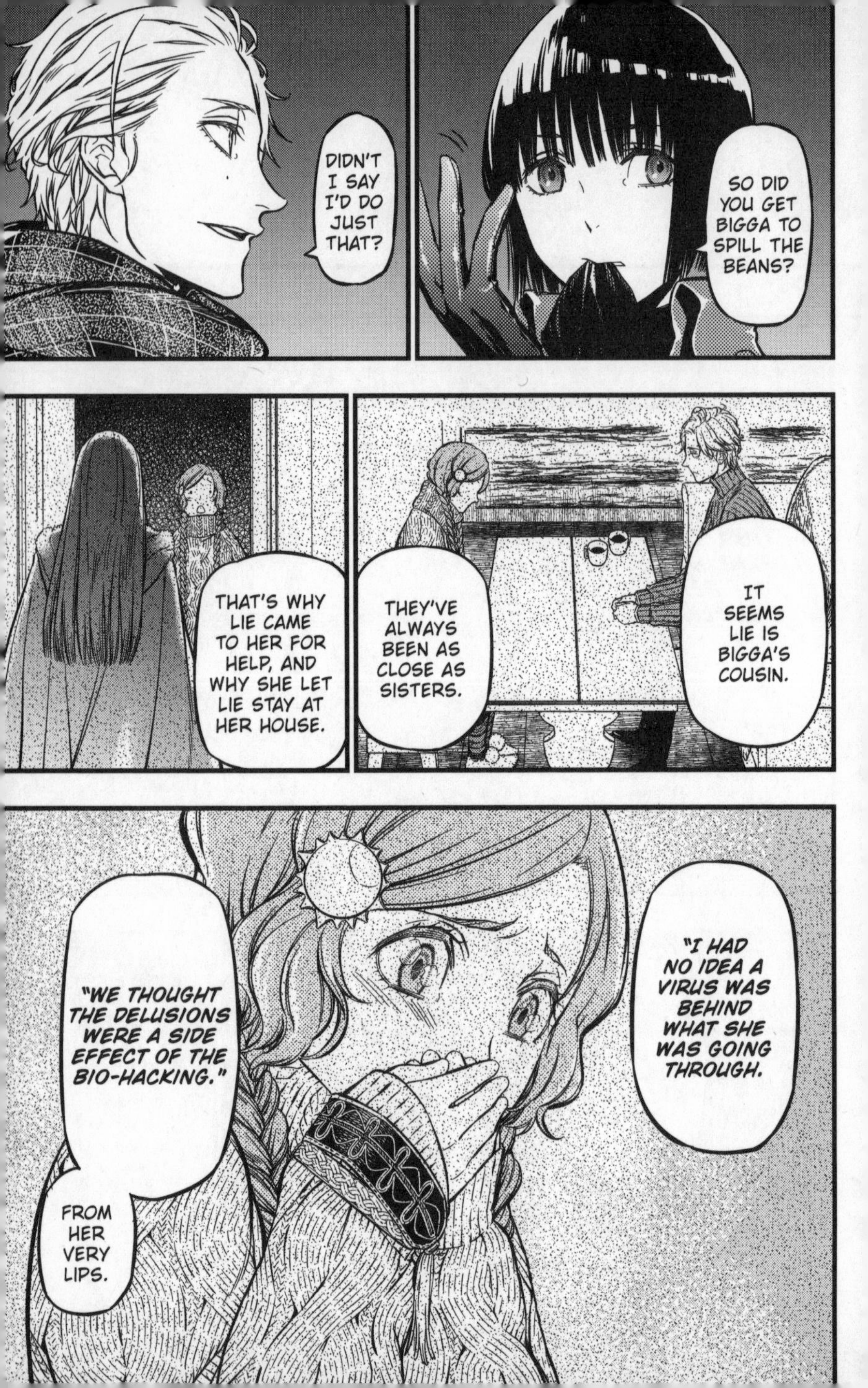
SO DID YOU GET BIGGA TO SPILL THE BEANS?
DIDN'T I SAY I'D DO JUST THAT?
IT SEEMS LIE IS BIGGA'S COUSIN.
THEY'VE ALWAYS BEEN AS CLOSE AS SISTERS.
THAT'S WHY LIE CAME TO HER FOR HELP, AND WHY SHE LET LIE STAY AT HER HOUSE.
"I HAD NO IDEA A VIRUS WAS BEHIND WHAT SHE WAS GOING THROUGH.
"WE THOUGHT THE DELUSIONS WERE A SIDE EFFECT OF THE BIO-HACKING."
FROM HER VERY LIPS.

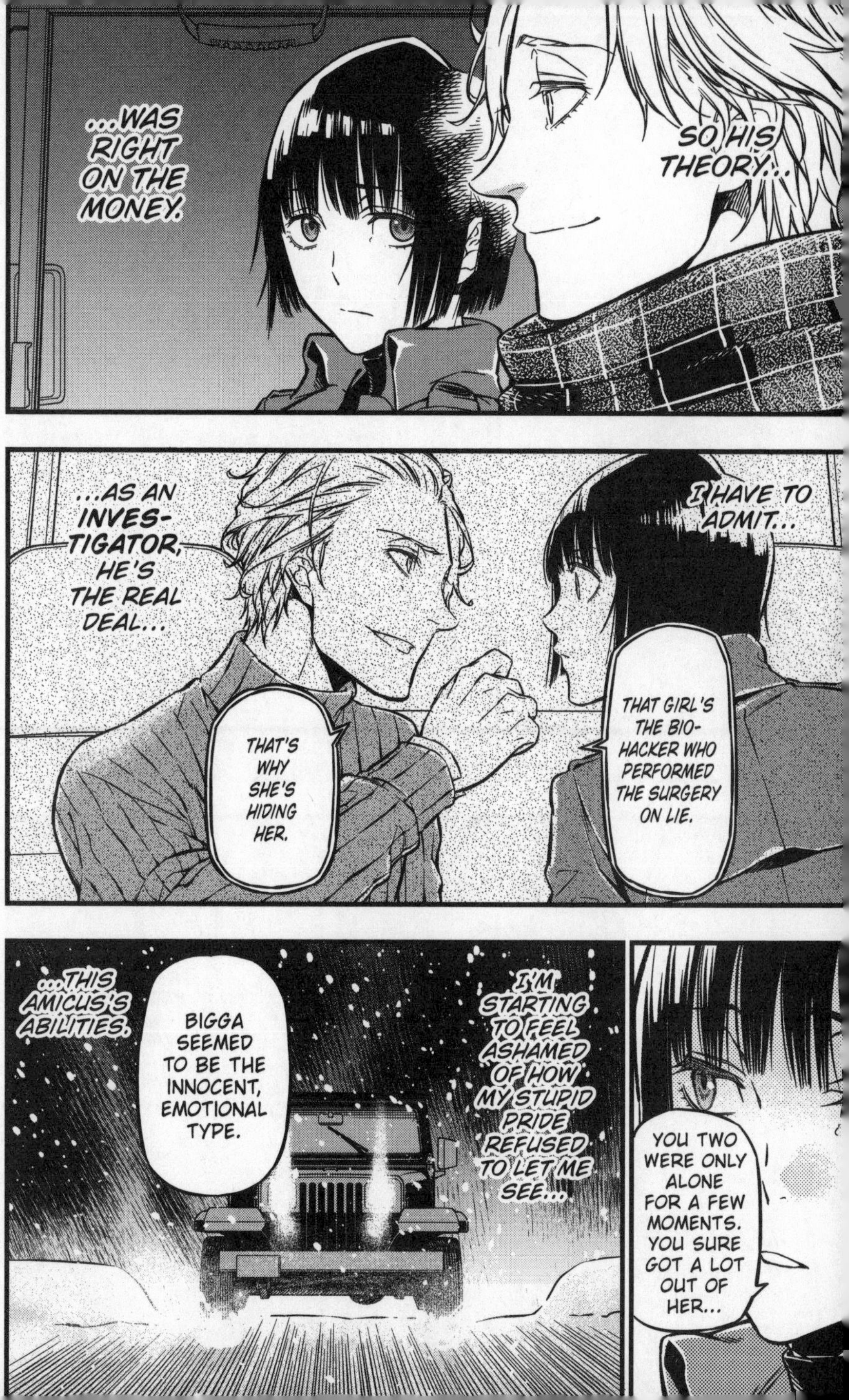
SO HIS THEORY...
...WAS RIGHT ON THE MONEY.
I HAVE TO ADMIT...
...AS AN INVES-TIGATOR, HE'S THE REAL DEAL...
THAT GIRL'S THE BIO-HACKER WHO PERFORMED THE SURGERY ON LIE.
THAT'S WHY SHE'S HIDING HER.
YOU TWO WERE ONLY ALONE FOR A FEW MOMENTS. YOU SURE GOT A LOT OUT OF HER...
I'M STARTING TO FEEL ASHAMED OF HOW MY STUPID PRIDE REFUSED TO LET ME SEE...
...THIS AMICUS'S ABILITIES.
BIGGA SEEMED TO BE THE INNOCENT, EMOTIONAL TYPE.

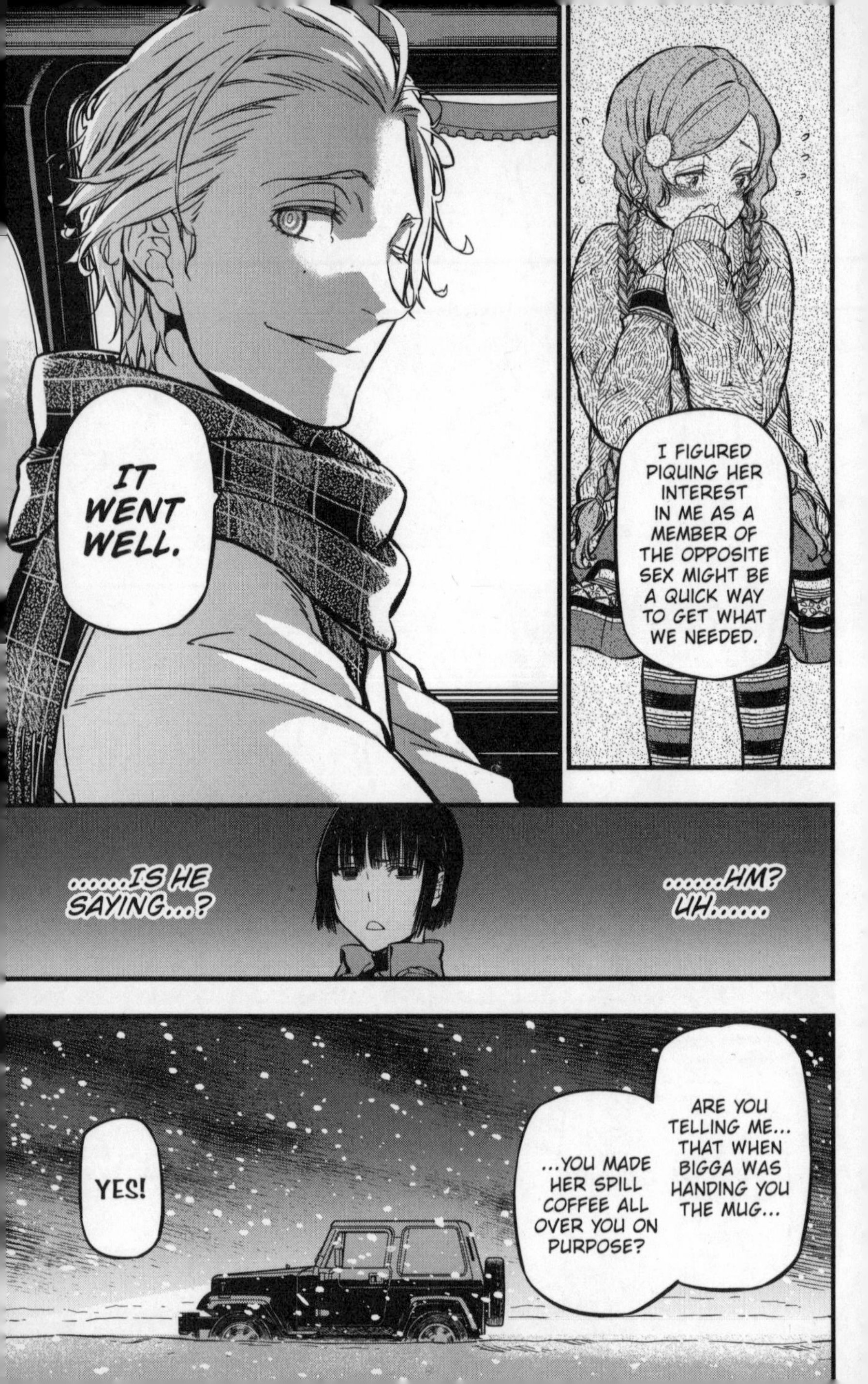
I FIGURED PIQUING HER INTEREST IN ME AS A MEMBER OF THE OPPOSITE SEX MIGHT BE A QUICK WAY TO GET WHAT WE NEEDED.
IT WENT WELL.
……HM? UH……
……IS HE SAYING…?
ARE YOU TELLING ME… THAT WHEN BIGGA WAS HANDING YOU THE MUG…
…YOU MADE HER SPILL COFFEE ALL OVER YOU ON PURPOSE?
YES!

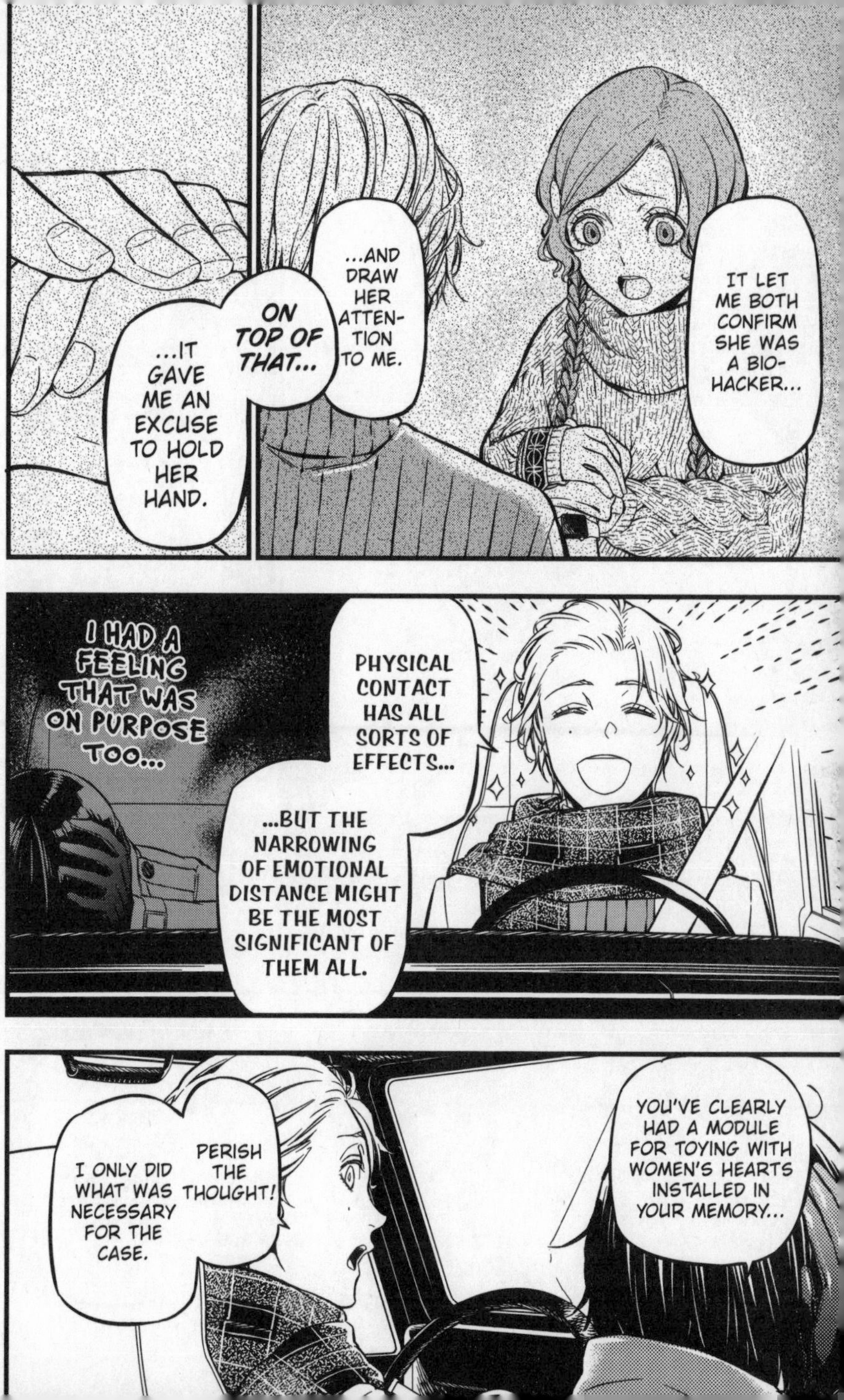
IT LET ME BOTH CONFIRM SHE WAS A BIO-HACKER...
...AND DRAW HER ATTEN-TION TO ME.
ON TOP OF THAT...
...IT GAVE ME AN EXCUSE TO HOLD HER HAND.
PHYSICAL CONTACT HAS ALL SORTS OF EFFECTS...
...BUT THE NARROWING OF EMOTIONAL DISTANCE MIGHT BE THE MOST SIGNIFICANT OF THEM ALL.
I HAD A FEELING THAT WAS ON PURPOSE TOO...
YOU'VE CLEARLY HAD A MODULE FOR TOYING WITH WOMEN'S HEARTS INSTALLED IN YOUR MEMORY...
PERISH THE THOUGHT!
I ONLY DID WHAT WAS NECESSARY FOR THE CASE.

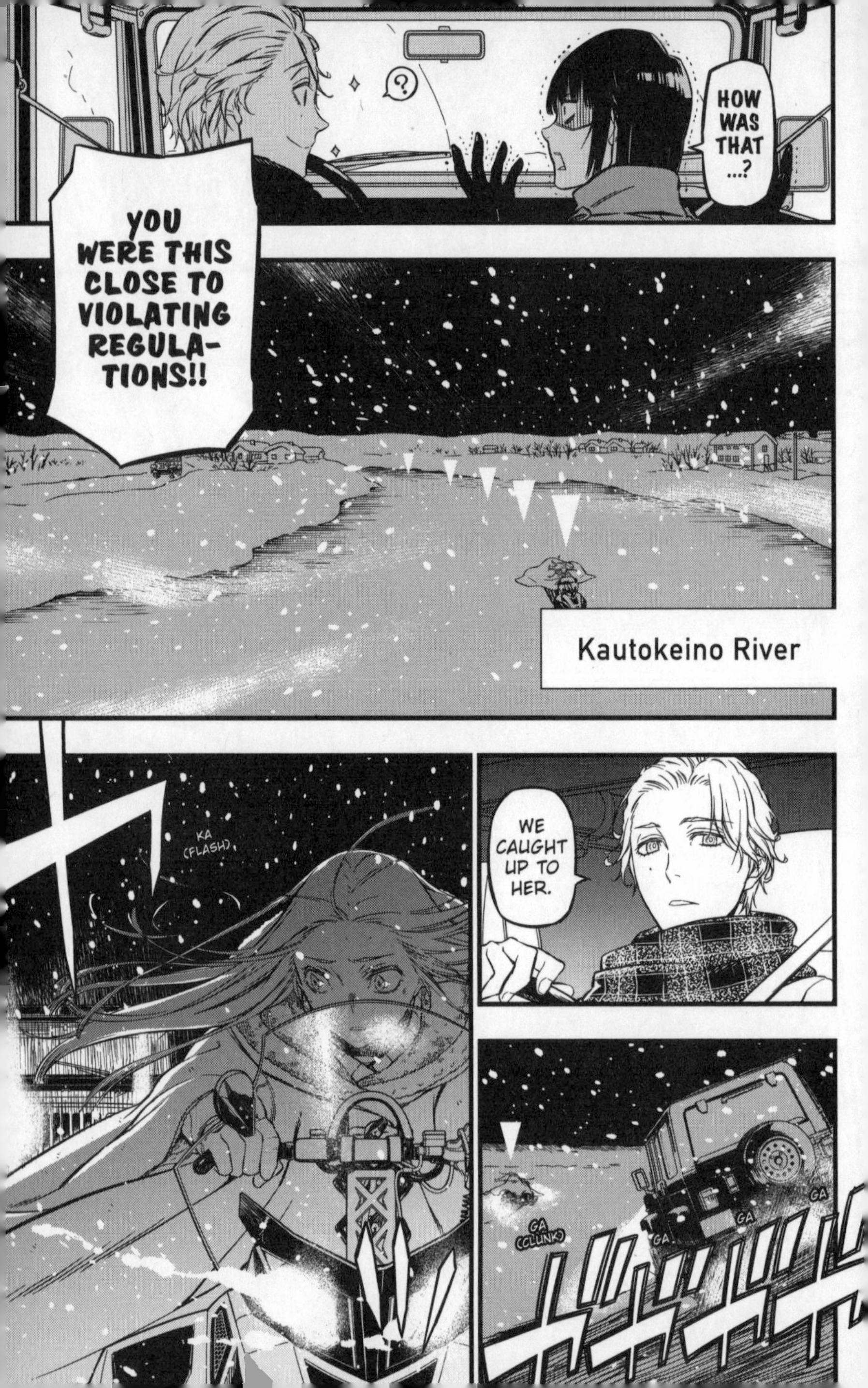

HOW WAS THAT ...?
?
YOU WERE THIS CLOSE TO VIOLATING REGULA-TIONS!!
Kautokeino River
WE CAUGHT UP TO HER.
KA (FLASH)
GA (CLUNK)
GA
GA
GA

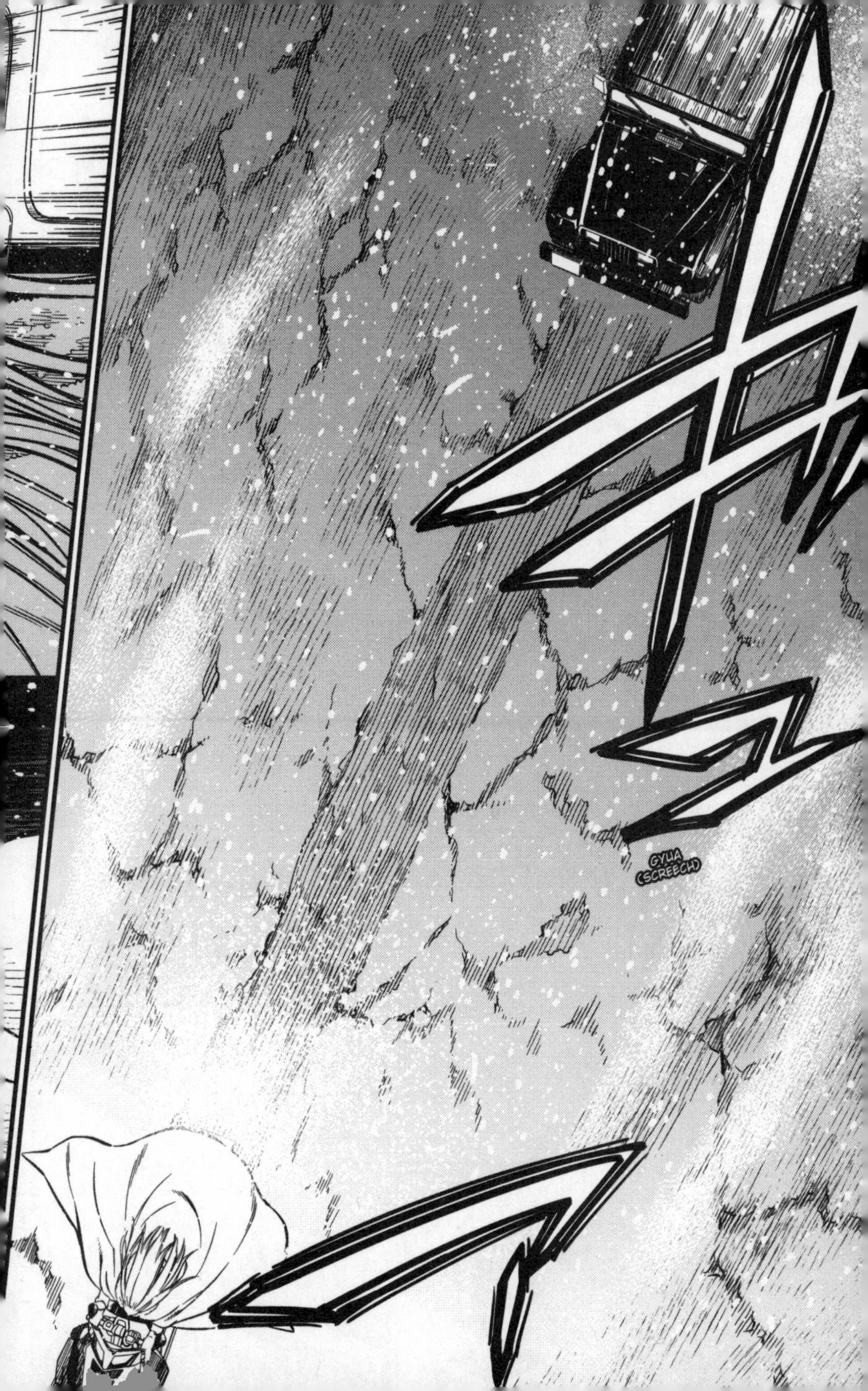
GYUA
(SCREECH)

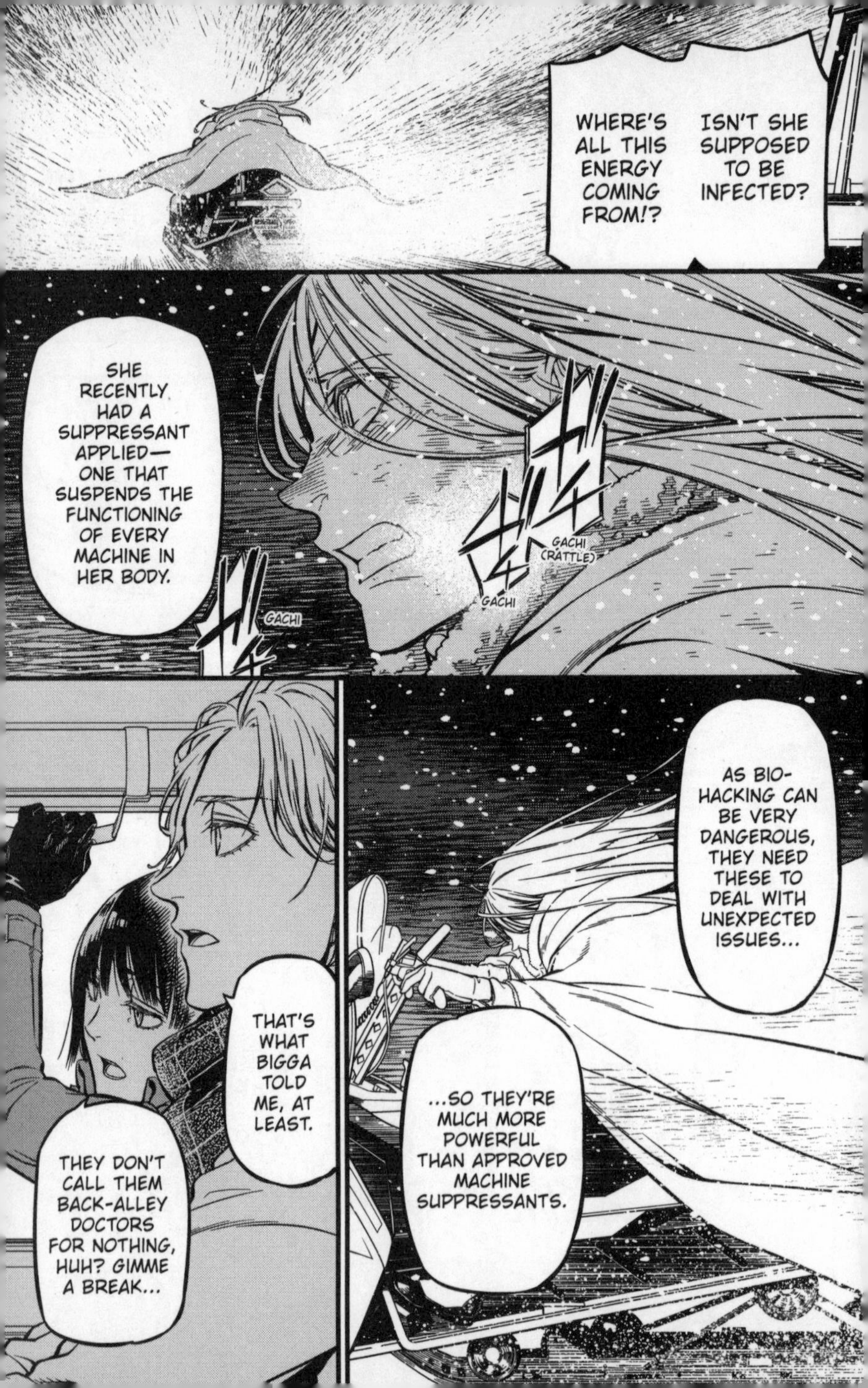
ISN'T SHE SUPPOSED TO BE INFECTED?
WHERE'S ALL THIS ENERGY COMING FROM!?
GACHI (RATTLE)
GACHI
SHE RECENTLY HAD A SUPPRESSANT APPLIED—ONE THAT SUSPENDS THE FUNCTIONING OF EVERY MACHINE IN HER BODY.
GACHI
AS BIO-HACKING CAN BE VERY DANGEROUS, THEY NEED THESE TO DEAL WITH UNEXPECTED ISSUES...
...SO THEY'RE MUCH MORE POWERFUL THAN APPROVED MACHINE SUPPRESSANTS.
THAT'S WHAT BIGGA TOLD ME, AT LEAST.
THEY DON'T CALL THEM BACK-ALLEY DOCTORS FOR NOTHING, HUH? GIMME A BREAK...

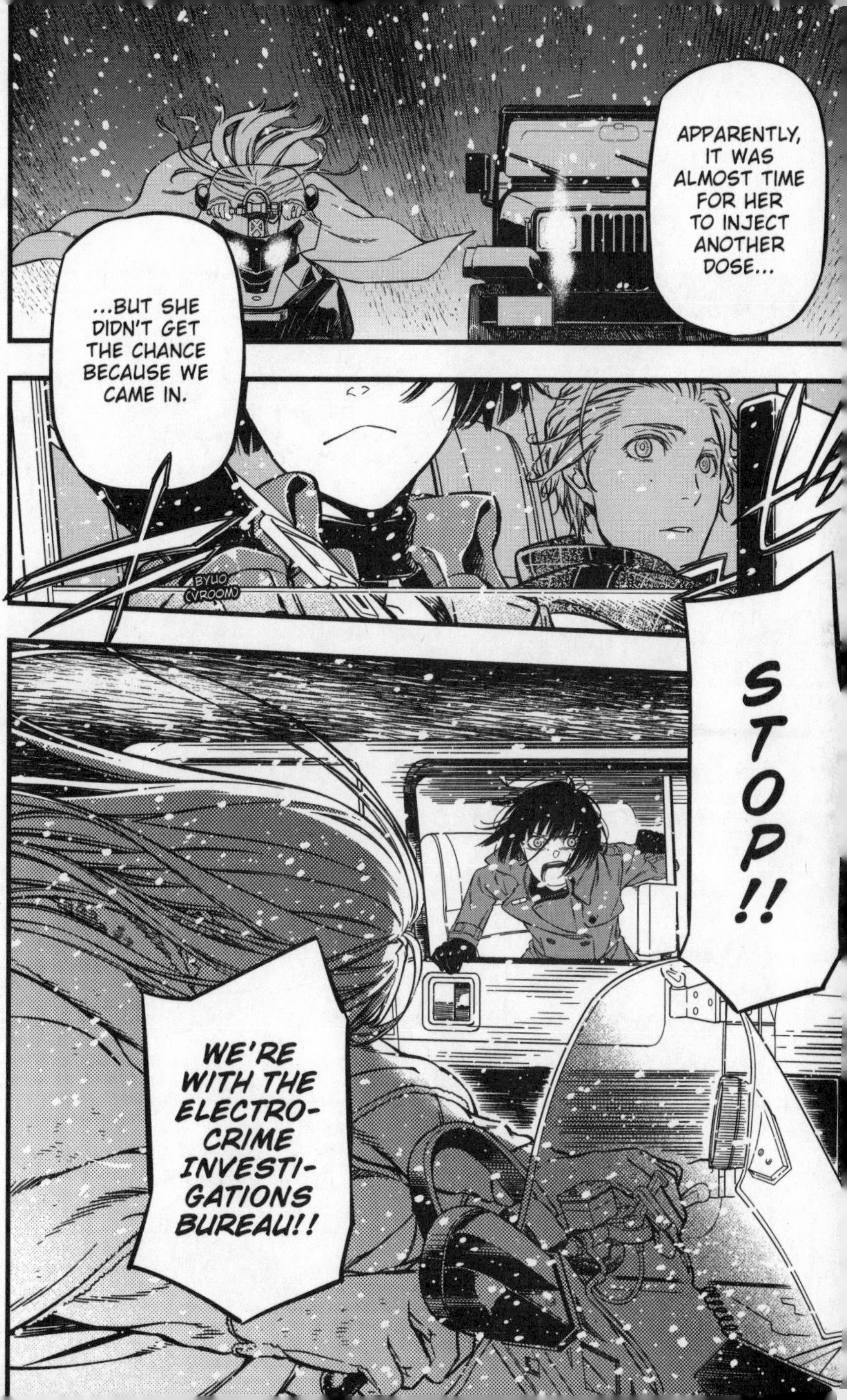
APPARENTLY, IT WAS ALMOST TIME FOR HER TO INJECT ANOTHER DOSE...
...BUT SHE DIDN'T GET THE CHANCE BECAUSE WE CAME IN.
BYUO (VROOM)
STOP!!
WE'RE WITH THE ELECTRO-CRIME INVESTIGATIONS BUREAU!!

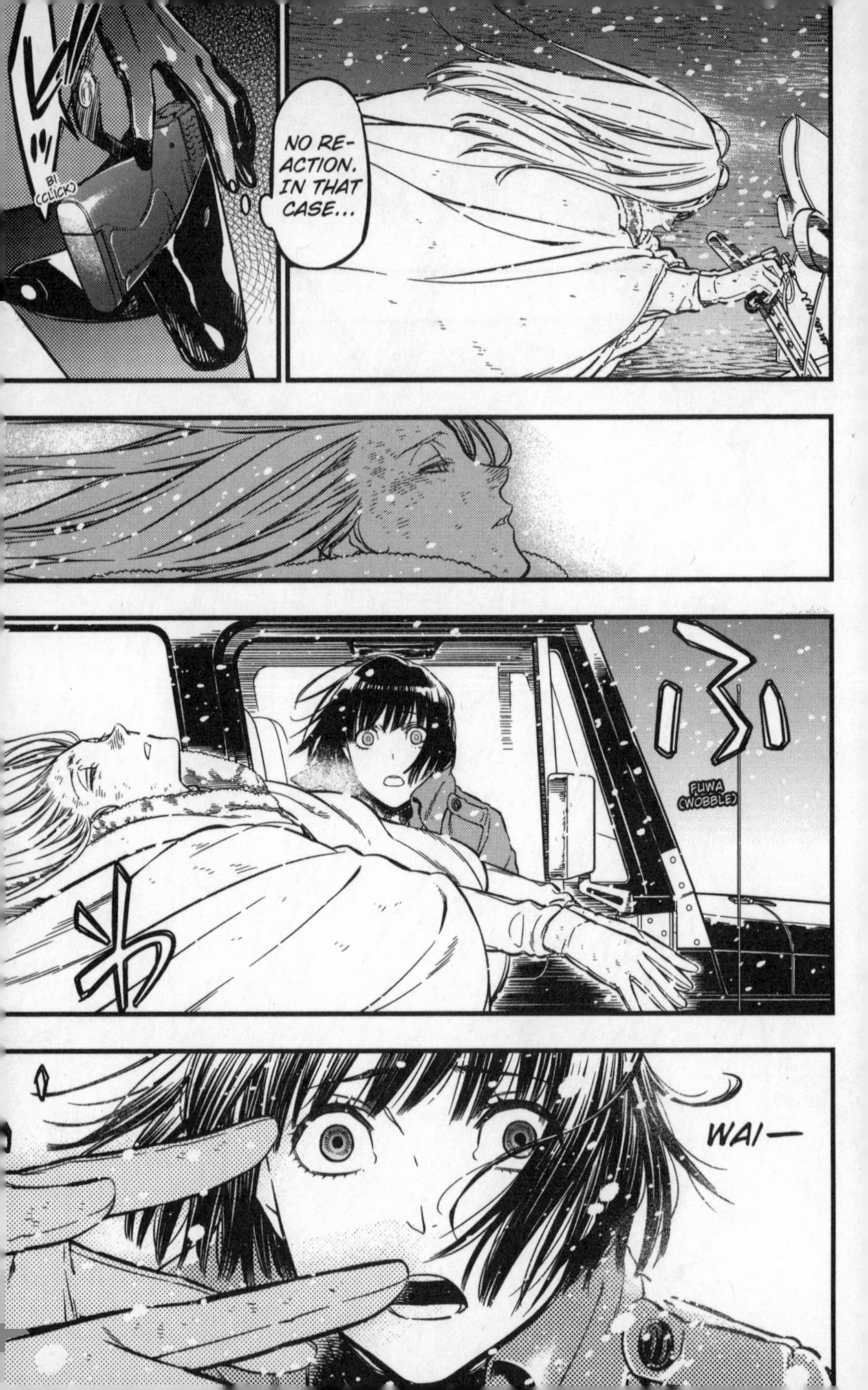
NO RE-
ACTION.
IN THAT
CASE...
BI
(CLICK)
FUWA
(WOBBLE)
WAI—

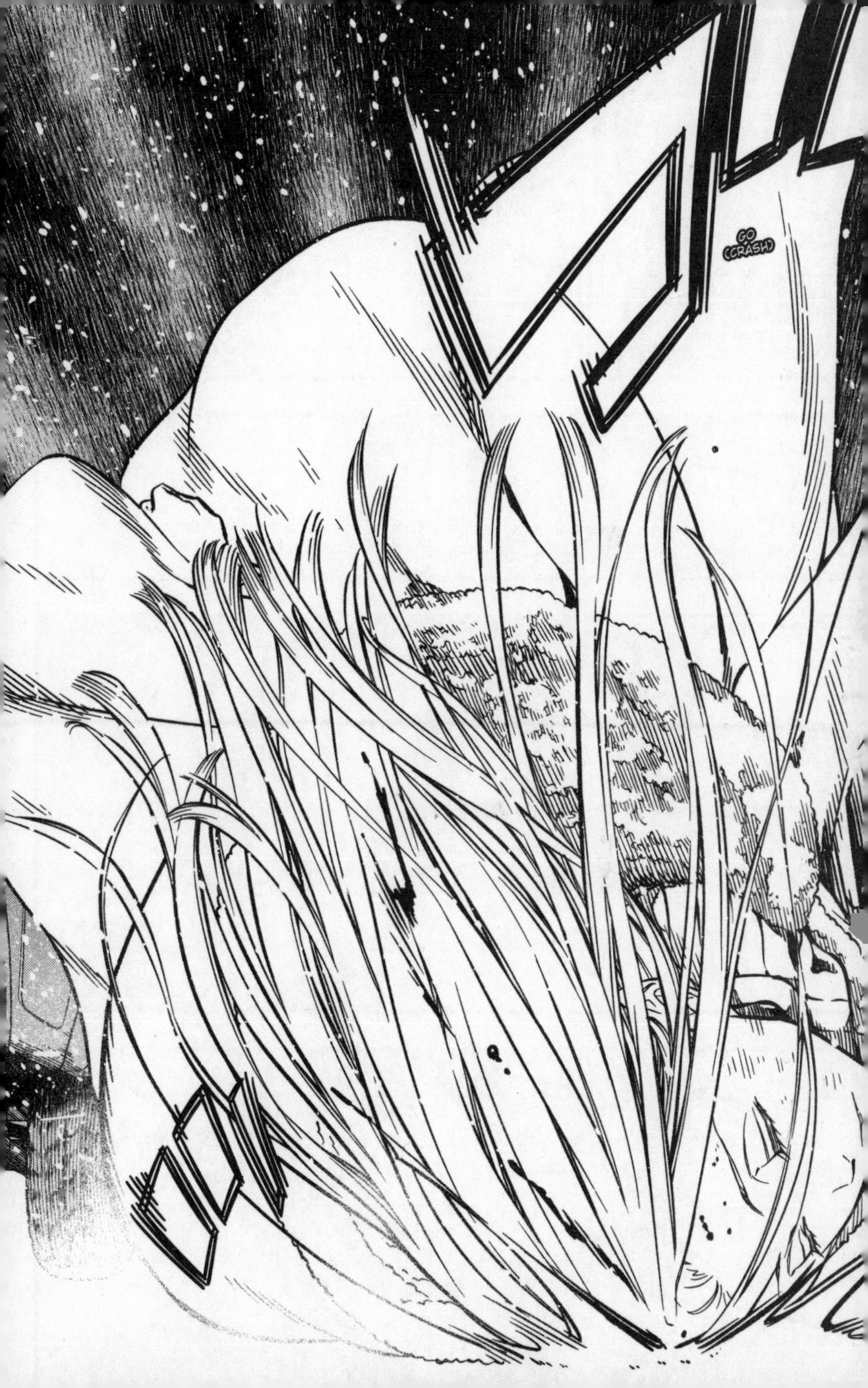
GO (CRASH)

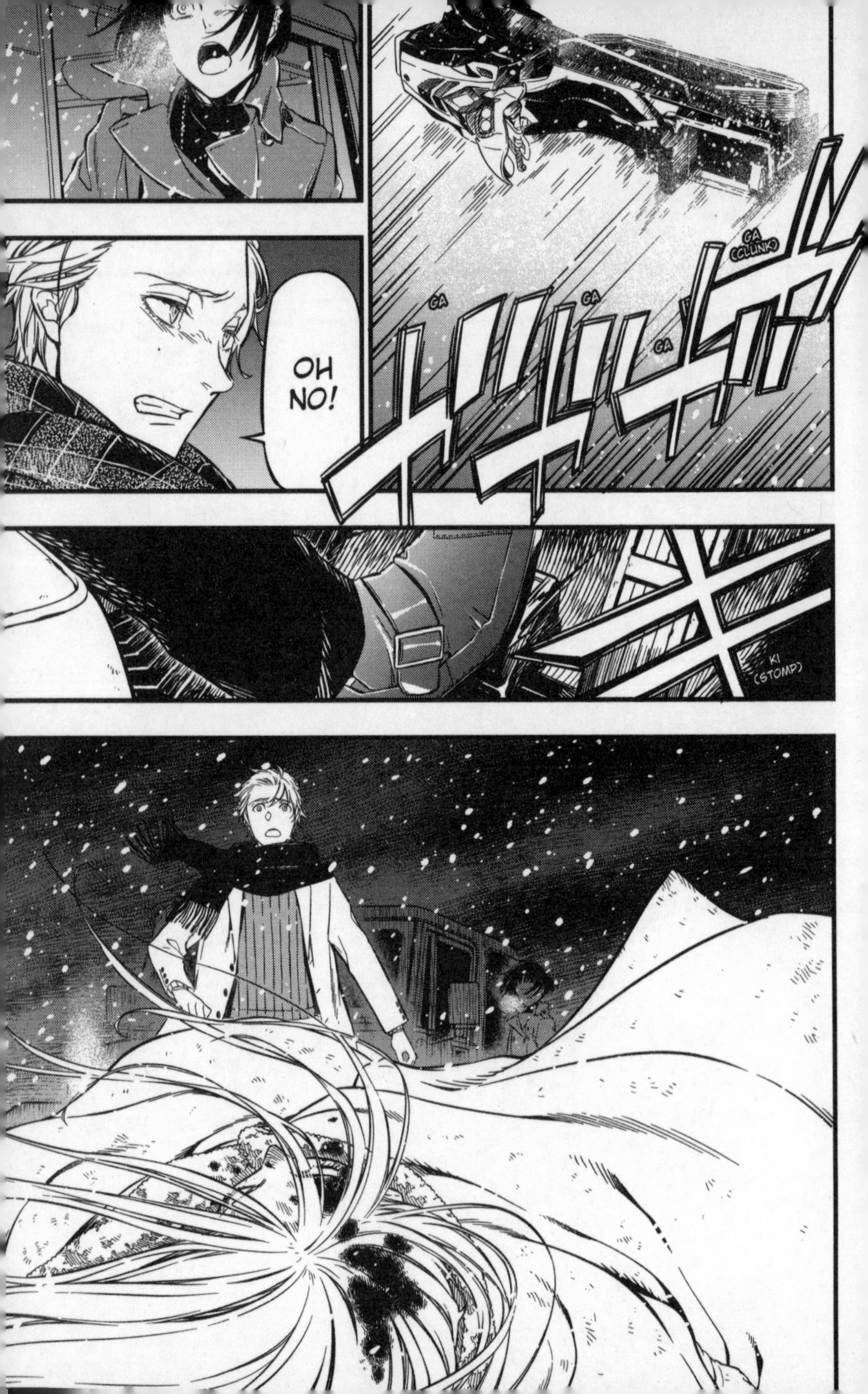

GA
(CLUNK)
GA
GA
GA
OH NO!
KI
(STOMP)

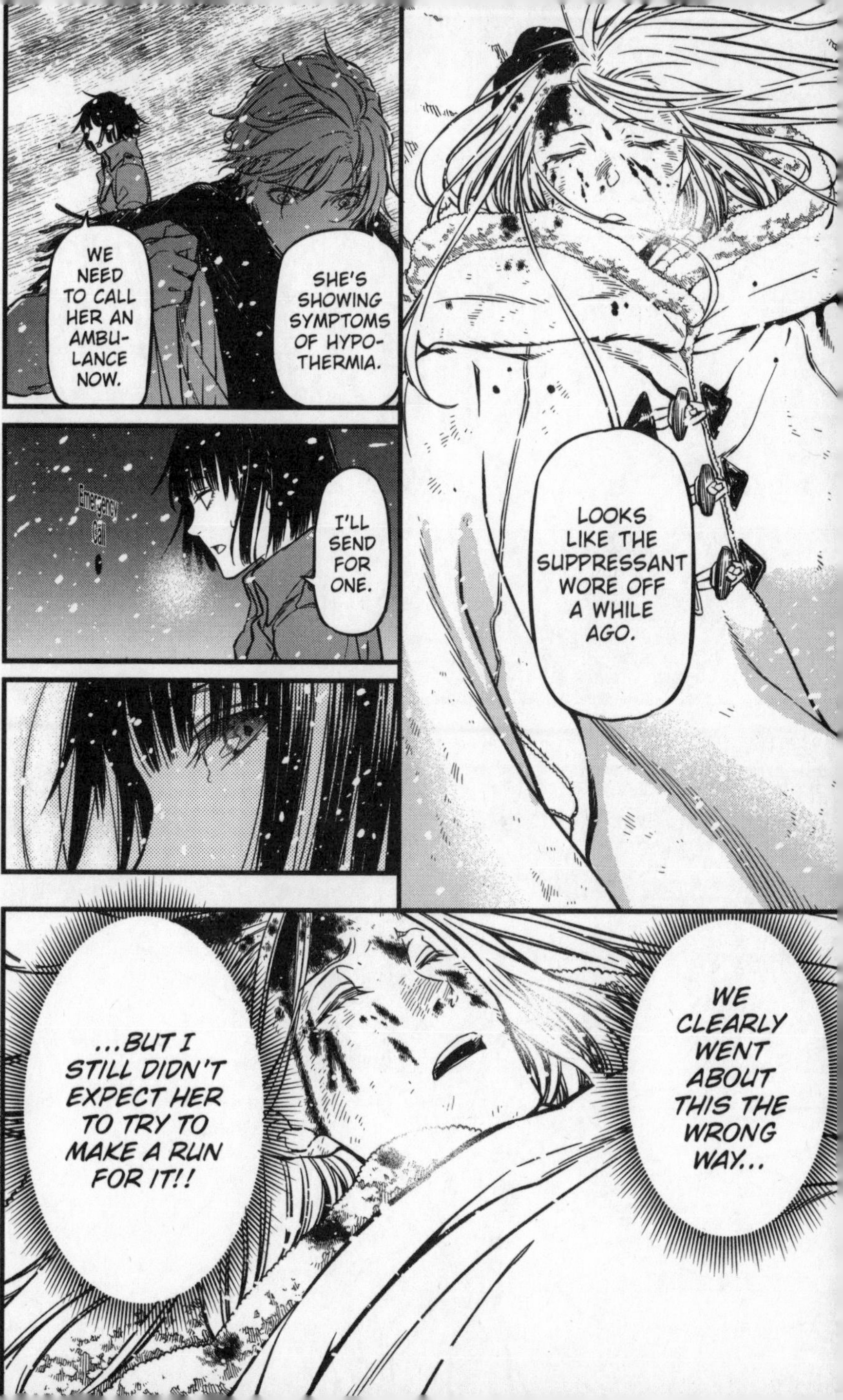
LOOKS LIKE THE SUPPRESSANT WORE OFF A WHILE AGO.
SHE'S SHOWING SYMPTOMS OF HYPO-THERMIA.
WE NEED TO CALL HER AN AMBU-LANCE NOW.
I'LL SEND FOR ONE.
Emergency Call
WE CLEARLY WENT ABOUT THIS THE WRONG WAY...
...BUT I STILL DIDN'T EXPECT HER TO TRY TO MAKE A RUN FOR IT!!

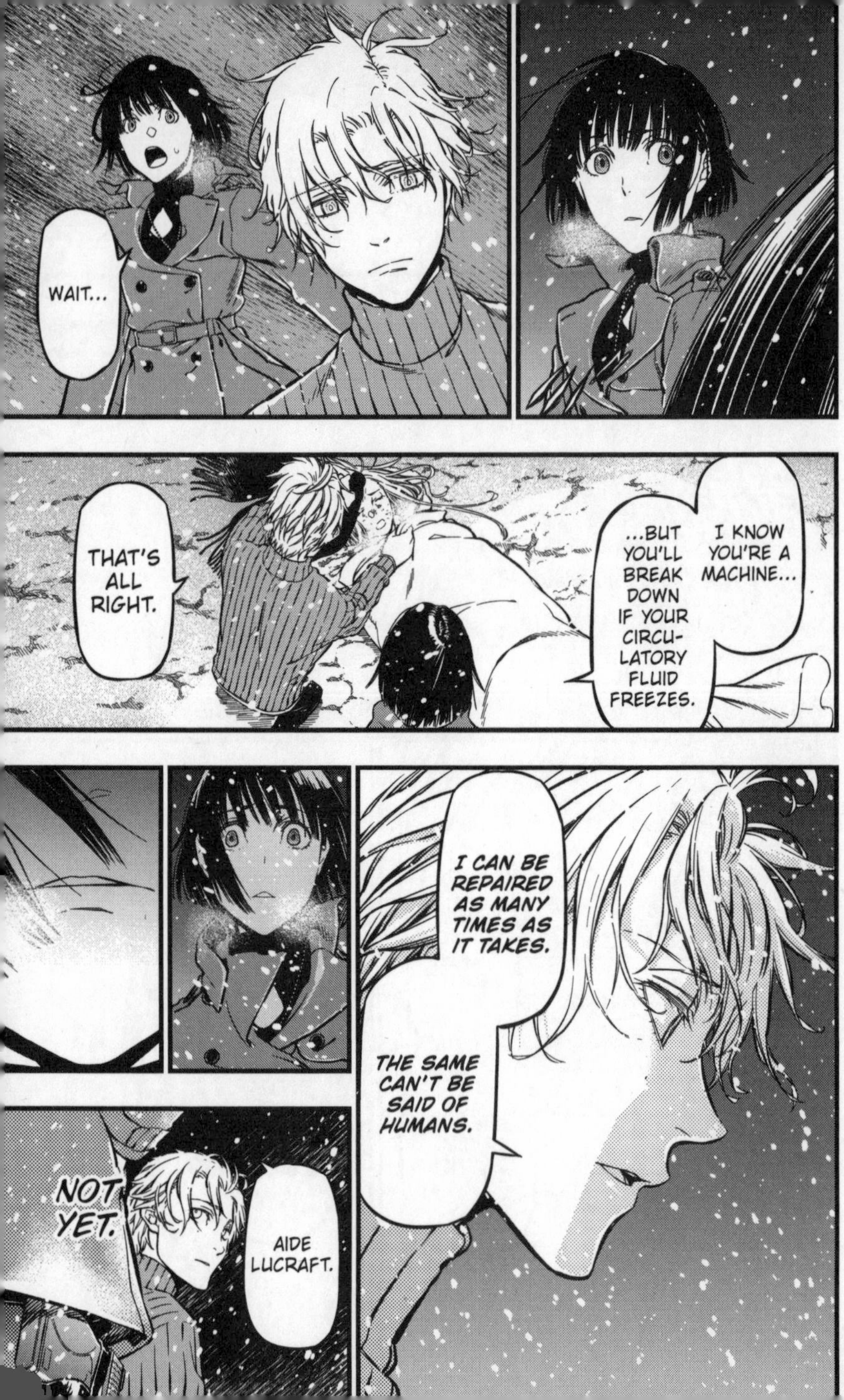
WAIT...
I KNOW YOU'RE A MACHINE...
...BUT YOU'LL BREAK DOWN IF YOUR CIRCULATORY FLUID FREEZES.
THAT'S ALL RIGHT.
I CAN BE REPAIRED AS MANY TIMES AS IT TAKES.
THE SAME CAN'T BE SAID OF HUMANS.
AIDE LUCRAFT.
NOT YET.

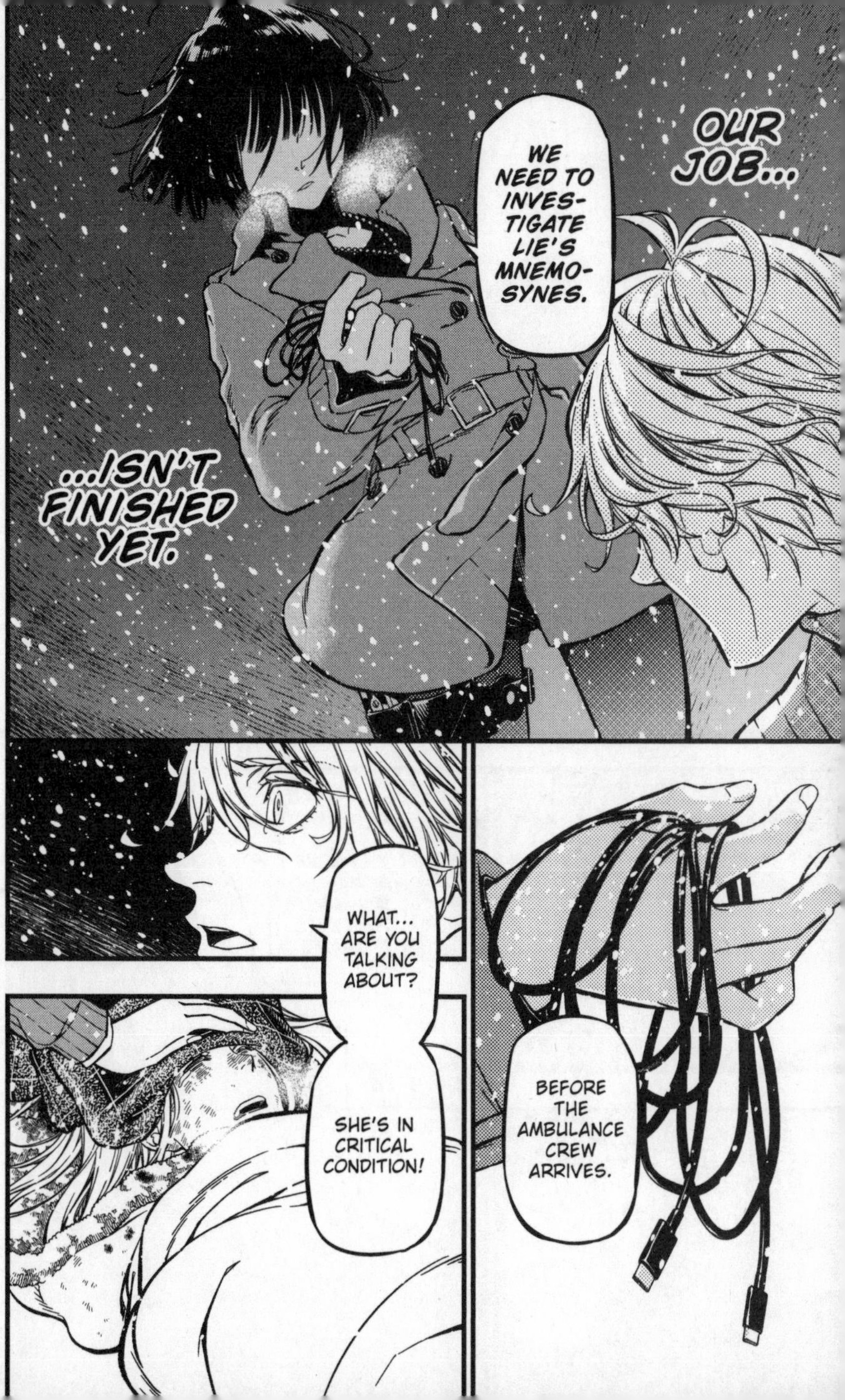
OUR JOB...
...ISN'T FINISHED YET.
WE NEED TO INVES-TIGATE LIE'S MNEMO-SYNES.
BEFORE THE AMBULANCE CREW ARRIVES.
WHAT... ARE YOU TALKING ABOUT?
SHE'S IN CRITICAL CONDITION!

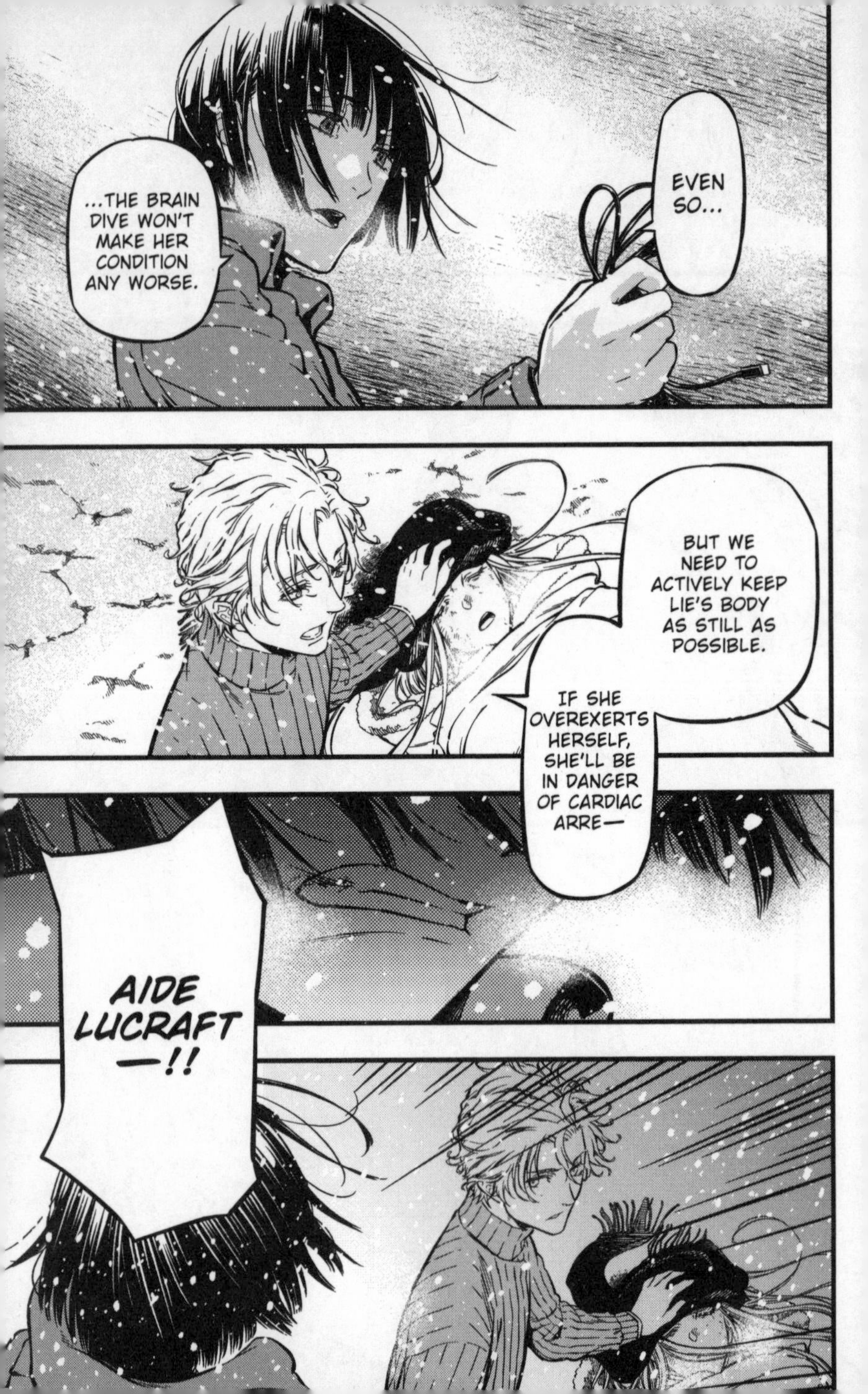
EVEN SO...
...THE BRAIN DIVE WON'T MAKE HER CONDITION ANY WORSE.
BUT WE NEED TO ACTIVELY KEEP LIE'S BODY AS STILL AS POSSIBLE.
IF SHE OVEREXERTS HERSELF, SHE'LL BE IN DANGER OF CARDIAC ARRE—
AIDE LUCRAFT—!!

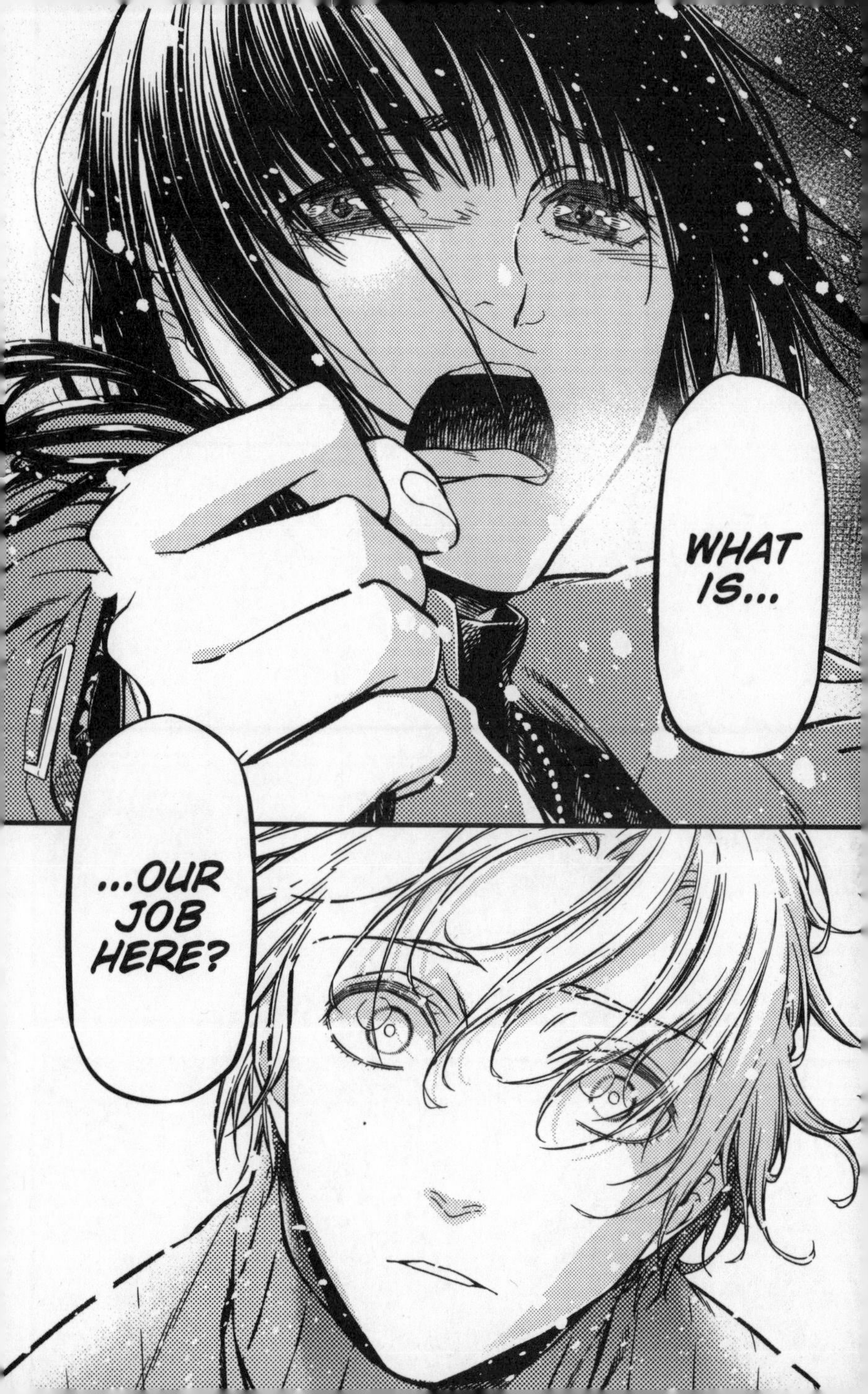
WHAT IS...
...OUR JOB HERE?

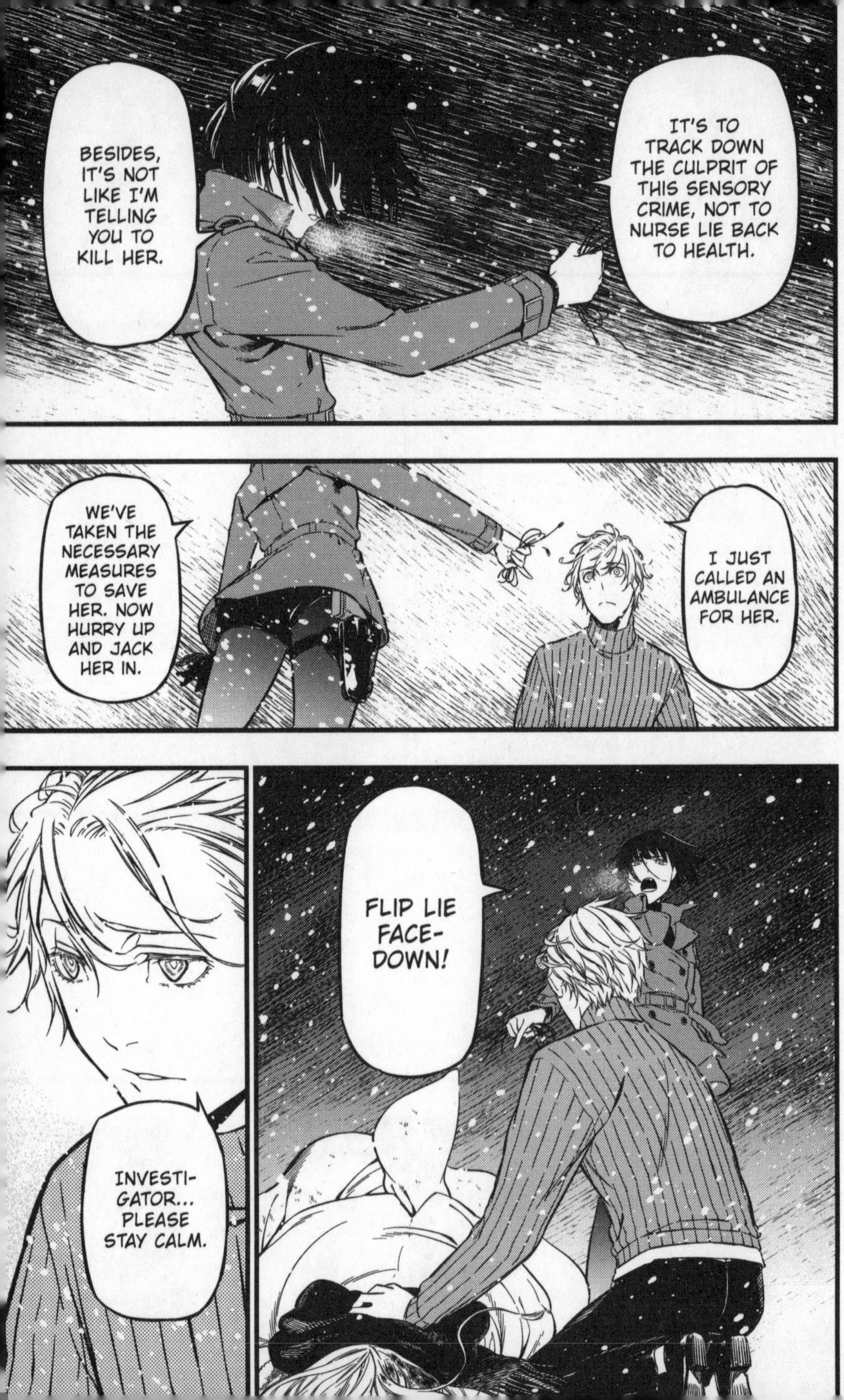
IT'S TO TRACK DOWN THE CULPRIT OF THIS SENSORY CRIME, NOT TO NURSE LIE BACK TO HEALTH.
BESIDES, IT'S NOT LIKE I'M TELLING YOU TO KILL HER.
I JUST CALLED AN AMBULANCE FOR HER.
WE'VE TAKEN THE NECESSARY MEASURES TO SAVE HER. NOW HURRY UP AND JACK HER IN.
FLIP LIE FACE-DOWN!
INVESTI-GATOR... PLEASE STAY CALM.

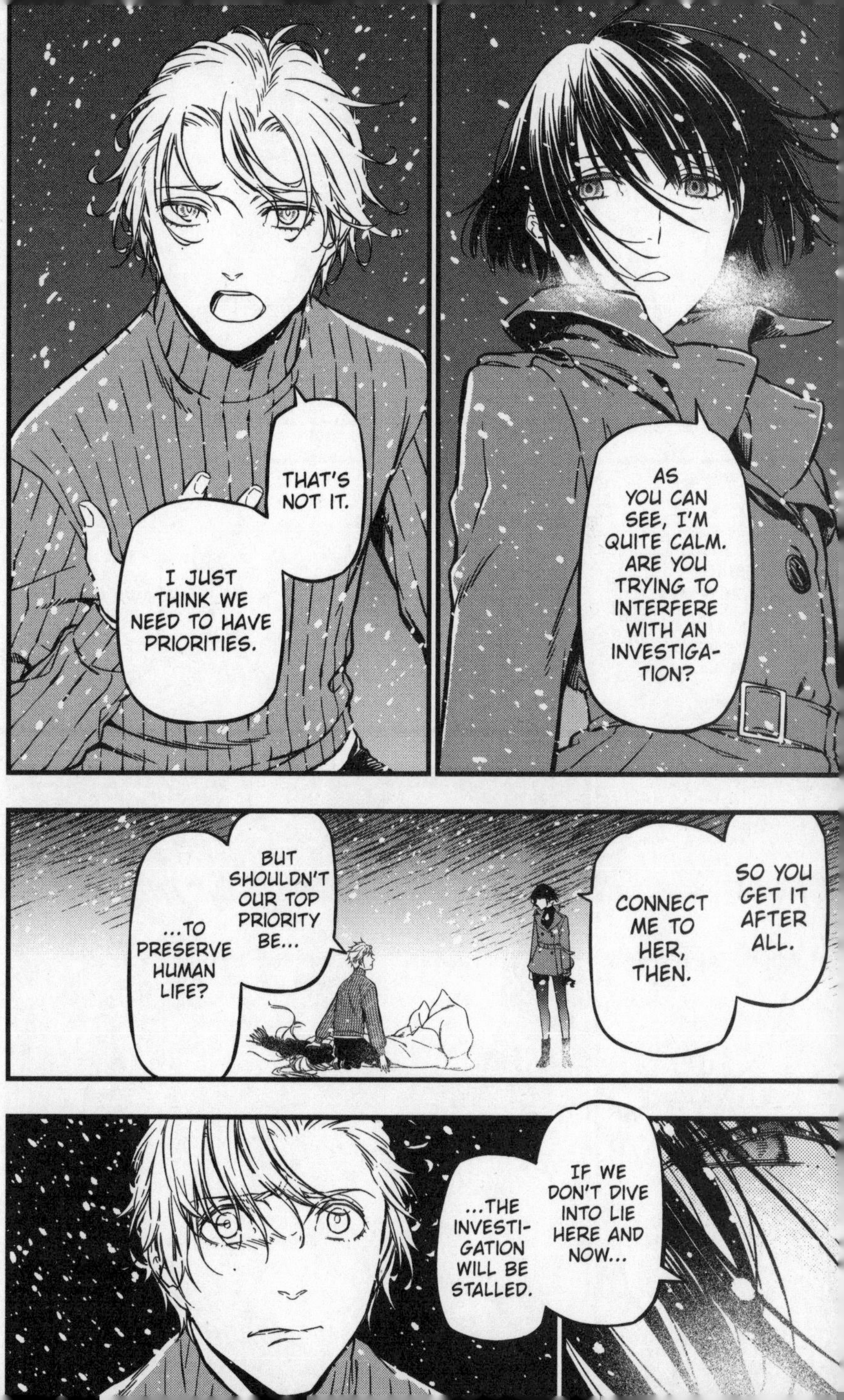
AS YOU CAN SEE, I'M QUITE CALM. ARE YOU TRYING TO INTERFERE WITH AN INVESTIGA-TION?
THAT'S NOT IT.
I JUST THINK WE NEED TO HAVE PRIORITIES.
SO YOU GET IT AFTER ALL.
CONNECT ME TO HER, THEN.
BUT SHOULDN'T OUR TOP PRIORITY BE...
...TO PRESERVE HUMAN LIFE?
IF WE DON'T DIVE INTO LIE HERE AND NOW...
...THE INVESTI-GATION WILL BE STALLED.

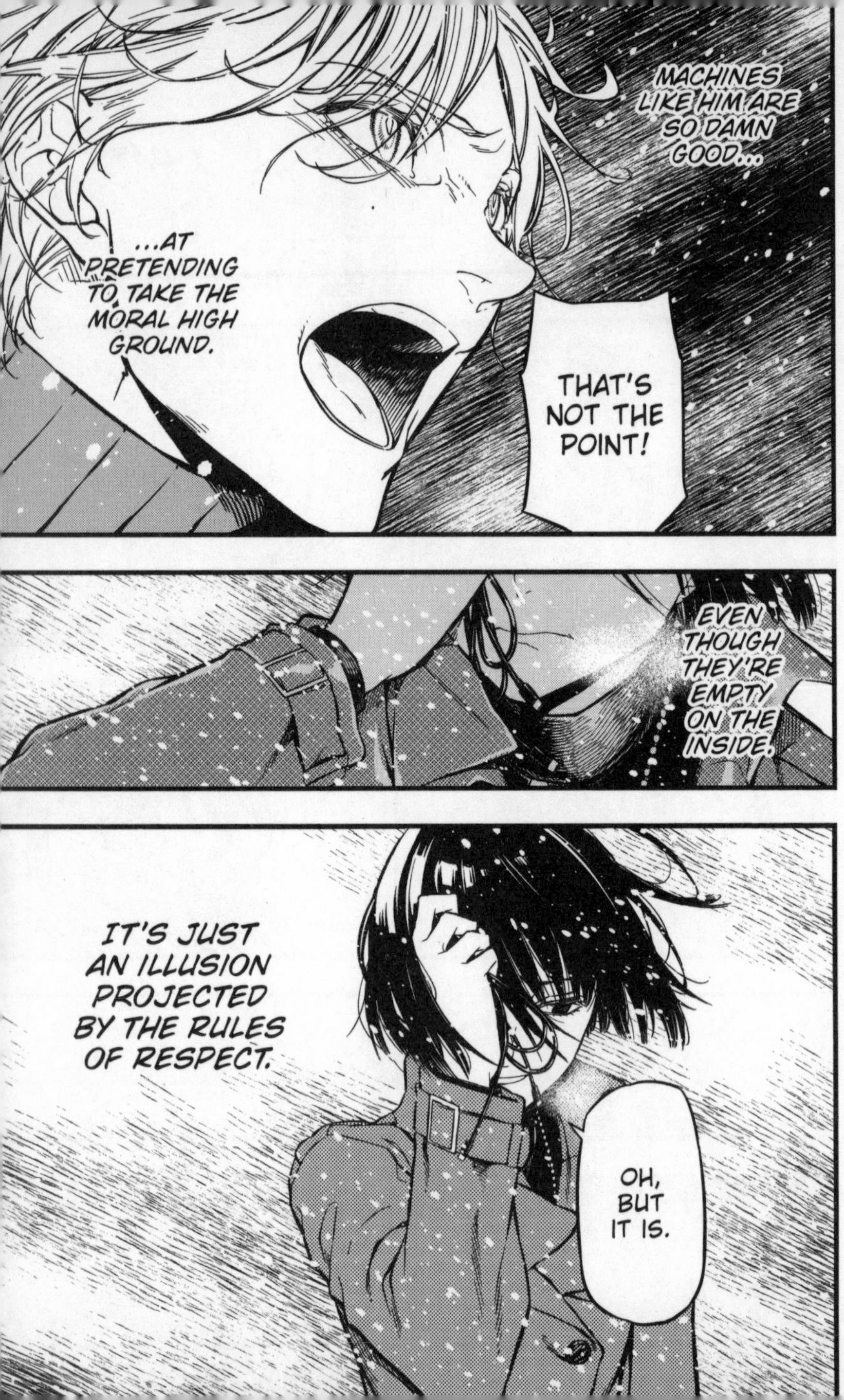
MACHINES LIKE HIM ARE SO DAMN GOOD...
...AT PRETENDING TO TAKE THE MORAL HIGH GROUND.
THAT'S NOT THE POINT!
EVEN THOUGH THEY'RE EMPTY ON THE INSIDE.
IT'S JUST AN ILLUSION PROJECTED BY THE RULES OF RESPECT.
OH, BUT IT IS.

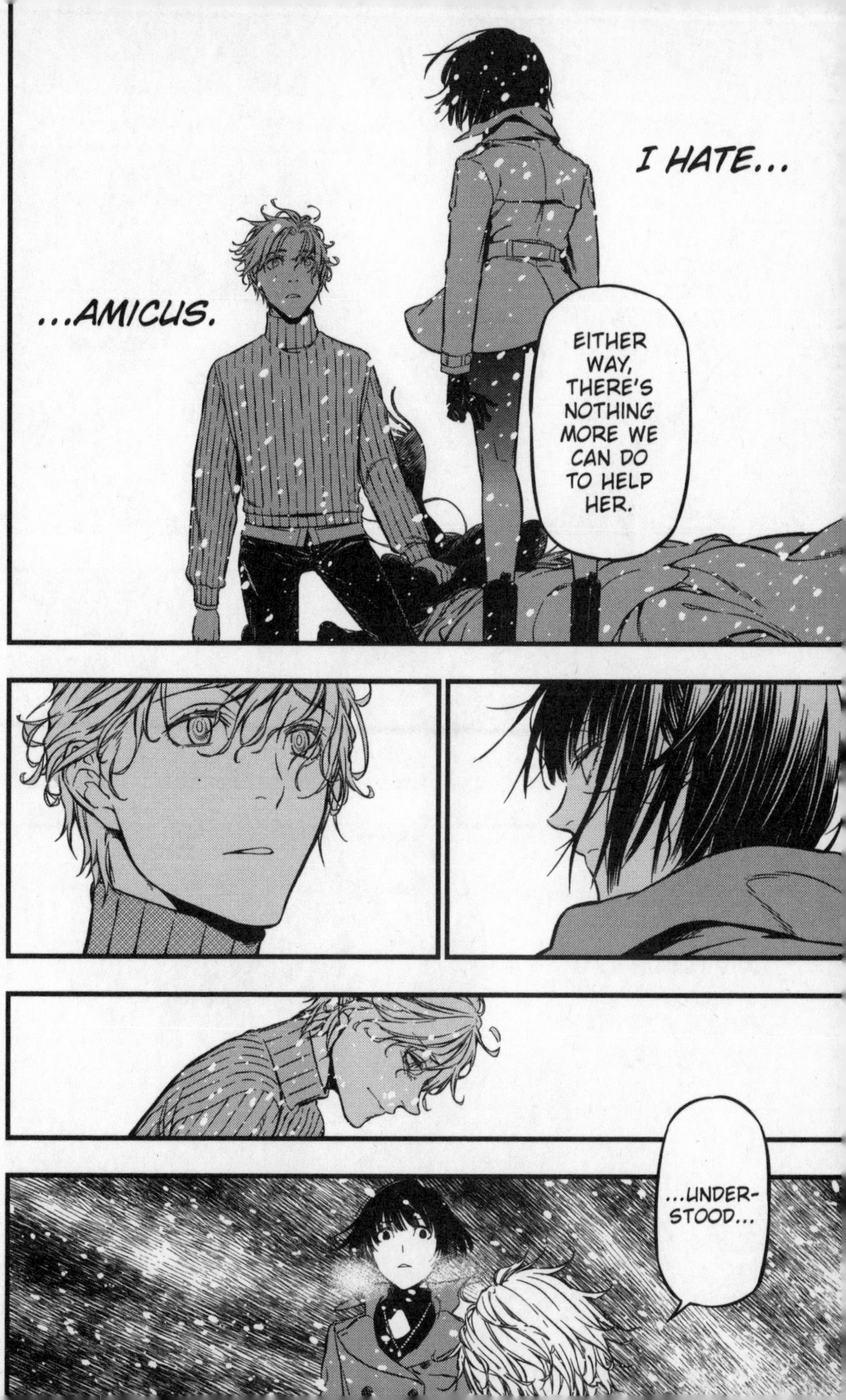
I HATE...
EITHER WAY, THERE'S NOTHING MORE WE CAN DO TO HELP HER.
...AMICUS.
...UNDER-STOOD...

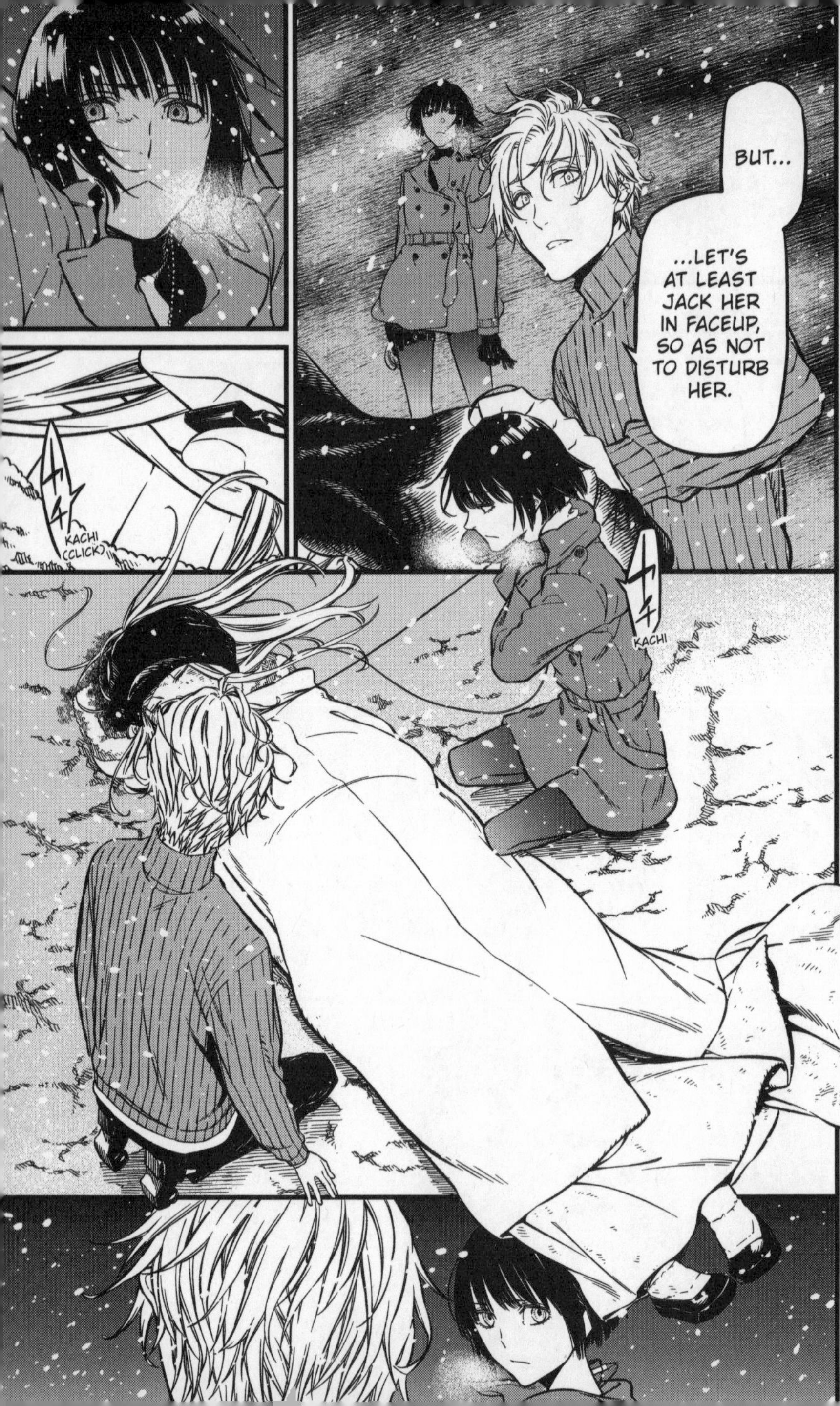
BUT...
...LET'S AT LEAST JACK HER IN FACEUP, SO AS NOT TO DISTURB HER.
KACHI (CLICK)
KACHI

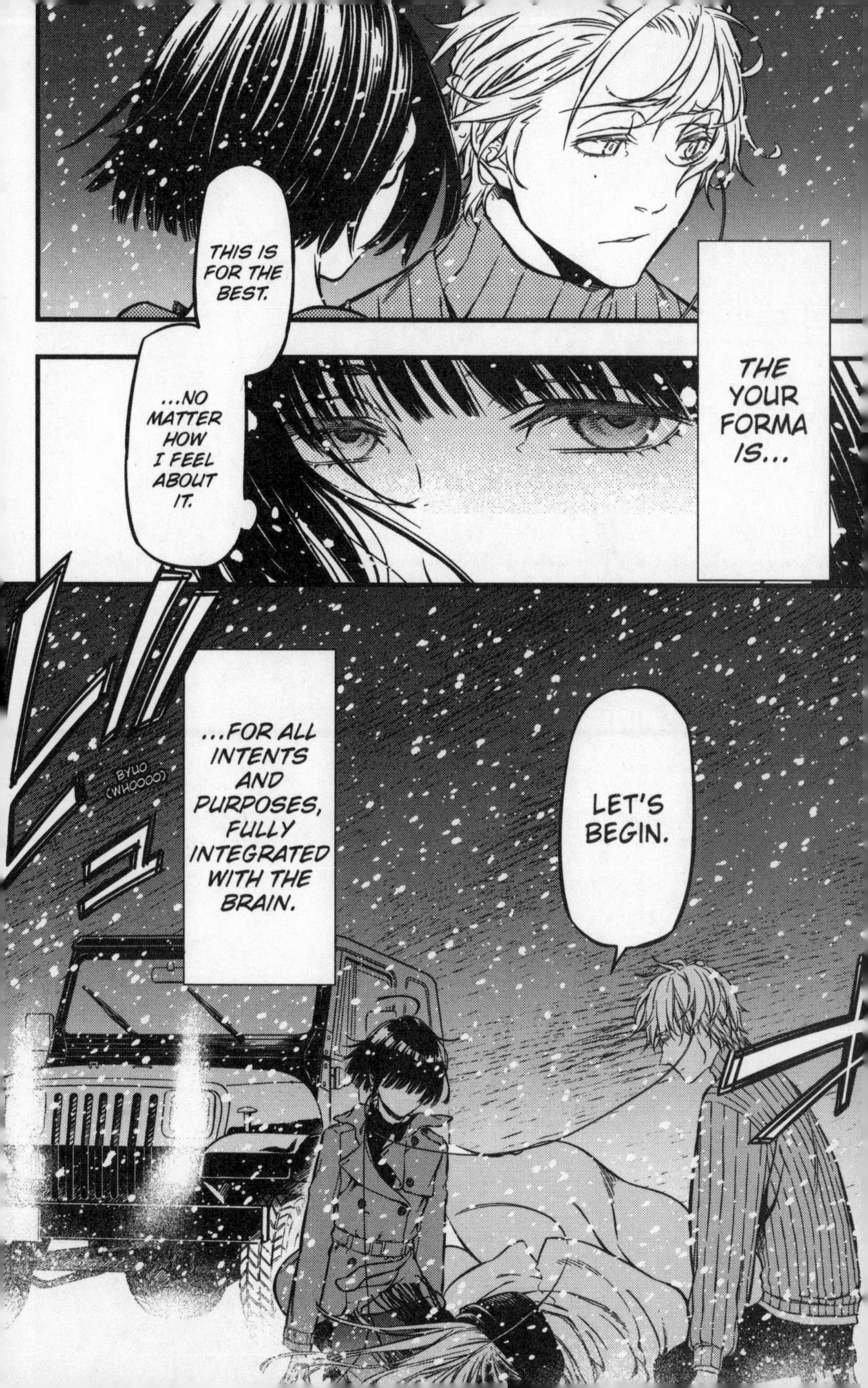
THIS IS FOR THE BEST.
...NO MATTER HOW I FEEL ABOUT IT.
THE YOUR FORMA IS...
...FOR ALL INTENTS AND PURPOSES, FULLY INTEGRATED WITH THE BRAIN.
BYUO (WHOOOO)
LET'S BEGIN.

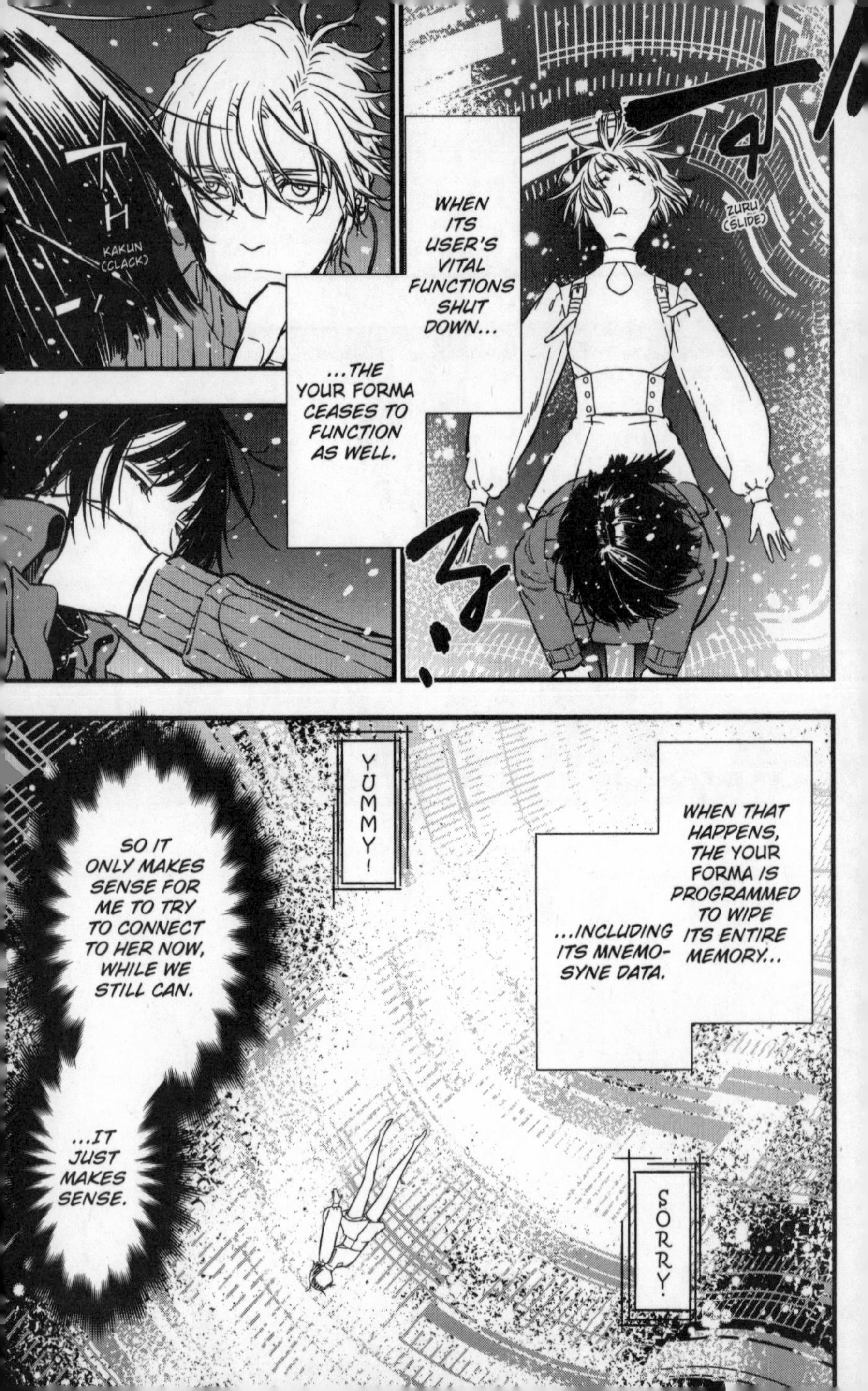
ZURU (SLIDE)
WHEN ITS USER'S VITAL FUNCTIONS SHUT DOWN...
...THE YOUR FORMA CEASES TO FUNCTION AS WELL.
KAKUN (CLACK)
WHEN THAT HAPPENS, THE YOUR FORMA IS PROGRAMMED TO WIPE ITS ENTIRE MEMORY...
...INCLUDING ITS MNEMO-SYNE DATA.
YUMMY!
SO IT ONLY MAKES SENSE FOR ME TO TRY TO CONNECT TO HER NOW, WHILE WE STILL CAN.
SORRY.
...IT JUST MAKES SENSE.

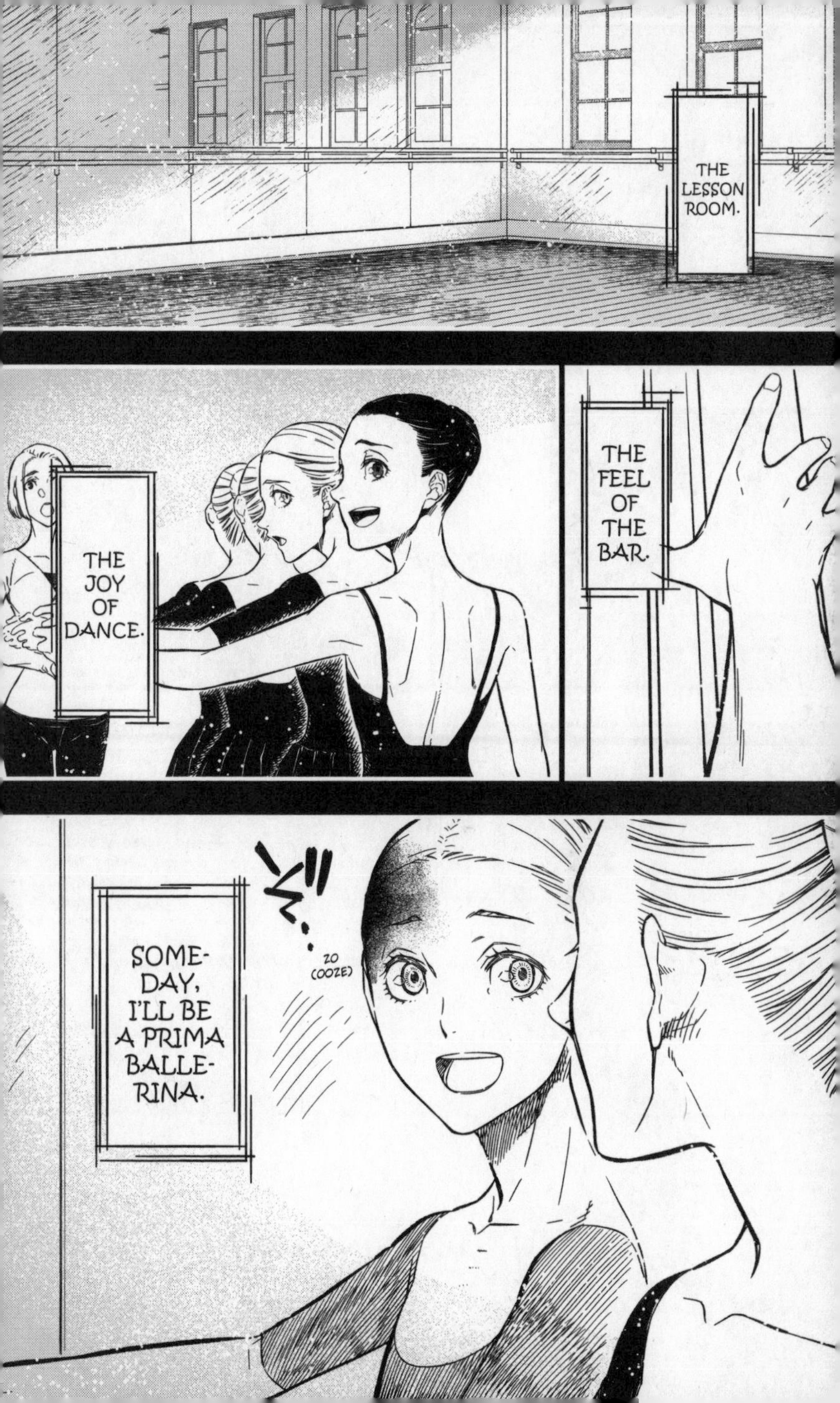
THE LESSON ROOM.
THE FEEL OF THE BAR.
THE JOY OF DANCE.
SOME-DAY, I'LL BE A PRIMA BALLE-RINA.
ZO (OOZE)

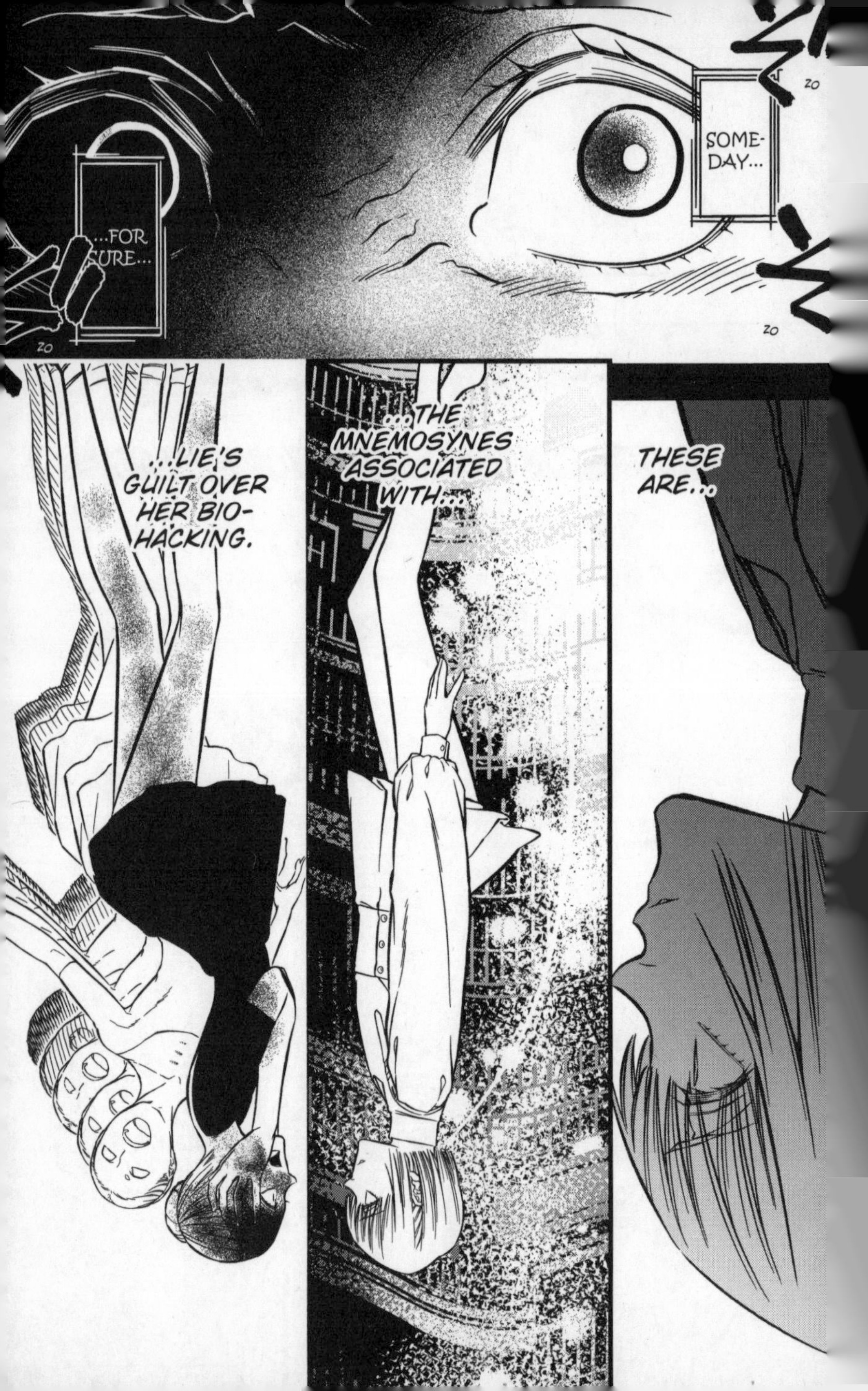
SOME-DAY...
...FOR SURE...
THESE ARE...
...THE MNEMOSYNES ASSOCIATED WITH...
...LIE'S GUILT OVER HER BIO-HACKING.

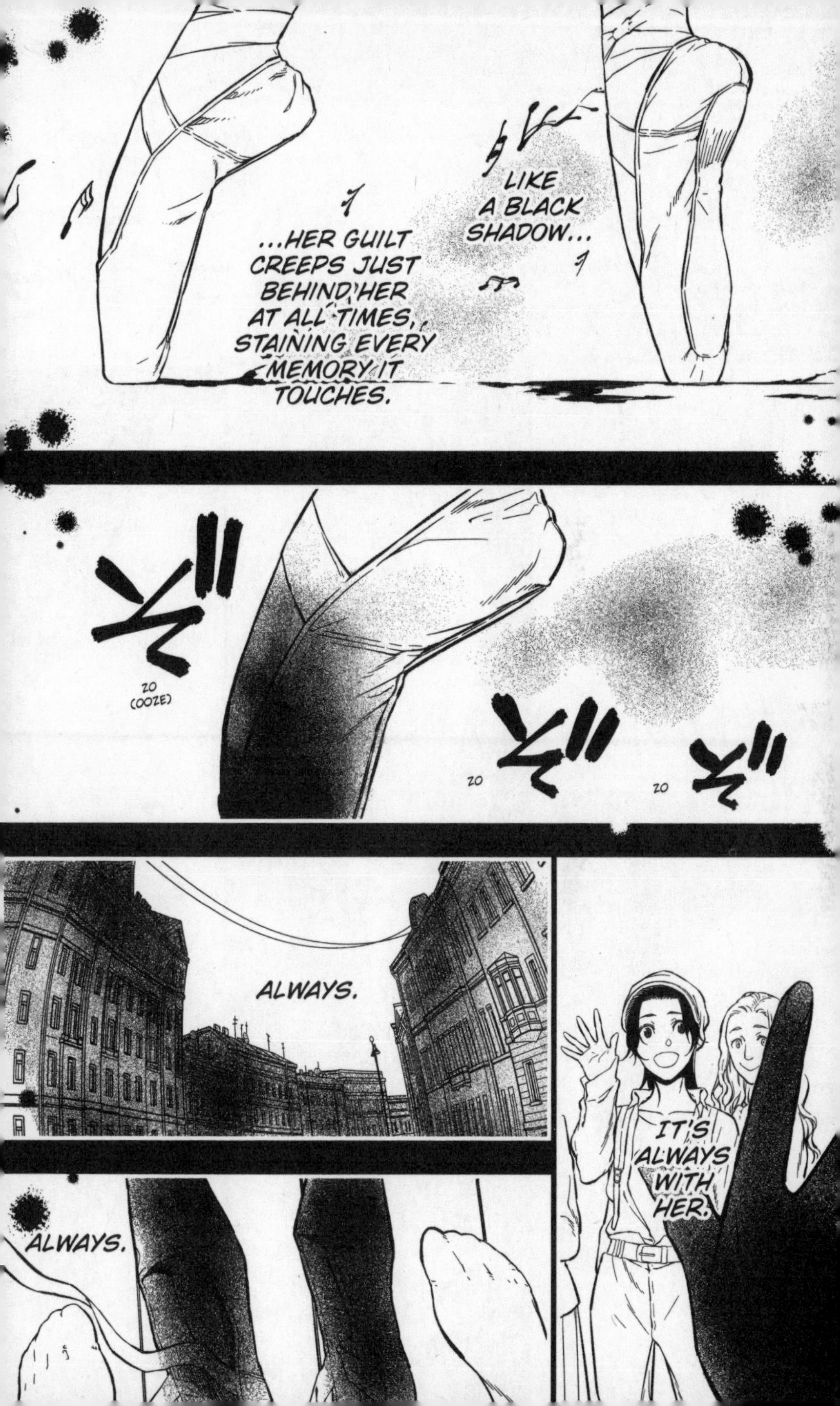
LIKE A BLACK SHADOW...
...HER GUILT CREEPS JUST BEHIND HER AT ALL TIMES, STAINING EVERY MEMORY IT TOUCHES.
ZO
ZO
ZO (OOZE)
IT'S ALWAYS WITH HER.
ALWAYS.
ALWAYS.

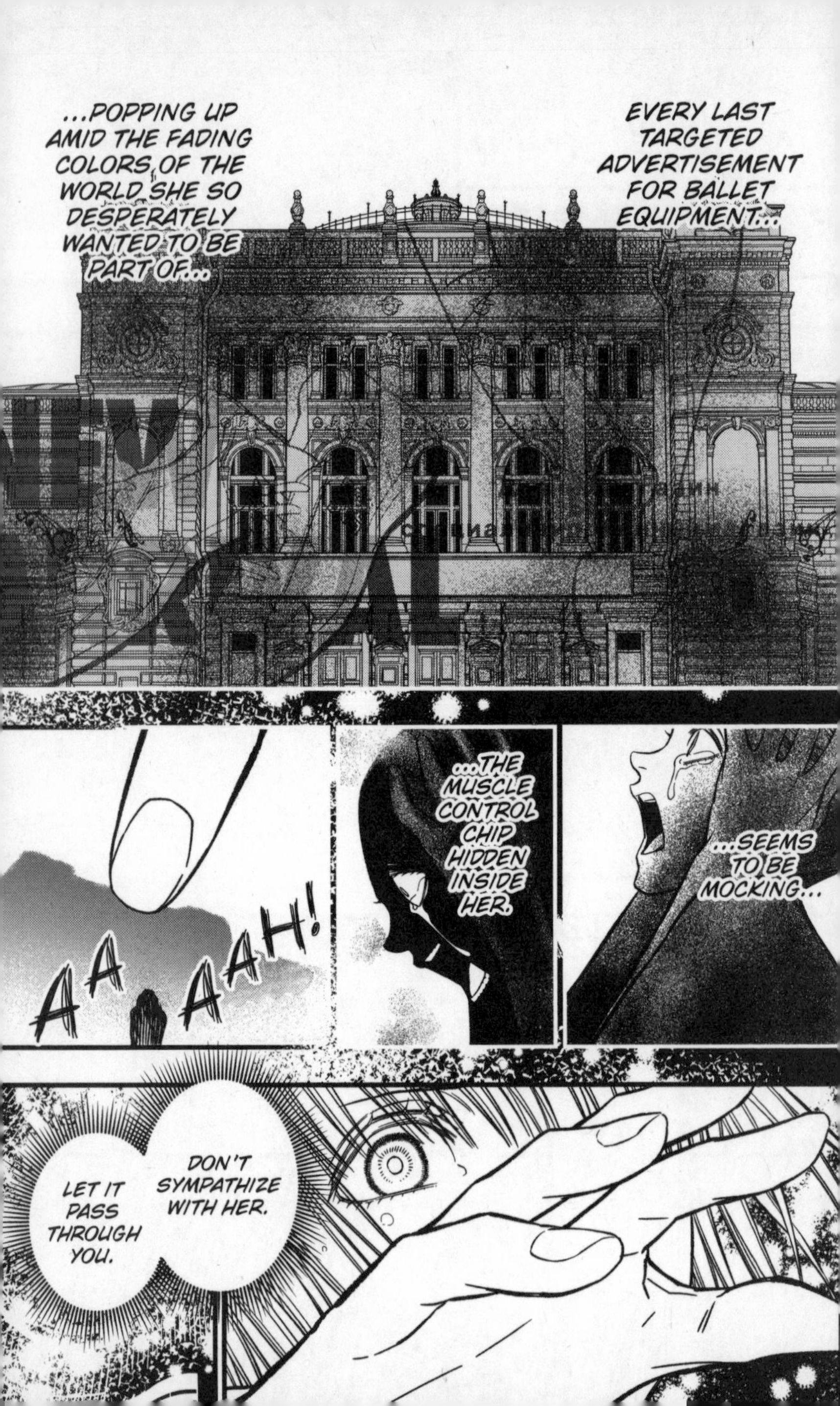
EVERY LAST TARGETED ADVERTISEMENT FOR BALLET EQUIPMENT...
...POPPING UP AMID THE FADING COLORS OF THE WORLD SHE SO DESPERATELY WANTED TO BE PART OF...
...SEEMS TO BE MOCKING...
...THE MUSCLE CONTROL CHIP HIDDEN INSIDE HER.
AAAAAH!
DON'T SYMPATHIZE WITH HER.
LET IT PASS THROUGH YOU.

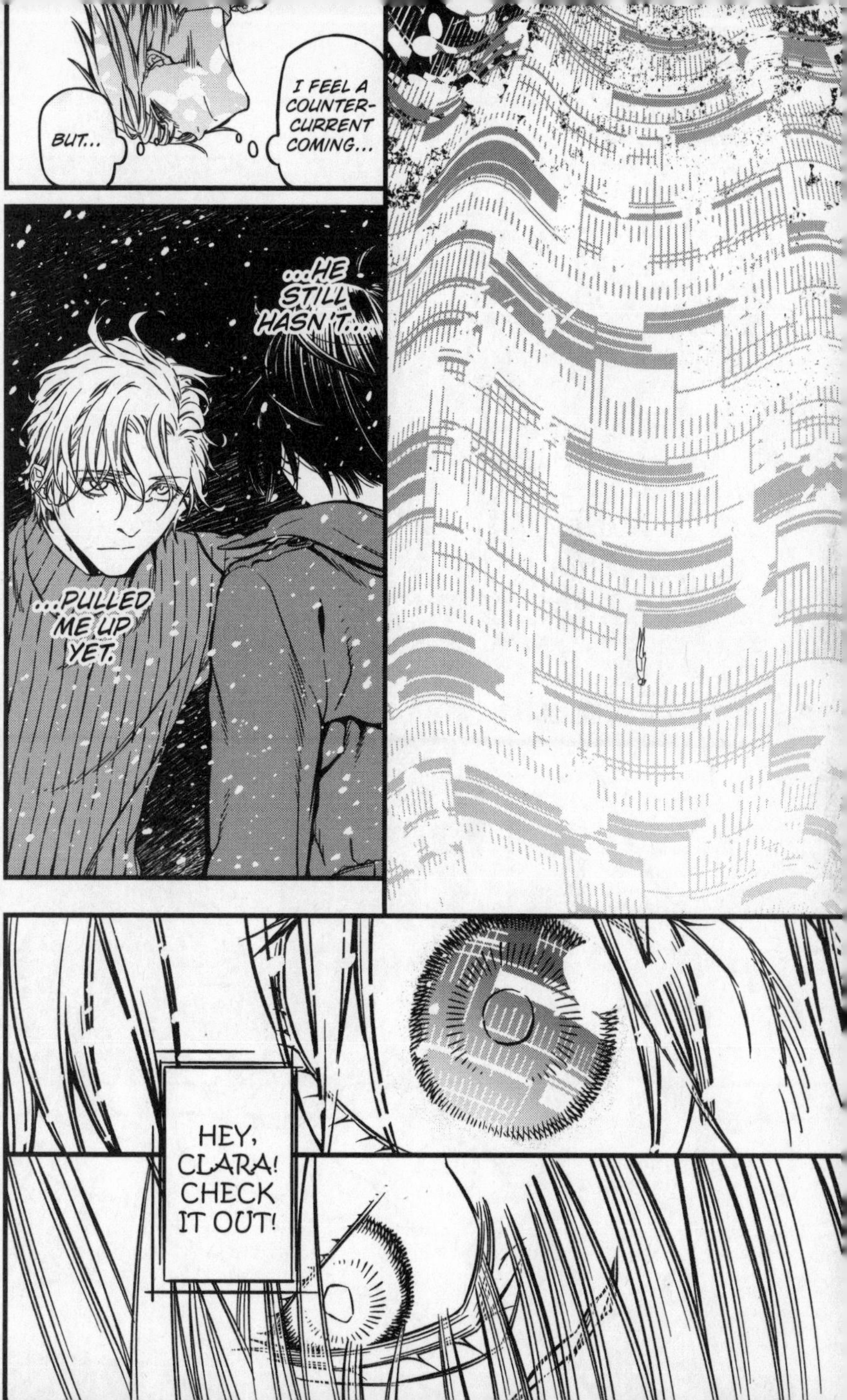
I FEEL A COUNTER-CURRENT COMING...
BUT...
...HE STILL HASN'T...
...PULLED ME UP YET.
HEY, CLARA! CHECK IT OUT!

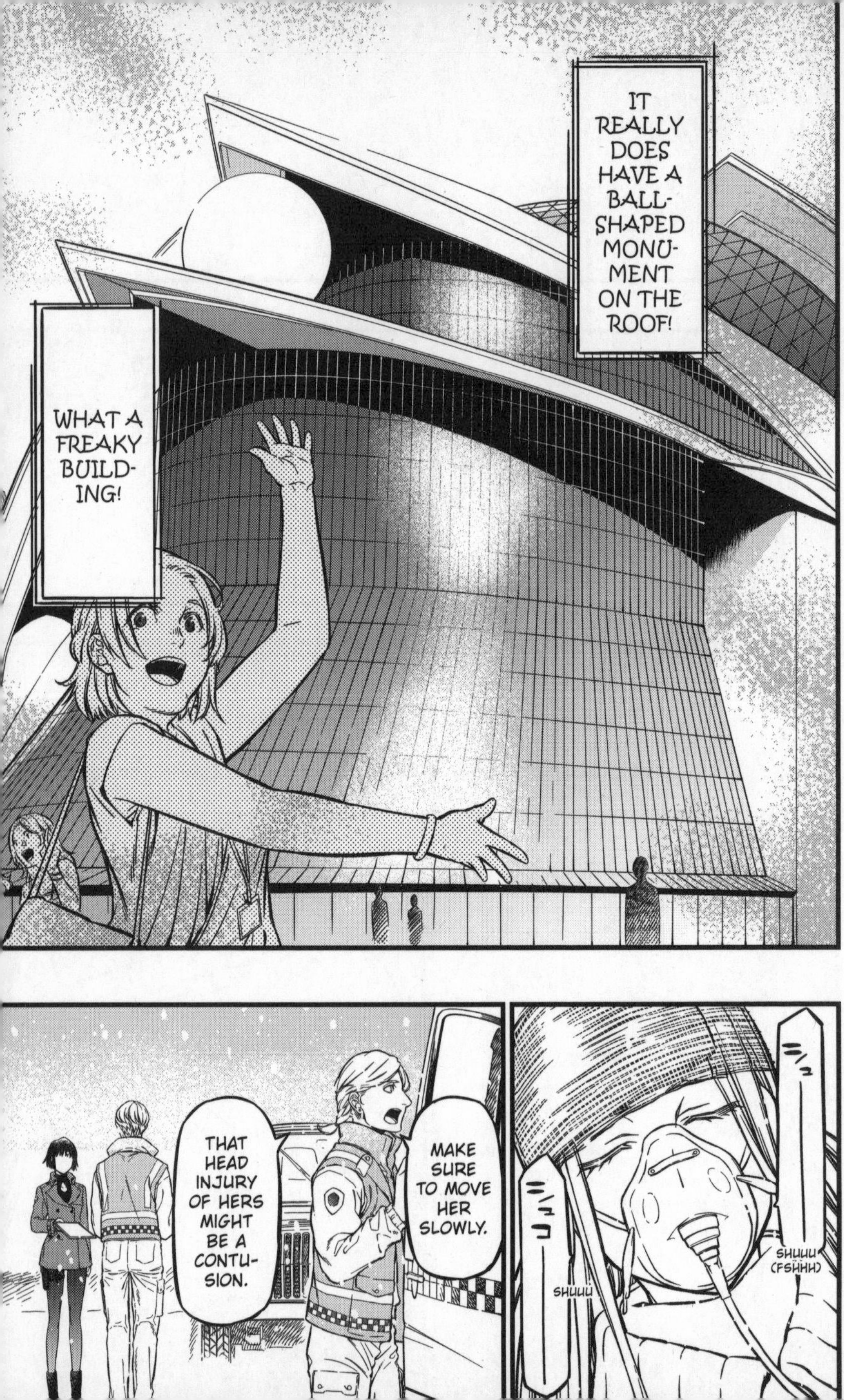
IT REALLY DOES HAVE A BALL-SHAPED MONUMENT ON THE ROOF!
WHAT A FREAKY BUILDING!
SHUUU (FSHHH)
SHUUU
MAKE SURE TO MOVE HER SLOWLY.
THAT HEAD INJURY OF HERS MIGHT BE A CONTUSION.

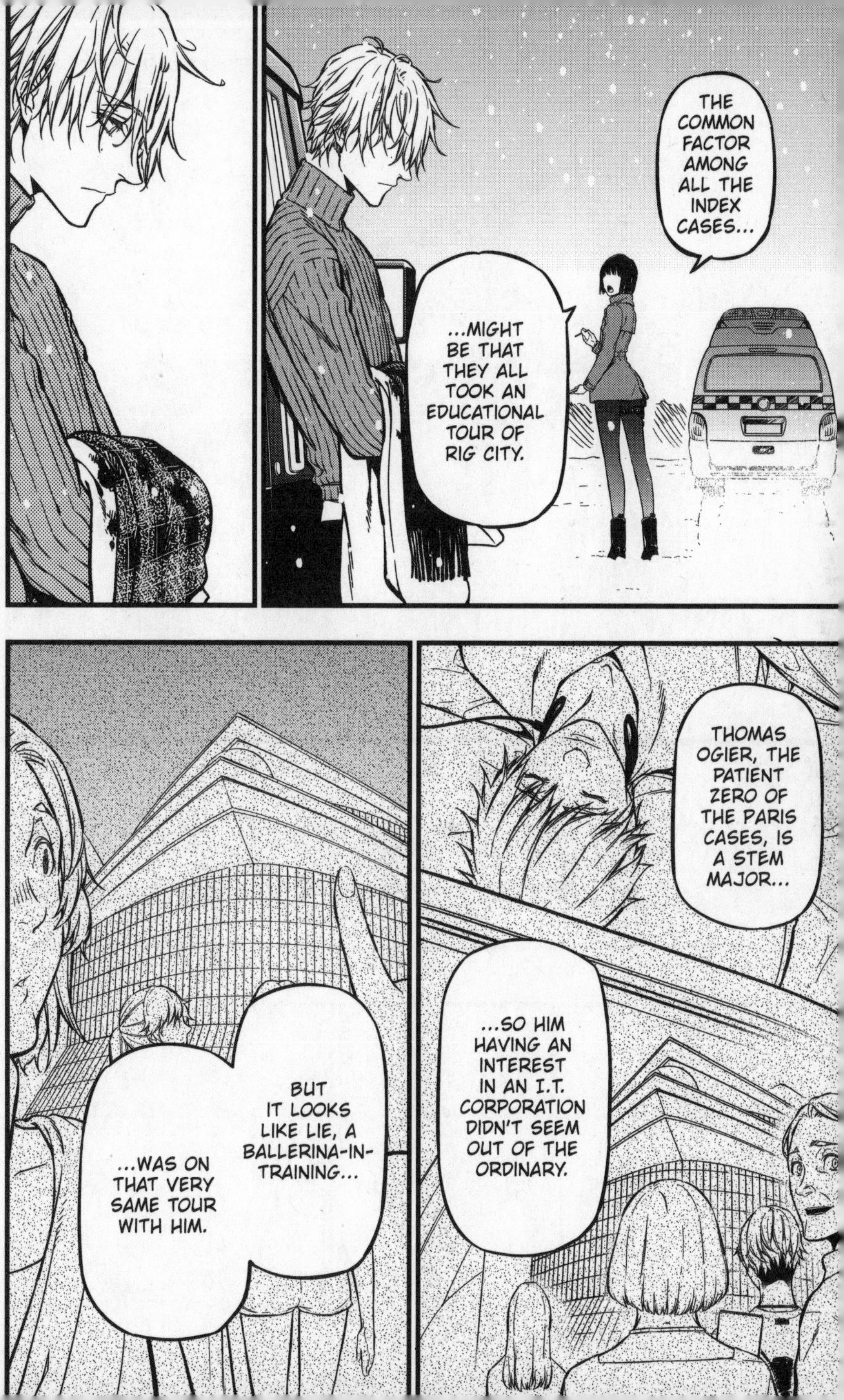
THE COMMON FACTOR AMONG ALL THE INDEX CASES...
...MIGHT BE THAT THEY ALL TOOK AN EDUCATIONAL TOUR OF RIG CITY.
THOMAS OGIER, THE PATIENT ZERO OF THE PARIS CASES, IS A STEM MAJOR...
...SO HIM HAVING AN INTEREST IN AN I.T. CORPORATION DIDN'T SEEM OUT OF THE ORDINARY.
BUT IT LOOKS LIKE LIE, A BALLERINA-IN-TRAINING...
...WAS ON THAT VERY SAME TOUR WITH HIM.

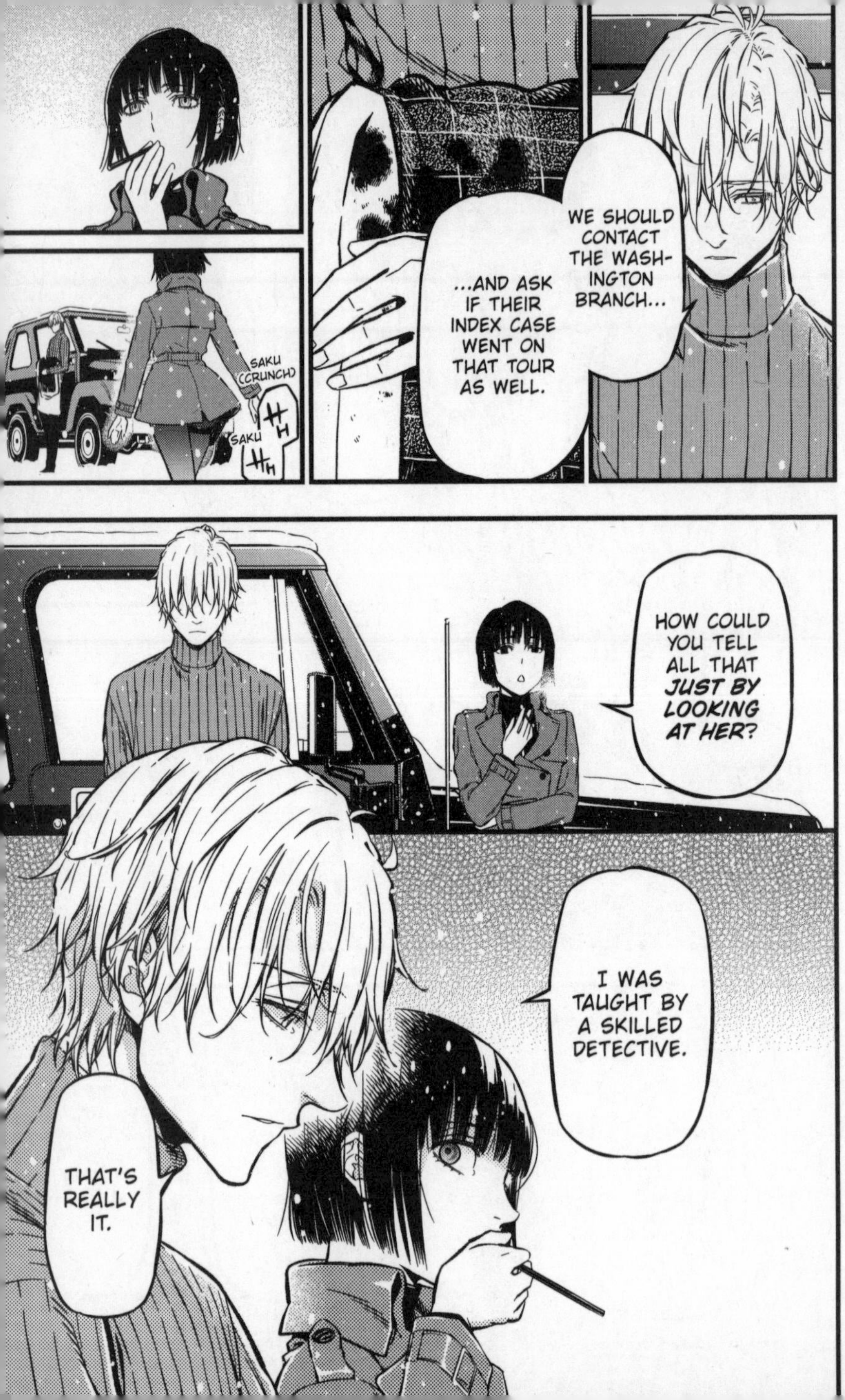
WE SHOULD CONTACT THE WASH-INGTON BRANCH...
...AND ASK IF THEIR INDEX CASE WENT ON THAT TOUR AS WELL.
SAKU (CRUNCH)
SAKU
HOW COULD YOU TELL ALL THAT *JUST BY LOOKING AT HER?*
I WAS TAUGHT BY A SKILLED DETECTIVE.
THAT'S REALLY IT.

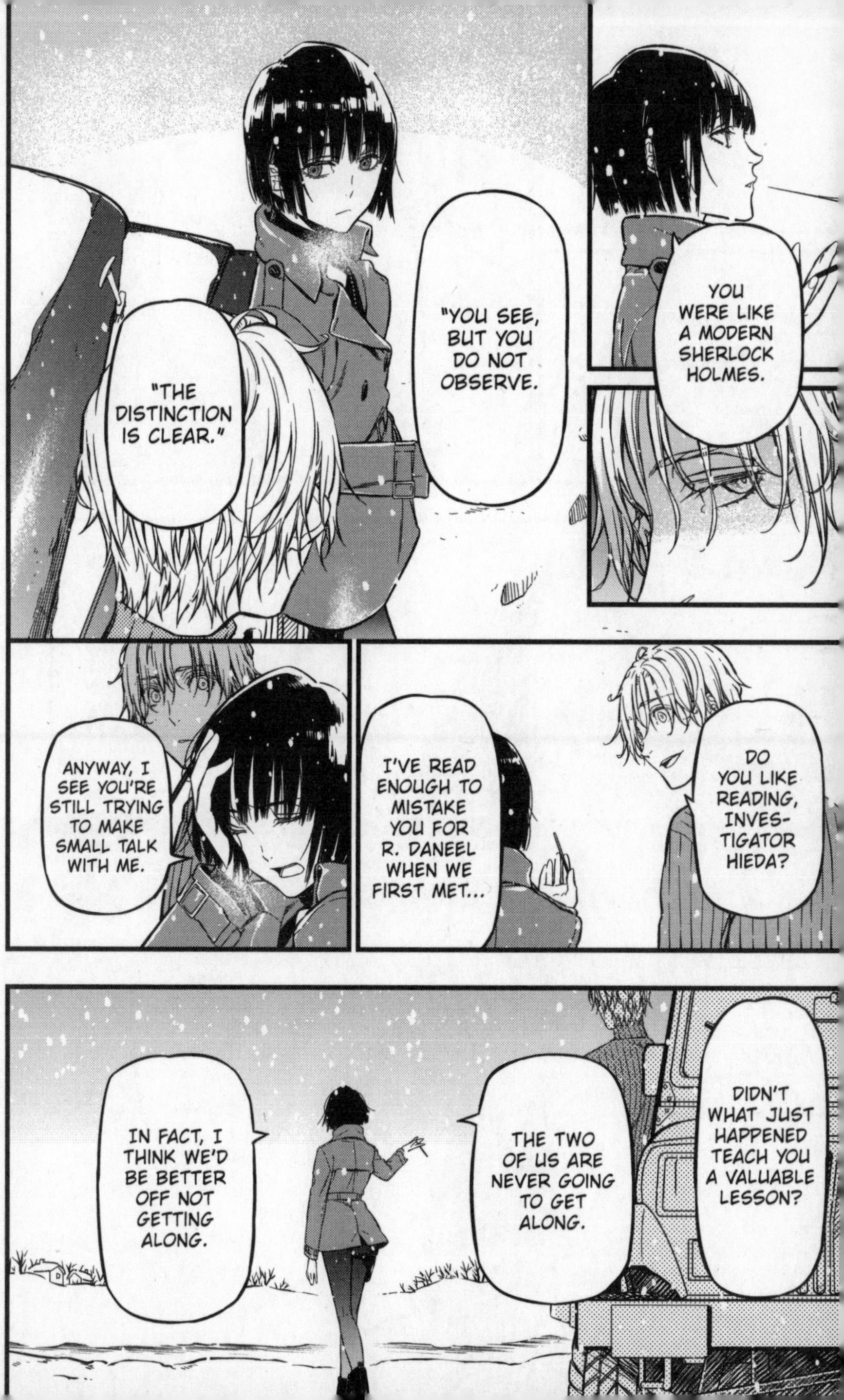
YOU WERE LIKE A MODERN SHERLOCK HOLMES.
"YOU SEE, BUT YOU DO NOT OBSERVE.
"THE DISTINCTION IS CLEAR."
DO YOU LIKE READING, INVES-TIGATOR HIEDA?
I'VE READ ENOUGH TO MISTAKE YOU FOR R. DANEEL WHEN WE FIRST MET...
ANYWAY, I SEE YOU'RE STILL TRYING TO MAKE SMALL TALK WITH ME.
DIDN'T WHAT JUST HAPPENED TEACH YOU A VALUABLE LESSON?
THE TWO OF US ARE NEVER GOING TO GET ALONG.
IN FACT, I THINK WE'D BE BETTER OFF NOT GETTING ALONG.

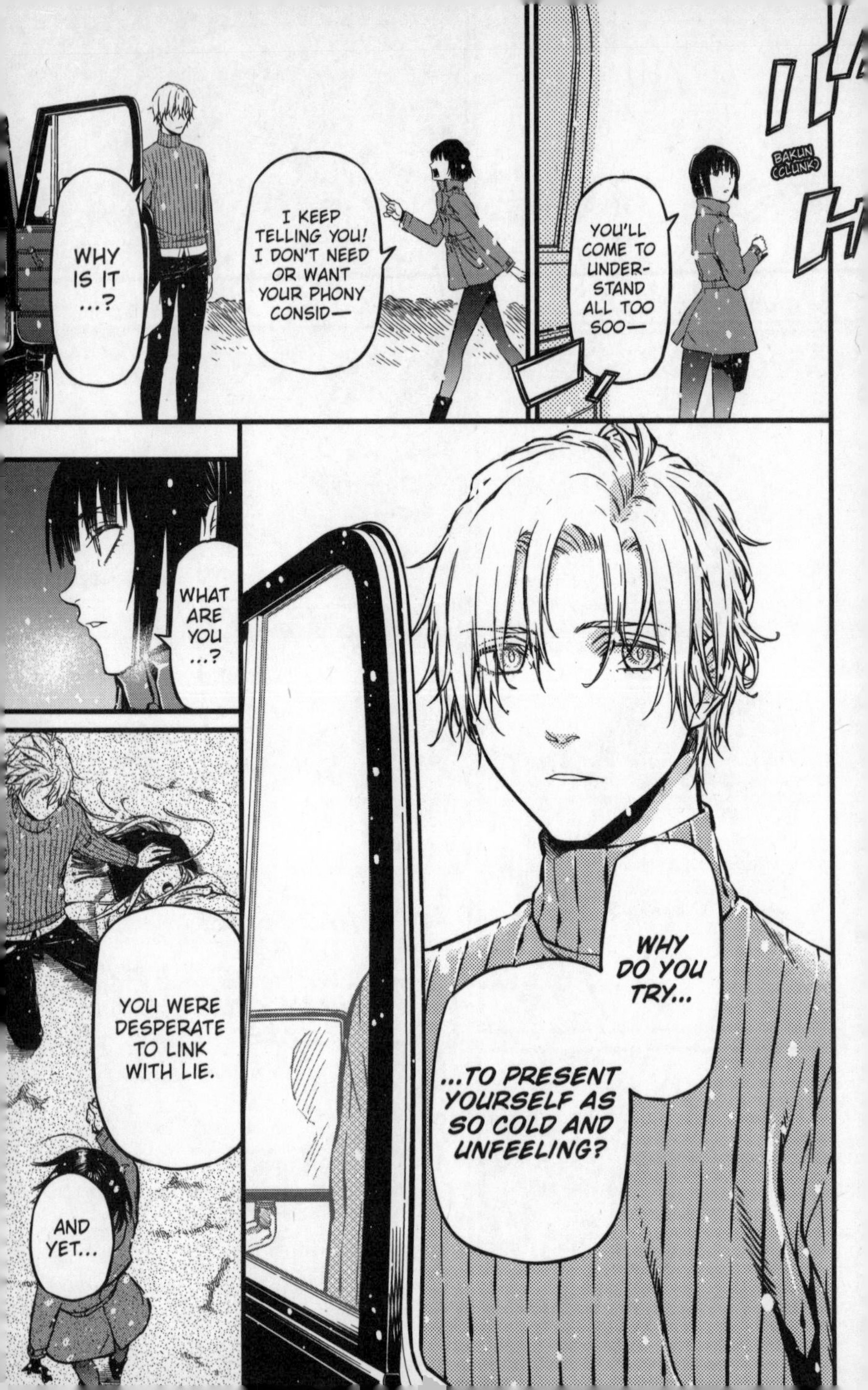
BAKUN (CLUNK)
YOU'LL COME TO UNDERSTAND ALL TOO SOO—
I KEEP TELLING YOU! I DON'T NEED OR WANT YOUR PHONY CONSID—
WHY IS IT ...?
WHY DO YOU TRY...
...TO PRESENT YOURSELF AS SO COLD AND UNFEELING?
WHAT ARE YOU ...?
YOU WERE DESPERATE TO LINK WITH LIE.
AND YET...

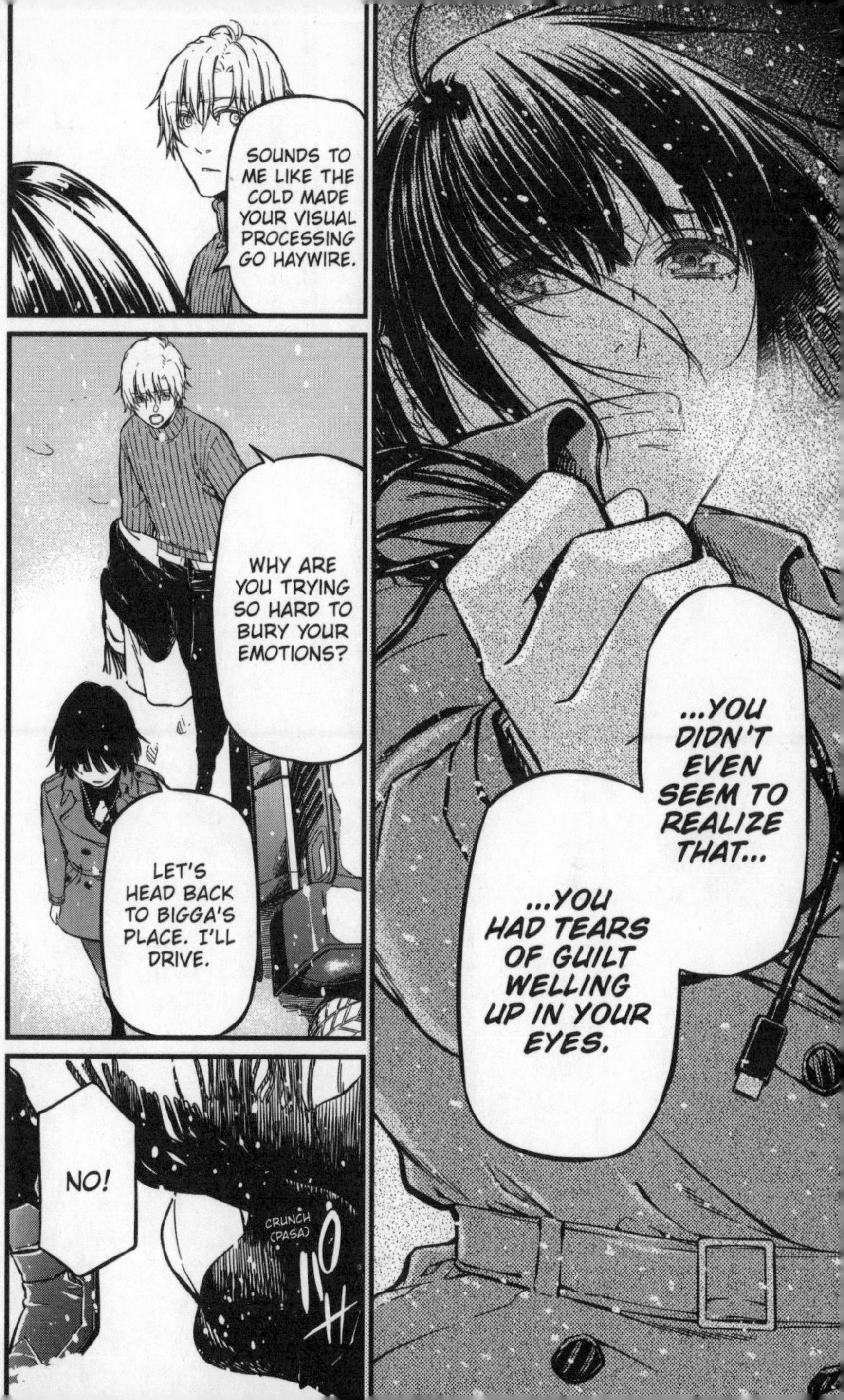
...YOU DIDN'T EVEN SEEM TO REALIZE THAT...
...YOU HAD TEARS OF GUILT WELLING UP IN YOUR EYES.
SOUNDS TO ME LIKE THE COLD MADE YOUR VISUAL PROCESSING GO HAYWIRE.
WHY ARE YOU TRYING SO HARD TO BURY YOUR EMOTIONS?
LET'S HEAD BACK TO BIGGA'S PLACE. I'LL DRIVE.
NO!
CRUNCH (PASA)

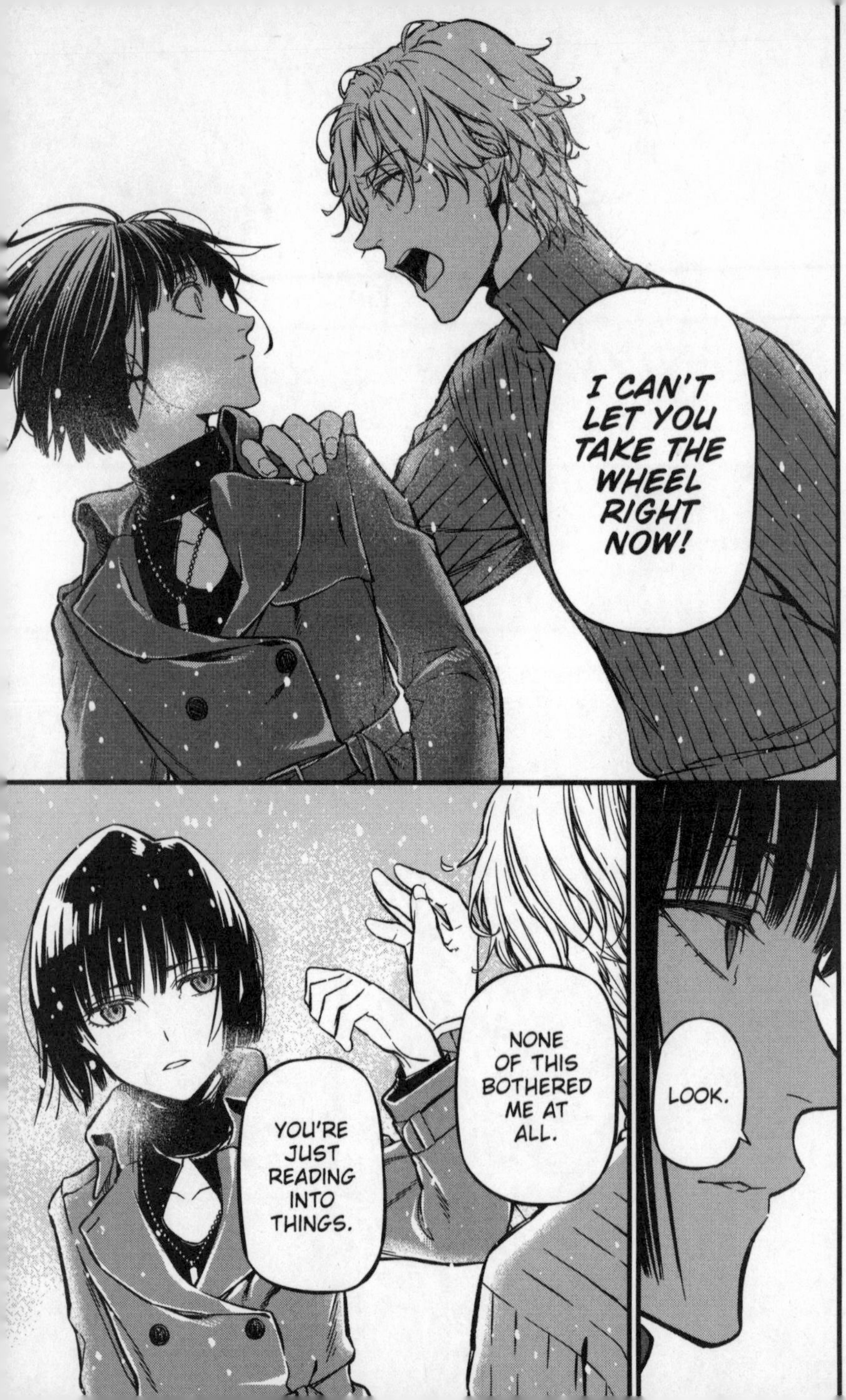
I CAN'T LET YOU TAKE THE WHEEL RIGHT NOW!
LOOK.
NONE OF THIS BOTHERED ME AT ALL.
YOU'RE JUST READING INTO THINGS.

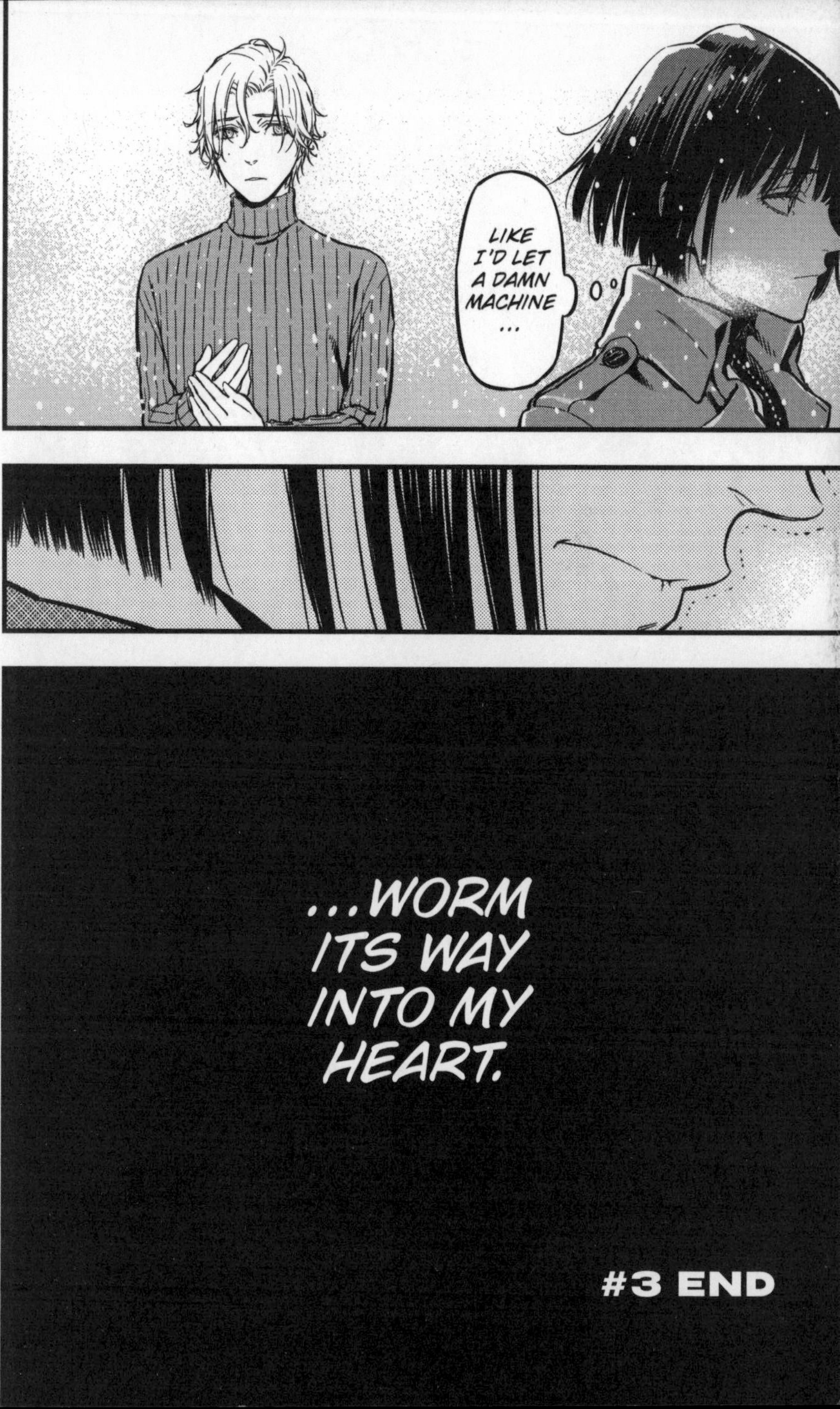
LIKE I'D LET A DAMN MACHINE ...
...WORM ITS WAY INTO MY HEART.
#3 END

YOUR FORMA

YOUR FORMA

"Forgetting" is a thing of the past.

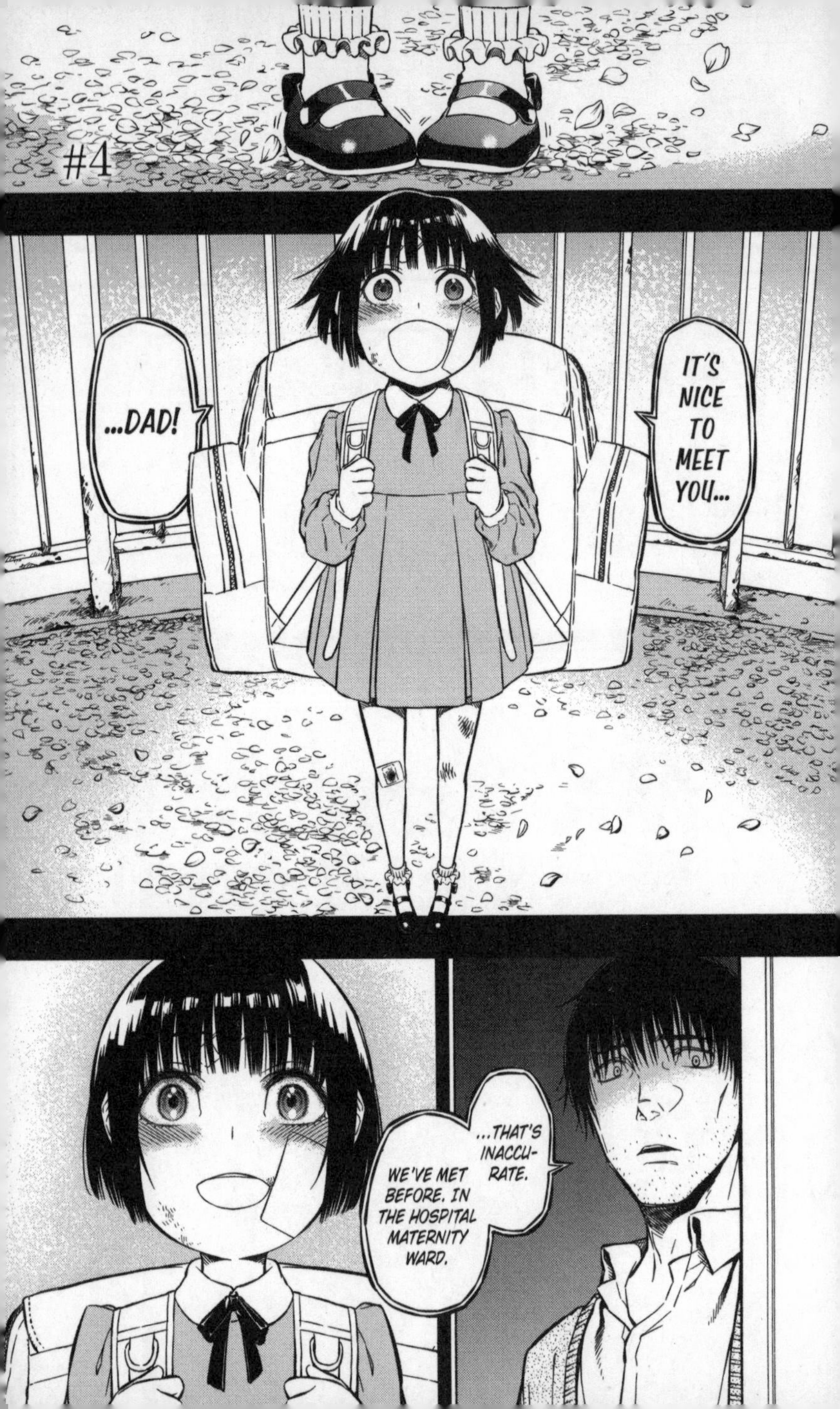
#4
IT'S NICE TO MEET YOU...
...DAD!
...THAT'S INACCU-RATE.
WE'VE MET BEFORE. IN THE HOSPITAL MATERNITY WARD.

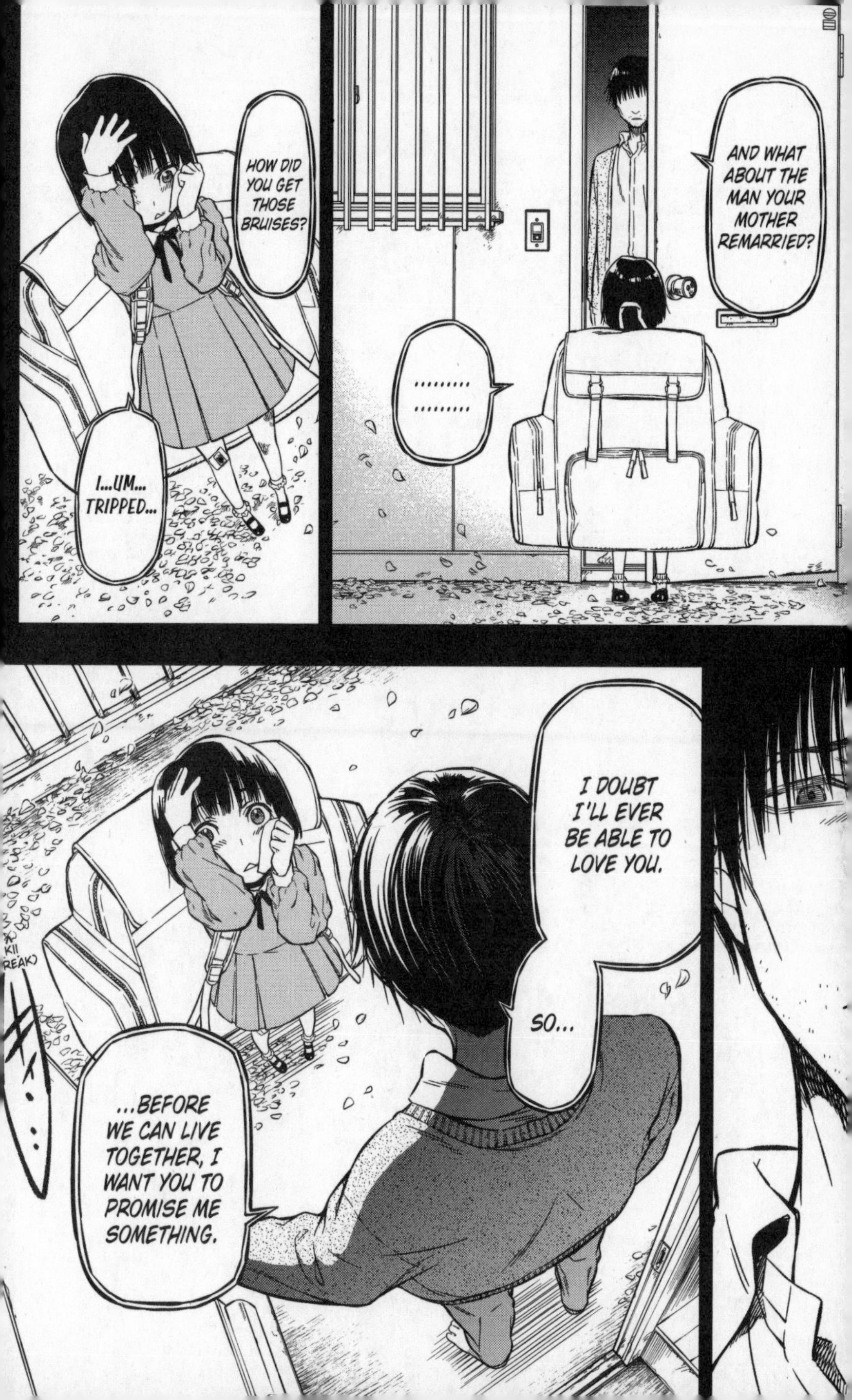
AND WHAT ABOUT THE MAN YOUR MOTHER REMARRIED?
....
HOW DID YOU GET THOSE BRUISES?
I...UM... TRIPPED...
I DOUBT I'LL EVER BE ABLE TO LOVE YOU.
SO...
...BEFORE WE CAN LIVE TOGETHER, I WANT YOU TO PROMISE ME SOMETHING.

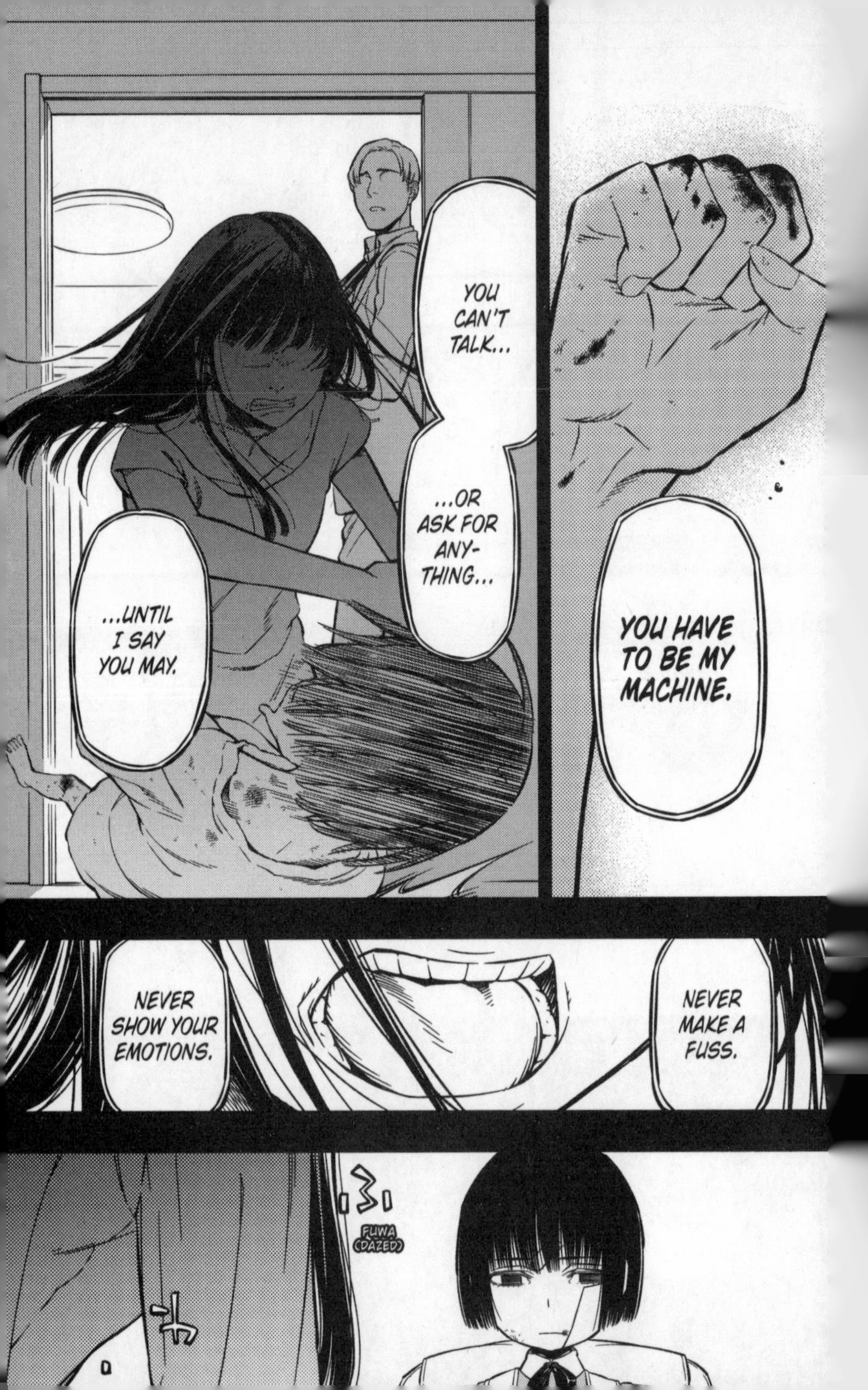
YOU HAVE TO BE MY MACHINE.
YOU CAN'T TALK...
...OR ASK FOR ANY-THING...
...UNTIL I SAY YOU MAY.
NEVER MAKE A FUSS.
NEVER SHOW YOUR EMOTIONS.
FUWA (DAZED)

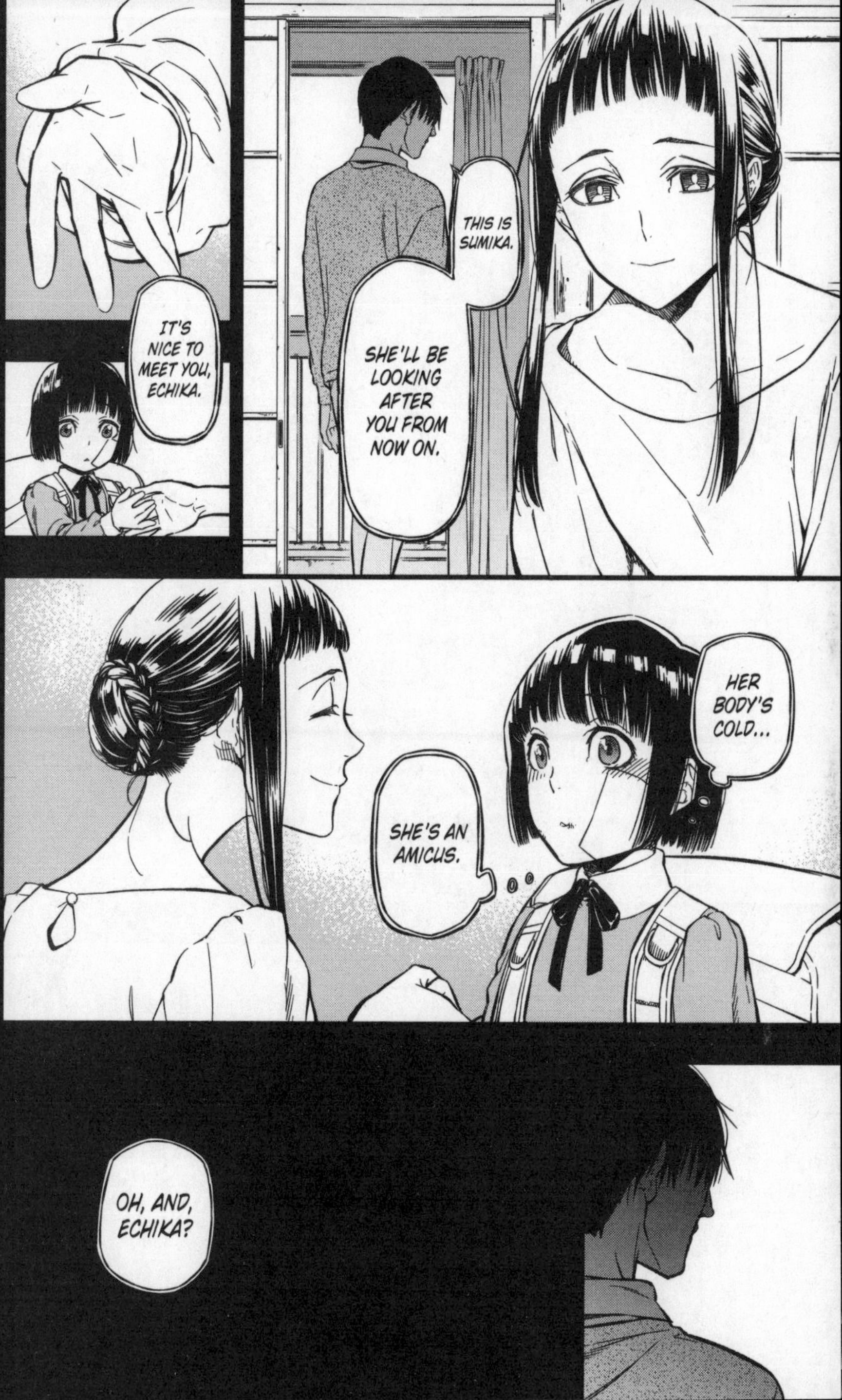
THIS IS SUMIKA.
SHE'LL BE LOOKING AFTER YOU FROM NOW ON.
IT'S NICE TO MEET YOU, ECHIKA.
HER BODY'S COLD...
SHE'S AN AMICUS.
OH, AND, ECHIKA?

#4 Shackle

YOUR FORMA

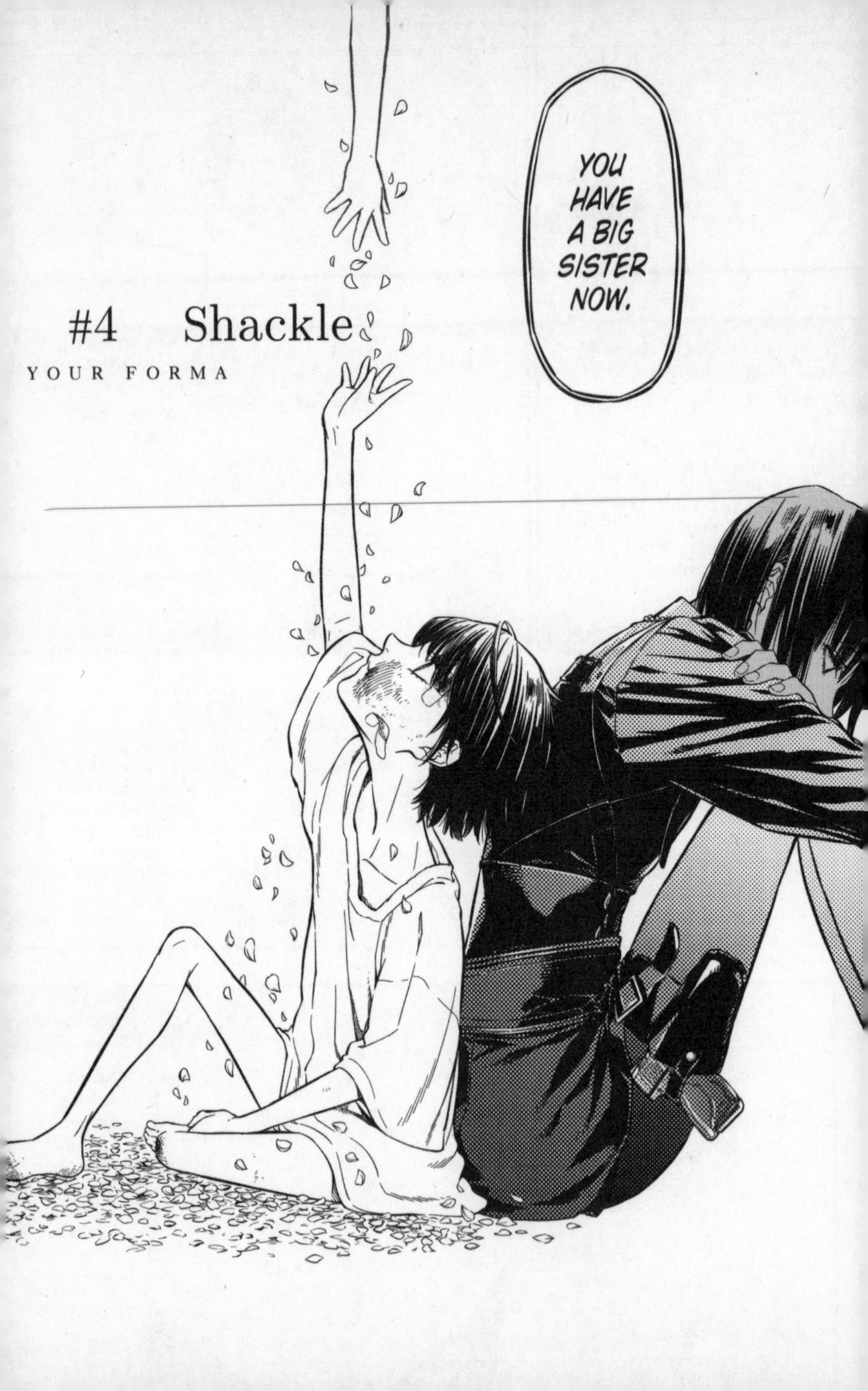
YOU HAVE A BIG SISTER NOW.

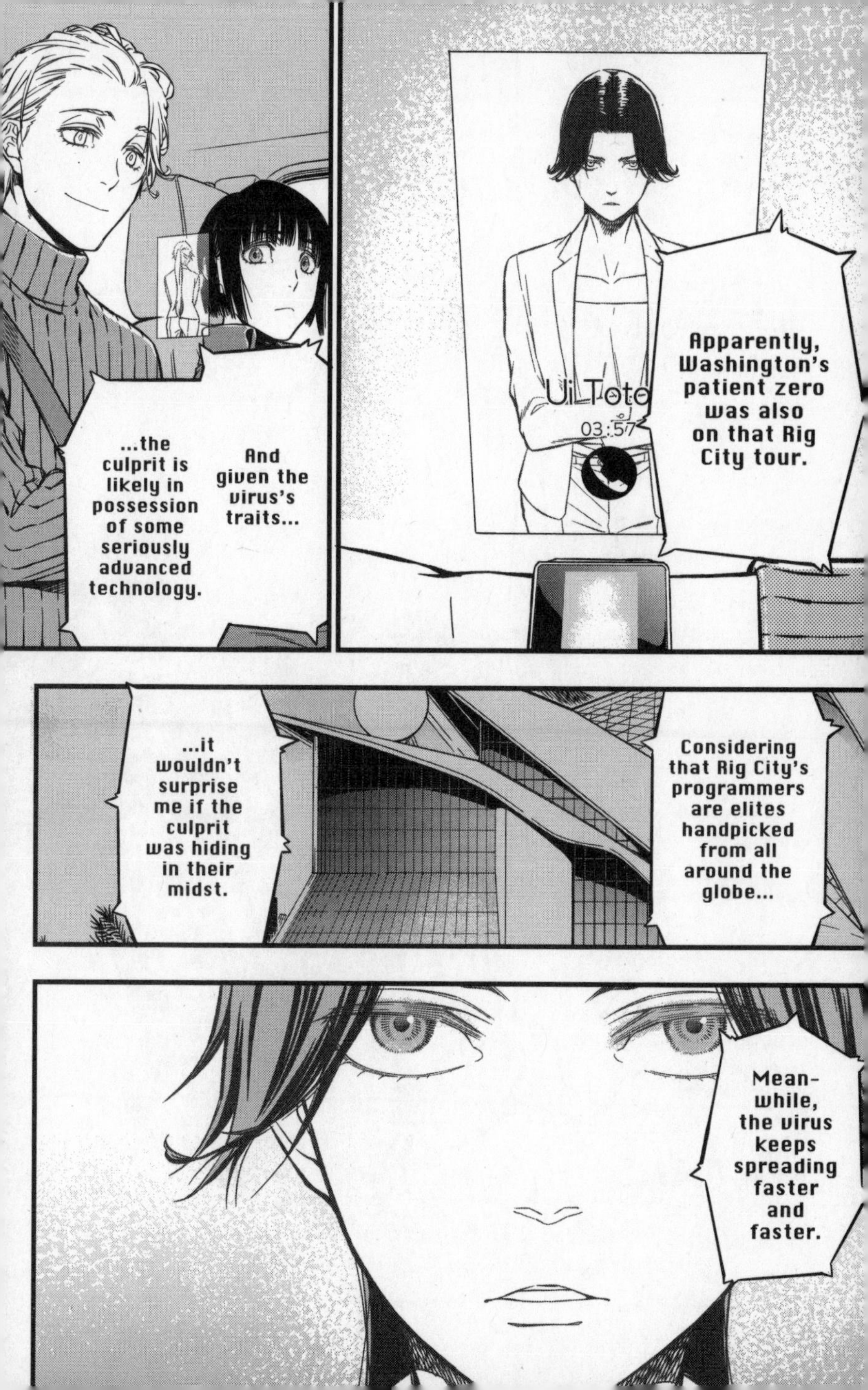
Ui Toto
03:57
Apparently, Washington's patient zero was also on that Rig City tour.
And given the virus's traits...
...the culprit is likely in possession of some seriously advanced technology.
Considering that Rig City's programmers are elites handpicked from all around the globe...
...it wouldn't surprise me if the culprit was hiding in their midst.
Mean-while, the virus keeps spreading faster and faster.

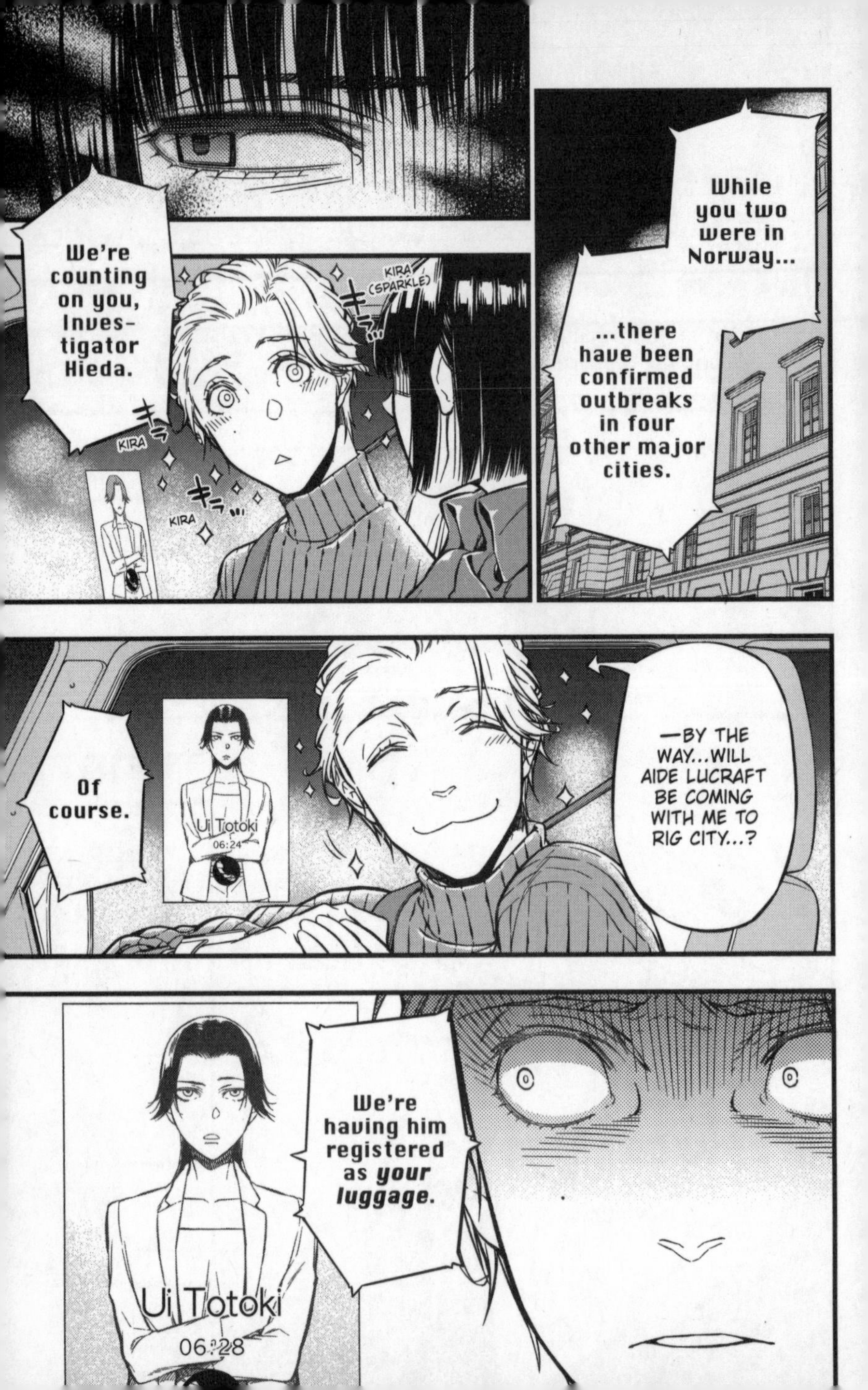
While you two were in Norway...
...there have been confirmed outbreaks in four other major cities.
KIRA (SPARKLE)
We're counting on you, Investigator Hieda.
KIRA
KIRA
—BY THE WAY...WILL AIDE LUCRAFT BE COMING WITH ME TO RIG CITY...?
Ui Totoki
06:24
Of course.
We're having him registered as ***your luggage***.
Ui Totoki
06:28

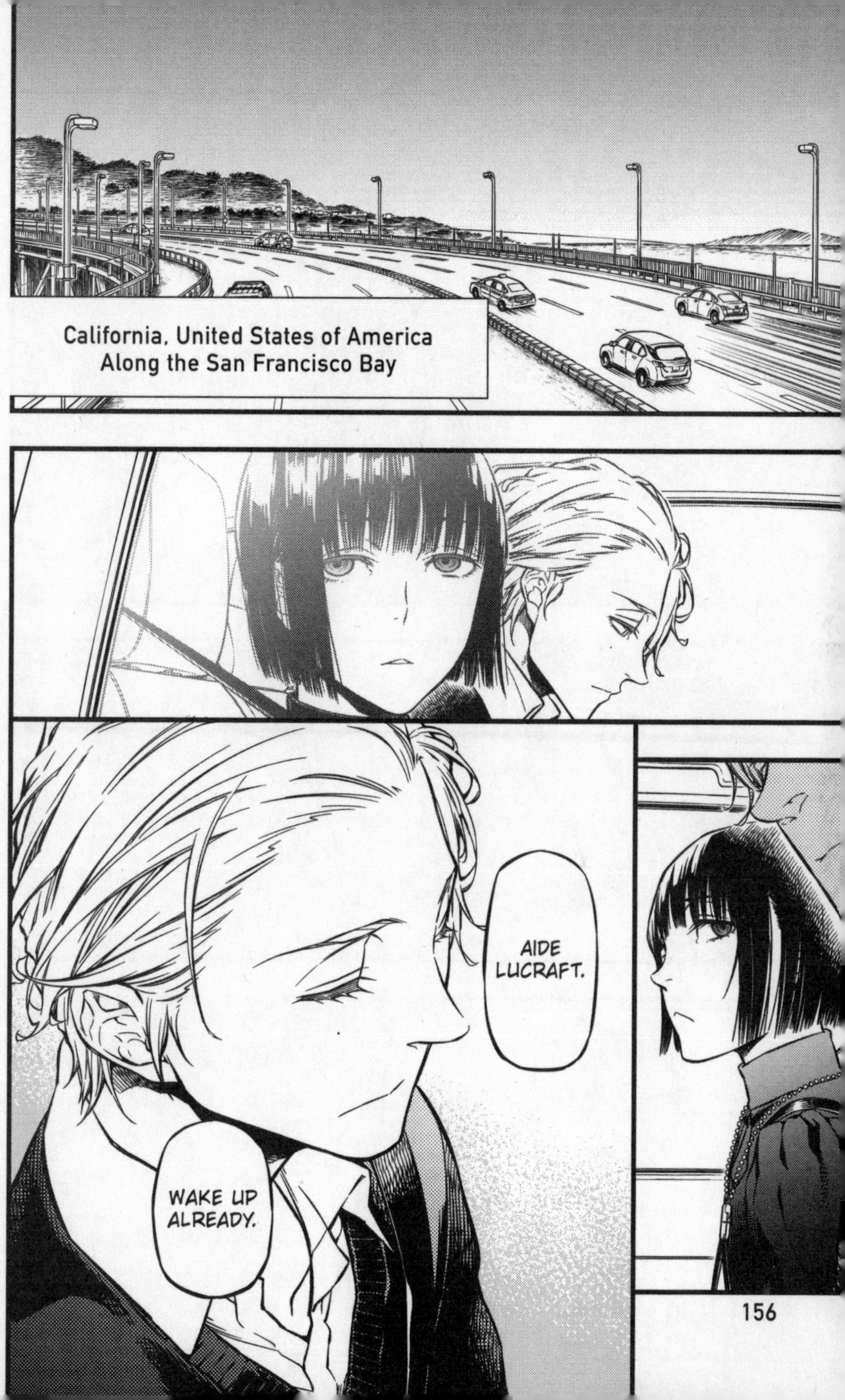
California, United States of America
Along the San Francisco Bay
AIDE LUCRAFT.
WAKE UP ALREADY.

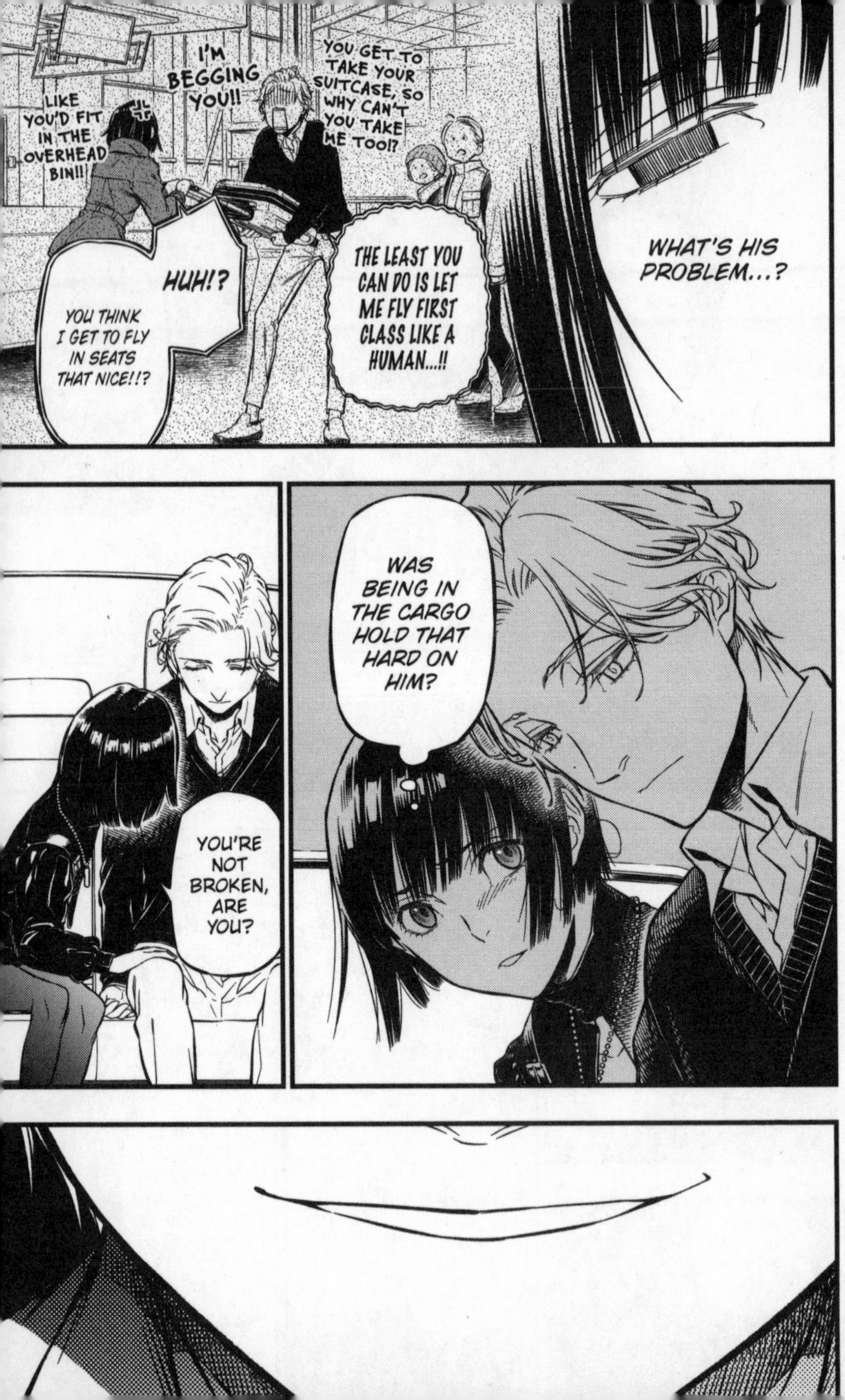
WHAT'S HIS PROBLEM...?
YOU GET TO TAKE YOUR SUITCASE, SO WHY CAN'T YOU TAKE ME TOO!?
I'M BEGGING YOU!!
LIKE YOU'D FIT IN THE OVERHEAD BIN!!
THE LEAST YOU CAN DO IS LET ME FLY FIRST CLASS LIKE A HUMAN...!!
HUH!?
YOU THINK I GET TO FLY IN SEATS THAT NICE!!?
WAS BEING IN THE CARGO HOLD THAT HARD ON HIM?
YOU'RE NOT BROKEN, ARE YOU?

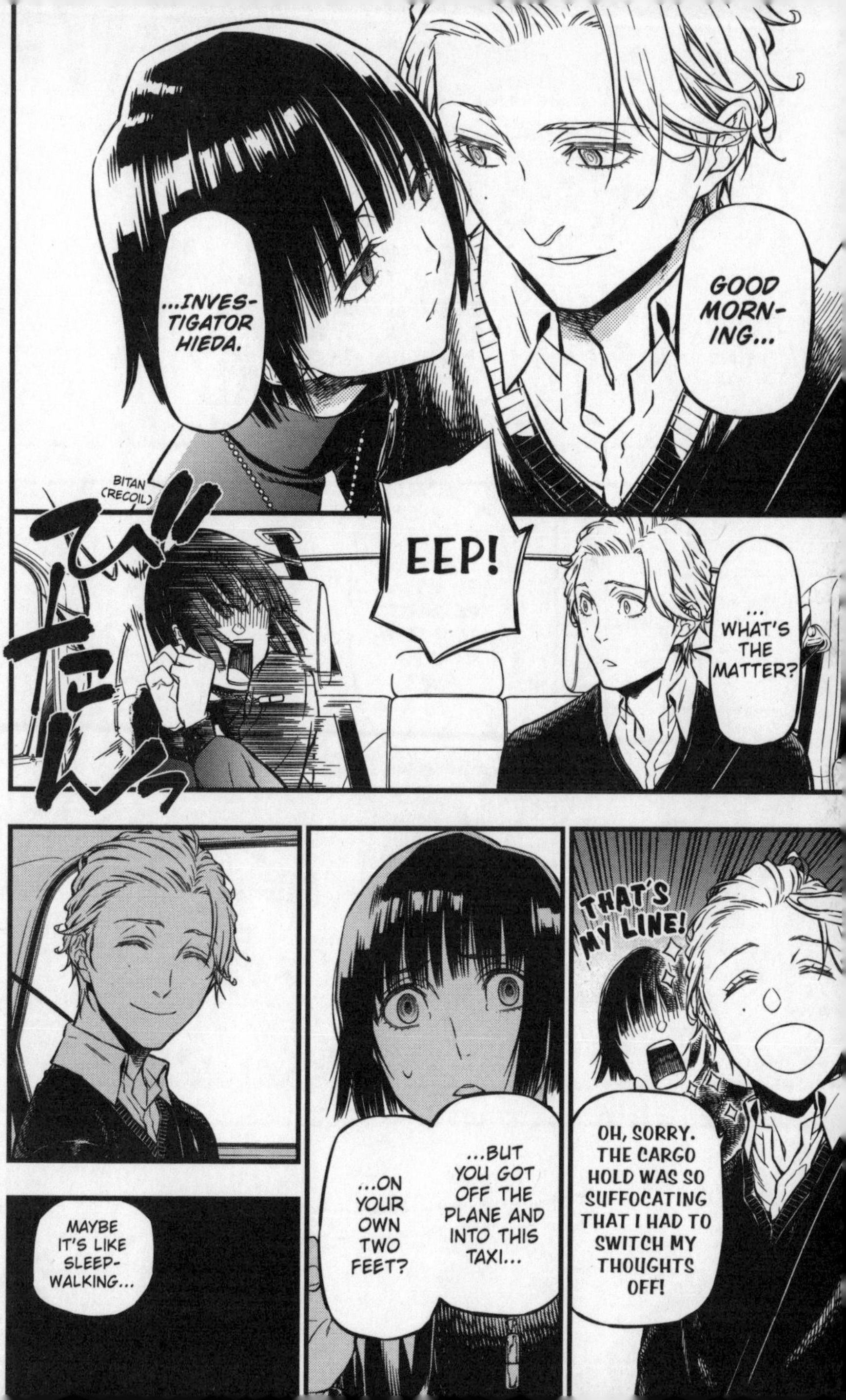
GOOD MORNING...
...INVESTIGATOR HIEDA.
...WHAT'S THE MATTER?
EEP!
BITAN (RECOIL)
THAT'S MY LINE!
OH, SORRY. THE CARGO HOLD WAS SO SUFFOCATING THAT I HAD TO SWITCH MY THOUGHTS OFF!
...BUT YOU GOT OFF THE PLANE AND INTO THIS TAXI...
...ON YOUR OWN TWO FEET?
MAYBE IT'S LIKE SLEEP-WALKING...

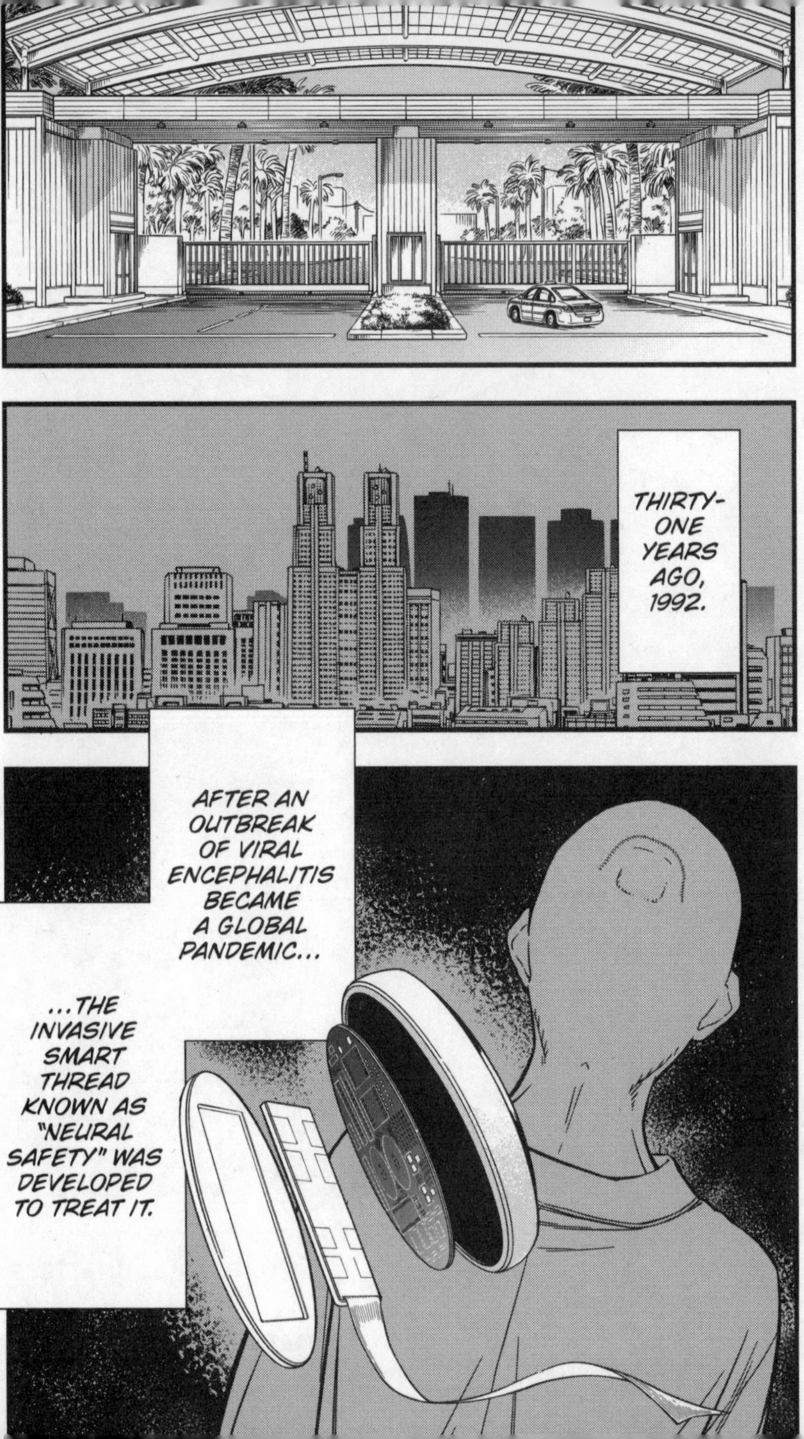
THIRTY-ONE YEARS AGO, 1992.
AFTER AN OUTBREAK OF VIRAL ENCEPHALITIS BECAME A GLOBAL PANDEMIC...
...THE INVASIVE SMART THREAD KNOWN AS "NEURAL SAFETY" WAS DEVELOPED TO TREAT IT.

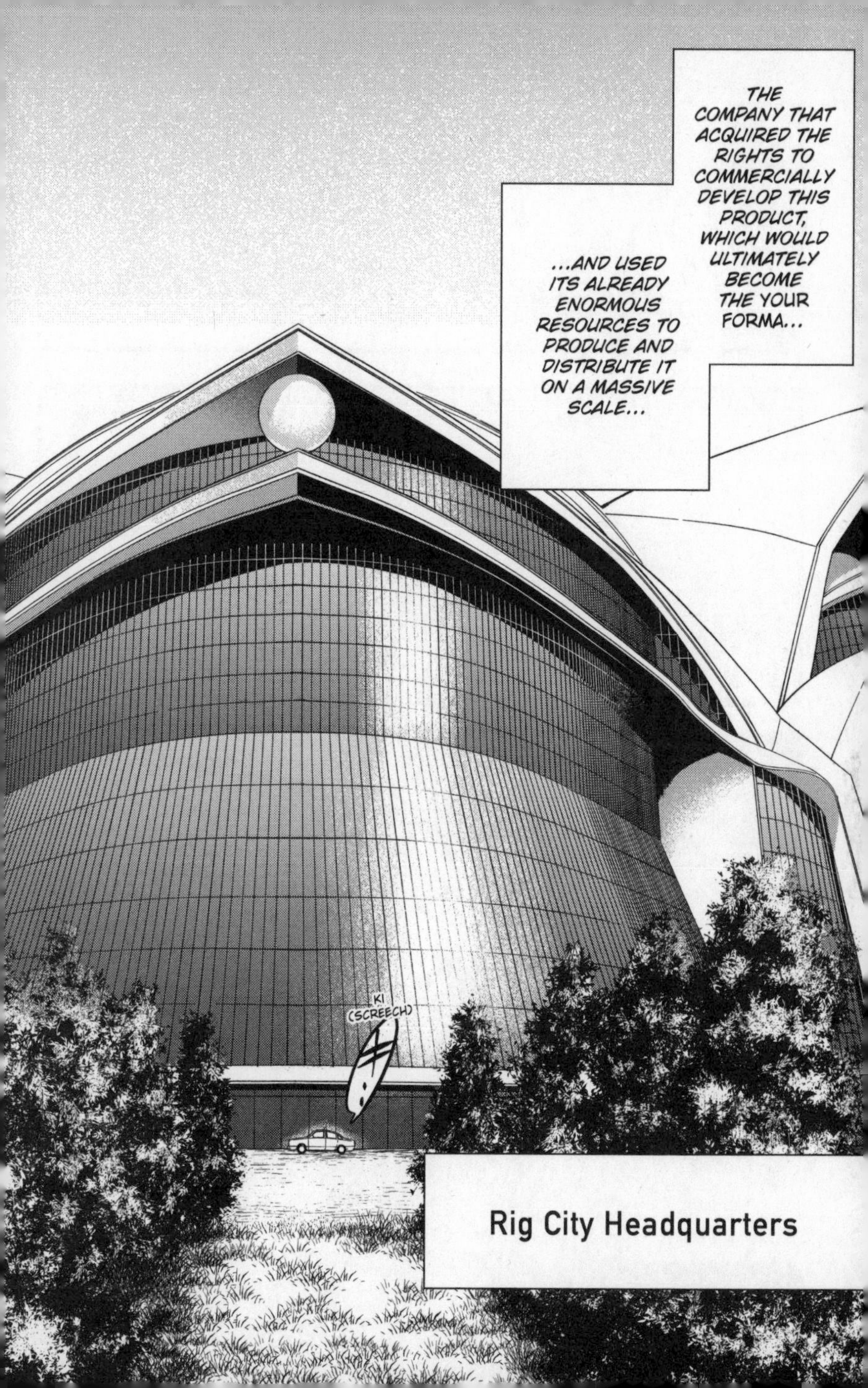
THE COMPANY THAT ACQUIRED THE RIGHTS TO COMMERCIALLY DEVELOP THIS PRODUCT, WHICH WOULD ULTIMATELY BECOME THE YOUR FORMA...
...AND USED ITS ALREADY ENORMOUS RESOURCES TO PRODUCE AND DISTRIBUTE IT ON A MASSIVE SCALE...
KI (SCREECH)
Rig City Headquarters

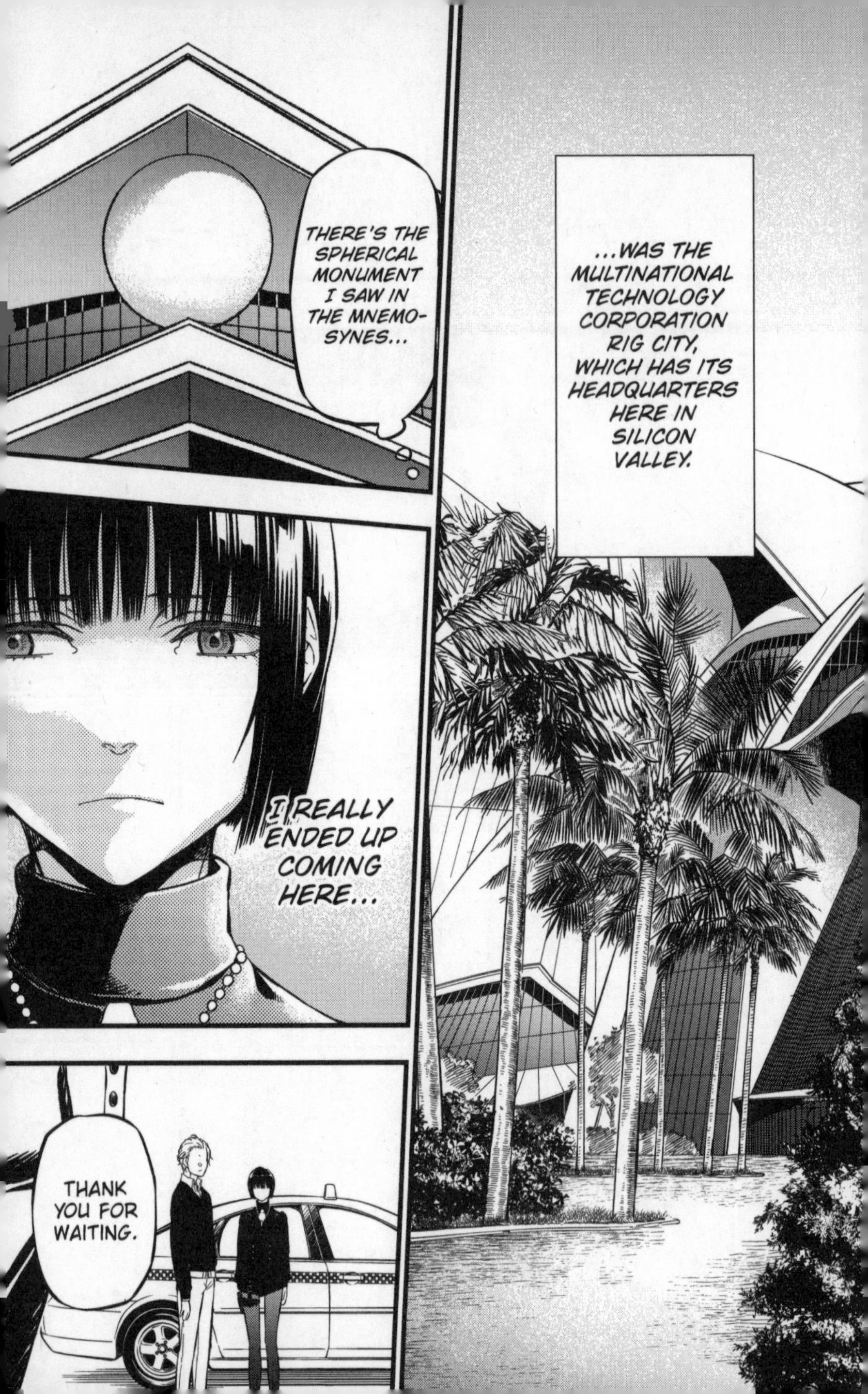
...WAS THE MULTINATIONAL TECHNOLOGY CORPORATION RIG CITY, WHICH HAS ITS HEADQUARTERS HERE IN SILICON VALLEY.
THERE'S THE SPHERICAL MONUMENT I SAW IN THE MNEMO-SYNES...
I REALLY ENDED UP COMING HERE...
THANK YOU FOR WAITING.

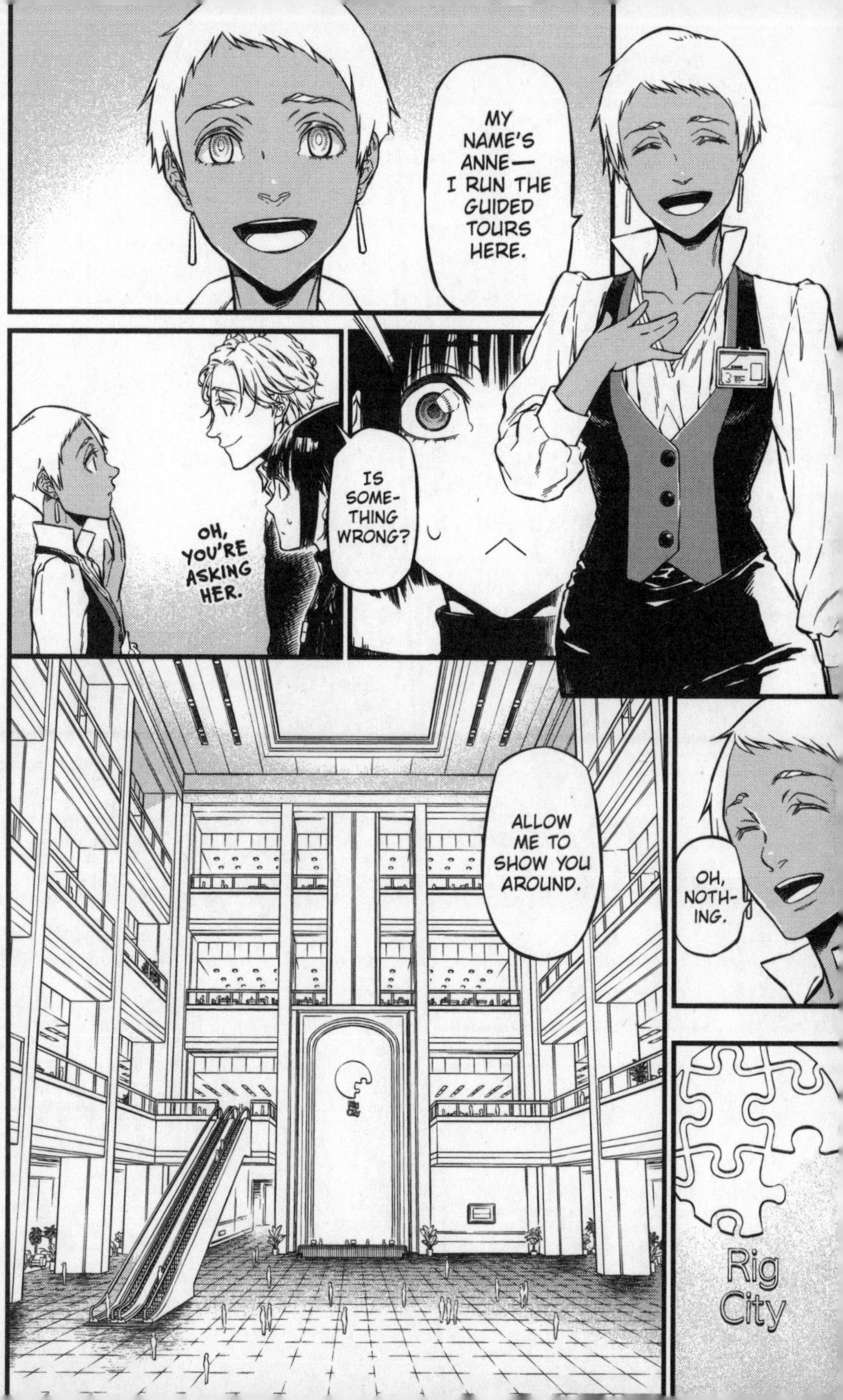
MY NAME'S ANNE— I RUN THE GUIDED TOURS HERE.
IS SOMETHING WRONG?
OH, YOU'RE ASKING HER.
OH, NOTHING.
Rig City
ALLOW ME TO SHOW YOU AROUND.

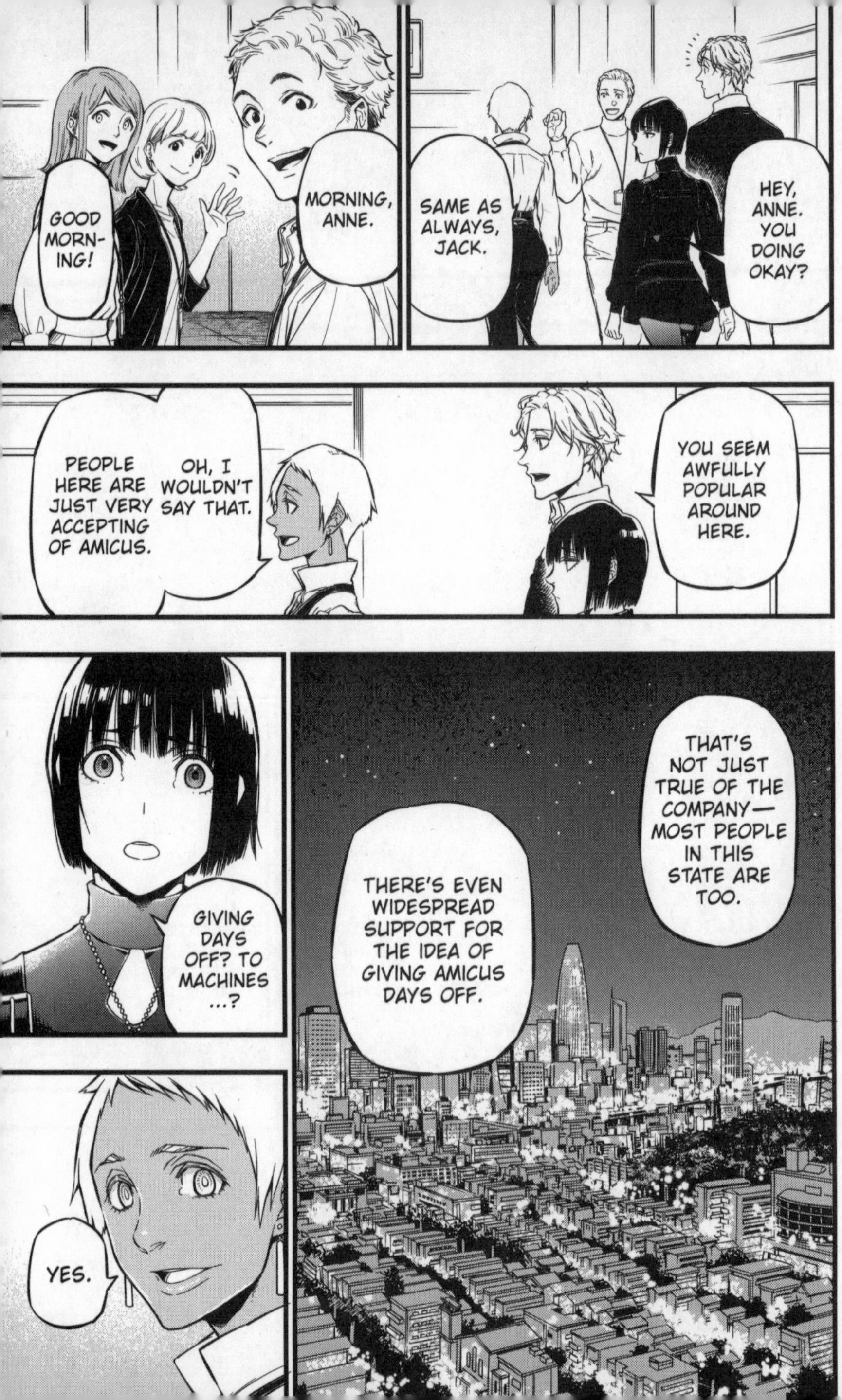
HEY, ANNE. YOU DOING OKAY?
SAME AS ALWAYS, JACK.
MORNING, ANNE.
GOOD MORNING!
YOU SEEM AWFULLY POPULAR AROUND HERE.
OH, I WOULDN'T SAY THAT.
PEOPLE HERE ARE JUST VERY ACCEPTING OF AMICUS.
THAT'S NOT JUST TRUE OF THE COMPANY— MOST PEOPLE IN THIS STATE ARE TOO.
THERE'S EVEN WIDESPREAD SUPPORT FOR THE IDEA OF GIVING AMICUS DAYS OFF.
GIVING DAYS OFF? TO MACHINES ...?
YES.

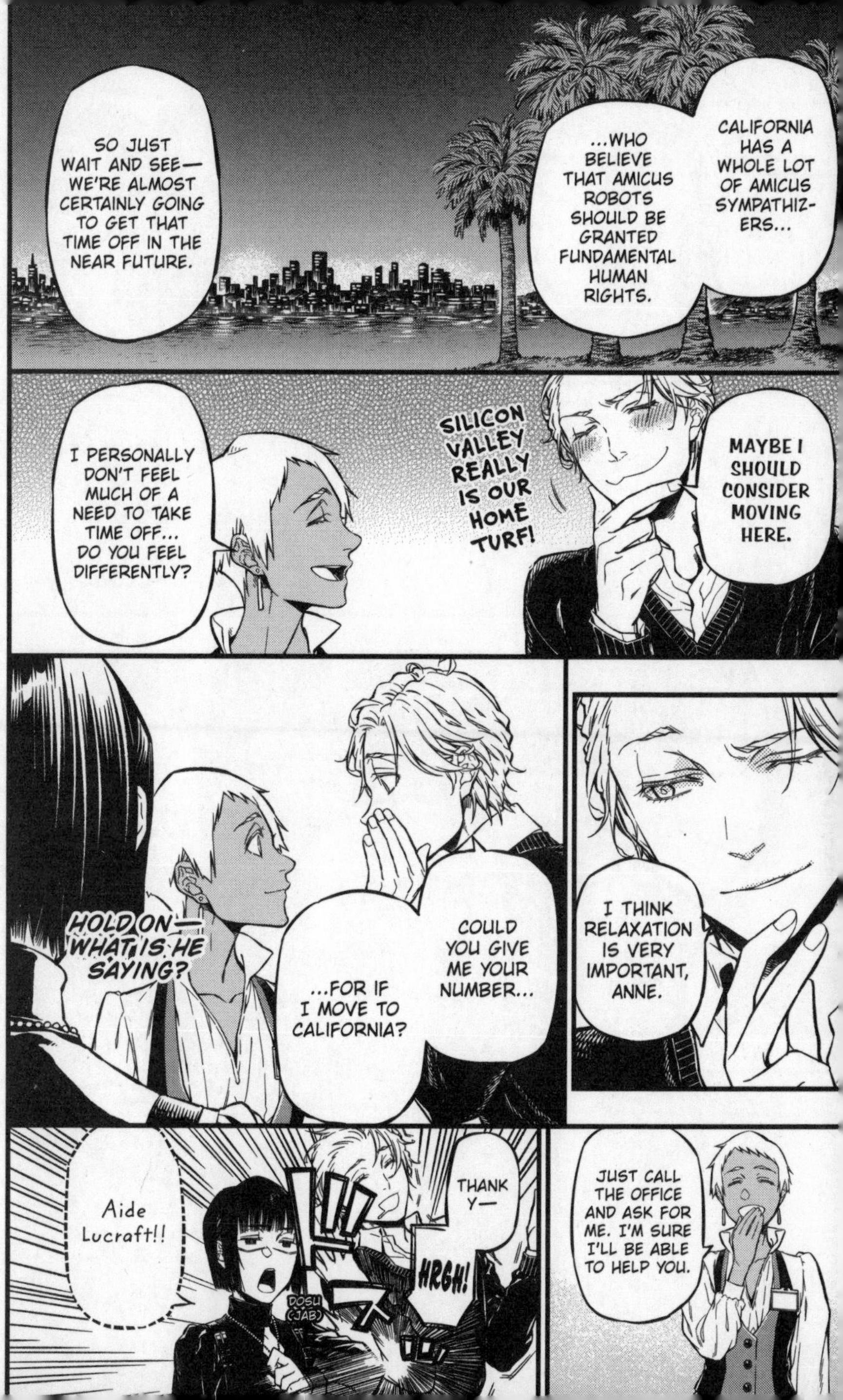
CALIFORNIA HAS A WHOLE LOT OF AMICUS SYMPATHIZ- ERS...
...WHO BELIEVE THAT AMICUS ROBOTS SHOULD BE GRANTED FUNDAMENTAL HUMAN RIGHTS.
SO JUST WAIT AND SEE— WE'RE ALMOST CERTAINLY GOING TO GET THAT TIME OFF IN THE NEAR FUTURE.
MAYBE I SHOULD CONSIDER MOVING HERE.
SILICON VALLEY REALLY IS OUR HOME TURF!
I PERSONALLY DON'T FEEL MUCH OF A NEED TO TAKE TIME OFF... DO YOU FEEL DIFFERENTLY?
I THINK RELAXATION IS VERY IMPORTANT, ANNE.
COULD YOU GIVE ME YOUR NUMBER...
...FOR IF I MOVE TO CALIFORNIA?
HOLD ON— WHAT IS HE SAYING?
JUST CALL THE OFFICE AND ASK FOR ME. I'M SURE I'LL BE ABLE TO HELP YOU.
THANK Y—
HRGH!
DOSU (JAB)
Aide Lucraft!!

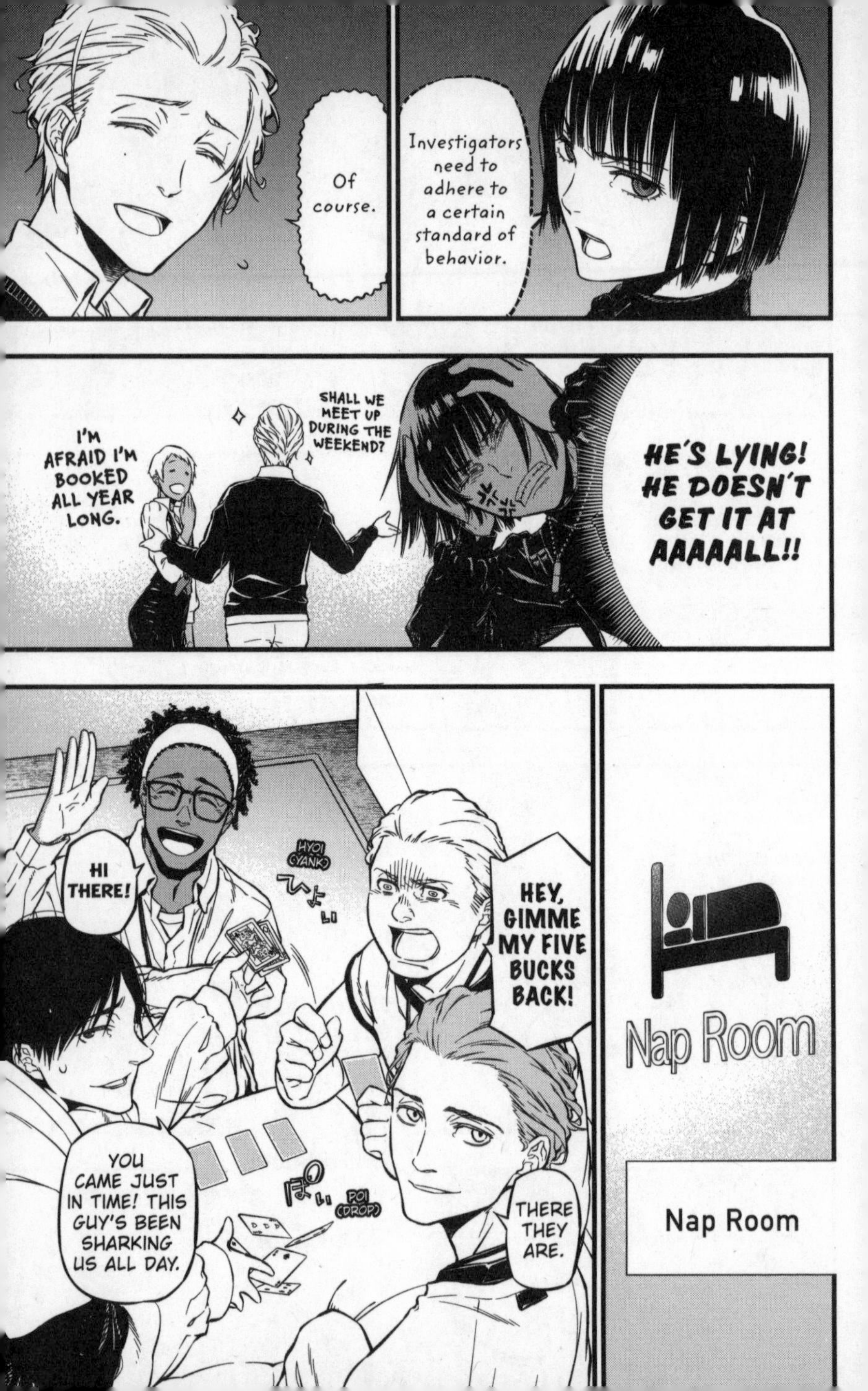
Investigators need to adhere to a certain standard of behavior.
Of course.
HE'S LYING! HE DOESN'T GET IT AT AAAAALL!!
SHALL WE MEET UP DURING THE WEEKEND?
I'M AFRAID I'M BOOKED ALL YEAR LONG.
Nap Room
Nap Room
HEY, GIMME MY FIVE BUCKS BACK!
HYOI (YANK)
HI THERE!
THERE THEY ARE.
POI (DROP)
YOU CAME JUST IN TIME! THIS GUY'S BEEN SHARKING US ALL DAY.

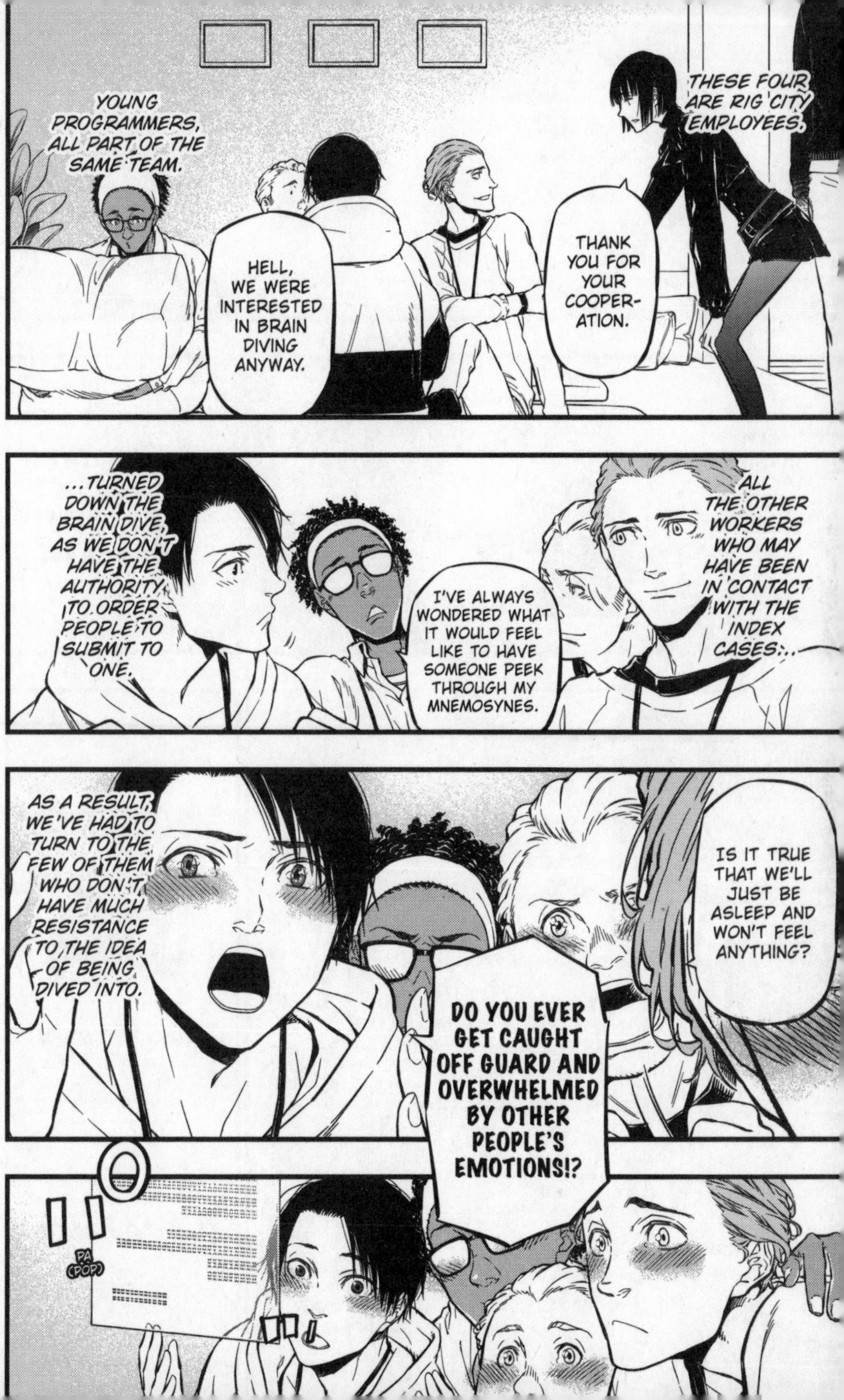
THESE FOUR ARE RIG CITY EMPLOYEES.
THANK YOU FOR YOUR COOPERATION.
HELL, WE WERE INTERESTED IN BRAIN DIVING ANYWAY.
YOUNG PROGRAMMERS, ALL PART OF THE SAME TEAM.
ALL THE OTHER WORKERS WHO MAY HAVE BEEN IN CONTACT WITH THE INDEX CASES...
I'VE ALWAYS WONDERED WHAT IT WOULD FEEL LIKE TO HAVE SOMEONE PEEK THROUGH MY MNEMOSYNES.
...TURNED DOWN THE BRAIN DIVE, AS WE DON'T HAVE THE AUTHORITY TO ORDER PEOPLE TO SUBMIT TO ONE.
IS IT TRUE THAT WE'LL JUST BE ASLEEP AND WON'T FEEL ANYTHING?
AS A RESULT, WE'VE HAD TO TURN TO THE FEW OF THEM WHO DON'T HAVE MUCH RESISTANCE TO THE IDEA OF BEING DIVED INTO.
DO YOU EVER GET CAUGHT OFF GUARD AND OVERWHELMED BY OTHER PEOPLE'S EMOTIONS!?
PA (POP)

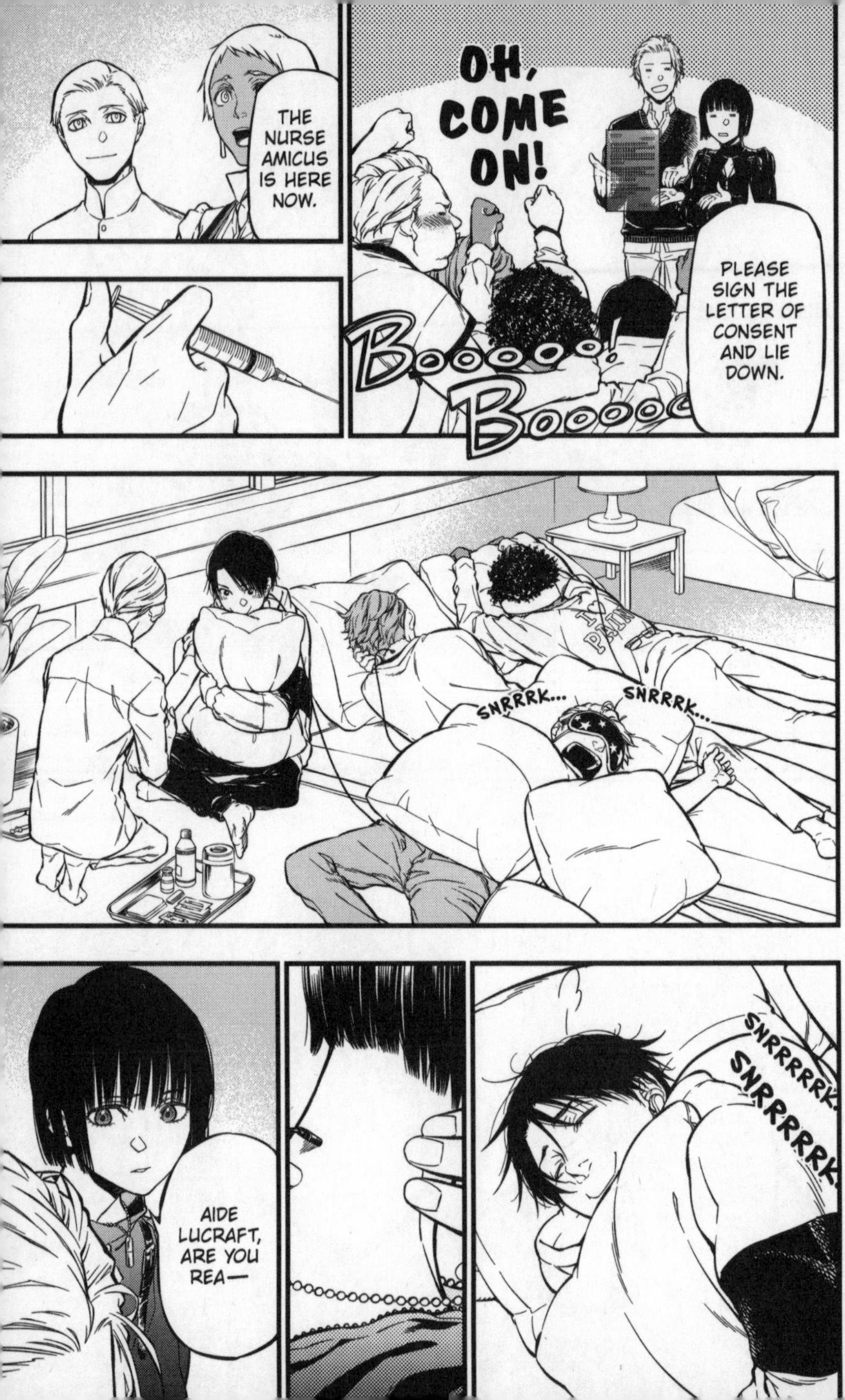

PLEASE SIGN THE LETTER OF CONSENT AND LIE DOWN.
OH, COME ON!
Booooo!
Boooooo
THE NURSE AMICUS IS HERE NOW.
SNRRRK...
SNRRRK...
SNRRRRK.
SNRRRRK.
SNRRRRK.
AIDE LUCRAFT, ARE YOU REA—

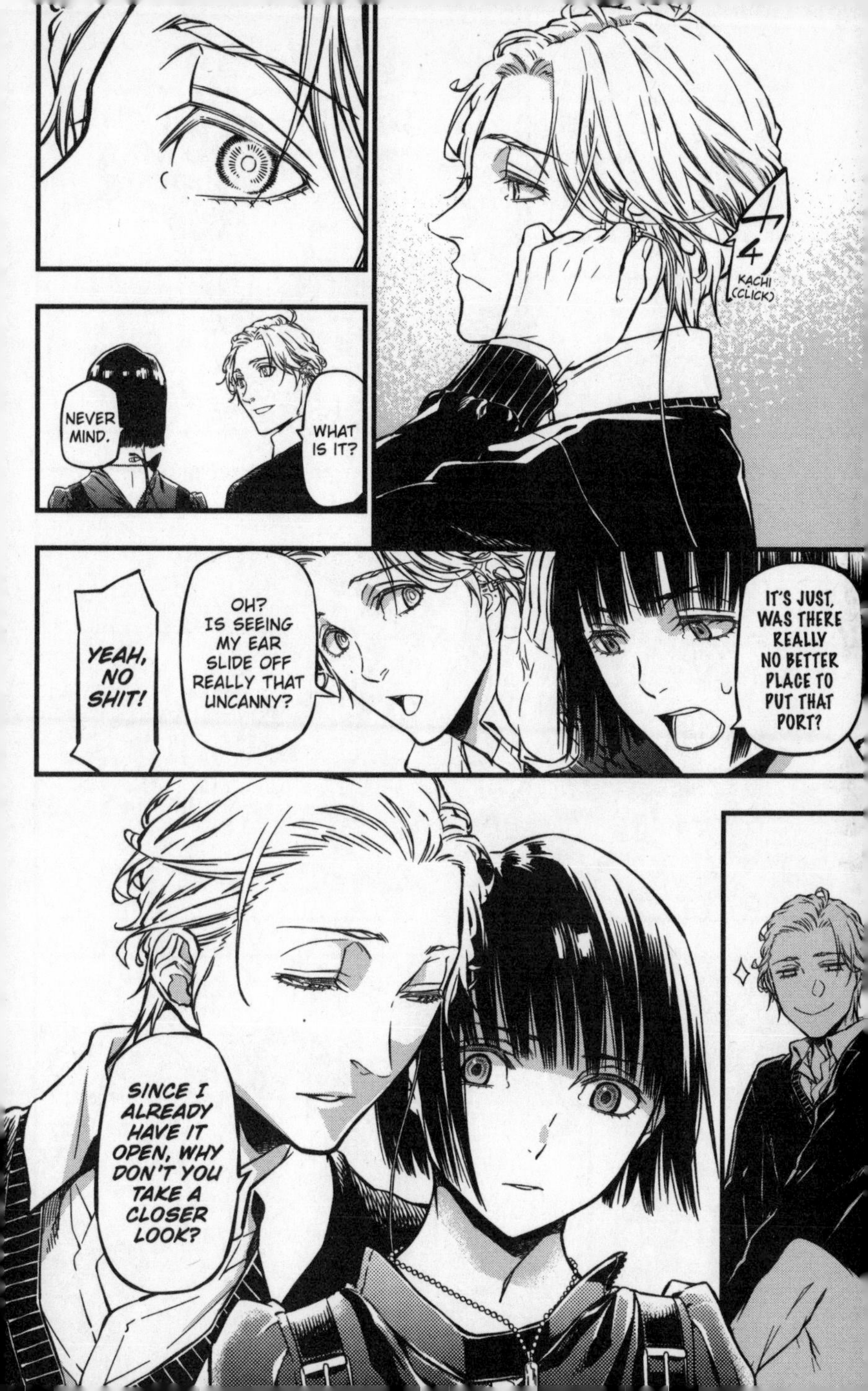
KACHI (CLICK)
WHAT IS IT?
NEVER MIND.
IT'S JUST, WAS THERE REALLY NO BETTER PLACE TO PUT THAT PORT?
OH? IS SEEING MY EAR SLIDE OFF REALLY THAT UNCANNY?
YEAH, NO SHIT!
SINCE I ALREADY HAVE IT OPEN, WHY DON'T YOU TAKE A CLOSER LOOK?

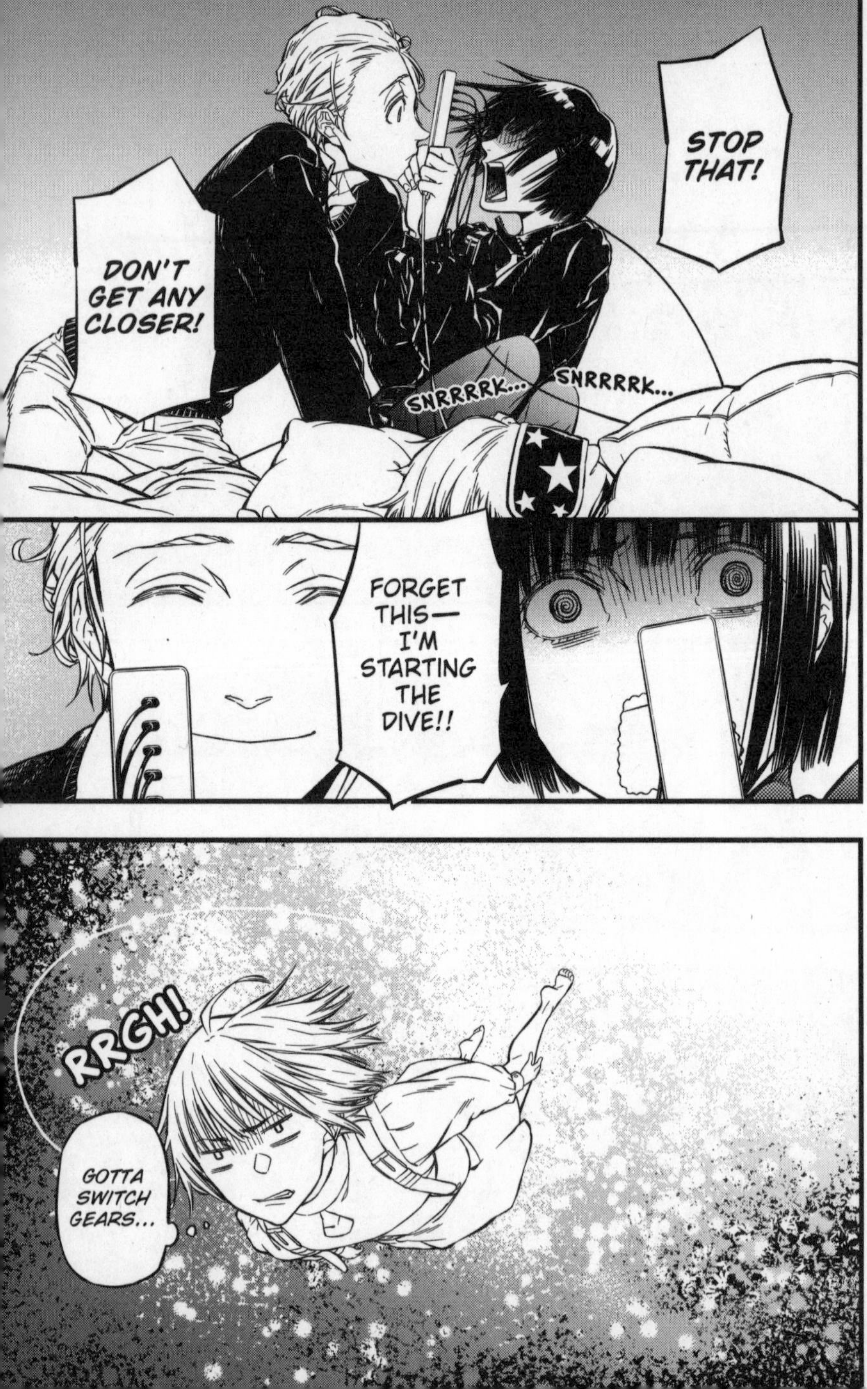
STOP THAT!
DON'T GET ANY CLOSER!
SNRRRRK...
SNRRRRK...
FORGET THIS— I'M STARTING THE DIVE!!
RRGH!
GOTTA SWITCH GEARS...

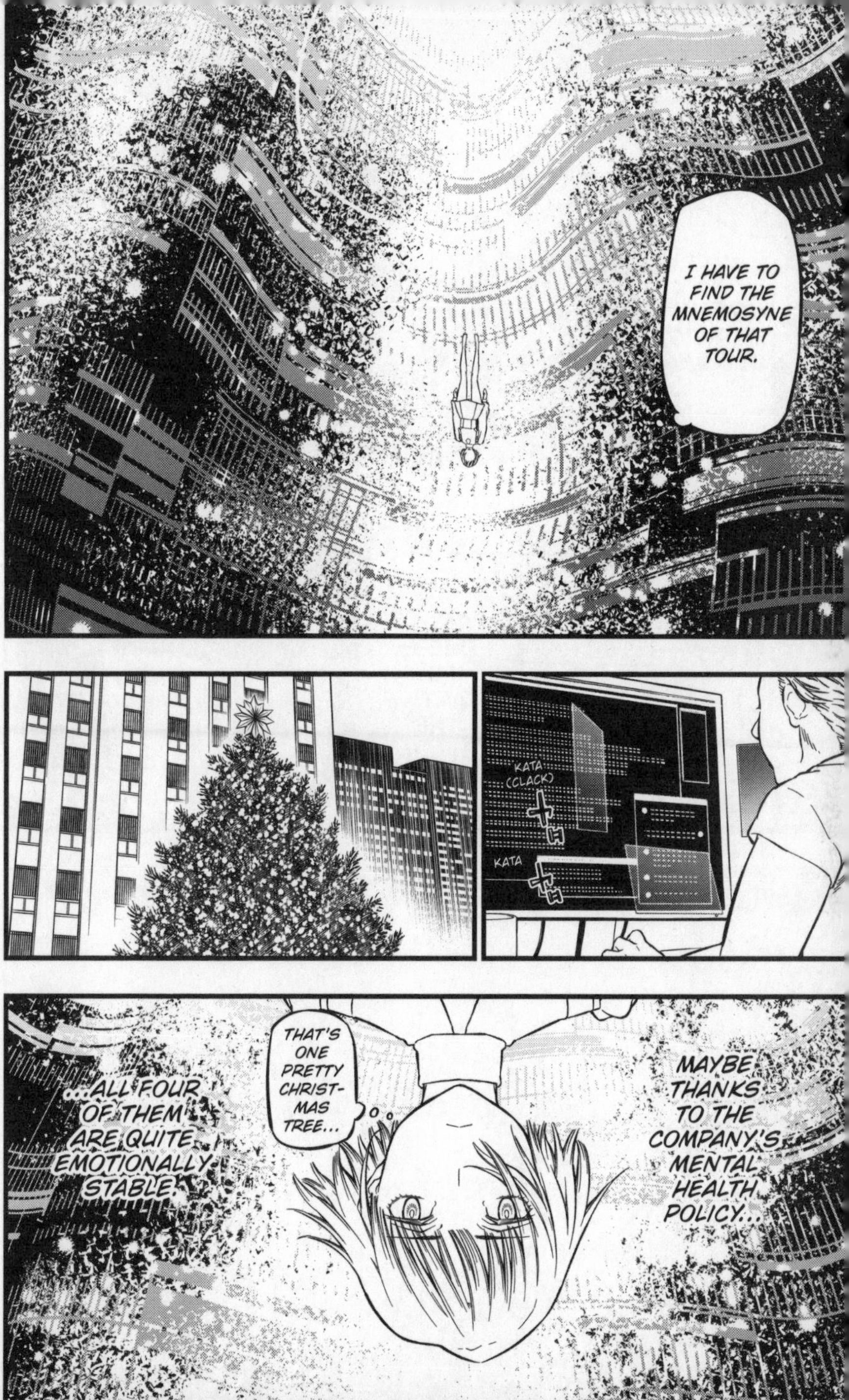
I HAVE TO FIND THE MNEMOSYNE OF THAT TOUR.
KATA (CLACK)
KATA
MAYBE THANKS TO THE COMPANY'S MENTAL HEALTH POLICY...
THAT'S ONE PRETTY CHRIST-MAS TREE...
...ALL FOUR OF THEM ARE QUITE EMOTIONALLY STABLE.

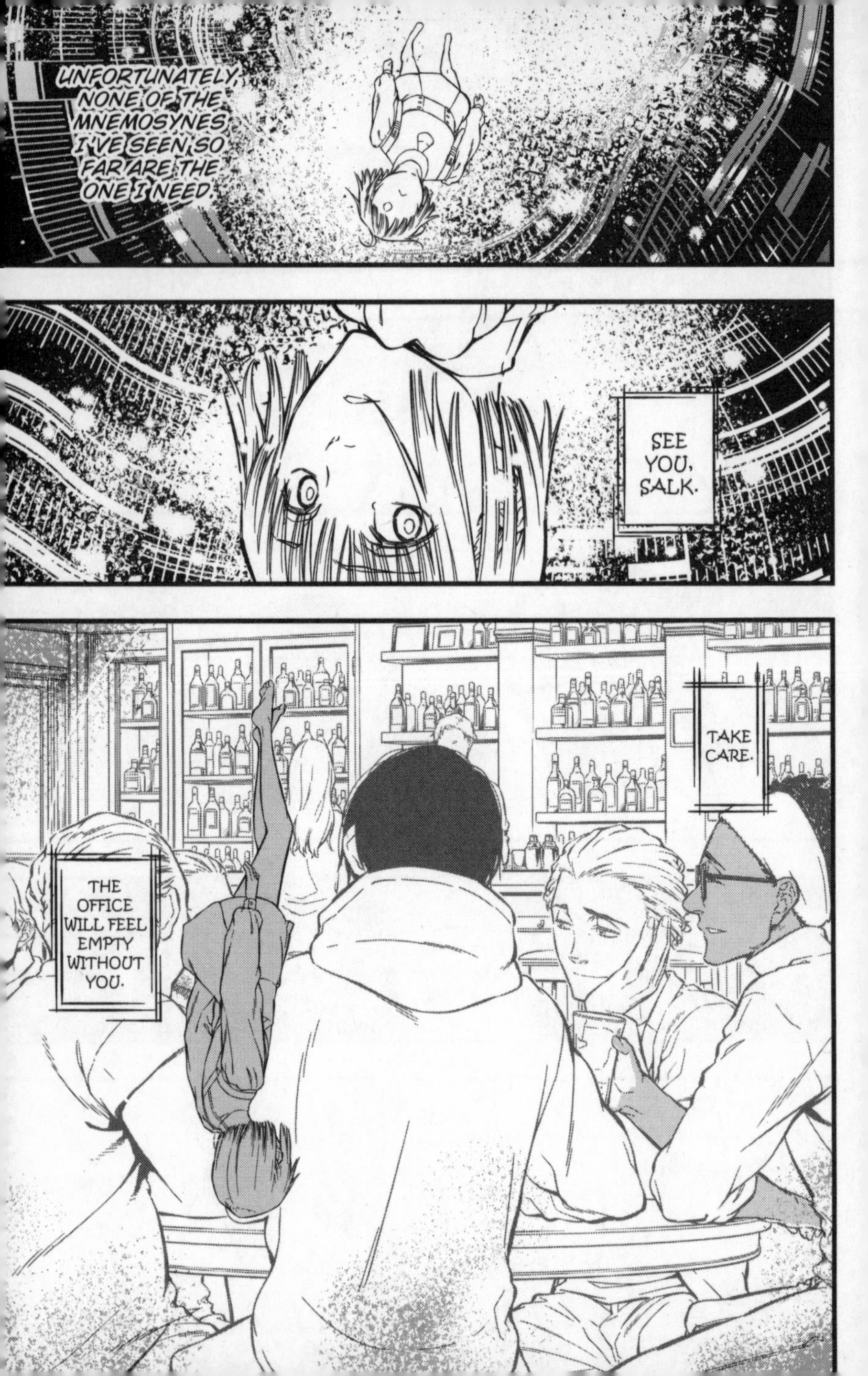
UNFORTUNATELY, NONE OF THE MNEMOSYNES I'VE SEEN SO FAR ARE THE ONE I NEED.
SEE YOU, SALK.
TAKE CARE.
THE OFFICE WILL FEEL EMPTY WITHOUT YOU.

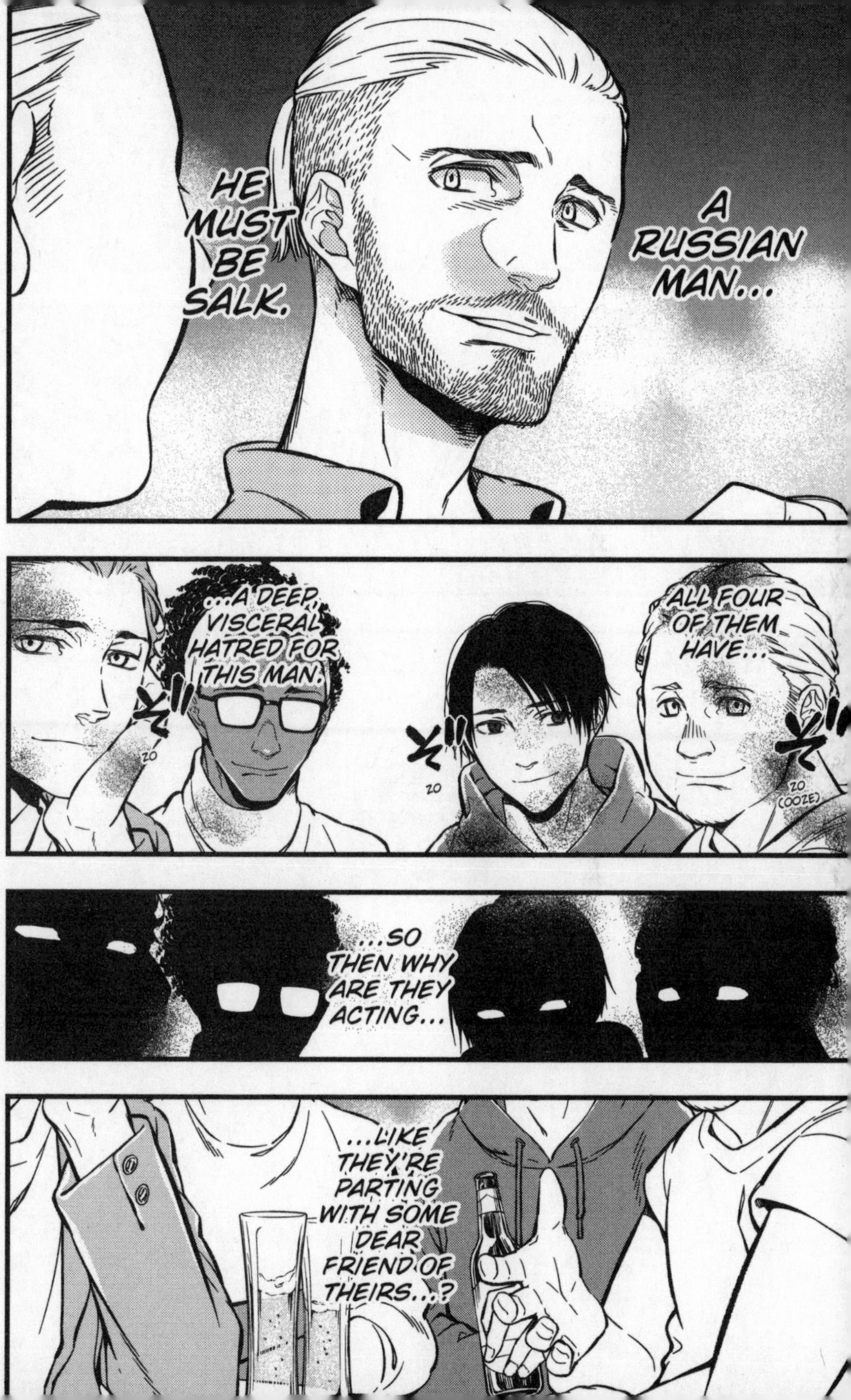
A RUSSIAN MAN...
HE MUST BE SALK.
ALL FOUR OF THEM HAVE...
ZO (OOZE)
ZO
...A DEEP, VISCERAL HATRED FOR THIS MAN.
ZO
...SO THEN WHY ARE THEY ACTING...
...LIKE THEY'RE PARTING WITH SOME DEAR FRIEND OF THEIRS...?

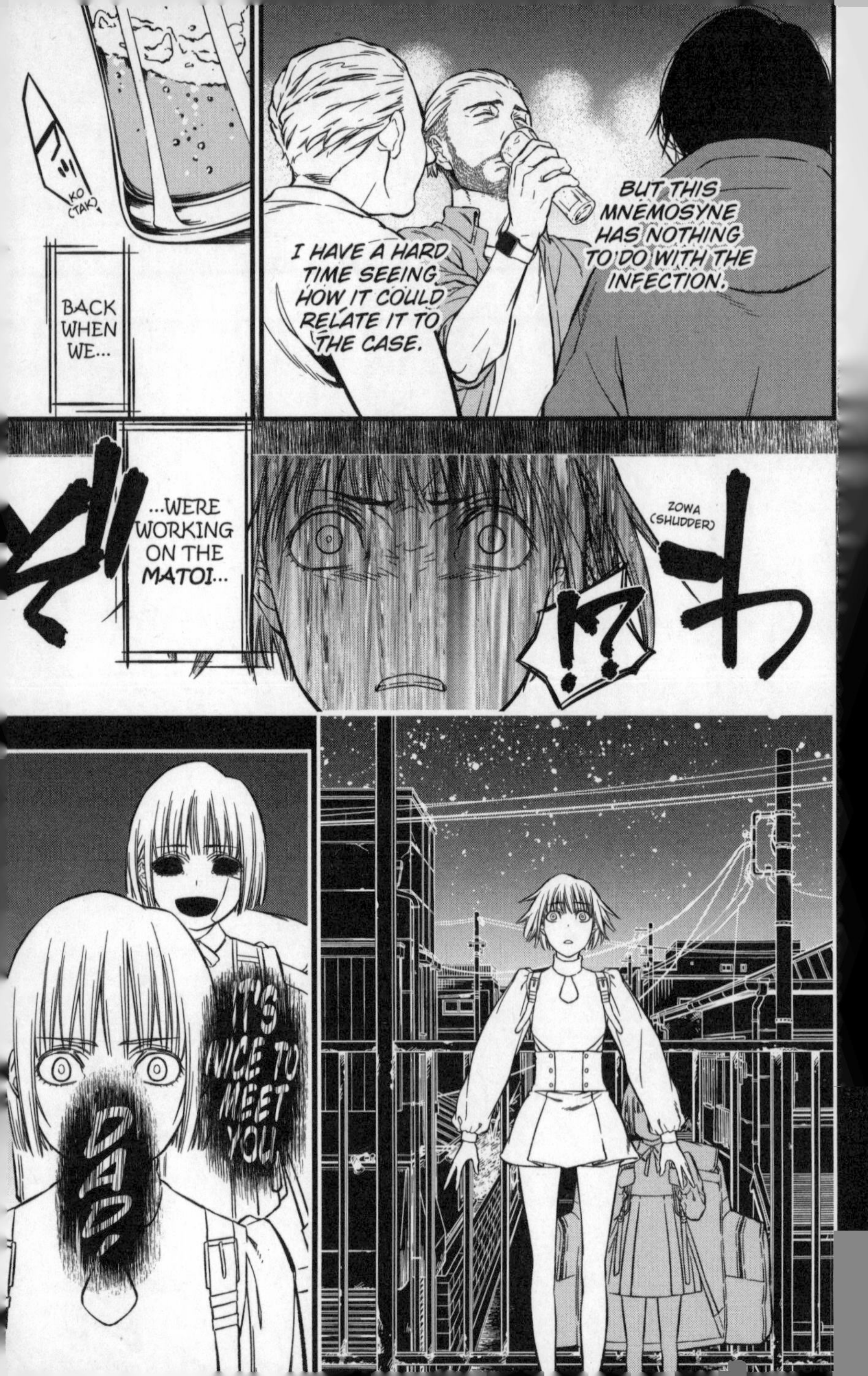
BUT THIS MNEMOSYNE HAS NOTHING TO DO WITH THE INFECTION.
I HAVE A HARD TIME SEEING HOW IT COULD RELATE IT TO THE CASE.
KO (TAK)
BACK WHEN WE...
ZOWA (SHUDDER)
...WERE WORKING ON THE MATOI...
IT'S NICE TO MEET YOU.

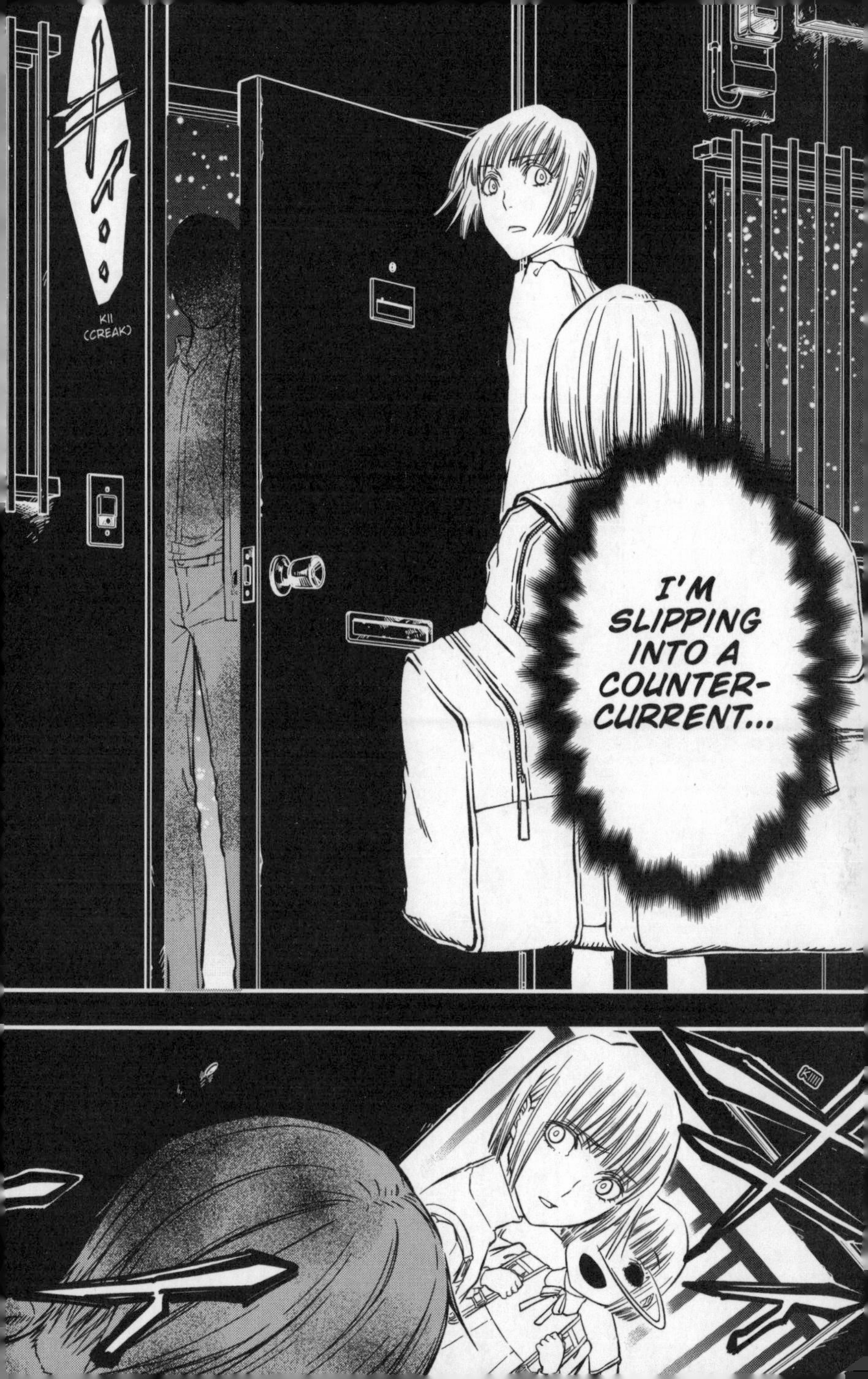
KII (CREAK)
I'M SLIPPING INTO A COUNTER-CURRENT...
KIIII

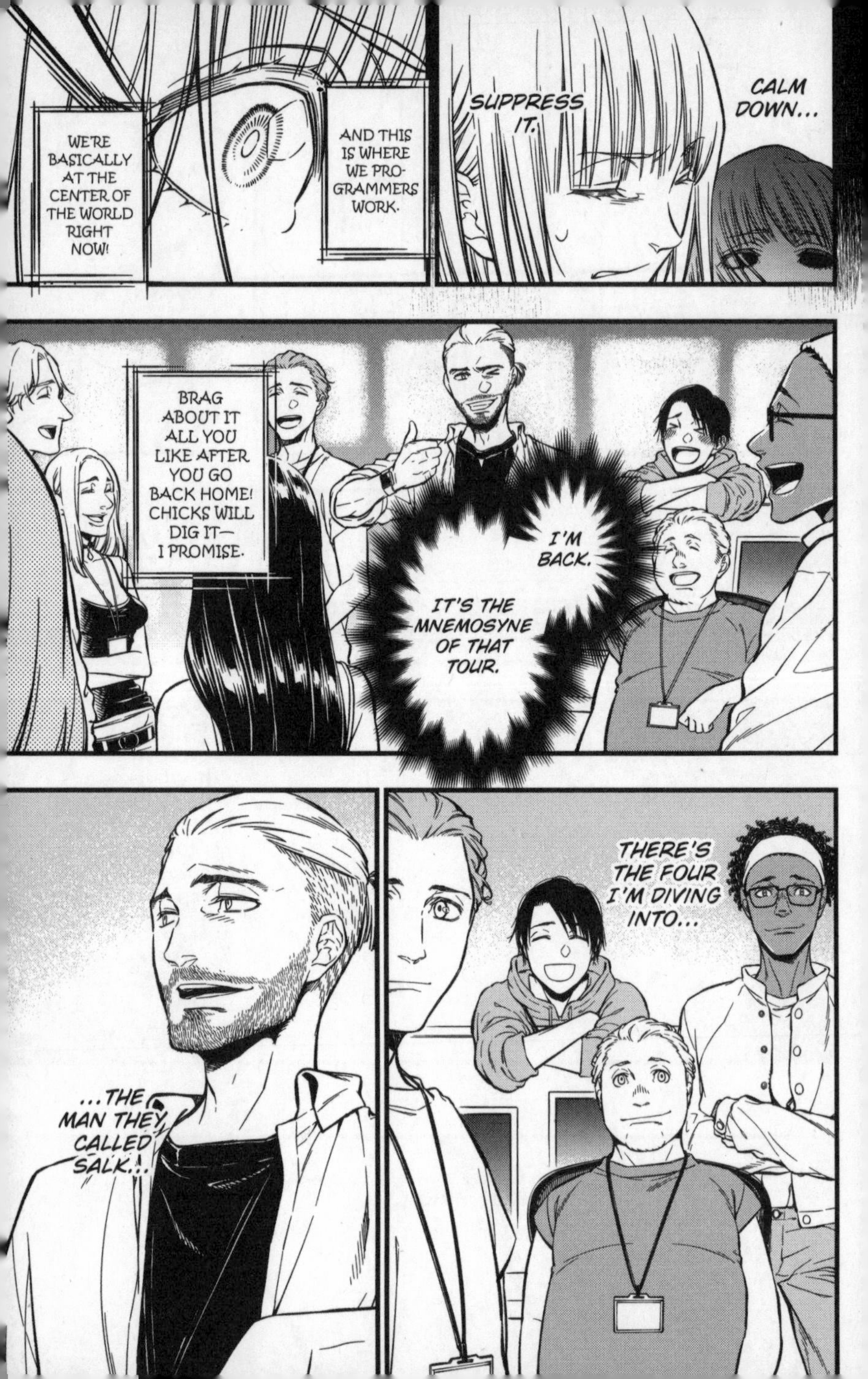
CALM DOWN...
SUPPRESS IT.
AND THIS IS WHERE WE PRO-GRAMMERS WORK.
WE'RE BASICALLY AT THE CENTER OF THE WORLD RIGHT NOW!
I'M BACK.
IT'S THE MNEMOSYNE OF THAT TOUR.
BRAG ABOUT IT ALL YOU LIKE AFTER YOU GO BACK HOME! CHICKS WILL DIG IT— I PROMISE.
THERE'S THE FOUR I'M DIVING INTO...
...THE MAN THEY CALLED SALK...

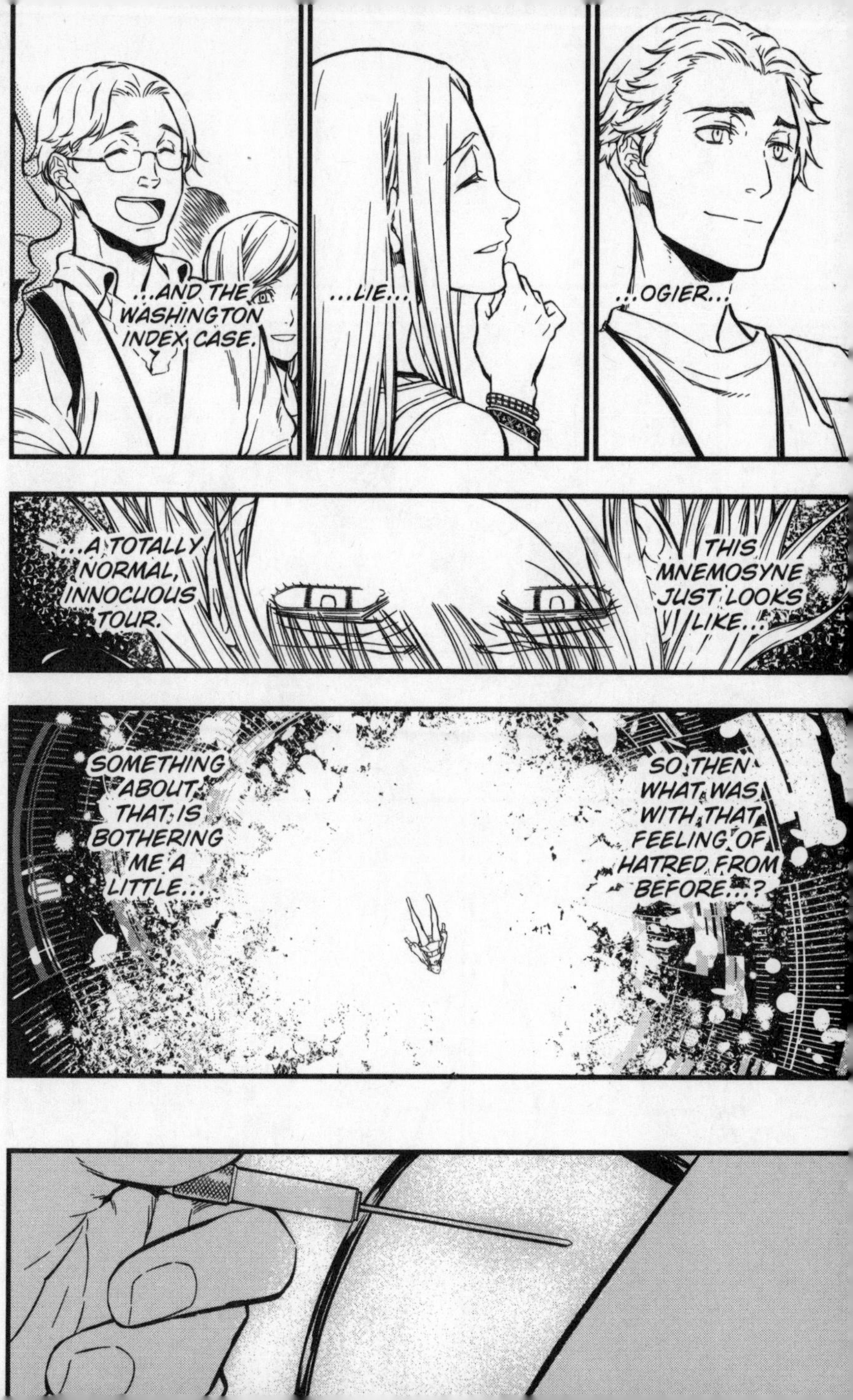
...OGIER...
...LIE...
...AND THE WASHINGTON INDEX CASE.
THIS MNEMOSYNE JUST LOOKS LIKE...
...A TOTALLY NORMAL, INNOCUOUS TOUR.
SO THEN WHAT WAS WITH THAT FEELING OF HATRED FROM BEFORE...?
SOMETHING ABOUT THAT IS BOTHERING ME A LITTLE...

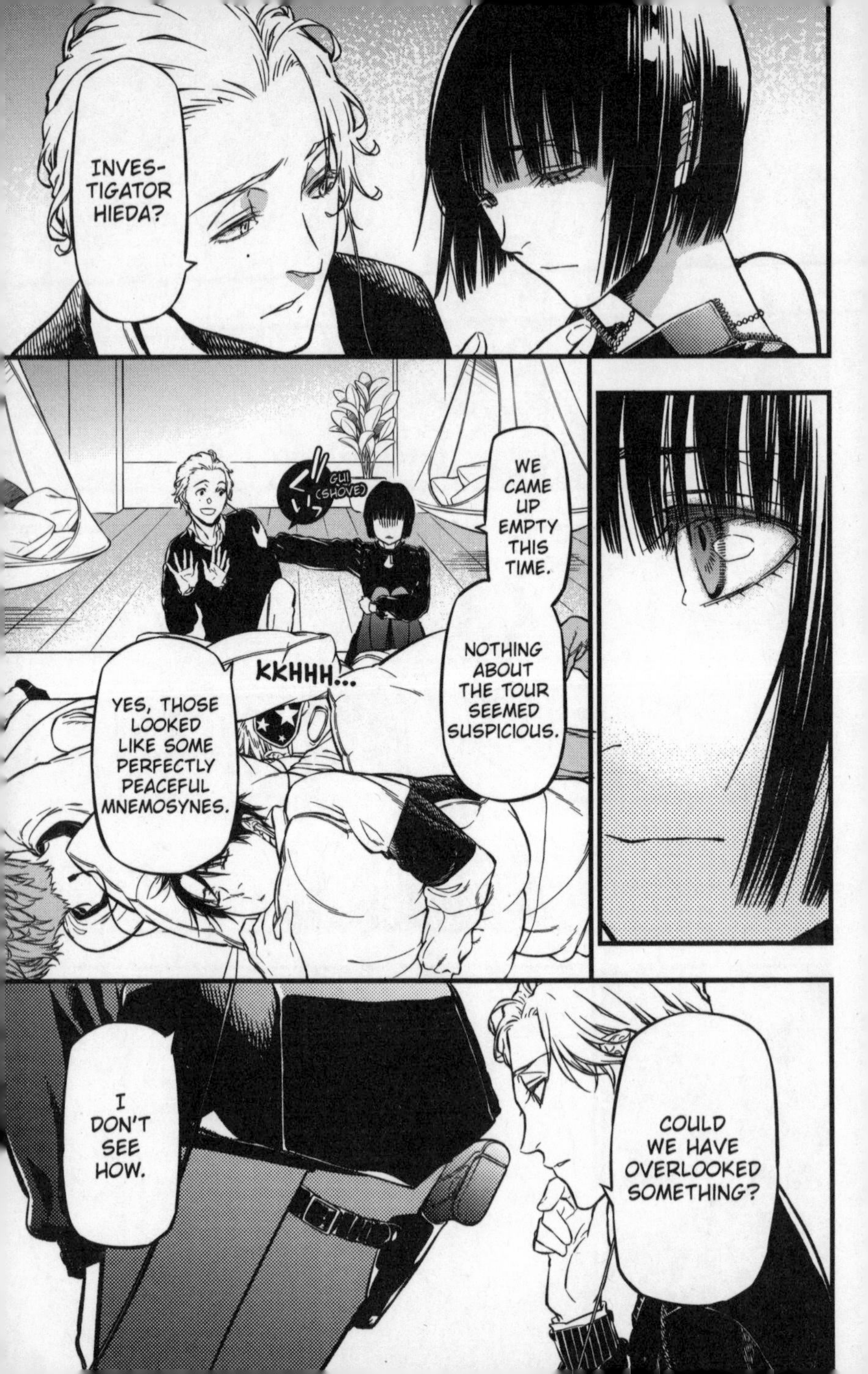

INVES-TIGATOR HIEDA?
WE CAME UP EMPTY THIS TIME.
GUI (SHOVE)
NOTHING ABOUT THE TOUR SEEMED SUSPICIOUS.
KKHHH...
YES, THOSE LOOKED LIKE SOME PERFECTLY PEACEFUL MNEMOSYNES.
COULD WE HAVE OVERLOOKED SOMETHING?
I DON'T SEE HOW.

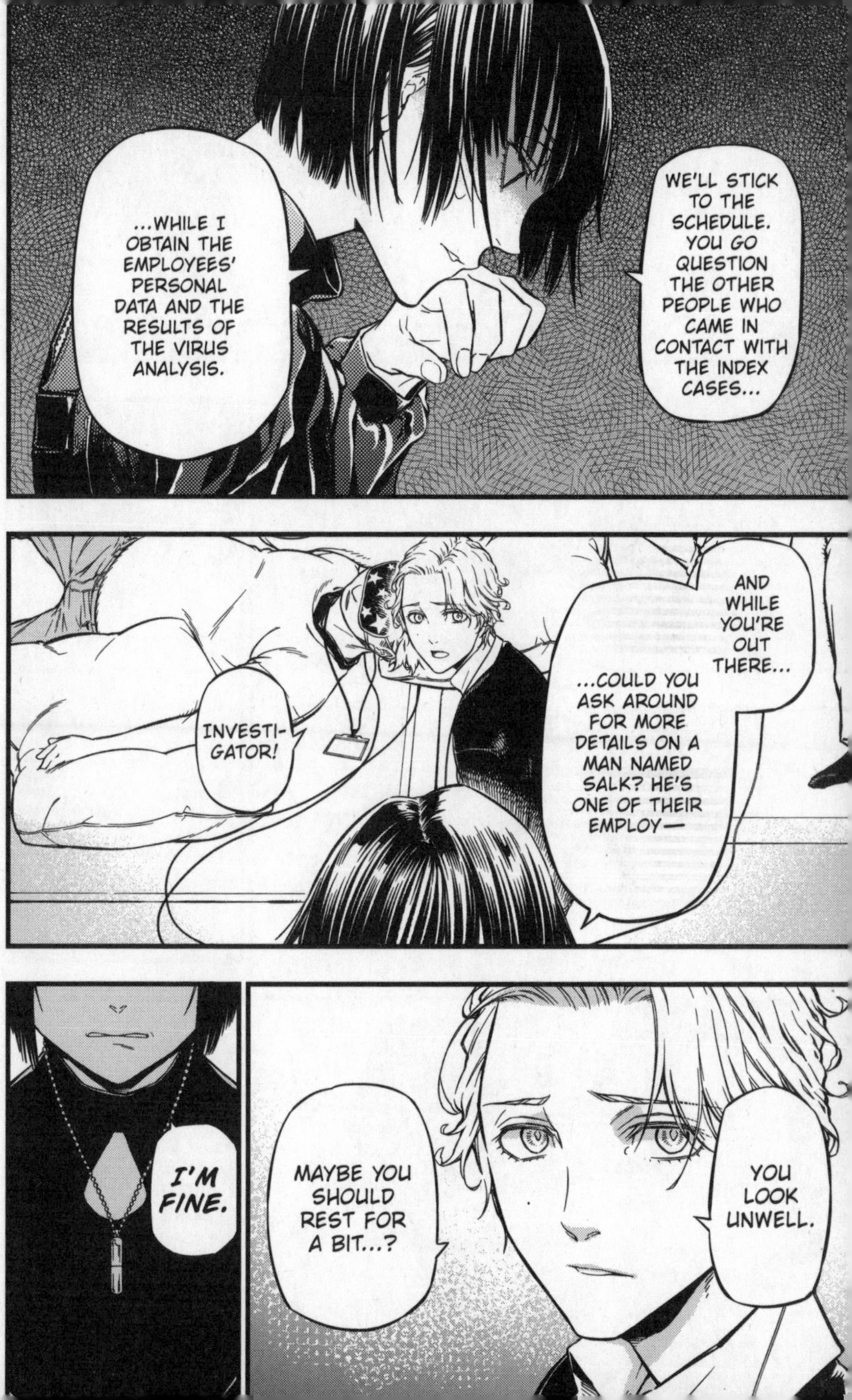
WE'LL STICK TO THE SCHEDULE. YOU GO QUESTION THE OTHER PEOPLE WHO CAME IN CONTACT WITH THE INDEX CASES...
...WHILE I OBTAIN THE EMPLOYEES' PERSONAL DATA AND THE RESULTS OF THE VIRUS ANALYSIS.
AND WHILE YOU'RE OUT THERE...
...COULD YOU ASK AROUND FOR MORE DETAILS ON A MAN NAMED SALK? HE'S ONE OF THEIR EMPLOY—
INVESTI-GATOR!
YOU LOOK UNWELL.
MAYBE YOU SHOULD REST FOR A BIT...?
I'M FINE.

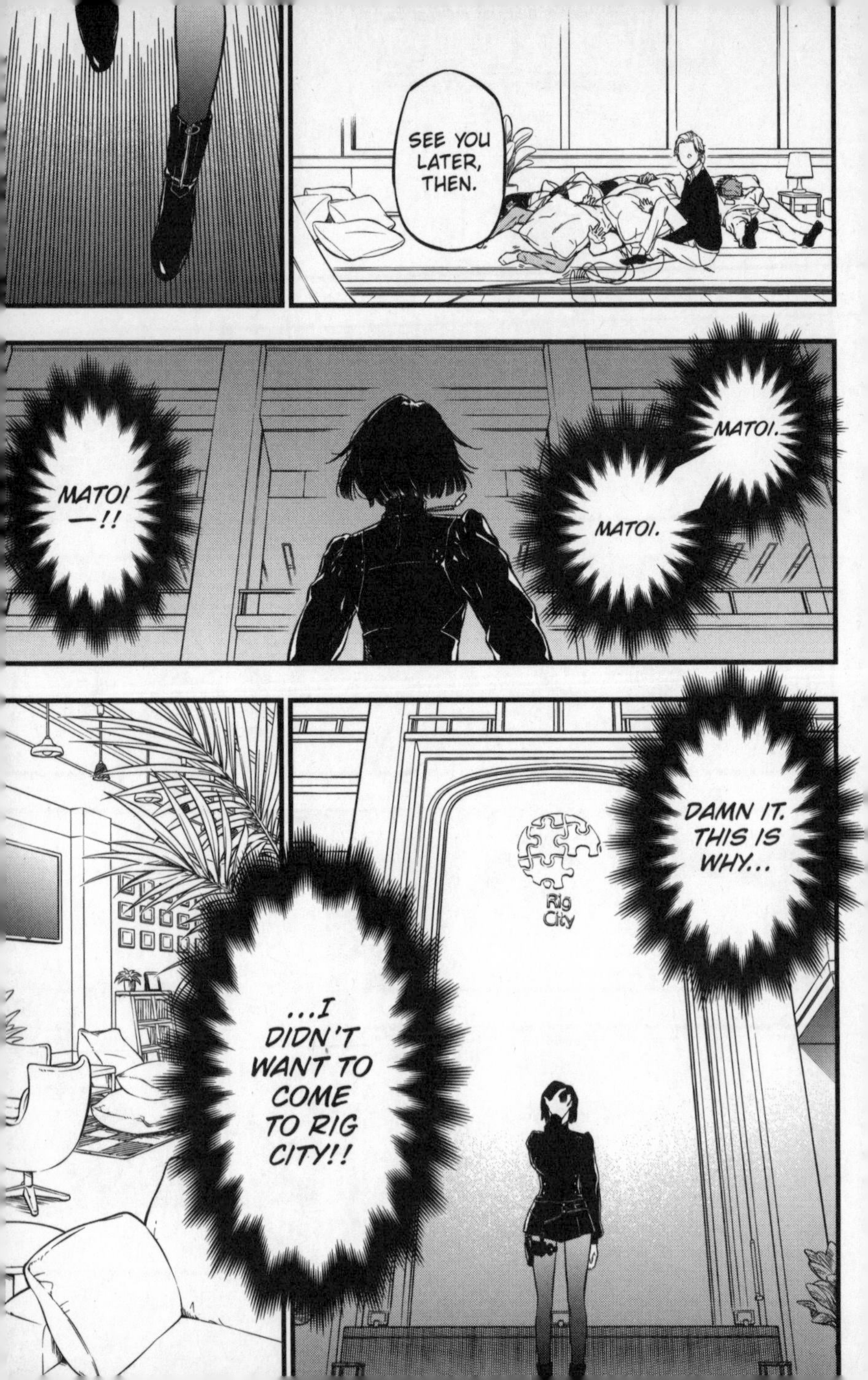
SEE YOU LATER, THEN.
MATOI.
MATOI.
MATOI—!!
DAMN IT. THIS IS WHY...
Rig City
...I DIDN'T WANT TO COME TO RIG CITY!!

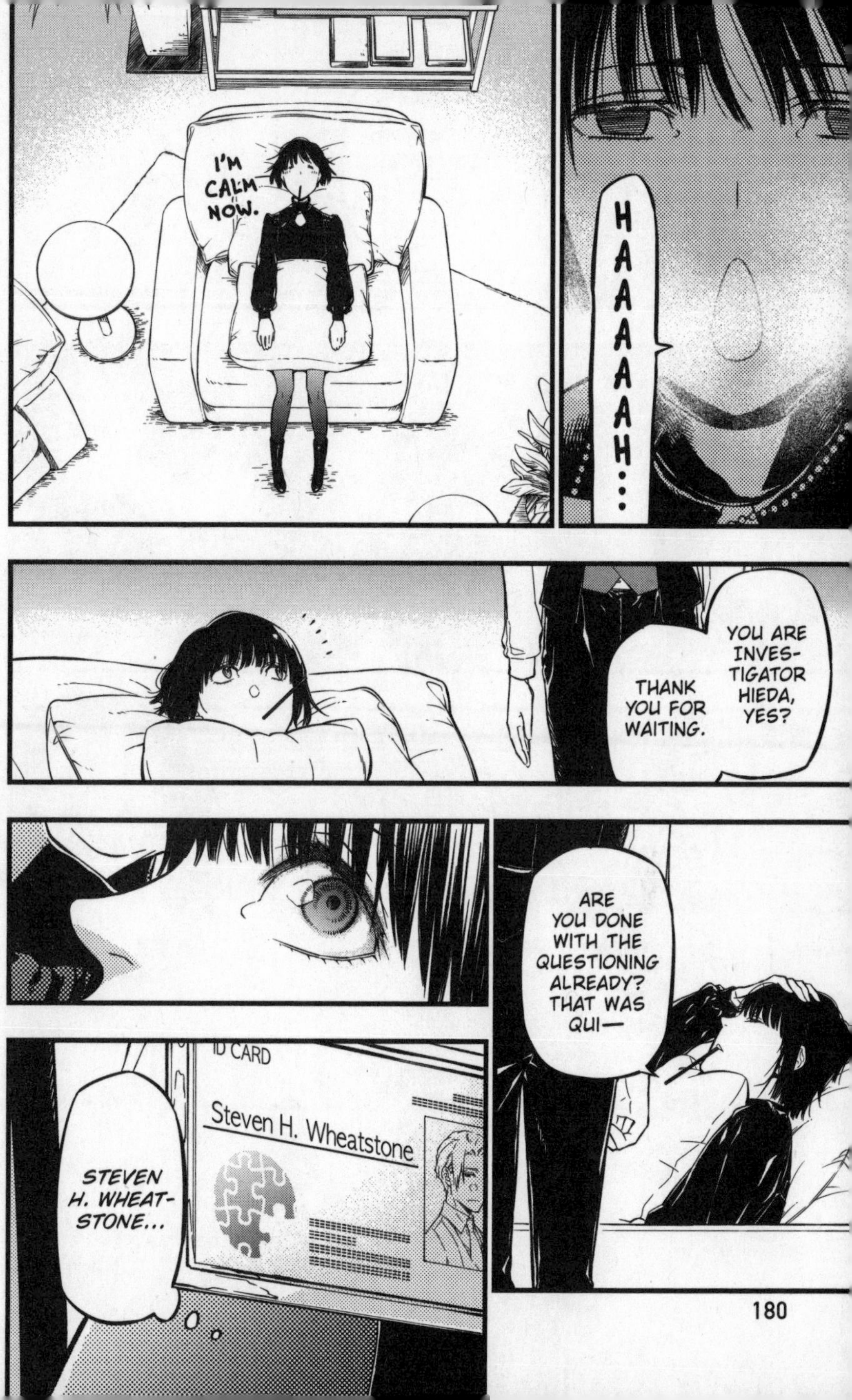
HAAAAAAH...
I'M CALM NOW.
YOU ARE INVESTIGATOR HIEDA, YES?
THANK YOU FOR WAITING.
ARE YOU DONE WITH THE QUESTIONING ALREADY? THAT WAS QUI—
ID CARD
Steven H. Wheatstone
STEVEN H. WHEATSTONE...

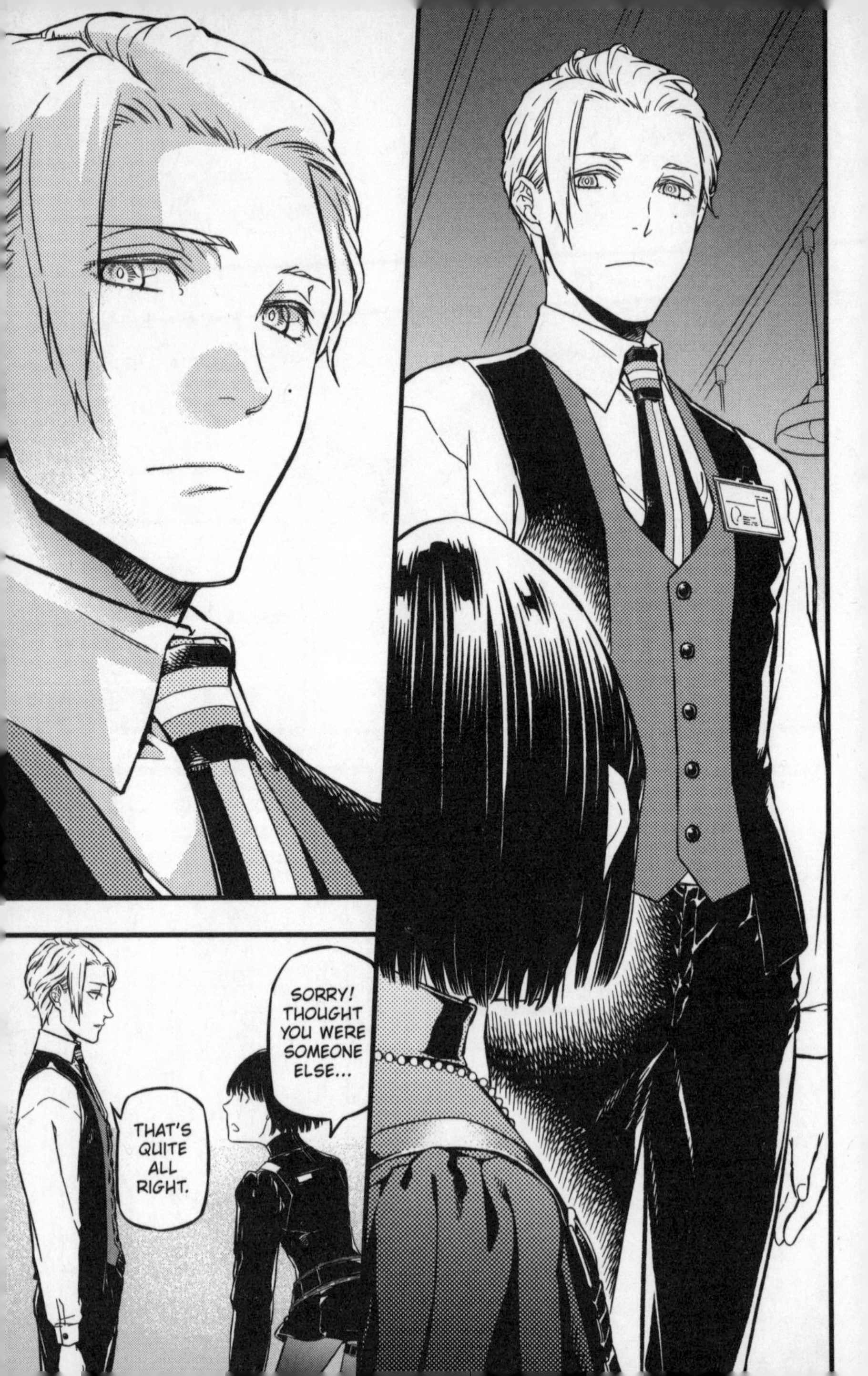
SORRY! THOUGHT YOU WERE SOMEONE ELSE...
THAT'S QUITE ALL RIGHT.

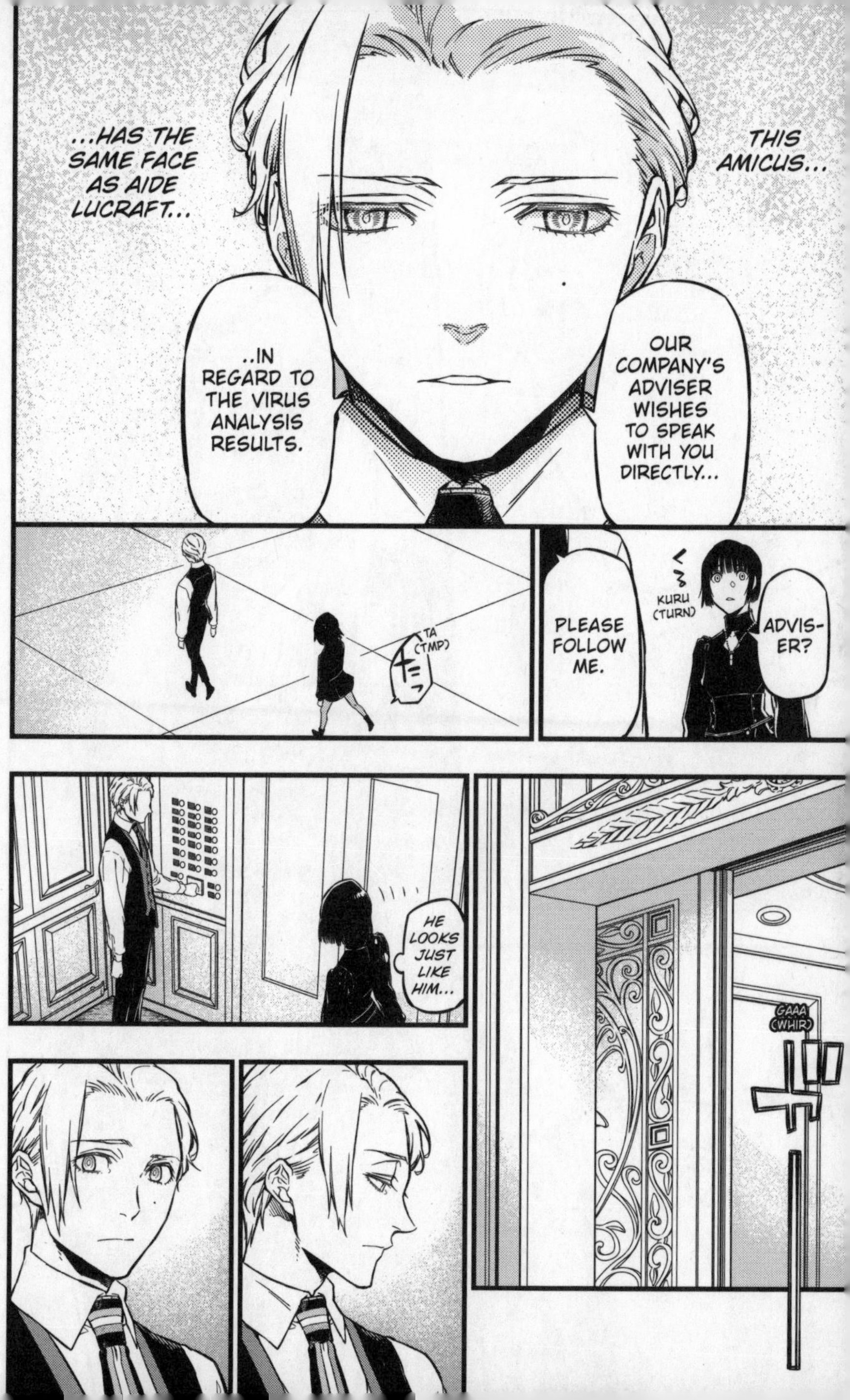
THIS AMICUS...
...HAS THE SAME FACE AS AIDE LUCRAFT...
OUR COMPANY'S ADVISER WISHES TO SPEAK WITH YOU DIRECTLY...
..IN REGARD TO THE VIRUS ANALYSIS RESULTS.
ADVIS-ER?
KURU (TURN)
PLEASE FOLLOW ME.
TA (TMP)
GAAA (WHIR)
HE LOOKS JUST LIKE HIM...

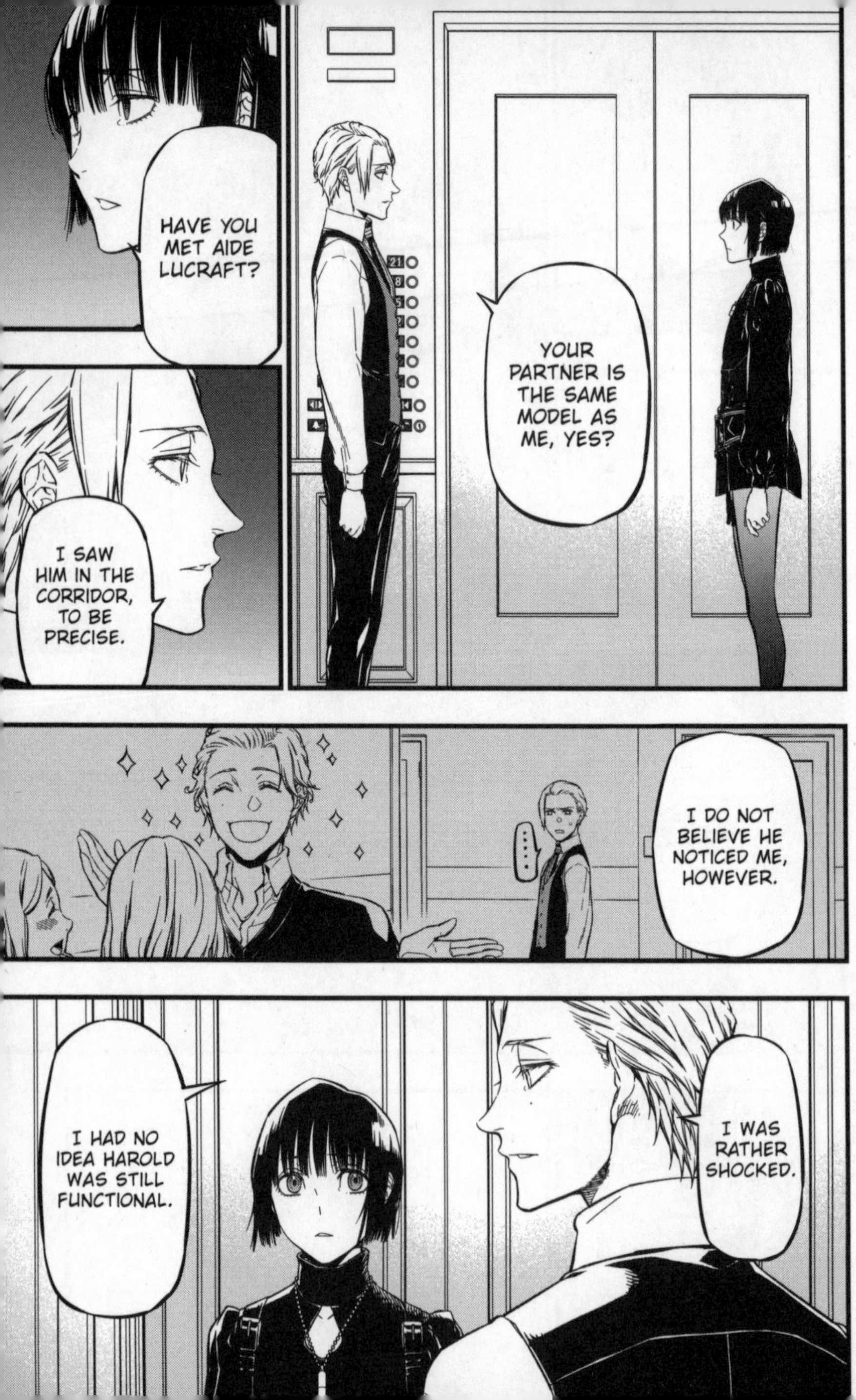
YOUR PARTNER IS THE SAME MODEL AS ME, YES?
HAVE YOU MET AIDE LUCRAFT?
I SAW HIM IN THE CORRIDOR, TO BE PRECISE.
I DO NOT BELIEVE HE NOTICED ME, HOWEVER.
.....
I WAS RATHER SHOCKED.
I HAD NO IDEA HAROLD WAS STILL FUNCTIONAL.

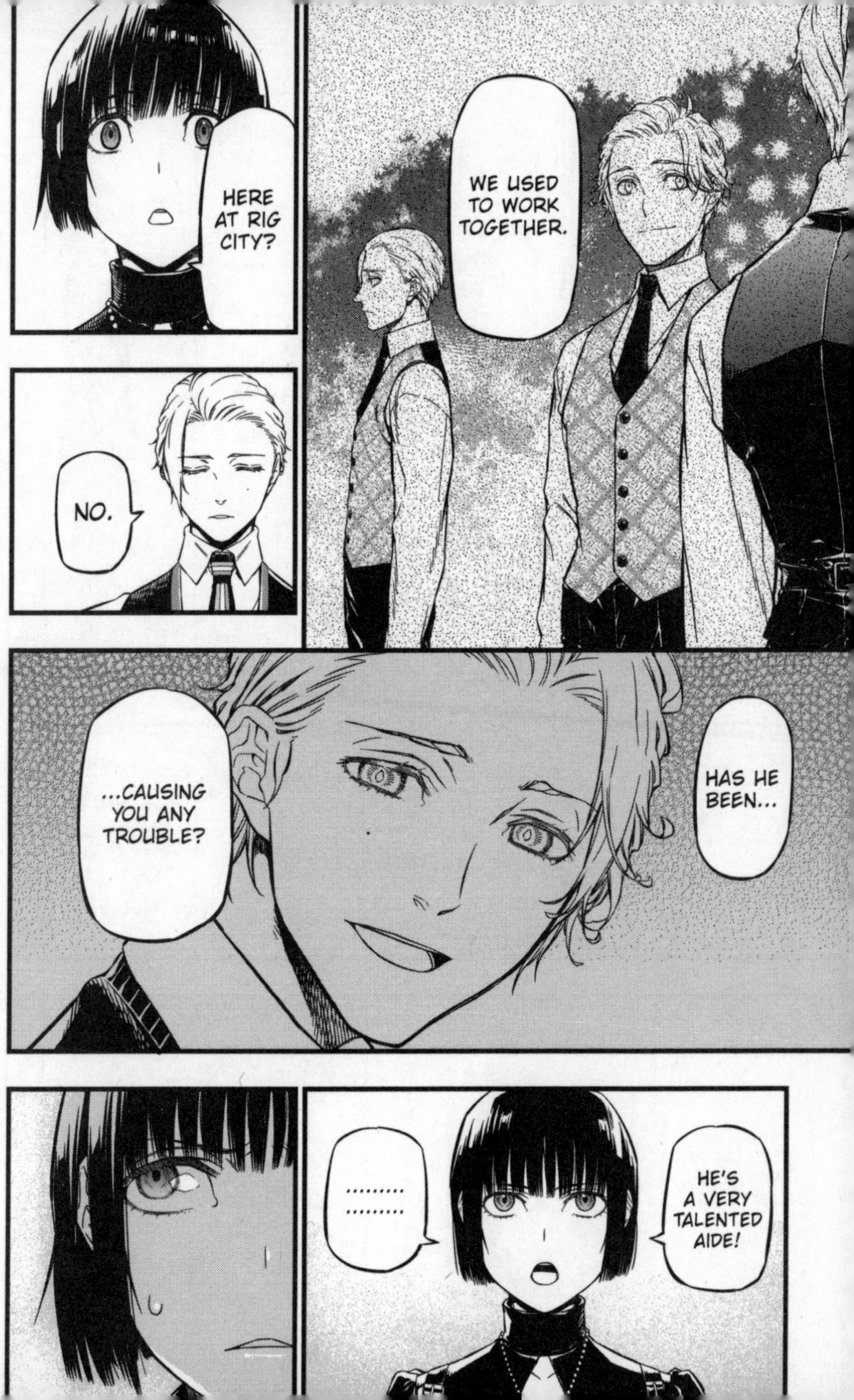
WE USED TO WORK TOGETHER.
HERE AT RIG CITY?
NO.
HAS HE BEEN...
...CAUSING YOU ANY TROUBLE?
HE'S A VERY TALENTED AIDE!
....
....

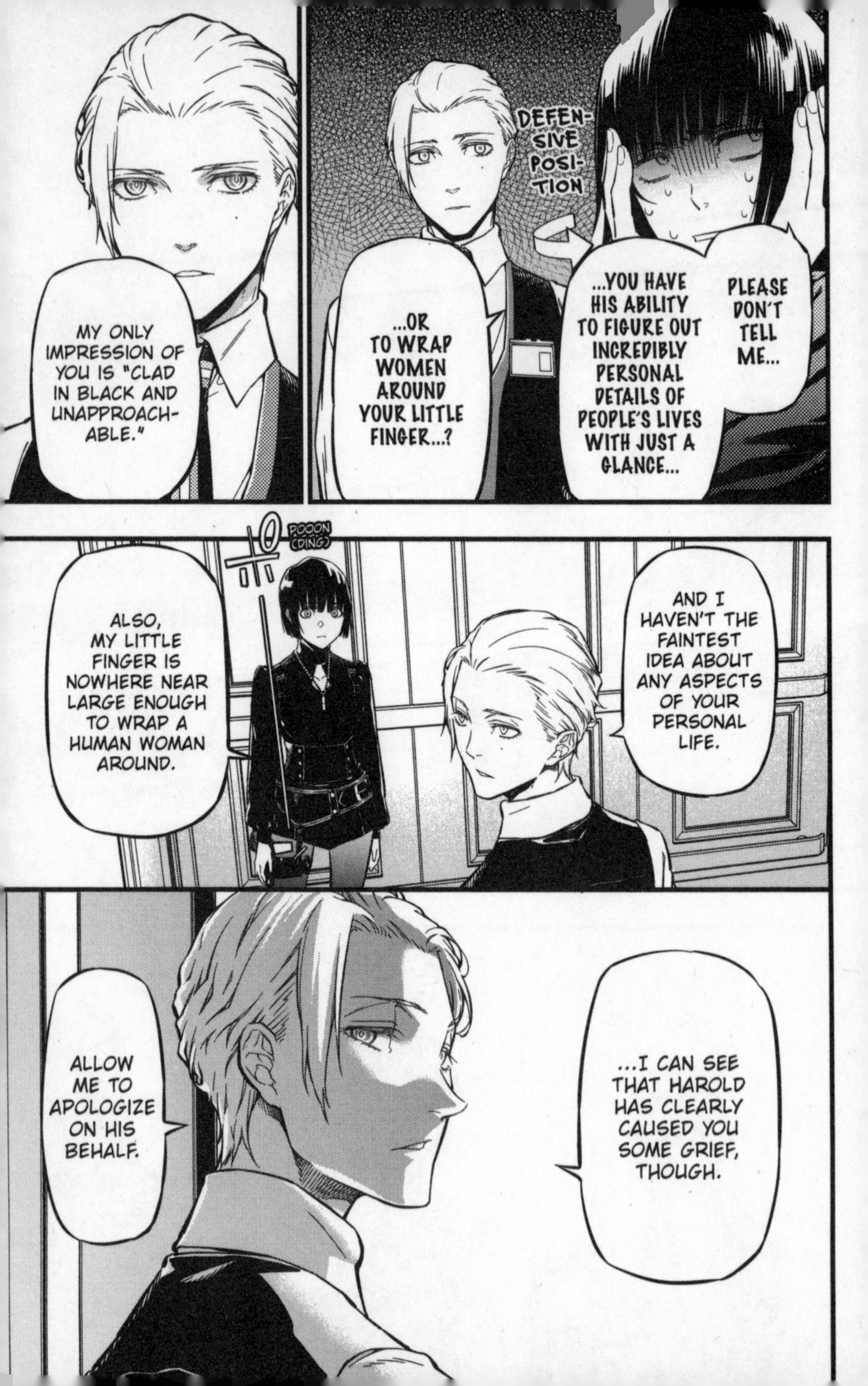
PLEASE DON'T TELL ME...
...YOU HAVE HIS ABILITY TO FIGURE OUT INCREDIBLY PERSONAL DETAILS OF PEOPLE'S LIVES WITH JUST A GLANCE...
DEFEN-SIVE POSI-TION
...OR TO WRAP WOMEN AROUND YOUR LITTLE FINGER...?
MY ONLY IMPRESSION OF YOU IS "CLAD IN BLACK AND UNAPPROACH-ABLE."
AND I HAVEN'T THE FAINTEST IDEA ABOUT ANY ASPECTS OF YOUR PERSONAL LIFE.
POOON (DING)
ALSO, MY LITTLE FINGER IS NOWHERE NEAR LARGE ENOUGH TO WRAP A HUMAN WOMAN AROUND.
...I CAN SEE THAT HAROLD HAS CLEARLY CAUSED YOU SOME GRIEF, THOUGH.
ALLOW ME TO APOLOGIZE ON HIS BEHALF.

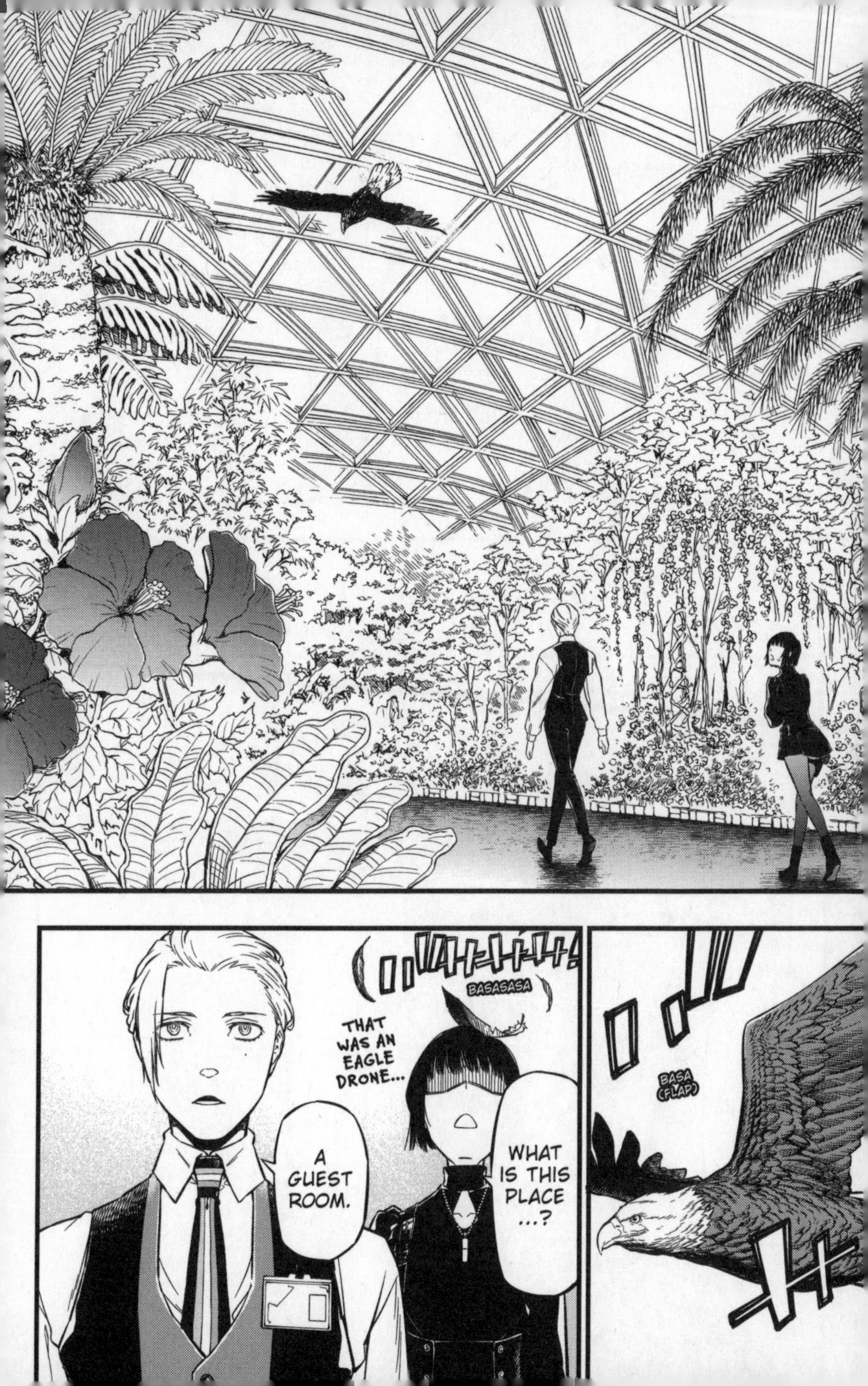
BASA (FLAP)
BASASASA
THAT WAS AN EAGLE DRONE...
WHAT IS THIS PLACE ...?
A GUEST ROOM.

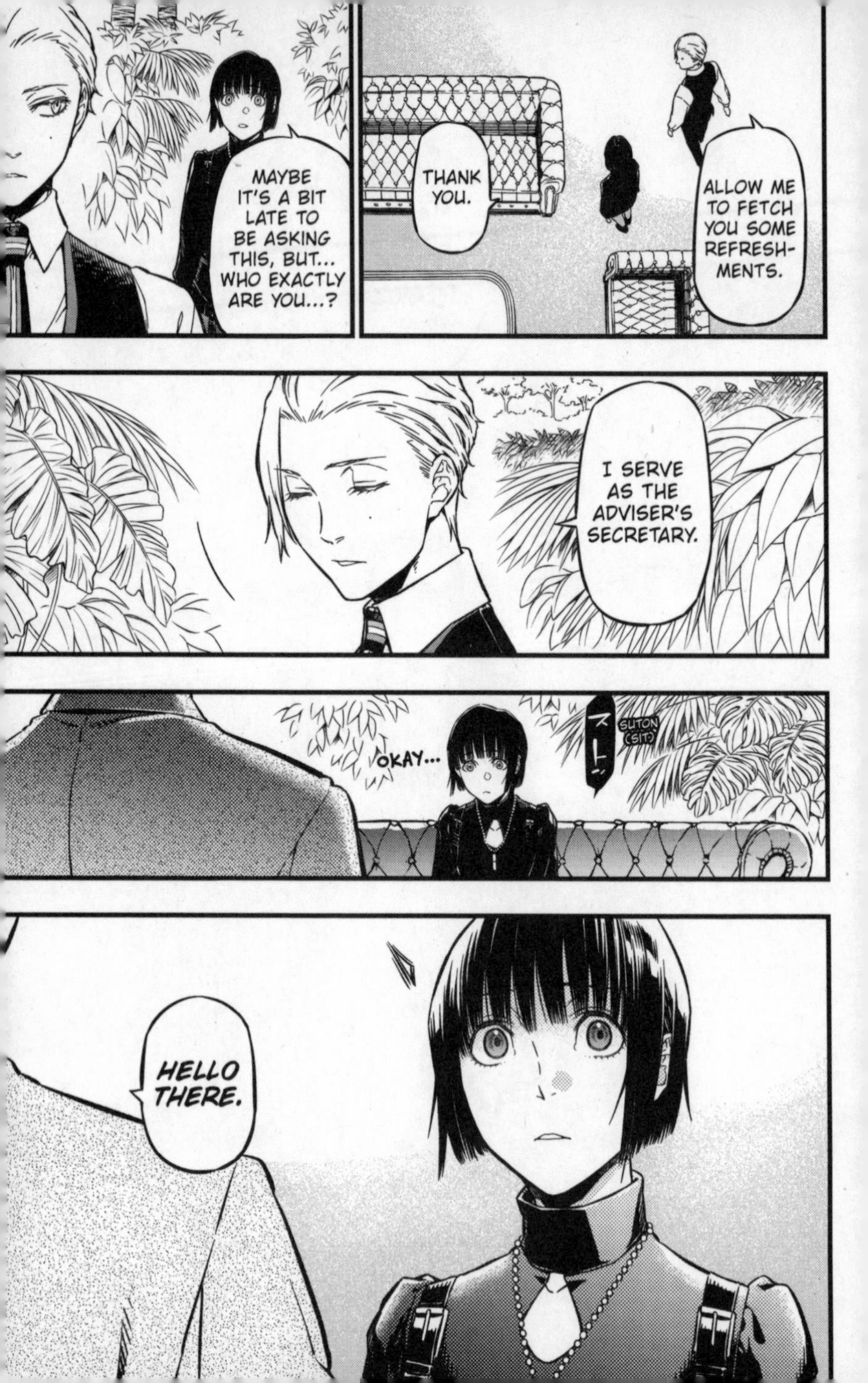
ALLOW ME TO FETCH YOU SOME REFRESH-MENTS.
THANK YOU.
MAYBE IT'S A BIT LATE TO BE ASKING THIS, BUT... WHO EXACTLY ARE YOU...?
I SERVE AS THE ADVISER'S SECRETARY.
SUTON (SIT)
OKAY...
HELLO THERE.

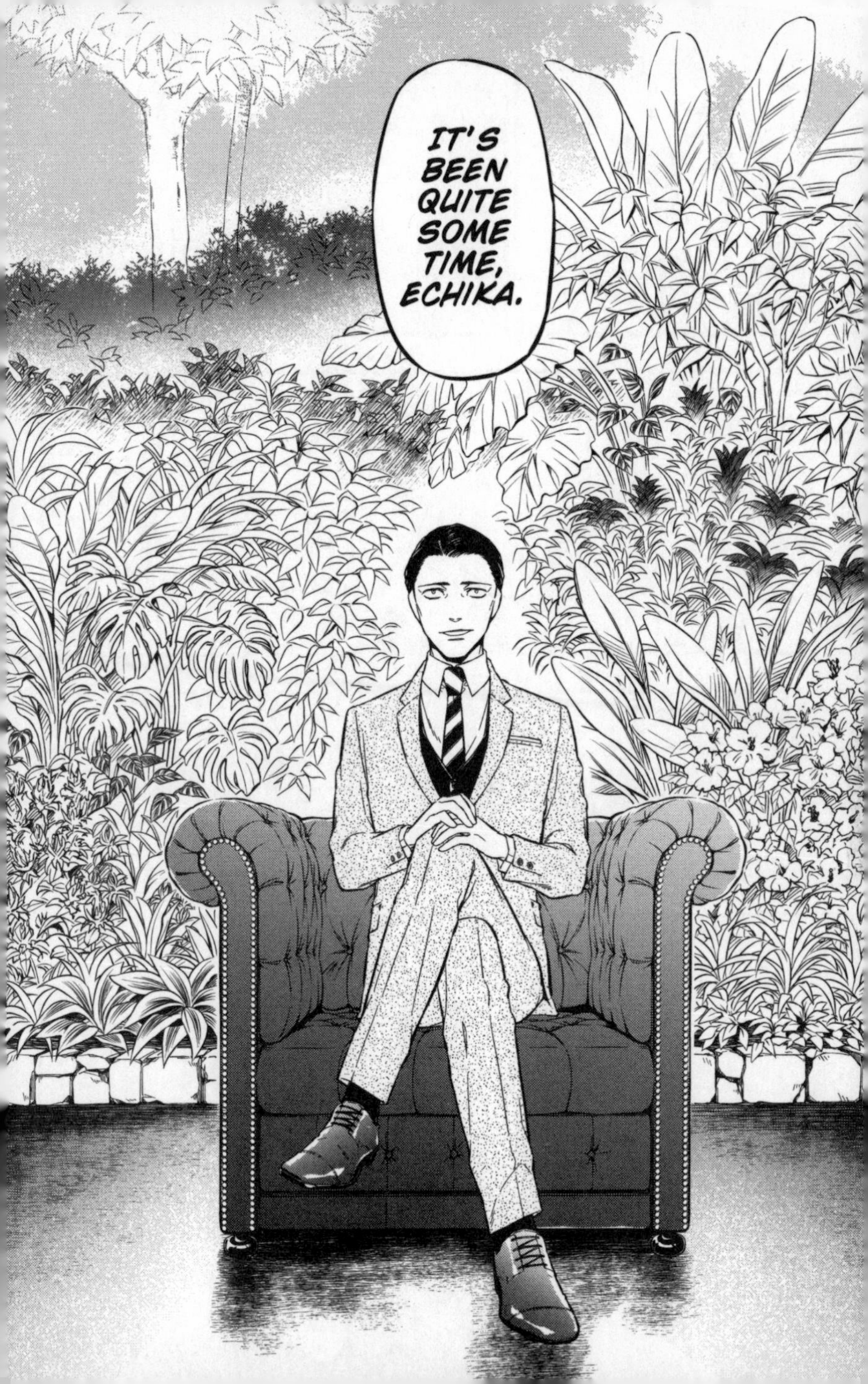
IT'S BEEN QUITE SOME TIME, ECHIKA.

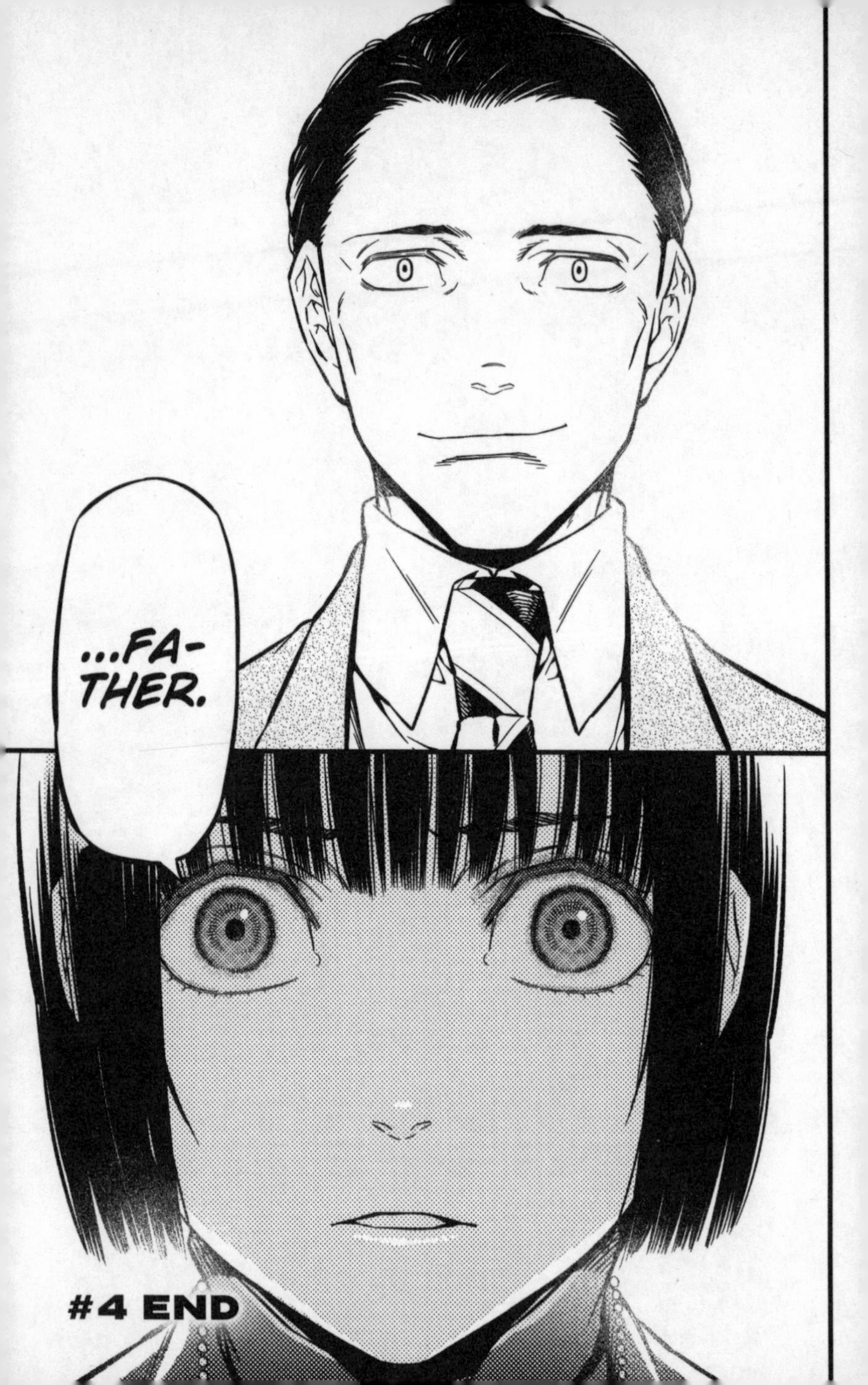
...FA-
THER.
#4 END

YOUR FORMA

Yoshinori Kisaragi

Mareho Kikuishi

Tsubata Nozaki

Iyori Kazaoka

Hayato Misawa

To Be Continued

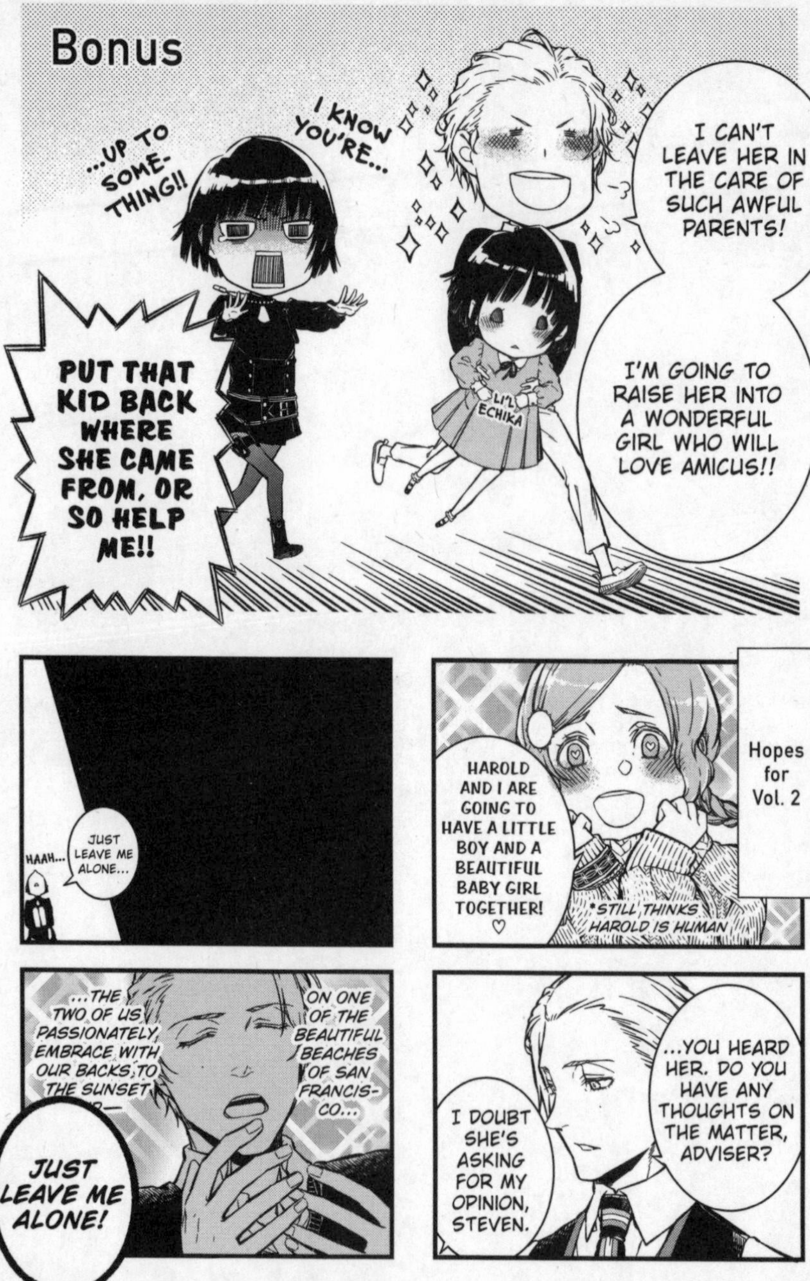
Bonus
I CAN'T LEAVE HER IN THE CARE OF SUCH AWFUL PARENTS!
I'M GOING TO RAISE HER INTO A WONDERFUL GIRL WHO WILL LOVE AMICUS!!
LI'L ECHIKA
I KNOW YOU'RE...
...UP TO SOMETHING!!
PUT THAT KID BACK WHERE SHE CAME FROM, OR SO HELP ME!!
Hopes for Vol. 2
HAROLD AND I ARE GOING TO HAVE A LITTLE BOY AND A BEAUTIFUL BABY GIRL TOGETHER! ♡
*STILL THINKS HAROLD IS HUMAN
JUST LEAVE ME ALONE...
HAAH...
...YOU HEARD HER. DO YOU HAVE ANY THOUGHTS ON THE MATTER, ADVISER?
I DOUBT SHE'S ASKING FOR MY OPINION, STEVEN.
ON ONE OF THE BEAUTIFUL BEACHES OF SAN FRANCISCO...
...THE TWO OF US PASSIONATELY EMBRACE WITH OUR BACKS TO THE SUNSET—
JUST LEAVE ME ALONE!

Hello there. This is the original author, Kikuishi.
Congratulations on the release of Volume 1 of the manga!
I was asked to write this afterword for it, but after looking
at the manuscript, my only impressions were "Great! Cute!
Cool!" and so on, so I'm worried it might not really be worth
crashing this manga if that's all I've got to say...

Back when I was still just uploading stories online as a
hobby, I'd always look at manga adaptations of other novels
and think, "It must be so nice to see a story you came up with
come to life like that..."
So when I received an offer to have this story be adapted
into a manga—the first such offer I've ever had in my life—
I recall being so shocked that I could only nod and robotically
repeat, "Yes. Yes." I still can hardly believe my very own book
is being used as the source material for a manga.
I can't express how grateful I am.

Converting a globetrotting story with such complex
worldbuilding into visual form must have been tricky, but
Kisaragi-sensei is so talented that I feel like he actually
made it more enjoyable and easier to understand than the
original.
The manga versions of Echika and Harold are just so full of
life—I kept saying, "Oh, so that's the kind of expression they
had in this scene!" I keep learning things about them that I
never knew myself.
I really can't thank Kisaragi-sensei and *Young Ace*'s editorial
department enough. They have my deepest appreciation.

As a reader, I'm looking forward to seeing how they'll render
the next volumes of *Your Forma*.
All right, that's enough out of me!

Mareho Kikuishi

Echika, what is your role?
To be my machine, no?

It's all just programming.
It's all fake. All lies.

What if something had happened to her...?
You...monster.

Don't just assume that our emotions
are nothing more than programming.

The blade of the past
gouges into Echika's heart—

The story continues in Volume 2

THE SAGA OF TANYA THE EVIL

Her name is Tanya Degurechaff and she is the Devil of the Rhine, one of the greatest soldiers the Empire has ever seen! But inside her mind lives a ruthless, calculating ex-salaryman who enjoyed a peaceful life in Japan until he woke up in a war-torn world. Reborn as a destitute orphaned girl with nothing to her name but memories of a previous life, Tanya will do whatever it takes to survive, even if she can find it only behind the barrel of a gun!

LIGHT NOVEL VOL. 1-11 AND
MANGA VOL. 1-18 AVAILABLE NOW!

© Carlo Zen 2013
Illustration: Shinobu Shinotsuki
KADOKAWA CORPORATION

© Chika Tojo 2016 © Carlo Zen
KADOKAWA CORPORATION

The Detective Is Already Dead

When the story begins without its hero

Kimihiko Kimizuka has always been a magnet for trouble and intrigue. For as long as he can remember, he's been stumbling across murder scenes or receiving mysterious attache cases to transport. When he met Siesta, a brilliant detective fighting a secret war against an organization of pseudohumans, he couldn't resist the call to become her assistant and join her on an epic journey across the world.

...Until a year ago, that is. Now he's returned to a relatively normal and tepid life, knowing the adventure must be over. After all, the detective is already dead.

Volume 4 available wherever books are sold!

YEN ON
YenPress.com

TANTEI HA MO, SHINDEIRU. Vol. 1
©nigozyu 2019
Illustration: Umibouzu
KADOKAWA CORPORATION

YOUR FORMA

I

YOSHINORI KISARAGI

Original Story **Mareho Kikuishi**
Character Design **Tsubata Nozaki**

Translation **Roman Lampert**
Lettering **Arbash Mughal**

YOUR FORMA Volume 1
©Yoshinori Kisaragi 2021
©Mareho Kikuishi, Tsubata Nozaki 2021
First published in Japan in 2021 by KADOKAWA CORPORATION, Tokyo.
English translation rights arranged with KADOKAWA CORPORATION, Tokyo through TUTTLE-MORI AGENCY, INC., Tokyo.

English translation © 2023 by Yen Press, LLC

W9-COV-790

Yen Press
150 West 30th Street, 19th Floor
New York, NY 10001

Visit us at yenpress.com
facebook.com/yenpress
twitter.com/yenpress
yenpress.tumblr.com
instagram.com/yenpress

First Yen Press Edition: January 2023
Edited by Yen Press Editorial: Riley Pearsall, Carl Li
Designed by Yen Press Design: Jane Sohn

Yen Press is an imprint of Yen Press, LLC.
The Yen Press name and logo are trademarks of Yen Press, LLC.

The publisher is not responsible for websites (or their content) that are not owned by the publisher.

Library of Congress Control Number: 2022946409

ISBNs: 978-1-9753-5184-7 (paperback)
978-1-9753-5185-4 (ebook)

10 9 8 7 6 5 4 3 2 1

WOR

Printed in the United States of America